Progress in
Historical Geography

STUDIES IN HISTORICAL GEOGRAPHY

General Editors Alan R. H. Baker
University Lecturer in Geography and Fellow of Emmanuel College, Cambridge

J. B. Harley
Lecturer in Geography at the University of Exeter

published

Alan R. H. Baker
John D. Hamshere
John Langton (editors)
Geographical Interpretations of Historical Sources: Readings in Historical Geography (1970)

Josiah Cox Russell *Medieval Regions and their Cities (1972)*

Alan R. H. Baker (editor) *Progress in Historical Geography (1972)*

in preparation

Australia: an Historical Geography Michael Williams

Celts, Saxons and Vikings: Studies in Settlement Continuity Glanville R. J. Jones

Change and Decay: The Great Agricultural Depression in Nineteenth-century Britain Peter J. Perry

English Market Towns before the Industrial Revolution J. H. C. Patten

English Provincial Cities of the Nineteenth Century David Ward

Finland, Daughter of the Sea Michael R. H. Jones

Historical Geography: an Introduction Alan R. H. Baker

Historical Geography of Rural Settlement in Britain Brian K. Roberts

A Social Geography of Britain in the Nineteenth Century D. R. Mills

South America: an Historical Geography D. J. Robinson

History through Maps J. B. Harley

Tithe Surveys Hugh C. Prince and Roger J. P. Kain

Progress in
Historical Geography

Edited by
Alan R. H. Baker

*University Lecturer in Geography
and Fellow of Emmanuel College, Cambridge*

David & Charles : Newton Abbot

ISBN 0 7153 5534 1

COPYRIGHT NOTICE

© Alan R. H. Baker and Contributors 1972

Set in Times New Roman
and printed in Great Britain
by Bristol Typesetting Company Limited
for David & Charles (Publishers) Limited
South Devon House Newton Abbot Devon

Contents

		Page
Figures		8
Preface		9

1 Rethinking Historical Geography   11
Alan R. H. Baker *(University Lecturer in Geography and Fellow of Emmanuel College, Cambridge)*

The challenge of change	11
Explorations in other disciplines	13
Statistical approaches in historical geography	17
Theoretical approaches in historical geography	21
Behavioural approaches in historical geography	24
Prospect of the past	28

2 Historical Geography in France   29
X. de Planhol *(Professor of Geography, University of Paris-Sorbonne)*

The growth and decline of French historical geography	29
The history behind geography	31
The geography behind history	36
Geographies of the past and changing geographies	37
The writings of Roger Dion	40

3 Historical Geography in Germany, Austria and Switzerland   45
Helmut Jäger *(Professor of Geography, University of Würzburg)*

Methods of approach	46
Historical physical geography	51
Historical human geography	53
Geographies of the past and landscape histories	60
Historical atlases	62

4 *Historical Geography in Scandinavia*   63
   S. *Helmfrid (Professor of Human Geography, Univer-*
   sity of Stockholm)
   Definition and delimitation   63
   Agrarian historical geography in Scandinavia   65
   Progress in selected fields of empirical study   67
       The prehistoric continuity problem   67
       The regression phase of the late Middle Ages   72
       Structural change and estate formation during the
       sixteenth and seventeenth centuries   72
       The phases of land clearance and colonisation   73
       The morphogenetic analysis of open-field landscapes   75
       Historical population geography   81
   Methodological progress   83
   Models in historical geography   86
   Prospect   89

5 *Historical Geography in Britain*   90
   Alan R. H. Baker
   Historical geography and the 'old' geography in Britain
   c. 1950   90
   Methodological explorations and empirical investigations
   within the traditional framework   95
   Historical geography and the 'new geography' in Britain
   c. 1970   101

6 *Historical Geography in the USSR*   111
   R. A. French (Lecturer in Geography, University
   College London and School of Slavonic and East
   European Studies)
   The revival of interest   111
   Historical physical geography   115
   Historical biogeography   117
   Landscape and ethnos   120
   Historical economic geography   123
   The fading revival   126

7 *Historical Geography in North America*   129
   A. H. Clark (Finch Professor of Geography, Univer-
   sity of Wisconsin)
   Introduction   129
   The philosophy and methodology of North American
   historical geography   130
   Regional historical geography   133
   Urban interests   134
   General topical studies   135
   Current fashions in methods and models   136
   Changing geographies and geographical change   137

'Cultural' geography and geographers 138
Morphological interests 139
Environment and perception 140
Historical geography in Canada 141
Conclusion 142

8 *Historical Geography in Australia and New Zealand* 144
R. L. Heathcote (Reader in Geography, Flinders University of South Australia) and M. McCaskill (Professor of Geography, Flinders University of South Australia)
Historical geography in Australia—the antecedents 145
Australian historical geography since 1945 148
    Themes 148
    Sources 150
    Techniques 151
    Methods 153
Historical geography in New Zealand—the antecedents 154
New Zealand historical geography since 1945 158
    Past geographies 160
    Geographical change 161
Assessment and prospect 165

9 *Historical Geography in Latin America* 168
D. J. Robinson (Lecturer in Latin American Geography, University College London)
Indigenous impediments and imperfections 168
Intellectual colonialism 172
Scales, areas and themes of research 175
Competition from allied disciplines 181
An outline for the future 184

10 *Historical Geography in Africa* 187
Kwamina B. Dickson (Associate Professor of Geography, University of Ghana)
Progress in historical geography in Africa 187
Possibility of an historical geography of Africa 190
Pre-colonial times 191
Colonial and post-colonial times 198
Source materials 203
Historical geography of Africa and models in human geography 205
Conclusion 206

Notes and References 207
Bibliography 275
Index 303

Figures

1 The wine trade of the eighteenth century in north-west
   Spain   33
2 The location of high quality vineyards in Burgundy   42
3 Regional studies of the traditional peasant economies and
   rural landscapes of Scandinavia   66
4 A graphical model of the evolution of rural landscape in
   eastern Östergötland, Sweden   68
5 Relict cultivation and settlement features in Njaerheim,
   Jarren   71
6 Border zones of particular relevance in the regional differentiation of rural landscapes in Scandinavia   74
7 Prehistoric settlement sites and variations in the phosphate
   content of the soils around Berga, Narke   84
8 The methodological framework of A. Harris, *The Rural
   Landscape of the East Riding of Yorkshire 1700–1850*
   (London, 1961)   97
9 A synoptic model system to show one mode of approach
   to the evolution of spatial patterns in human geography   105
10 Some approaches to historical geography   107
11 Availability of Reports from British Consuls in South
   America, 1820–1900   180
12 Culture areas of Africa   192
13 Distribution of population in Ghana (based on the 1960
   Census of Population)   200
14 Major trade routes in Ghana in the eighteenth century   202

Preface

THE LAST TEN to fifteen years or so have seen profound changes in the philosophy and methodology of geography as a whole. A review of some recent developments within the field of historical geography in particular is both a necessary and, it is hoped, a worthwhile undertaking. Such a review could have been organised in a number of ways—for example, by topics or by periods or by places. But it seemed important to ensure a wide coverage of the literature and not to base the review only on publications available in the English language. For this reason each contributor was invited to examine the ways in which, and the extent to which, historical geographers in his region, country or 'school' had over the last twenty-five years been adapting to new problems, new methodologies, new techniques and new sources. They were asked to identify the fundamental progress that had been made in the study of historical geography rather than to provide a bibliographical review of all studies published during the period. Inevitably, the coverage provided by this book is incomplete; not all regions, countries and 'schools' have been included. But the coverage is intended to be wide enough to provide a general indication of the nature of recent studies in historical geography.

In a possibly presumptous but not deliberately dogmatic opening chapter I have attempted to outline the ways in which I believe the study of historical geography is changing now and is likely to change in the future. Such is the diversity of outlook among historical geographers that one will probably

9

regard the views expressed in this chapter as heretical while another will perhaps consider them to be orthodox. For the former the Bastille is no prison, while for the latter the Bastille has already been successfully stormed. But if this chapter encourages both to think constructively about the subject, then it will have achieved its purpose.

I would like to express my warm thanks to the contributors for their willing co-operation. Contributors from Europe—Staffan Helmfrid, Helmut Jäger, and Xavier de Planhol—I came to know not only as colleagues but as friends from contact begun and renewed at conferences, at Würzburg in 1966 and at Liège in 1969. Tony French, Les Heathcote and David Robinson were at University College London while I was on the staff there before coming to Cambridge in 1966. It was also at University College that I first met Andy Clark on one of his visits to the College. Professor Dickson and Professor McCaskill I know only by their public writings and personal correspondence. To all of them I owe my gratitude, for without their assistance this book could not have been produced.

To Professor H. C. Darby I also owe a great debt, both for his constant encouragement and stimulus over more than a decade and for allowing the facilities of the Department of Geography at Cambridge to be called upon to assist the editorial work involved in preparing this book for the press. I am particularly indebted to Miss Helen Gibson for typing the edited text so efficiently.

To my wife, Sandra, I owe my thanks for providing both considerable help in preparing the bibliography and confident assurance that there was light at the end of the tunnel.

ALAN R. H. BAKER

Emmanuel College
Cambridge
Le quatorze juillet, 1971

1

Rethinking Historical Geography

By ALAN R. H. BAKER

THE CHALLENGE OF CHANGE

IT IS, PARADOXICALLY, the future that matters most in the study of historical geography. For a discipline to flourish it needs to be flexible. But the future is not usually regarded as the province of an historical geographer. Any discussion of the changing nature of historical geography, of the necessity for adaptation, will be admittedly partial, personal and possibly idiosyncratic. None the less, historical geography is a profession. Those who profess a religious faith recognise that their profession dies unless it is renewed by frequent rediscovery of its reason for being. In the case of historical geography the need is for a rethinking of its philosophy and methodology. Rethinking should be, of course, a constant and routine intellectual process.[1] This present essay is a contribution to, but not synonymous with, that process.

Since 1960—when the present writer graduated—there has been a change of paradigm taking place within geography, a model-based paradigm replacing the old, predominantly classificatory, geographical tradition.[2] The changes involved have been disagreeable, even agonising, to those committed to the old paradigm.[3] Trends within the discipline as a whole have not all been equally discernible within historical geography in particular.[4] The 'stresses' created by the new geography have not been followed immediately by adaptations within historical geography to reduce the 'strain' on its functioning. Historical geography has a long relaxation time.

None the less, signs of the 'strain' have of late become

increasingly obvious. The last four years in particular have seen a growing awareness of the problem. In 1967 C. T. Smith suggested that historical geography might be on the threshold of a new major task; D. Harvey drew attention to the unfortunate gap that had developed between scholarly studies of specialist historical geographers and the analytical techniques of human geographers concerned with contemporary distributions; and L. W. Hepple warned that the trend away from Kant and exceptionalism and the new emphasis on generalised models might leave historical geography rather isolated if it continued to emphasise uniqueness, detail and Hartshornian philosophy.[5] In 1969 R. M. Newcomb argued that while the historical geographer need not be the most *au courant* member of his disciplinary clan he cannot allow himself to become technologically redundant.[6] Newcomb's methodological stocktaking examined twelve approaches to historical geography, but his description of particular approaches as either traditional or new modes confused rather than clarified the issues. More perceptive was Harvey's dissection of the temporal modes of explanation in geography.[7] A new classificatory framework—into real, perceived and theoretical geographies of the past—was outlined by A. R. H. Baker, R. A. Butlin, A. D. M. Phillips and H. C. Prince.[8] This framework has subsequently been elaborated in detail by Prince.[9]

In 1970 the hindrances to a marriage between the traditional empirical and the new theoretical approaches in historical geography were discussed by A. R. H. Baker, J. D. Hamshere and J. Langton; the ease of oversimplifying the crucial issues was noted by J. H. C. Patten; and the changing nature of today's studies of yesterday's geographies was described for a wide audience.[10] But the need for rethinking has been most strongly voiced in two book reviews. M. J. Bowden referred to the widening rift between geography and historical geography.[11] W. A. Koelsch asserted the need to face squarely the current intellectual crisis in historical geography by the development of new research strategies which are authentic in terms of the newer paradigms of both geography and history.[12] These vividly expressed views have not gone unchallenged. R. C. Harris, for example, has claimed that the historical geographer's concern should be one of synthesis rather than analysis.[13] The debate continues.[14]

In the limited space of this essay, it is clearly impossible to examine in detail the issues involved in this debate. What is attempted instead is a sketch of the trails which, in the view of the writer, need to be more thoroughly explored by historical geographers in the future than they have been in the past. A map of these trails will appear, it is to be hoped, after more detailed survey.[15] An assumption is necessary here: that methodologically the main advances can be expected from an increased awareness of developments in other disciplines, from a greater use of statistical methods, from the development, application and testing of theory, and from exploitation of behavioural approaches and sources.

EXPLORATIONS IN OTHER DISCIPLINES

Rethinking becomes necessary because orthodox doctrines have ceased to carry conviction. As far as historical geography is concerned, this involves a questioning of the adequacy of its traditional methods and techniques. It requires going back to the beginning and rethinking basic issues about what have become such elementary matters as cross-sections, vertical themes and historical scholarship.[16] As recently as 1965 the reconstruction of past geographies was being described as 'the most orthodox and unexceptional view of historical geography'.[17] The limitations of the method have previously been examined and accepted but now its validity, especially as a means of studying geographical change, is being fundamentally questioned.[18] The same is true of narrative methods which provide only 'loose, weakly explanatory, non-rigorous modes of temporal explanation'.[19] It is even true of the canons of historical scholarship on which the study of historical geography is based. Prince has launched an extreme attack on this last orthodoxy by asserting that in the study of the processes of geographical change the scholarly techniques perfected by historians, patiently acquired and only recently mastered by some geographers, are unrewarding if not irrelevant. The claim of historical scholarship to elucidate the truth of the past is, in Prince's view, constantly undermined

B

by its own methods.[20] This latter view must be regarded as extreme if only because any use of historical documents will inevitably demand scholarly circumspection. Scholarship is certainly relevant, but it should no longer be viewed as adequate on its own.

The links between historical geography on the one hand and economic and social history on the other hand have traditionally been close, and some support for the questioning of these orthodoxies in historical geography is not surprisingly to be found in the recent literature of economic and social history. A review of research in these fields, for example, commented that as far as its techniques are concerned much economic and social history is based on sources and methods for which the classic Rankean discipline of historical investigation does not provide a very adequate guide.[21] The amassing of large collections of facts, not overlooking the smallest details, has inevitably led, as Prince has pointed out, to an impasse in historical geography: the more fully and precisely the facts are known the more certain is the conclusion that no interpretation will exactly fit them.[22] On the other hand, the accumulation of facts by economic and social historians has not resulted simply in more traditional narrative history. Increasingly, the application of systematic techniques of analysis to historical problems has meant that economic and social historians have been less concerned with narrative history, or unique sequences of events 'for their own sake', and more with comparative themes in historical processes.[23] Classical historical narrative is seen by R. F. Berkhofer as being no longer possible: 'The complexity of behavioural interaction seen by modern social theorists disallows both the single narrative viewpoint and the haphazard explanation that have constituted traditional narrative history'.[24]

Even when examining ostensibly unique events, the approach of many economic and social historians has been conditioned by an awareness of analytical relationships, of the need to make these explicit and of the attractions of fitting them into relatively general frameworks.[25] There exists a vast literature on the problem of historical generalisation, a literature with which most historical geographers could usefully make themselves more familiar.[26] Some notes on the subject by W. O. Aydelotte constitute an illuminating point of entry into this largely alien world.[27] For E. R. Leach, rethinking in anthropology meant moving away from a classificatory paradigm towards generalisations, away from the examination of comparative social structures towards the identification of generalised, mathematical, structural pattern.[28] A similar movement is to be seen in archaeology.[29]

If there are lessons to be learned about generalisation in the writing of historical geography, there are others to be learned about the study of change. The prolonged discussion of 'cross-sections' and 'vertical themes' in historical geography seems to have taken place largely in ignorance of very similar discussions in most other social sciences about the particular methodological problems associated with 'synchronic' and 'diachronic' studies.[30] Discussion of the compromise solutions in historical geography to the problem of reconciling both aspects of time—as setting and as sequence—would surely have benefited from a greater awareness of solutions to the same problem in other disciplines.[31] One recent suggestion is that the apparent impossibility of writing simultaneously about the two dimensions of time might well be the historian's equivalent of the natural scientist's principle of indeterminacy.[32]

On the whole, historical geographers have ignored the conceptualisations of the nature of change devised by other social scientists. 'In so far as they have paid any attention to this matter they have adopted a more or less Clarkian view of it as the difference between before-and-after data, or viewed it cinematographically as a series of sequent cross-sections . . . this methodology is inadequate for a *study* of change (as opposed to a *description*—though even for this it would still probably be unsatisfactory). It only allows us to extrapolate between two fixed points in time, without providing much insight into the dynamics of change. If we want to investigate change, then we must devise categories of change for our study: we must focus our attention on events *of* change rather than on events *in* change.'[33] Considerable assistance in this task is likely to be obtained by foraging systematically in the literature of other disciplines. Within social anthropology, for example, the historical approach has been represented by two main branches: social evolutionists tended to 'explain' institutions in terms of a line of progress through immutable stages from earlier forms, while social diffusionists sought in any particular setting the origins of institutions in terms of the effects of external contacts and connexions. The historical approach within sociology flourished in America where fruitful links were promoted with prehistory, archaeology and sociology. In Britain it was the sociological tradition rather than the historical which received most forceful advocacy: reacting against the methods of the evolutionists and diffusionists, Radcliffe-Brown asserted the relative irrelevance of the past for the present which he considered was to be understood in terms of its own contemporary structure.[34] Links between history and anthropology have not been as close in Britain as in America, nor have links between geography and anthropology.[35] The links between history and anthropology have recently been discussed at a conference in Edinburgh and there are clear benefits to be reaped in historical geography. The major focus of economic anthropology, for example, is on the comparative study of regional and local economic systems, ranging from those of isolated, technologically primitive communities to those of peasants strongly influenced by industrialisation. The field covered includes such topics as land tenure, the methods and organisation of production, entrepreneurship, the operation of markets and spheres of exchange, the distribution of wealth in relation to social status—both the methods and results of such research possess much of relevance to historical geographers.[37] The social anthropologist's concern with 'social change' and his view of the diachronic approach as the most tightly controlled type of comparative analysis make his work of particular relevance to those attempting to examine processes of geographical change.[38] Sociological studies of 'social change' would equally repay closer attention.[39]

Renewed attempts to measure change are being made in economic history. A checklist of questions to ask when endeavouring to measure change has been advocated by Berkhofer as follows:[40]

1 Delimitation of the sequence—when did it start?
2 The order of the sequence in relation to time—what followed what?

3 The order of the occurrence—why did it happen in that sequence?
4 The timing of the sequence—why did it occur when it did? Why did not something else occur? (These questions help to establish the sufficient as well as the necessary conditions for the sequence.)
5 The rate of change—how long did the entire sequence take? Were certain elements of it faster or slower than others?

With the addition of an occasional 'where?' to incorporate the spatial component, such a checklist could usefully serve an historical geographer analysing processes of geographical change. From answers to these questions would come the measurement of change. 'Although full answers to these questions demand techniques of quantification not yet available to historical analysts in many cases, still the remembering of the questions as a checklist will produce better quantitative histories of changes over time.'[41] Examination of the relevance of system theory to the study of change has led Langton to a similar conclusion, for he has argued that system theory provides a series of three process models—simple action systems, uncontrolled feedback systems, and controlled feedback systems—which provide the necessary organising concepts to analyse change at any level of abstraction. Moreover, in its presentation of these models as a progressive sequence, system theory points clearly to the limitations of the simpler conceptualisations of process by making explicit the nature of the change-producing mechanisms which they omit and to the consequences of their omission.[42] To a considerable extent, however, advances in the understanding of processes shaping spatial patterns depend upon our being able to measure those processes.

STATISTICAL APPROACHES IN HISTORICAL GEOGRAPHY

The application of statistical techniques in historical geography is still in its youth, while in some other branches of geography it has already reached maturity. Mathematical techniques will probably never be so widely used in historical geography as elsewhere in geography: its practitioners tend to be non-mathematical by inclination as well as by training, and much historical data is not amenable to mathematical analysis. The use of parametric techniques, which require normally distributed data and accurate measures of central tendency and dispersion, is not appropriate to many historical data because much of this is not normally distributed and does not represent a random sample. Non-parametric techniques are of much greater relevance. While one can point to a number of studies in historical geography making judicious use of mathematical tools of description and analysis, it is still the case that many historical sources could be made to yield much more than hitherto by the further application of relevant mathematical procedures.[43]

Particularly convincing evidence that this is indeed the case is provided by the recent experience of economic and social history. One of the most significant trends in this field of late has been the pursuit of quantification. Economic history has, of course, always been concerned with quantities but these have traditionally been embodied in simple basic series of raw data related to traditional concepts. What is particularly striking about the new emphasis on quantitative economic history is both its tendency to use increasingly sophisticated statistical techniques and its tendency to organise the painstaking collection of a variety of statistical data with reference to relatively new concepts.[44] There has been a very lively debate among historians about the merits and limitations of both quantitative economic history and econometric history, but when all the reservations have been made it is clear that quantification has shown itself to be a powerful tool in historical analysis.[45] It ought equally to be so in much historical geographical analysis. Furthermore, the role of quantification in relation to economic and social history is, it has been argued, in some respects becoming so different in degree that the enquiry becomes different in kind. Historical scholarship is itself being partly refashioned by the drive for quantification. None the less, the greater the application of mathematical processing to raw data and the more ambitious the conclusions which are sought by such methods, the more rigorous must be the critical evaluation of the original data. The need for that meticulous analysis of sources that has been the hall-mark of the professional historical scholar is increased not lessened.[46]

Quantification in history may be of greater relevance to historical geographers interested in processes of geographical change than are those aspects of quantification in geography which have concerned themselves with identifying static structural geometries.[47] Identical spatial distributions or geometries may be generated by very different processes. The relations between form and process are therefore likely to be nonsymmetric, as G. Olsson has pointed out, and it follows that arguing from form to process is often dangerous and that specification of functional relationships is more important than specification of the geometric properties of a spatial phenomenon.[48] To date, however, there has been very little accomplished in geography in the construction of dynamic models of spatial form.[49] The 'tremendous potential' noted by Harvey for developing more realistic, stochastic, models of spatial development over time and of giving such models a quantitative mathematical expression constitutes a considerable challenge to those interested in geographies of the past as well as to those interested in geographies of the present.[50]

The early flush of enthusiasm over the use of Monte Carlo simulation has now waned into a more modest assessment of its utility.[51] The role of accident, or chance, cannot be denied but it has the disadvantage of actually explaining nothing.[52] Harvey has pointed out that assuming probabilistic mechanisms involves us in some conceptual difficulties. In general it adds nothing to the rigour of explanations of particular situations and it can only add rigour if we are prepared to pay the price of mapping the varied phenomena we are dealing with into the calculus of probability.[53] Within this framework, simulation procedures—like the counterfactual method—should be regarded as an extension of the comparative method of traditional historical scholarship.[54] As such, they deserve still closer attention by geographers concerned with the development of cultural forms over space and through time. This is equally the case with Markov-chain models.[55] A serious difficulty in applying a Monte Carlo model to the simulation of, say, industrial location patterns is finding a suitable basis for establishing the spatial probability framework. Another is that in reality the occupation of any location by, say, an

industrial plant may alter the probability that other locations
will be occupied. This latter difficulty might be accommodated
in a Markov-chain type of model, which allows for the probability of development at a particular time and place to be
related to what has gone before.[56]

A basic need, then, is for a change of attitude towards
historical data, for the replacement whenever possible of im-
pressionistic surveys of data by appropriate quantitative
techniques. Even when the data does not appear to be amenable to statistical treatment, the possibility should be examined
of employing a quasi-quantitative method called Bayesian
statistics. Bayses' theorem can be used 'in order to convert
prior degrees of belief, taken with the evidence supplied by the
data, into posterior degrees of belief'.[57] In other words, it
makes possible the testing of hypotheses against qualitative
evidence. To take an example of the sort of problems which
might be handled within a Bayesian framework. In a study of
the diffusion of agricultural innovations in, say, seventeenth-
century England an historical analyst might, on the basis of
his knowledge of innovation diffusion theory, hold a degree of
belief that certain spatial adoption patterns existed in the
period and place he is studying. The actual patterns of crop
and livestock production revealed in the evidence, notably
probate inventories and farm accounts, become the observed
events which, combined with the prior probabilities, can yield
posterior degrees of belief. There is an unexplored trail here
awaiting adventurous historical geographers.

When inadequacies of the historical data entirely preclude
their mathematical *analysis,* the alternative of a mathematical
approach should prove of value. This involves determining
the relationships and sets of relationships among phenomena
rather than being concerned with the particular characteristics
of the phenomena themselves. It would also seem to require
explorations into topology, a non-metrical form of mathematics, and the expression of these relationships in symbolic
logic.[58] The affinities here would lie less with the approach
to model-building in economics and much more with that in
anthropology. Anthropological models can rarely be subjected
to quantitative treatment.[59]

THEORETICAL APPROACHES IN HISTORICAL GEOGRAPHY

The search for generalisations about the processes of geographical change, in particular for generalisations that can be validated mathematically, requires a careful framing of the questions to be asked of the available data. The framing of questions, the establishment of hypotheses, in turn depends upon the available theory. Quantification is no substitute for cerebration. Aydelotte has aptly summarised the position: 'Theory plays an essential role in intellectual advance; collection of facts by itself is inadequate and may, if theory is neglected, actually retard or impede understanding. It is unfortunately the case that a number of empirical studies have not produced results proportionate to the labour expended on them, since they were not addressed to significant problems and the objectives for which they were undertaken were insufficiently considered in theoretical terms. Indeed, the assiduous pursuit of an ostensibly strict empiricism may act as a soporific and prevent our giving critical consideration to more general problems of interpretation.'[60] The historical geographer somehow has to fashion his empirical data, abstracted and analysed with all the skills at his command, into something coherent and meaningful. He has, at some stage, to decide what were the necessary and sufficient conditions which led to one event rather than another, for this is what constitutes explanation in historical terms. Invariably, as the historical geographer searches the historical record, he brings to bear upon that record certain expectations about what ought or ought not to have happened. In good historical research these expectations are changing constantly as new information becomes available. But it is also reasonable to change these expectations as more and more theory becomes available. In short, theory is the main means by which we codify and analyse our expectations. 'Theory should not be thought of as some kind of panacea which is going to solve all of the complex problems of historical explanation in geography. It is, rather, the means we use for sorting and sifting through our own expectations and of determining the sometimes quite complex implications of those expectations.'[61] A knowledge of theories current in the other social sciences could be a source of new ideas and perspectives enabling historical geographers to appraise their own problems differently and could suggest new questions that it might be illuminating to investigate. Theories can usefully direct enquiries.[62]

It is, none the less, illogical to criticise, as Prince has done, the works of R. Dion and H. C. Darby for their lack of theoretical content when they are explicitly and intentionally empirical. Such works can only be judged as pieces of empirical, historical scholarship: they were not written as case studies in the investigation of geographical change and cannot be evaluated on these terms.[63] Prince's strictures on the 'inadequacy of inductivism' appear especially misplaced when one realises that system theory is itself an empirical method. As P. A. Samuelson has observed, there is no substitute for empirical analysis in the study of non-equilibrium situations because a life-time could be spent in analysing the behaviour patterns which are hypothetically possible in such conditions.[64] An empirical bias is inevitable in system theory given its concern with diachronic analysis, with the study of non-equilibrium conditions.[65] A logical consequence of empirical analysis is the induction of generalisations. 'Induction is the process most fundamental to the historical approach.'[66] T. Hägerstrand's first model of the spatial diffusion of innovations was inductively derived.[67] Generalisation can be inductive: 'it consists in perceiving possible general laws in the circumstances of special cases; it is guesswork, a gamble, you may be wrong or you may be right, but if you happen to be right you have learnt something new altogether'.[68] The identification of empirical regularities and relationships of a sufficiently general nature to warrant the status of laws or quasi-laws is a challenging and worthwhile task.

In practice, however, the inductive and deductive approaches to scientific enquiry are inseparable.[69] 'Deductive theory needs frequent reference to the real world if it is to have any practical and interpretative value, just as empirical inquiry directed toward lawlike statement must feed on more abstract theory.'[70] Indeed, it would be highly misleading to suggest that theories are first arrived at by a deductive process and then tested. As H. M. Blalock points out, 'the actual process is much more fluid than this and undoubtedly always involves an inductive effort. One formulates the best theory he [*sic*] can in the light of existing evidence. He [*sic*] then should formalise this theory in order to spell out its implications. These implications are then checked against new data and the theory modified'.[71]

The problems involved in the development of theory *ab initio* within an historical framework are considerable. A first problem, which is common to all academic enquiry, is that any large-scale model of the operation of complex cause and effect processes through time is fraught with fundamental difficulties, notably those of feedback which can only partially be overcome by the use of model sequences, comprising connected sub-models which individually incorporate only short spans of time.[72] A second problem is that it will rarely be that data pertaining to all the parameters and variables that are relevant to such process models can be quantified. There is little or no hope of writing the kind of theory which will be adequate to explain *in toto* what actually happened to, say, the French wine industry during the nineteenth century. The more grandiose the attempt to develop theory in historical geography, the less satisfactory it seems likely to be.[73]

More harvest is probably to be reaped in the application and testing of theory derived from other branches of geography and from other social science disciplines. The view has, of course, recently been expressed that geographical theory is essentially derivative, concerned with elaborating economic, sociological, political and psychological theory in a spatial context.[74] One can disagree with this and yet still hold the view that, given the enormous difficulty of understanding the interrelationships that make up particular parts of the surface of the earth, generalisations from social science that simplify the task should be seized.[75] This involves the retrogressive application of concepts and theories in order to illuminate aspects of the past rather than of the concepts and theories themselves. A recent book by D. Ward on nineteenth-century American cities is an excellent example of this particular theoretical approach in historical geography.[76] Somewhat but not so very different is the *retrospective* testing of concepts and theories in the laboratory of the past in order to illuminate aspects of those concepts and theories rather than of the past. Some social anthropologists view history in this way,[77] although some economic historians view the testing of economic theory as part of economics not of economic history.[78] J. M. Blaut has argued that if geography is to become a generalising science, 'it must take its comparisons where it finds them, comparing here-now with there-then as well as there-now. If one wishes to classify the matter of farming systems, cities or floods, and to discover the laws that generate and differentiate each class, one accomplishes less than half the task by investigating only those examples co-existing at a given time'.[79] The longer the time-span over which a model remains valid, the more confidence we may place in it as indicating fundamental spatial structure. The past has been used, for example, by J. C. Hudson and others to test a general location theory for rural settlement and by D. Sibley to test the hypothesis that steady state characteristics are maintained during urban growth.[80] These two approaches—retrogressive and retrospective—to theory in historical studies can, of course, most usefully be combined. J. P. Lewis' *Building Cycles and Britain's Growth* (1965) employs theoretical models to interpret the historical record and uses the historical record to test the models.[81] There can be no doubt that in historical geography there are many facts looking for theories with which they may be more fully understood; it is equally the case that in the social sciences as a whole there are many theories looking for facts with which they may be more rigorously tested.

BEHAVIOURAL APPROACHES IN HISTORICAL GEOGRAPHY

The search for generalisations about the processes of geographical change, in particular for generalisations that can be validated mathematically and that can be set in an appropriate theoretical framework, requires analysis of data at the lowest possible level of generalisation and at the relevant level of decision-making. Increasingly, human geographers concerned with analysing the contemporary scene are finding it necessary to adopt a behavioural approach.[82] Olsson has recently suggested that the widespread dissatisfaction with existing geographical theories may be due to a preoccupation with spatial patterns and a neglect of small-scale generating processes.[83] Hägerstrand has commented that nothing truly general can be said about aggregate regularities until it is made clear how far they remain invariant for organisational differences at the micro-level.[84]

A concern with behavioural postulates leads inevitably to an increasing emphasis on the analysis of individual and small group behaviour and it would seem at first sight that inadequacies of his sources might lead an historical geographer to conclude that such an approach to his own chosen problems was impossible. Dead men do not answer questionnaires and much of the surviving historical data relates to aggregate rather than individual behaviour. It is certainly the case that aggregate patterns of, for example, agricultural land use, population migration and the location of industry have been the primary concern of many historical geographers. But before declaring the impossibility of any alternative approach to problem solving in historical geography, it behoves us to inquire of cognate disciplines how they have reacted to this seemingly intractable problem.

Most of the contributors to a recent conference on the relevance of models for social anthropology were convinced that a closer specification of narrower social contexts was likely to be a more fruitful line of advance than a search for sweeping generalisations.[85] But, of course, their interests were not primarily historical by nature. Of greater significance is K. C. Chang's advocacy in archaeology of the study of local social groups, self-contained in terms of the day-to-day interactions of the people concerned. He suggested analysis of the community—a camp, a village or a town—as the archaeologocial unit of behavioural meaningfulness. Since, in Chang's view, the concept of community concerns people in the flesh-and-blood sense, which cannot be retrieved archaeologically, he suggests the concept of settlement to substitute for it: 'A settlement is not a logical abstraction, nor can it be characterised by a listing, however sophisticated, of artefact types. It delineates an empirical reality, a physical unit of deposition which is composed of cultural *things* abandoned in specific spatial relationships.'[86] Within history, Berkhofer has explored in depth both the need for and the problems in attempting a behavioural approach to historical analysis.[87] Links between history and sociology have become stronger of late, while social history itself has developed into a systematic study of social structure and social change, incorporating an analysis of changes in organisation, techniques, ideas, and values.[88] There is a tendency for economic history, which in the past generation received most of its conceptual impetus from economics, to adopt more specifically social analysis.[89]

The possibilities, then, of analysing the decision-making process in historic time should not be underestimated. Focusing attention on the decision-making unit rather than on aggregate geographical patterns will involve examining more closely than hitherto the records of individual units, such as families, farms, and firms. It will involve looking afresh at the historical sources traditionally used by geographers as well as investigating new sources. Even descriptive accounts and diaries can be analysed systematically. Content analysis and similar methods can be expected to be used increasingly by historical geographers.[90]

Very little attention has yet been paid to the decision-making process in models of spatial development and much more is to be hoped for.[91] It is, therefore, almost paradoxical that Prince should assert that perhaps the greatest advance in historical geography in recent years has been achieved by viewing the past through the eyes of contemporary observers and by rediscovering the evaluations they made of the objects they observed.[92] Historical geographers have long been interested in the perception of past environments by their contemporaries.[93] Indeed, the topic has a long pedigree: for example, in her book on *England in Transition,* published in 1931, Dorothy George wrote: 'To counteract our bad habit of reading history backwards and looking at the past only from the standpoint of the present, we must read the contemporary books, for their point of view as well as for their information. Far the best authority for early eighteenth-century England is Defoe'.[94] A paper in 1952 by W. Kirk on historical geography and the behavioural environment made explicit a view of the world that was implicit in the writings of a number of other workers.[95] Studies of the historical perception of environments have grown in number of late and Prince has provided an elegant appraisal of these excursions into 'imagined worlds of the past'.[96] R. J. Chorley has gone so far as to suggest that environmental perception provides 'one useful means by which historical geography can find a secure and relevant place in contemporary developments in the subject as a whole'.[97] It is now widely accepted that considerable parts of any cultural landscape are obviously the result of human actions, that behind these actions lie ideas about the images of reality, and that an historical geographer comes to understand a landscape by studying these ideas and images. But the approach to the past through the concept of perception has its limitations. No matter how well an historical geographer understands what men in the past thought about their environments, this remains the actors' viewpoint. Reconstructing this viewpoint is part—but only one part—of the task of any historian, who must go on to analyse the total situation according to the observers' view as well.[98] A behavioural approach in historical geography involves more than reconstructing 'imagined worlds of the world'.

By emphasising the importance of the decision-making unit, of individuals rather than of aggregates, there inevitably develops an awareness of the role of particular peoples and events. Both the general and the particular event lie within the field of interest of the historical geographer and here perhaps he associates himself more closely with history than with the developing model-based human geography which lacks interest in the unique event. The position has recently been summarised by J. E. Vance: 'It would be incorrect to hold that no regularity can be anticipated in the experiential (historical) approach to geographical analysis. Human behaviour is far from being unstructured and quixotic. It is subject to shared responses to common situations. At the same time, individual solutions to situations can be expected, and the study of the experience of man in shaping resolutions for problems has two logical concerns: that with the *commonly shared responses* and that with the *exceptional acts*'.[99] Historical geographers have an important contribution to make in developing the 'historical language' band of the epistemological spectrum.[100] As with history, historical geography may be of generalised and comparative interest in one approach and of intrinsic interest in another, but both contribute to each other and are by no means incompatible in techniques or philosophical background.[101] None the less, the 'intrinsic interest' team has had a good innings and it is perhaps now time for the 'generalised and comparative interest' school to bat.

PROSPECT OF THE PAST

The ideas and trends presented in this essay have implications for research and teaching in historical geography which cannot, for reasons of time and space, be discussed fully here. An increasingly quantitative, theoretical and behavioural analysis (or if not analysis, then approach) in historical geography would have many repercussions. It would involve a change of kind rather than of degree in the writing of historical geography. This despite the fact that many, and notably Marc Bloch, have long advocated the adoption of more explicitly comparative work, of more explicitly problem (rather than source material) based work, and of more explicitly interdisciplinary research.[102] It would, moreover, link historical geography more closely to the rest of the subject. The dichotomy between historical geography and geography could be broken down, to be replaced by historical studies in the branches of systematic geography. Studies in, for example, 'historical agricultural geography', 'historical urban geography' and 'historical economic geography' seem to offer possibilities of fundamental development, particularly in terms of a better understanding of the processes by which geographical change through time may take place.[103] Such an organisation of the subject would view historical geography as a means towards an end rather than as an end in itself. The task now ahead— not least for the present writer—is to narrow the gap between rhetoric and reality, profession and practice.

2

Historical Geography in France

By XAVIER DE PLANHOL

THE GROWTH AND DECLINE OF FRENCH
HISTORICAL GEOGRAPHY

MORE THAN ANY other, the French school of geography has
been imbued with history. Although French geography had a
richly encyclopaedic tradition,[1] towards the end of the nineteenth century geography in the university became distinctively
a branch of historical studies. Paul Vidal de la Blache (1843–
1918), generally acknowledged as the father of French university geography, was initially an historian. In university teaching, geography has only slowly and partially broken away
from its very close links with history. Until 1942, the principal
competitive examination conducted by the State for admission
to teaching posts in universities and high schools (*l'agrégation*)
remained a joint examination in history and geography. Even
today in university courses, the link between the two continues
to be a strong one. History remains compulsory for the
Diplôme Universitaire d'Etudes Littéraires in geography and
likewise geography is still compulsory for the history diploma
(corresponding approximately to first degree standard in
British universities).

Paradoxically, one consequence of these particularly close
links has been that historical geography has never been
viewed in France as a separate branch of geography and it has
hardly developed distinctive methods. It could be argued that
in France all geography has, for a long time, been more or
less historical and that historical geography as such has not

C

existed. All of the great regional monographs, which until about 1940 constituted the greater part of the work of French geographers, included an important retrospective section and many had organisational frameworks which contrasted traditional ways of living (usually in the context of the zenith of settlement in the countryside in the eighteenth and early nineteenth centuries) with the modern situation. History, as an explanatory element, was inseparable from the all-embracing description which remained the ideal of the French school of geography until the middle of the present century.

This situation has altered considerably during the last twenty or so years. The expansion of geography in an increasing variety of directions, the growing specialisation in university chairs, the orientation of research towards general problems, often tackled within a regional framework but with an intention other than that of describing the whole—in sum, these trends have strained the traditional bonds between geographical analysis and historical interpretation. Most French geographers today are turning either towards physical geography (especially geomorphology) or towards the economic geography of urban and industrial societies whose roots do not penetrate so far into the past as those of rural and agrarian societies.

With this great upsurge and diversification of activity, one would have expected historical geography in France to elucidate its distinctiveness and improve its techniques. In fact, such a tendency is hardly discernible. The original links with history for a long time kept geographers in a subordinate position and French geographers seem to have preserved in relation to history a certain inferiority complex, associated with a certain rancour, which reveals itself increasingly in an inclination to believe that geography can only establish itself in opposition to history and not in conjunction with it. How often, during the last two decades, have we heard of young French geographers anxious to know if the role which they have attributed in their researches to historical antecedents has been considered excessive? There exists one school of thought which considers that in the modern world the cultural landscapes of industrialised countries have shaken off the past so rapidly that it no longer deserves the attention of geographers, who should concentrate their efforts instead on the analysis of social and economic processes at work today. The physical *milieu,* the relationships between man and the physical environment, are likewise discredited by some. Very significant in this respect is the work of one of the most vigorous influences in modern French economic geography, Paul Claval, who has clarified this attitude towards the past. Having himself a substantial historical knowledge and often appropriately including in his writings references to earlier forms of regional organisation,[2] he believes nonetheless that geography should concentrate on the study of modern economic activity and on prospective approaches.[3] Many young French geographers share this viewpoint. Humanitarian concern of the socially aware about the efficiency of the urban way of life and illusory ideas of the personally ambitious about influencing public affairs combine in leading some geographers to treat historical geography with the scorn usually poured on anything considered to be old-fashioned.

It must, regretfully, be said that French historical geography today seems to be in large measure a residual discipline. It has not established a set of principles. Its progress depends on isolated individuals following their own initiatives. Historical geography has, it is true, produced some notable studies. It still produces them. But one would have expected more in view of the particularly propitious environment in which historical geography in France developed.

THE HISTORY BEHIND GEOGRAPHY

A major stream of activity and ideas nonetheless persists, notably in one current which today represents the basic legacy of the French tradition of regional studies, namely studies in the agrarian geography of particular areas. The role of historical interpretation is still fundamental to such works. One must here refer to many useful studies and note the quasi-comprehensive coverage of numerous monumental publications in this field during the last twenty-five years.[4]

A methodological change is discernible in the way authors presented the results of their researches. The orthodox reconstruction of an ancient, 'traditional', phase of occupation of the land, a necessary preface and introduction to the study of modern changes, dominated the work of M. Derruau on the Grande Limagne,[5] of M. Chevalier on part of the Pyrenees,[6] of X. de Planhol on southern Anatolia,[7] of S. Lerat on the *pays* of the Adour[8] and of B. Janin on the alpine Valley of Aosta.[9] This was also the approach of S. Daveau in his examination of historical influences on the formation of the Franco-Swiss border in the Jura which served as an introduction to a geographical study comparing ways of life on both sides of the frontier.[10] It was also the approach of A. Huetz de Lemps in a massive work on viticulture in north-west Spain, nearly half of which was concerned with its historical evolution and which included some maps showing the exact extent of vine-growing in areas from which it has now disappeared as well as maps of former commercial routes (Fig 1).[11] R. Lebeau, in a book on the southern Jura, likewise discussed the former economy before describing modern activities.[12]

A new methodological emphasis has been demonstrated, however, in a number of studies. Following E. Juillard, who in his study of the rural economy in the plain of Basse-Alsace described the then present-day conditions in the first part of his book before studying their antecedents and evolution in the second part,[13] several authors have reversed the orthodox, chronological, order of exposition. This is not a matter of experimenting with a way of presenting material; it is the result of a deliberate intention strictly to limit study of the past to those elements of it which are necessary to an understanding of the present. A desire to reconstruct the entire geography of the past is clearly replaced here by a retrospective approach which restricts itself to explaining phenomena discernible in the present. In this way P. Brunet, in his book on the rural landscape of the heart of the Paris Basin, deferred until the *third* section of the book examination of the development of large farm holdings which he had identified in the *first* section as the characteristic trait of the region's economy today and whose independence of physical factors he had demonstrated in the *second* section.[14] Even within the examination of this development (an examination which occupies nearly half of the book), the discussion was strictly against the flow of time. Elements of interpretation were sought retrogressively

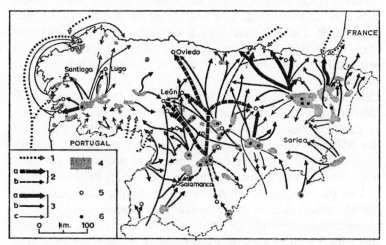

Fig 1   The wine trade of the eighteenth century in north-west Spain (after
A. Huetz de Lemps, 1967, 503)

1   Wine coming from Portugal, France, Andalusia or Catalonia
2   White wines from the Tierra de Medina
   a   Principal flows
   b   Secondary flows
3   Other wines from north-west Spain
   a   Principal flows
   b   Flows of average importance
   c   Minor flows
4   Areas producing surplus wines for sale
5   Important wine exporting centres
6   Main centres of wine consumption
Trade in certain quality wines (Peralta, Frontignan) is not shown
on this map

in earlier and earlier periods: in the role of the growth of
Paris in the last few centuries, which Brunet showed to have
been a weak influence on the process of farm enlargement;
then in the medieval periods which he considered to have
been essential to the process; finally in the large Gallo-Roman
estates with which the later large farms had little affiliation.
Similarly it was only after having studied the present problems
of the countryside around Toulouse that R. Brunet sought
their origins in earlier periods.[15] History in these cases has
been put exclusively at the service of geography. This trend is
carried further in those studies whose method of presentation

involves completely rejecting historical reconstructions which, although subordinated, are still features of the works just cited. In P. Flatrès' study of the agrarian geography of countries on Europe's Atlantic fringe, historical explanation is essentially woven into the fabric of different chapters.[16] A similar approach is seen in the works of A. Fel on the Massif Central,[17] of R. Livet on Basse-Provence,[18] and even of H. Desplanques on Umbria in which the author has traced back successive phases in the changing patterns of settlement since the Middle Ages, to which he attributes particular importance.[19] Permeating these books, historical geography *per se* is not unmistakably detectable at any one point in them.

The distinctiveness of historical geography is much more readily observable in more specialised studies not aiming to be as comprehensive as the works just discussed. But such specialised studies are few. Retrospective study of arrangements of fields and farmsteads for their own sake has rarely been attempted in France. The most active centre of such work is the University of Rennes, where the research and teaching of A. Meynier over the last thirty years and more, together with the studies he has encouraged and directed, have resulted in a thorough investigation of the fields of Brittany. Emphasis has been placed on the identification of periods when landscapes of open fields, in large measure shrouded under *bocage* since the eighteenth and nineteenth centuries, were much more important than they are today.[20] The map which Meynier has provided of open fields in Brittany and of their former extent has shown that their present concentration on the littoral is only a residual feature.[21] They have persisted into the present-day in such locations thanks to the use of marine shells as fertiliser, whereas they have disappeared along with cereal cultivation on the acidic soils of the interior. Meynier has been able to refute the conjectures which saw this coastal concentration of open fields in Brittany as a consequence of its colonisation by peoples coming by sea.[22] Large-scale maps of genetic elements of field and settlement patterns have been a further interesting product of Meynier's work.[23] The only other systematic study has been at Nancy, where J. Peltre has applied (for the first time in France and to field and settlement patterns in Lorraine)[24] the morphometric analysis of agrarian landscapes developed in Sweden by D. Hannerberg and his school.

Studies of other areas have been fragmentary and isolated. A number have, however, been devoted to Mediterranean regions, a traditional area of interest for French geographers and historians. Particularly worth noting are the studies of Roman centuriations in Tunisia, based principally on the interpretation of aerial photographs.[25] These have, moreover, promoted some interesting methodological discussions revolving around the possibility of safely attributing to the Roman period landscape vestiges identified and mapped from aerial photographs.[26] An entirely different approach, using land surveys listing properties in geographical sequence, has been used to reconstruct a Hittite field pattern of the second millennium BC in the high plateaux of central Anatolia. This was in the early stages of the process of parcellation of a *Blockflur*. Evidence from Assyrian sources and the Bible demonstrated the existence of open fields and of communal agrarian practices in the ancient Near East.[27]

The contribution of French historians to retrospective studies of agrarian structures has been piecemeal and far from systematic. It is, nonetheless, to the work of an historian that one turns for the first demonstration of the tardy (ie late medieval) development of the communal system of agriculture.[28] More recently, other historians have re-examined and discussed the earliest evidence for the appearance of regulated cultivation over large areas: C. Higounet for the Ile-de-France in the thirteenth century; R. Fossier for Picardy, where he has been able to distinguish stages in development very clearly (the appearance of cultivation based on furlongs in 1220 and in 1229; an example of a regulated cultivation based upon the division of a village territory into three equal parts in 1248; a general refashioning of the pattern of parcels and regrouping of fields between 1260 and 1300).[29] But these studies, decisive though they are for geographers preoccupied with restrospective studies of agrarian landscapes, remain of only marginal interest to historians.

THE GEOGRAPHY BEHIND HISTORY

The French school of history has been impregnated with geography as much as that of geography has been with history. But the attitude of historians towards geography has for a long time been a mixture of condescension and mistrust. Since L. Febvre strongly asserted, in the face of Ratzelian determinism, the primacy and autonomy of human actions, there has developed among both historians and geographers in France considerable scepticism about any claim to the direct influence of geographical factors upon the course of history.[30]

Particularly during the 1930s, as part of a strong reaction against certain Anglo-Saxon excesses,[31] there was established a veritable dogma about the unchanging nature of climate in historical time or at least about the absence of important climatic fluctuations. So research which, early in the 1950s, attributed the former extension of olive cultivation in Anatolia in the classical epoch to a period of less rigorous winter extremes, seemed to be exceptional.[32] One can now find evidence that this view of climate as more or less unchanging has been completely abandoned in the excellent work of E. Le Roy Ladurie. This has produced results of major importance for glaciology and geomorphology in throwing light for the first time on the existence of a phase of ice-retreat during the fourteenth and fifteenth centuries in between the two glacial advances of the medieval (c.1150–1300) and modern (c.1600–1850) periods.[33] But Le Roy Ladurie's consideration of the implications of these climatic changes for agrarian history remains an isolated contribution.[34] There has, it is true, been a useful review of the influence of climatic fluctuations on the migrations of peoples in ancient and medieval times.[35] But in the final analysis the climatic factor is only part of the explanation. Even in marginal regions such as those of the Near East, human influences are essentially dominant in the history of vegetation. It is, for example, to the pressure of population in peasant societies during periods of peace that one has to attribute the principal phases of woodland destruction in Anatolia and Iran.[36]

In any case, the problem of geographical determinism is no

longer presented in simple terms. A 'geographical history' of Islam which examined social mechanisms, themselves linked to religious concepts, for explanations of advances and retreats of both nomadic and sedentary ways of life in the arid regions of the ancient world, also emphasised the initial physical factors which influenced the development of those mental attitudes in both the desert of Arabia and its oases where Islamic religion was born. But it is in the context of a general concept of the settlement of land that it is necessary to consider physical influences (such as relief and vegetation cover) whose impact is not to be denied at a regional scale.[37] Only rarely have French historians paid attention to basic physical influences. The clearest recognition of their role is undoubtedly seen in studies in historical demography, which have become more numerous in recent years. One such of the plain of Forez in the eighteenth century contrasts the deficit of its demographic balance-sheet with the excessively mountainous nature of its environment and draws from this important conclusions about the decline or growth of agriculture in the two regions being studied.[38] This sort of approach is only just beginning to be extended to the Middle Ages, where it will certainly be productive.

GEOGRAPHIES OF THE PAST AND CHANGING GEOGRAPHIES

While it is not necessarily a matter of identifying inevitable relationships, geography is in fact always considered to some degree in the writings of French historians. This is especially the case when they take the form of retrospective reconstructions in which, for a particular period, a large part of the description is of settlement and land use, of marketing and trading activities. This last topic dominates the imposing picture by F. Braudel of the Mediterranean world during the second half of the sixteenth century.[39] It is also seen in a remarkable reconstruction of trading and exchange routes of the Moslem world contained in a posthumous work of M. Lombard, which succeeds in elucidating for the first time the economic balance of the whole of this vast world and the nature of its relations with the African, Asiatic and European worlds, thanks to its combined use of literary, archaeological and numismatic evidence.[40] Geography always underpins works of this kind. A review of our knowledge of West Africa in the Middle Ages has appeared with a geographical title.[41] In the field of rural studies these general descriptions can in turn lead to further major discoveries and interpretations. A reconstruction of the rural economy of Portugal at the end of the eighteenth and the beginning of the nineteenth century in turn resulted in the identification of an entirely new type of open field cultivation: a three, four or even five course rotation with only one course of cultivation for two, three or four of fallow.[42] This arrangement strongly suggests that the development of rotations here had entirely different origins from those of cerealisation (*Vergetreidung*) usually suggested in continental Europe. Such rotational systems in the Mediterranean areas would have been linked to the need to arrange the pasturage of transhumant sheep flocks separately from the arable lands, as is proved by the fact that fallow lands were frequently knocked down at auctions for sheep flocks not belonging to the village community.

The other orthodox approach to history—that of following change through time—does not necessarily involve the elaboration of geographical cross-sections. But geography is not entirely absent from a group of studies which concern themselves with the changing nature of societies in relation to their use of resources. Particularly important in this context are studies of 'colonial' history in North Africa and in South America which analyse the modification of European agriculture in the face of different environments[43] and which are hardly distinguishable in their approach from specifically geographical studies of similar societies.[44] This evolutionary approach allows the identification of interactions which escape a static analysis. For example, a study of the rural history of Upper Provence in the early Middle Ages threw considerable light on the problem of the development of transhumance, especially in demonstrating the late appearance of direct transhumance which emerged initially within the framework of ecclesiastical estate economies in the lowlands and for which there is only clear evidence at the beginning of the modern period.[45]

In fact these two approaches, static and dynamic, are often

usefully combined, especially by those writers concerned with
earlier periods for which archaeological and place-name mapping is a fundamental tool in reconstructing stages of colonisation. Such studies are compelled to trace change by a series
of maps of a single region for successive periods. This method
was used by L. R. Nougier in his reconstruction of the phases
of Neolithic colonisation in western Europe[46] and has been
systematically employed by J. P. Millotte for the region of the
Jura and the plains of the Saone[47] and of prehistoric Lorraine.[48] These studies have emphasised the contrast between
the distribution of settlement along valleys during the Bronze
Age and the later spread of settlement onto the limestone
plateaux, associated perhaps with a drier phase but much
more certainly with the impact of a predominantly pastoral
migratory people. For more recent periods, R. Fossier has
used archaeological and place-name evidence to reconstruct
the Celtic, Gallo-Roman and Medieval phases of colonisation
in Picardy.[49] Following the settlement of the Celtic period,
concentrated along valleys, and a notable expansion onto the
cereal-growing limon of the plateau during the Gallo-Roman
period within a framework of large estates, there occurred an
important phase of colonisation between the end of the sixth
and the middle of the eighth century, the demographic and
economic aspects of which remain uncertain. The same methodological combination can be extended to more general problems at an almost national scale.[50] Archaeological investigation
is also an indispensable tool, even for recent periods, in such
areas as North Africa where literary evidence is scarce.[51]

Rural settlements have received preferential treatment from
historical geographers but one cannot separate them from their
urban, administrative and transportation frameworks. Some
syntheses have been undertaken with this in mind.[52] Following
a general study by a geographer of the formation and development of the road network of France[53] have come regional
monographs.[54] The distribution of industries in the past[55] and
of religious ideas[56] have been carefully studied. But all this
work to date remains fragmentary. It seems, however, that a
period of co-ordinated efforts is now beginning with the
appearance of carefully documented regional historical atlases
dealing with the various aspects of historical development

from the prehistoric to the present periods.[57] One hopes that these efforts will develop rapidly, thus at last providing a coherent framework for French studies in historical geography.

THE WRITINGS OF ROGER DION

Historical geography in France is, it appears, paradoxically both everywhere and nowhere. One person, however, deserves special attention. As indicated in the slant he has given to his writings and in the title ('Historical Geography of France') which he has given to his chair at the Collège de France, Roger Dion is the only French geographer who has systematically embraced historical geography and placed an historical perspective at the centre of all his work. Fortunately his has been an original, productive, often extremely ingenious mind which has succeeded in introducing geographical explanation into the most obscure and most remote aspects of the past. His work, apart from his major books, is widely scattered in numerous articles in a variety of journals often of limited circulation.[58] But it is easy nonetheless to detect some important themes in his work.

The first phase of Dion's career was devoted to retrospective studies in agrarian geography. This period began with broad studies contrasting agrarian 'civilisations' of the North and of the Mediterranean region.[59] The explanations contained in these works are no longer acceptable but the studies themselves remain classics, notably because of their splendid description of the communal agricultural system of northern France and of the individualistic agriculture of the west and south. This phase of Dion's work was concluded with a synthesis which clearly demonstrated the stages of colonisation in the sedimentary basins of Hercynean Europe.[60] He elucidated the selective nature of the colonisation, the initial preference for calcareous plateaux, with their certain and regular cereal harvests, in contrast to the less attractive regions of clays and sands, and the consequential predominance of grouped settlements in the former areas and of dispersed settlement (an index of tardy colonisation) in the latter areas. Dion has only once returned to the historical geography of agrarian landscapes, in a short but brilliant paper showing the relative nature of the concept of a *bon pays* in the context of the *Champagne crayeuse,* an attractive region under the old economy because of its light and warm soils but becoming less so with the coming of the agricultural revolution of the eighteenth century when it was devoted to woodland again because of the local lack of manure and the unsuitability of the soils for fodder crops.[61]

These early interests in settlement and agriculture opened out into a geography of territorial boundaries, based on the particular case of France but of general importance, emphasising the role of 'forest frontiers' and of the negative nature of agricultural areas in the development of political boundaries.[62] At the same time Dion offered what is still a classic interpretation of the hill-top settlements of the Mediterranean. He associated them with a tree-crop economy, the only one which allowed factors of insecurity their full reign because of the long time it takes to recreate orchards, in contrast to the areas of cereal economy in northern Europe where insecurity has been much less important and which have never systematically resorted to defensively sited settlements, disturbances and troop movements only involving the loss of one year's harvest.[63]

A second main theme of Dion's work has been study of the development and location of French vineyards, especially those producing good quality wines. This viticultural phase spread over twenty years, produced many individual studies and culminated in a masterly synthesis.[64] The underlying theme is the dominance of human factors in the development of vineyards. It is fallacious to believe that the location of vineyards, especially those producing high quality wines, is associated with physical factors of soils and favourable sites. That this is not so is shown by examples such as the vineyards of the Bordeaux region where rightly famous wine-producing areas have developed under a humid and foggy climate. In fact, the problem is to disentangle for each vineyard the physical conditions of its emergence and the human elements, to reconstruct the social conditions (for example, the role of aristocratic or religious influences, or of an urban bourgeoisie) and the commercial circumstances (proximity of markets and of trade routes, the expansion or contraction of

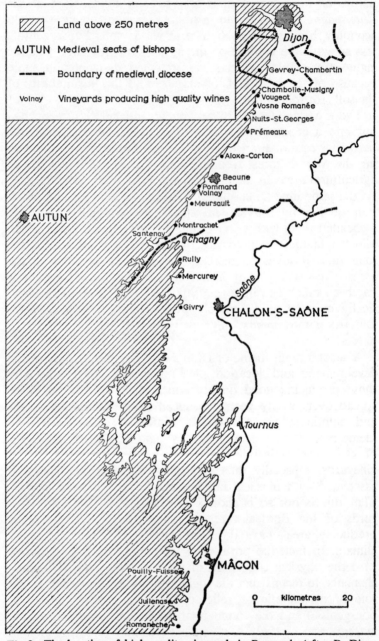

Fig 2 The location of high quality vineyards in Burgundy (after R. Dion, 1951, 128)

particular outlets) which led to such a costly enterprise. The
location of vineyards is a problem in historical geography. The
most striking example is undoubtedly the explanation of the
location of the high quality vineyards in Burgundy, whose
extent corresponds exactly with that part of the Burgundian
hills which, at the time of the creation of great vineyards in
the first and second centuries AD, was part of the territory of
Autun, then a rich and prosperous centre, whereas the rest
of the hills have no vineyards of equivalent renown (Fig 2).[66]
Other examples are those vineyards located on the main
routeways or close to markets: the vineyards of the north of
France (of the Paris region, of the Meuse, Moselle, and Rhine)
developed during the Middle Ages river-based export trade
to the regions of the north, and the vineyards of Orléans and
Sancerre were linked to the commercial prosperity of these
old towns and to the routeway of the Loire.[67] In one field
particularly dear to all Frenchmen,[68] the viticultural geography
of Dion has sought an explanation of the present in the past.

For the last twelve or so years, a third theme (previously
touched upon in some of Dion's earlier publications) has held
the attention of the doyen of French historical geography.
Dion has recently concerned himself with the great land and
sea routes of antiquity. Here too, the method adopted is
original and fruitful. Reconstruction of the major arteries of
the past and the identification of localities and peoples, for too
long attempted by purely philological methods, are only possible when seen against the relevant framework of human
geography, the commercial activities of the period. Dion has
in consequence been able to put forward new and ingenious
solutions to historical and geographical enigmas insoluble by
orthodox methods. It is worth having a look at a few
examples. The considerable disagreement in early sources
about the location of *Cassitérides,* which has provoked considerable debate among scholars, is undoubtedly explained
quite simply in the fact that this name has been used in turn
to refer to several 'islands of tin', in association with the
changing sources of supply.[69] A similar kind of solution has
been applied to the problem of the Ligurians, supposedly
the predecessors of the Celts in Gaul. Linguists, anthropologists and prehistorians have tried in vain to solve this problem

which practically disappears when one realises that this name has in fact designated not a well-defined people but barbaric populations for whom modern Liguria, hardly recognised in antiquity before the Roman period, has certainly been the final resting-place. It is by the identification of a river name with that of a major traditional commercial artery, which in fact did not follow the river throughout its course, that one can interpret texts which have remained incomprehensible, like that of Herodotus which locates the source of the Danube in the Pyrenees.[70] The same approach makes it possible to distinguish what is true and what is fiction in the *Periploi* or legendary voyages. Dion has re-examined the problem of *Thulé* and resolved the apparent contradictions in the works of Pytheas by showing that the word had undoubtedly been used by him with two different meanings, one much more restricted than the other.[71] Finally, Dion has provided a hopefully definitive end to one of the many controversies surrounding the geography of the Odyssey in showing that the Cyclops and Lestrygons, *cannibales factices,* were in the Homeric poem only a satirical and pejorative invention aimed against the people of Corinth and Megara, a part of the rivalries of the period of Greek colonisation.[72]

The significance of these findings is clear. That part of the past whose purely historical sources are precisely the most contradictory and deceptive has been seen with a new understanding. Historical geography, in the writings of Dion, has ceased being an auxiliary science to geography or to history and has become a fully autonomous discipline justifying its existence by its results. But this particular approach, this distinctive method, remains an isolated case. It is a great pity that Dion, because of the marginal position of the Collège de France in relation to the University of Paris, has not influenced young French geographers to the extent that work of such richness deserved.

3

Historical Geography in Germany, Austria, and Switzerland

By HELMUT JAGER

SINCE THE NINETEENTH century historical geography in the German language area has developed in close contact with a complete range of allied subjects related to historical-geographical problems. From this interdisciplinary co-operation, it received substantial impulses and historical geography has in turn contributed to both these subjects and the various branches of the geography of the present. Particularly close relationships link historical geography with history, above all with regional history and the history of law, economic and social history, as well as prehistoric archaeology, history of the dark ages, medieval archaeology, onomastic science and historical folklore studies. In addition it has close ties with vegetation history and several branches of pedology. Owing to its broad scope the subject is an integral part of an interdependent network of academic disciplines. In order to facilitate an easier comprehension of this survey, the essential spheres of historical geography are presented one after the other and exemplified with a few publications, particularly those of recent years. The important and long-established research into local and regional history in the German language area has produced an abundance of significant works relevant both to historical geography as well as to regional history. Since mention can only be made of a few of them here, the reader is referred to the annual bibliographies in the *Blätter für Deutsche Landesgeschichte*.

D

METHODS OF APPROACH

Historical geography is an empirical science using predominantly *regressive methods*. By this is understood all those techniques which start with certain observable landscape features and on this basis draw conclusions about earlier conditions. The retrospective method, which the present author, with A. R. H. Baker, considers as orientated towards the present, is identical with the genetic or historic-evolutionary approach of German cultural geography.[1] This leads to a treatment in vertical themes as applied in F. Mager's *Waldgeschichte Ostpreussens vom 13. Jahrhundert bis zur Gegenwart*.[2] Historico-evolutionary studies can explain earlier or present-day conditions of a *geomer*,[3] in as much as they are determined by historical heritage. The related retrogressive method which is orientated towards the past, was for instance applied by H. and G. Mortensen in their investigation of the eastern part of East Prussia around 1400.[4] This method, which aims to establish regional cross-sections, must be combined with the genetic method if earlier conditions are also to be interpreted geographically.

Since Meitzen, genetic analysis of field systems has formed a central theme in German historical geography. The advances achieved since the end of World War II rest first on the considerable increase in field-studies applying new methods of terrain investigation, and secondly in the increasingly sophisticated methods of evaluating documentary and cartographic sources. Thus the analysis of deeds and records has developed just as much as the application of numerical techniques, so that it has been possible to explain the origin of Central European field systems, even the complex 'open fields' (*Gewannfluren*) of the type found in South Germany, Austria, and Switzerland.

Static-formal analysis proceeds from the assumption that the division of the farm land into parcels as shown on the earliest cadastral maps and estate plans is essentially the same as that which existed at the time of the original laying-out of land pattern. Such a permanency of the land pattern, however, rarely exists. It is so, possibly, in the case of the high medieval *gereihte Hufen,* ie where the land of each holding being of rectangular shape adjoins that of their neighbours so as to form a row, or in the case of even later foundations.

Morphogenetic analysis by W. Müller-Wille and others considers the land layout even of the earliest cadastral maps normally as the result of a long and involved development.[5] With the help of farm categories, field names, the shapes of the parcels and other items, an analysis of the land pattern as it existed around 1800 is carried out, its division into individual (topographic) components is established and an attempt is made to ascertain their age. By means of an analysis of the spatial juxtaposition of parts of the entire field parcel complex, it arrives at conclusions as to their chronological sequence. It is however, as a rule, not possible to ascertain the field layout of the Middle Ages with any certainty, unless archival studies succeed in establishing connexions between *Flurbezirke* (the largest units of the field pattern complex), *Parzellenverbände* (groups of parcels, eg furlongs) or individual parcels and exact dates.

The *typological method* takes as its starting point the empirically established fact that certain forms of farm land layout may be correlated with particular stages in landscape development. Thus, for example, in Europe the minutely-chequered field patterns, whose individual parcels are characterized by straight or irregular outlines, followed by banks or walls, date back to the pre-industrial phases of landscape history. Densely built-up nucleated settlements of irregular layout (*Haufendörfer*) are typically late forms of long development. However, when working with purely morphological characteristics, one has to remember that some unrelated developments giving rise to similar forms did occur. To establish comprehensive cultural and historical landscape typology, such as demanded by E. Winkler,[6] will at any rate only be possible after further considerable additions to our knowledge.

The *comparative method* uses the results of research from well-defined areas where the development of the land layout is well documented and draws conclusions in respect of earlier conditions of other areas with similar structures, but inadequate documentation. H. Mortensen's analogical method is an example of this approach: he investigated certain problems of north-west German settlement research with the aid of results gained from studies of eastern Central Europe.[7] A further example of this method is the comparison of old hamlets in Western and Central Europe having in-field and out-field systems.[8] Investigations employing the comparative method have to ask about the norms of cultural landscape phenomena and processes before any conclusions may be drawn on the basis of analogies. Even then it must be constantly borne in mind that any conclusions will be merely probabilities rather than well-founded certainties; however, in many cases the comparative method makes an important advance towards achieving conclusive results.

The *method of retracing* (*Rückschreibung*) developed by A. Krenzlin and based on material from southern Germany, relates cadastral maps of the nineteenth century and earlier documents referring to land ownership and other evidence having information about the farm land to each other in such a manner that a restrospective analysis of the ownership of each individual parcel is carried out.[9] Thus it was possible to reconstruct even the earliest ownership units dating back to the high or early Middle Ages and link them genetically with the farms of the nineteenth century. A similar method was used by H. Bachmann, who aided by genealogical diagrams, retraced the ownership of north Tirolean farms right back to the sixth century, ie the time of the first arrival of the Bavarian settlers.[10]

The *association method* introduced by J. K. Rippel uses statistical means to reconstruct the historical development and the spatial structural changes of a land pattern complex beginning with the earliest cadastral maps of the area.[11] The following items are evaluated: the overall pattern of the village land (*Flurgefüge*) with reference to the soil and relief, also the field names, and the various shapes and sizes and the position of the individual plots of land in relation to the settlement. Particular note is taken of the association of parcels and larger units of the village land to particular classes of farms. The holdings' parcels of the eighteenth and nineteenth century are co-ordinated with the help of the combinatory evaluation of statistical distribution tables with those of the older holdings whose structure is derived by means of this method.

Besides the many techniques used also in studies of the geography of the present, there are also some specifically related to historical geography; however, some of the latter it shares with other neighbouring disciplines, in particular with history and its ancillary sciences.

Historico-geographical *field research* which concentrates on the investigation of extant vestiges of earlier landscapes, has had a new impetus in recent years. Its uppermost concern is to recognise, localise, describe, and interpret material as well as functional relics of earlier cultural landscapes, in the present point of time and space. In a broader sense, all phenomena which no longer fully conform to the present day socio-economic and political interplay of forces may be classified as such relics.

Since the earlier cultural landscapes were founded on a natural physical landscape, any extensive investigation must take account of this by studying the former physical nature by means of an historical physical geography, which investigates the earlier conditions of rivers, plant associations, soils and climate. The concept developed by H. Mortensen of the quasi-natural land forms lies somewhere between historical physical and historical cultural geography.[12] These land forms are the outcome of the quasi-physical moulding of the surface triggered off by anthropogenous interference. After man has created certain pre-conditions the relief then develops in conformity with natural physical laws. This theory was preceeded by various investigations, among them that of R. Käubler on the anthropogenous valley forms of the loess area of Saxony. As examples from a larger group of works, which combine physical and cultural geographical methods, mention may be made of investigations into soil erosion and the origin of minor relief features within historical time, natural or man-made. Study of the latter has been much stimulated by the results of research into deserted settlements. The mapping of abandoned fields has unearthed a whole range of agricultural relict features in the countryside. Some of these are for example ridge and furrow, terraced fields with sloped balks, further boulder banks, stone rows, heaps of stones gathered from the fields, earth banks and dry stone walls. Morphographic, morphogenetic, pedological, and stratographic studies of abandoned fields have proved of great assistance in the investigations of the existence of former arable farming and its intensity in certain areas. An extensive work by W. Müller-Wille deals with field patterns of the Dark Ages.[13] A. Semmel has developed a pedological method to prove the existence of former arable in areas without relict features.[14] This lends itself particularly to the study of deserted fields now covered by forest. Relict features are of assistance in deserted settlement research also in the important problem of the localisation of deserted settlements themselves; such relics are for instance: remains of buildings, features indicative of settlement on the surface of the ground (eg house platforms), wells, potsheards, burnt clay and other traces of occupance; further converging sunken tracks, ruderal plants (eg nettles) and certain elements in the soil (phosphate). Advances have been considerable where geographical and archeological methods have been linked together, as W. U. Guyan, among others, demonstrated in his research.[15] In a broader sense the abandoned buildings of former workshops and industrial installations also come under the heading of deserted settlements. Some branches of industry can look back at a long history of development, during which time their locations, the nature of their technical equipment and of the areas associated with their economic activity have altered considerably. Other industries, which were at one time important, have long since disappeared. Several investigations in recent years have examined former industries and their relict remains.[16]

Finally, part of the research into old roads and highways falls within the scope of historico-geographical field studies, and it has been furthered in recent years particularly by the co-operation of geographers and historians. H. Krüger's works on the oldest road map of Germany, together with the work of others, bear witness to the high status of historico-geographical archival and documentary studies. D. Denecke's extensive investigation employing field and archival data is the best and most up-to-date introduction to the study of ancient roads and highways in the German language area.[17]

It is beyond the scope of a brief survey such as this to give a more detailed account of all other methods of field research. Further techniques may only be summarily listed with reference to introductory publications. Combined researches in historical geography and pedology have been so successful in recent years that one may expect much more in the future from this direction.[18] Insights into the antropogenous changes in the vegetation, and into former land use, have been gained by means of interpretations of pollen diagrams. Fundamental for Central Europe in this respect is the still significant work by F. Firbas. Historico-geographical results are also obtainable from various techniques in plant sociology and forest history, as particularly instanced in several works by D. Krausch and H. Rubner.[19]

Of the less well known methods concerned with the evaluation of cartographic, pictorial and written sources, it may suffice to point to the *metrological* and *quantitative methods*. In the recent past these methods were considerably influenced by the works of Scandinavian geographers; because the material available in Germany is rather unlike that in Sweden, German studies differ from the Swedish in both their methodology and their content. Even though the material available in Central Europe is not as good as in Sweden, to judge by the rewarding work of recent years, further progress in the future is promising.[20]

Of techniques concerned with the evaluation of pictorial material which are still being developed mention must be made of *aerial photographic interpretation*. The *Institut für Landeskunde* of the *Bundesforschungsanstalt für Landeskunde und Raumforschung*, which possesses a large collection of aerial photographs, has in recent years issued a number of publications in some of which historical geography has also been touched upon.[21]

HISTORICAL PHYSICAL GEOGRAPHY

According to our concept of geography a general historical geography has evolved over the past decades analogous to general geography as such. It is principally represented in H. Jäger's *Historische Geographie* (1969). In view of the mutual interrelationships of almost all the geographical phenomena and processes, it is not enough to study individual phenomena in isolation. Examination of historical settlements, field patterns, workshops and other elements will only be satisfactory when the research is carried out in connexion with all those factors which conditioned and influenced them. Historical settlement geography is, for example, nothing else than an historical human geography which emphasises the study of settlements. Obviously they must be examined in association with physical geographical, technological, social, political, and economic factors.

Since historical geography has to do primarily with landscapes of historical and late prehistoric periods, it must concern itself with changes in physical geographical conditions, including those wrought by man. E. Neef examined in a general way the changeability of the physical environment whilst Jäger contributed a summary of physical conditions in medieval times. Recent publications on the question of man's influence upon the vegetation of Central Europe have been discussed by E. Glässer. G. Hard has repeatedly dealt with the influence of man on particular plant associations.[22]

As there is such a range of climatic areas in Central Europe, eg humid soils in the north west, dry regions in the centre and the south west, and since the high mountains have a well-defined upper limit of settlement, any lasting climatic changes must have far reaching consequences for settlement and land-use. For this reason, examinations of climatic changes in historical times, such as have been published by H. Flohn,[23] arouse great interest. A larger work by R. Fels concerns itself in a more general context with man-induced relief changes, soil erosion, changes of river courses, and climatic and coastal changes.[24] Coastal changes are discussed in a whole series of works on salt marsh studies, which largely due to W. Haarnagel have developed into a distinctive branch of physical and human geography. D. Hafeman has carried out research related to sea-level changes in historical time. Fluctuations of rivers and their impact on the regional settlement structure have been examined chiefly by H. Wilhelmy and H. Dongus.[25]

The findings of historical physical geography are fundamental to the study of past landscapes and also to works on the geographical bases of history. After a considerable period of stagnation research into this set of problems has been revitalised by C. Goehrke.[26]

HISTORICAL HUMAN GEOGRAPHY

So many contributions to historical human geography have appeared in recent years that only a few can be mentioned here as examples of the various aspects. Papers on genetic aspects make up the majority of publications. Advancing from the more formalistic 'morphology of the cultural landscape', which O. Schlüter had conceived even before World War I and in the inter-war period, studies of functional and socio-economic aspects have especially been developed owing to advances in methodology. This can be seen in the comprehensive paper by H. Bobek on social and economic development as well as in various publications concerned with smaller areas.[27] This stronger inclination towards the functional and socio-economic aspects explains why periodicals like the *Zeitschrift für Agrargeschichte und Agrarsoziologie* have published for years contributions by geographers and have given special prominence to geographical literature in their review sections.

In the field of settlement geography further refinements in regressive methods, the increased emphasis on archival studies and the results of research on deserted settlements have brought considerable advances. The high standard of methodology in geographical research into deserted settlements which goes right back to the work by Alfred Grund of 1901, the results of which are still largely valid today, has also intensified research in other disciplines into aspects of deserted settlements.

Taking account of geographical problems and using modern techniques of inquiry, C. Goehrke has initiated an historical examination of deserted settlements in Russia. Since deserted settlement research has up until now neglected many areas in Central Europe, regional examinations are capable of yielding surprising results of general significance. W. Janssen has carried out an investigation of the deserted settlements of the Rhineland using evidence of juxtaposition of settlement and castle, a work which is a fundamental introduction to the study of deserted settlements in this region. Valuable stimuli arose from collaboration with medieval archeology, which is likely to be intensified in the future. W. D. Hütteroth has shown to what extent advantage can be taken of the combined methods of geographical research into deserted settlements developed within the German language area, in relation to such research in countries outside Europe.[28] The papers read at the Würzburg Symposium of 1966 and the published material of the Working Party on the Terminology of the Agricultural Landscape testify to the international co-operation in the field of historical geography.[29]

A large part of the research concerned with dwellings and buildings, a branch of study whose justification has been undisputed for decades, belongs also to historical settlement geography. Authoritative contributions have been made by A. Krenzlin and by K. H. Schröder, and by R. Weiss from the points of view of both folk-lore and geography. Important material is also contained in G. Eitzen's survey and the series *Haus und Hof deutscher Bauern*. Since geography's concern with buildings is investigation according to their appearance and functional role in a socio-economic space, there is no difficulty in offsetting the geographical research on buildings both according to subject matter and method against the research in this field carried out by other disciplines.[30] H. Bobek and E. Lichtenberger have demonstrated in their large work on Vienna how to apply successfully geographical research on buildings in urban geography. Amongst recent examples of genetic urban geography is I. Leister's treatise on the city of Marburg. Besides monographs which deal with individual cities comprehensive works have also appeared. E. Keyser emphasises the importance of the layout as evidence of the development of cities without, however, abandoning the vital point of connecting it with documentary evidence. In this context P. Schöller's work on German towns, which has strong genetic leanings, must also be mentioned. For the historic small towns of the present a major problem for their continued existence is their integration within the modern functional regional structure. If they do not succeed in retaining their function as central places they will gradually lose all or most of their urban facilities and institutions. It is for that reason that several investigations over the past few years have concerned themselves with the problems of small towns of medieval origin. Historical urban geography is particularly closely related to local and regional history. In recent years the latter has produced various important works amongst which city atlases, genetic town maps in regional historical atlases and the book of German towns, edited by E. Keyser, with its regional volumes contain much material of great geographical relevance.[31]

Other studies which deal with towns under historico-geographical aspects are devoted to towns outside the German language area. R. Stewig showed in his work on Byzantium—Constantinople—Istanbul that it is necessary when investigating a world metropolis to take account of the time dimension. E. Wirth in his comparison of the cities of Damascus, Aleppo and Beirut goes back right into Hellenistic-Roman times. H. Wilhelmy contributed an historico-geographical work on the cities and towns of South America.[32]

Important publications dealing with topics of historical agricultural geography have already been mentioned; the comprehensive textbook by G. Schwarz contains numerous references to publications dealing with the origin of rural settlements and field patterns. Amongst the principal problems which have been solved in recent years is that of the origin of the *Gewannflur* (open fields). Although it had been established by research some time ago that it was a late form at the end of a long process of development, important questions concerned with chronology of the development, the initial forms from which it developed, and the mechanism of its changes had remained unanswered. As the works by A. Krenzlin and L. Reusch which were based on data from Lower Franconia have demonstrated, *Gewannflur* was not laid out simultaneously with the foundation of a settlement nor did it originate through a successive addition of *Gewann* (strip field) to *Gewann;* it was rather the final stage of a long development starting with field patterns consisting of large blocks or wide strips which became gradually more and more divided into smaller parcels.[33] These results have been confirmed by a number of investigations in other parts of

Germany. To the problems not yet finally solved belongs the question of the role that the so-called Frankish state colonisation played in southern Germany, and thematically allied with it, the phenomenon of early planned settlement and related types in that region. Planned settlements in southern Germany dating from the high and late medieval periods have been investigated primarily by K. Fehn.[34]

In recent years the active north-west German group of researchers connected with Müller-Wille has rather moved away from the *Langstreifen Theorie,* the hypothesis until then held that fields of long strips formed the original pattern of land divisions of the most ancient of our present settlements. In more recent investigations a division into blocks has been considered to have been the primary form in this area also; the long groups of strips within these having come about later as a dominant feature, the results of a secondary development. As a result of more refined methods of mapping deserted fields, M. Born[35] has also moved away from the earlier *Langstreifen Theorie.* A very convenient approach to research connected with the historical types of field patterns east of the Elbe is provided by works by A. Krenzlin, B. Benthien and O. August.[36]

In contrast to the many publications which deal with the origin of field patterns there are rather fewer concerned with systems of cultivation of past periods. A first important preliminary is to establish an inventory and to interpret extant antiquated systems, such as has been done by W. Kuls, A. Herold and W. A. Gallusser. Forms of field pattern and settlement types as well as land use systems of ancient character and other groups of historico-geographical objects are being investigated in central Slovakia by W. Sperling and F. Žigrai and are represented on a number of maps in the *Atlas der Deutschen Agrarlandschaft* edited by E. Otremba.[37]

As far as the investigation of dwelling places is concerned the starting point of research is the experience that settlements change rather rapidly. Research involves consideration of changes in economic, social, demographic, political and technological factors; these variables are all intertwined with each other in a system of interdependence whose elucidation is one of the tasks of historical geography. As recent works concerned with the origin of settlements have shown, the relatively numerous forms of dwelling places and field patterns are merely different stages in the development of rather fewer types; consequently only investigations which use a genetic approach are capable of leading to a full understanding. For the sake of economy of labour as well as for reasons inherent in the subject matter, the investigation of dwelling places goes hand in hand with research into field patterns so that most publications cited above also contain relevant information about the origin of dwelling places. It is established that some of our *Haufendörfer* (irregular nucleated villages) originated from *Weiler* (hamlets) and many of these in turn from *Einzelhöfe* (isolated farms); however, one must remember that a farm holding of the early historical period or the Dark Ages frequently possessed quite a different socio-economic organisation as a farm holding of the high or late Middle Ages or particularly the modern period. Phases of expansion and regression of settlement were not uncommon.

The structural changes in agriculture of the nineteenth century were particularly decisive for the present-day geography of Central Europe. H. Jäger has studied these changes particularly in Main Franconia and C. Borcherdt the Bavarian agricultural scene of the early nineteenth century while to H. Hahn we are indebted for a map of land use around 1820 together with a commentary—a contribution towards a map of the economy of the Rhineland of that time. An informative study by H. Pape showed how strongly a town which has since grown to a city exceeding 200,000 inhabitants was in 1828 still embedded in its agricultural region and involved with it.[38]

As far as specialised agricultural production is concerned the most intensive work has been on viticulture, its spatial development and the later shrinkage of the vine-growing area. K. Schröder has looked into the influences which viticulture has exerted on the forms of dwellings, settlements and field patterns for an extensive part of south-west Germany. R. Winkelmann using many and diverse unpublished documents has investigated the development of viticulture in the Rhine rift valley from its beginnings until the present. Other publications, although historical in their conception, are relevant to historical geography. K. Tisowsky has demonstrated in the

case of the southern Steigerwold the extent to which fluctuations in the area under vine from the sixteenth century onwards were determined by economic and social forces. The
first comprehensive survey of the once considerable viticulture
in Lower Lusatia has been produced by H. Krausch; it is based
on the interpretation of old maps, documents, pictorial presen-
tations and field evidence and is thus at the same time an
exemplary model of the combined historico-geographical
techinique. To H. Hahn we owe the most comprehensive work
on the German vine-growing areas. A more recent paper by
S. Morawetz investigates the pronounced recession of viticulture in south-western Styria resulting from socio-economic
changes.[39]

Since about 30 per cent of the total area of Germany,
Austria, and Switzerland is covered by forests, since their
locations are frequently an inheritance of earlier cultural
landscapes and since in the past in particular there existed
close relationships between forests and settlement, much attention has been paid in historical geography to forests. A starting point for any investigation into the distribution of woodland, heath and swamp is still the great work by O. Schlüter,
even if in some regions modifications would be necessary on
the strength of later research. A milestone in conception and
in content is F. Mager's great work on the forest in ancient
Prussia as a sphere of economic activity. H. Rubner and H.
Krausch in their research on forests link findings of plant
sociology, climatic history and pedology with results gleaned
from a meticulous examination of documentary sources. The
correlations between phases of advance and phases of regression of the cultural landscape on the one hand and changes in
the distribution of tree species found somewhat more rarely on
the other hand have been demonstrated by H. Jäger. The
influence of state legislation on the distribution of forests,
their composition and type has been investigated by H.
Hendinger, H. Jäger and F. Tichy. C. Troll has concerned himself in a comprehensive way with forests in Germany and
their former and present utilisation by man and has thus not
neglected to consider the historico-geographical conditions. W.
Abrahamczik's detailed investigation is fundamental as regards
the Alps.[40]

In a perusal of the extensive literature on historical geography one is initially under the impression that little attention has been paid to problems of historical industrial geography. In fact much has been done although, as a rule, questions of industrial geography have been dealt with in the context of more general human geographical investigations. Some relevant publications have already been pointed out in a different connection (p. 50). Other works which are exemplary models for the integration of a genetic industrial geography within treatises in human geography of a more general character have been produced by H. Overbeck, G. Mertins, and G. Ritter.[41]

Special problems arise in the compilation of maps of the economic geographies of the past. Comprehensive coverage, exact location of the items, and quantitative data are rare. For this reason a Sub-Commission of the *Akademie für Raumforschung und Landesplanung* is looking into the problems of historical economic maps. The emphasis of the work is placed on maps of the nineteenth century, when industrialisation spread through Central Europe. There are close ties between this Sub-Commission and a working group of historians on the history of industrialisation. The result of an interdisciplinary collaboration is an economic map of the Rhineland about 1820.[42]

Modern political geography differs considerably from the earlier approach which had concerned itself first and foremost with the physical bases of states and their politics, with the territories according to size, shape, location and differentiations and furthermore with the growth of states and groups of states. It dealt largely with problems which belong to the field of political science and developed in a deterministic way which led ultimately into a cul-de-sac. In the emerging new political geography the question which stands foremost is that of the spatial efficiency of political institutions. Research concerned with regional planning in the past also relates to political geography: an appropriate Commission of the *Akademie für Raumforschung und Landesplanung* in which geographers and historians collaborate has already produced eight volumes.[43]

Because of its temporal remoteness from the processes which shaped the cultural landscape of the past, historical geography is in a position to study the results of the influence of political institutions on the landscape. It is thus capable of obtaining results which enable it to suggest a basis for a new political geography. Advances in this direction are offered by F. Huttenlocher in his attempt to identify the spatial after-effects of policies of the former territories of Germany; by F. Metz in the last section of his paper on the bishopric and monastic house of Speyer and in particular by H. Overbeck, G. Pfeifer, P. Schöller, W. Fricke and H. Lamping.[44]

GEOGRAPHIES OF THE PAST AND LANDSCAPE HISTORIES

A separate branch of historical geography is concerned with the reconstruction of *Altlandschaften* (past landscapes). In its earlier stages of development the most important contributions in this branch have been made by Gradmann, Schlüter, Mortensen, and Schott. The term *Altlandschaft* denotes a relatively self-contained *geomer* of the prehistorical or historical past which has undergone changes by human occupance. Since in practice this research field is usually concerned with landscape conditions of the pre-historic or early historical past it has close ties with prehistoric and medieval archaeology and with the history of climate. The collaboration with pedology and the study of the development of the vegetation cover has proved particularly fruitful. Only a few works have achieved the ultimate aim of reconstructing the geographical conditions of a whole state or a large part of one at a particular point in the past, but there are many publications which have furnished contributions towards it. A. Schulten's restrictive conception has not found a response. According to him an historical regional geography of the Iberian Peninsula would have the sole task of evaluating most meticulously all points of information contained in the written sources of the classical period but do no more than this.[45]

Because of the incompleteness of the written records, which persisted well into the Middle Ages, this method can at best lead to a mere skeleton of a regional historical geography. Schulten himself did not succeed in getting beyond a good collection of material which because of the incompleteness of the written records, taken on its own, could never lead to a complete regional geography. More comprehensive and closer to an historical regional geography, since sources dating from periods later than the classic one are also evaluated, are the chapters by E. Kirsten dealing with the historical regional geography in the work of many volumes by A. Philippson on Greece.[46]

The work by H. and G. Mortensen on the settlement of the eastern part of East Prussia about 1400 in its use of many methods, including the regressive and restrospective ones, comes much closer to the aim of an historical regional geography as a comprehensive geography of a past period. G. Oberbeck almost achieved it when he depicted the medieval cultural landscape around Gifhorn in maps and texts. If F. Herzog in his work on the Osnabrück region in the eighteenth and nineteenth centuries had paid greater attention to towns and trade it would have amounted to an historical regional geography in the true sense.[47] Limited aspects of an historical regional geography are contained in investigations which deal genetically with the development of some groups of objects or of certain regions. Works of this kind usually combine 'horizontal' and 'vertical' sections and thereby come close to landscape histories as a separate class of historico-geographical account. It is difficult to say whether geographers usually avoid the expression 'landscape history' because the investigations are bound more strongly to the retrospective method (cf p 46) whose main concern is the present, or because they wish to avoid the word 'history' in a geographical account. However there can be no doubt that landscape history is a branch of the field of geography, just as the history of the development of plant life is a branch of botany, or the history of the earth is a branch of geology. Among the geographers who consciously and purposely call some of their works 'landscape histories' are F. Mager, W. U. Guyan, E. Winkler, and H. Jäger.[48]

W. Hütteroth in his important work on central Asia Minor deals with the subject quite deliberately very much along landscape historical lines. In his introduction he poses the question whether the concept of cultural landscape developed on the basis of conditions in Western and Central Europe should still be used in regions with much less dynamism of

E

landscape change. Numbering among the instructive examples which—apart from that by Hütteroth—apply the historico-geographical method developed in Central Europe to regions outside Europe are studies by G. Pfeifer on cultural landscapes in the New World, by F. Tichy on cultural landscape origins in Mexico and an interesting investigation of settlement in the lands of the Russian Cossack armies.[49]

Cross-sectional landscape reconstructions which in themselves are steps towards regional historical geographies, in particular if they are supplemented by discussions of the genetic implications, are to be found in so many good regional studies that only a few can be listed.[50]

HISTORICAL ATLASES

The plan of an historical atlas of the Austrian Alpine lands proposed by the Austrian geographer Richter in 1896 gave the first impetus to a whole series of regional historical atlases. From the beginning geographers and historians have collaborated on these works, which have become more sophisticated in both the questions tackled and in method. Regional historical atlases not only summarise cartographically the results of investigations over decades, they are also instruments of research which lead to new insights and methods of inquiry. The research report and bibliography by G. Franz cites over 400 publications from the present and former German language area. Amongst them are to be found besides the atlases also individual thematic maps, map series and papers concerned with historical cartography.[51]

In their topics, the historical regional atlases frequently embrace all important aspects of geography, from the physical basis to settlement, population, communications, economy and administration. Most of these atlases are complemented by memoirs which are often detailed monographs. Hence these atlases together with their accompanying memoirs form historical geographies of a special kind, always of a very high standard. By combining maps and text both the spatial description of the past as well as the genetic explanation of the respective conditions are mastered successfully.

4

Historical Geography in Scandinavia

By STAFFAN HELMFRID

DEFINITION AND DELIMITATION

THERE EXISTS NO stringent definition of historical geography that clearly separates it from other branches of systematic geography. In a sense all geographical research which takes into consideration geographical change over time could be called historical, and historical geography would then be just the dynamic approach to geographical problems. Even in the present volume, authors have expressed different views upon the delimitation of historical geography.[1]

Geography as a discipline has always profited by pragmatic approaches to philosophical problems, and a pragmatic definition of historical geography is therefore preferred by the present writer. The most typical feature of historical geographical research is that it has to rely upon historical evidence, either directly or indirectly man-made features of landscape, maps or written sources, more or less randomly preserved and inherited from past generations. This type of evidence differs in one fundamental way from source material produced by the living generation and generally used in contemporary research in human geography. It is a completed record, which can get lost or be damaged, but not be renewed or completed. Usually special training added to the basic geographical one is needed to be able to read and use this type of record. Special methods are also needed to bridge more or less random gaps in data series; silent witnesses must be interpreted.

The delimitation of different branches of systematic geography is relevant only for empirical work. All theoretical and methodological progress within geography and its neighbouring sciences bears as much upon historical geography as upon other fields of geographical research. This essay confines itself to empirical work and to methodological and theoretical progress developing from empirical work within historical geography.

For the present purpose a further limitation of the subject to be treated is needed. Historical geography in the Scandinavian countries, most of which experienced the effects of industrialisation and urbanisation only during the last hundred years, has mainly been concerned with agrarian historical geography.[2] Although the profound changes of society and landscape within this recent period of transformation offer vast fields for urgent historico-geographical research, the main stress of work until now has been upon the exploration of traditional rural societies and landscapes prior to the land reforms preceding the Industrial Revolution. From the second half of the eighteenth century, land reforms in all Scandinavian countries dissolved village communities, nucleated settlements and open-field patterns. Early predecessors of this process of modernisation have been traced in Southern Jutland as early as 1710.[3] Legislation first occurred in Sweden in 1757, was more radical and compulsory in 1803 and was then modified in 1827. Danish landlords started village dissolution in the 1760s, and legislation in Denmark was passed in 1781. Finland, which shared the fate of Sweden as part of the realm until 1809, completed its land reforms by the laws of 1881 and 1916. In Norway the redistribution of farms and fields was generally carried through in the second half of the nineteenth century.

This fundamental process of change, which is documented in an immense wealth of records, has so far attracted surprisingly little interest from historical geographers. It will certainly prove to be an extremely rewarding field for systematic study.[4]

AGRARIAN HISTORICAL GEOGRAPHY IN SCANDINAVIA

Modern historical geography in Scandinavia, as here defined, builds upon a great number of solidly founded local studies and regional surveys. Idiographic in scope, these basic studies unveiled the wealth of historical evidence and provided detailed descriptions of rural economies and landscapes, especially during the period from about 1640 to the middle of the nineteenth century. In the 1930–40s most Scandinavian geographers were engaged in this exploratory search into the past. The spatial coverage of the main works of this type is shown in Fig 3. Single village studies and more superficial regional surveys have not been included in this account.

A few of the works cited pointed ahead to a general shift of interest from mainly source-material-based exploration of the past towards more specifically problem-based analysis. Methodological and theoretical questions of the whole subject increasingly attracted the attention of human geographers. The introduction of new quantitative techniques and more sophisticated theorising, ie what has been called the shift to 'modern geography', occurred in Sweden in the 1940-50s. New fields of research called for attention, not least the fundamental questions of today's and tomorrow's spatial organisation of society. Historical geography was affected in two ways by this shift, quantitatively in a negative sense as a majority of the young generation of human geographers turned to problems of modern society and qualitatively in a positive sense as the new methods and theories were applied also in this field. Like human geography as a whole, historical geography experienced the cross-fertilising of empirical, theoretical and methodological work. A review and evaluation of early analytical studies and approaches to models of the historical evolution of fields and settlement patterns in Scandinavia was given by S. Helmfrid in 1962.[5] The author identified a number of the most relevant problems in modern agrarian historical geography and contributed to their solution through analysis on both macro- and micro-scales. Both from the point of view of its agrarian history and its richness in historical evidence, and above all in its cadastral plans from 1633 onwards, the

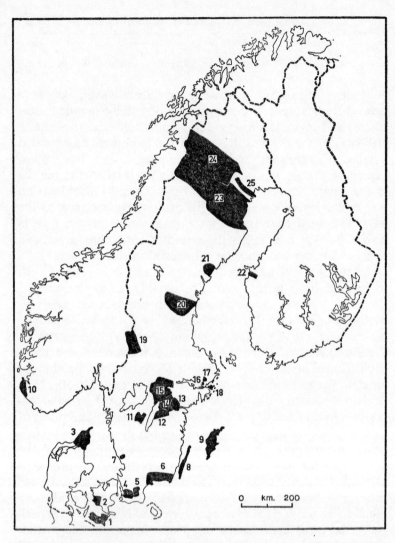

Fig 3   Regional studies of the traditional peasant economies and rural
landscapes of Scandinavia:
1   Widding, O. *Markfaellesskab og landskifte* (Copenhagen, 1949)
2   Hansen, R.-Steensberg, A. *Jordfordeling og usskiftning* (Copenhagen, 1951)
3   Hansen, V. *Landskab og begyggelse i Vendsyssel* (Copenhagen,
1964)
4   Dahl, S. *Torna och Bara* (Lund, 1942)
5   Kristoffersson, A. *Landskapsbildens förändringar i norra och
östra de len av Färs härad under de senaste tvåhundra åren*
(Lund, 1924)

6 Björnsson, S. *Blekinge. En studie av det blekingska kultur-landskapet* (Lund, 1946)
  Torbrand, D. *Johannishus fideikommiss intill 1735* (Uppsala, 1963)
7 Stenström, N. G. *Slöinge och Elftra socknar 1600–1870* (Lund 1945)
8 Göransson, S. *Village planning patterns and territorial organiza-tion. Studies in the Development of the Rural Landscape of Eastern Sweden (Oland)* (Uppsala, 1971)
9 Moberg, I. *Gotland um das Jahr 1700* (Stockholm, 1938)
10 Rønneseth, O. *Frühgeschichtliche Siedlungs-und Wirtschafts-formen im südwestlichen Norwegen* (Neumünster, 1966)
11 Lindgren, G. *Falbygden* (Uppsala, 1939)
12 Helmfrid, S. *Östergötland 'Västanstånt'. Studien über die ältere Agrarlandschaft und ihre Genese* (Stockholm, 1962)
13 Wennberg, A. *Lantbebyggelsen i nordöstra Östergötland 1600–1875* (Lund, 1947)
14 Bergsten, K. E. *Östergötlands bergslag* (Lund, 1946)
15 Hannerberg, D. *Närkes landsbygd 1600–1820* (Göteborg, 1941)
16 Forssell, E. *Kulturlandskapets utveckling i Sollentuna från 1500-talet till början av 1900-talet* (Stockholm, 1938)
17 Lagerstedt, T. *Näringsliv och bygd i Seminghundra härad vid 1630-talets slut* (Uppsala, 1942)
18 Hedenstierna, B. *Stockholms skärgård. Kulturgeografiska under-sökningar i Värmdö gamla skeppslag* (Stockholm, 1949)
19 Nilsson, Y. *Bygd och näringsliv i norra Värmland* (Lund, 1950)
20 Bodvall, G. *Bodland i norra Hälsingland* (Uppsala, 1959)
21 Westin, J. *Kulturgeografiska studier inom Nätra-, Näskeoch Utbyåarnas flodområden samt angränsande kusttrakter* (Lund, 1930)
22 Smeds, H. *Malaxbygden* (Helsinki, 1935)
23 Bylund, E. *Koloniseringen av Pite lappmark intill år 1867* (Uppsala, 1956)
24 Hultblad, F. *Overgång från nomadism till agrar bosättning i Jokkmokks socken* (Lund, 1968)
25 Enequist, G. *Nedre Luledalens byar* (Uppsala, 1937)

western part of the plain in Östergötland is an extremely rewarding area for this type of study.

PROGRESS IN SELECTED FIELDS OF EMPIRICAL STUDY

The prehistoric continuity problem
  The classical continuity problem of southern Scandinavian rural settlements through the Migration period (AD 400–600) was clearly formulated by M. Stenberger in his thesis on Öland (1933). The numerous desolate early iron-age field- and fence-systems with their house foundations on the island of

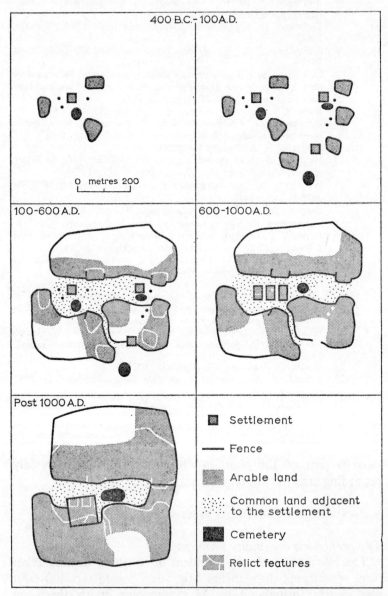

400 B.C. - 100 A.D.

0 metres 200

100-600 A.D.

600-1000 A.D.

Post 1000 A.D.

◨ Settlement

— Fence

▨ Arable land

∷ Common land adjacent
   to the settlement

▩ Cemetery

▧ Relict features

Fig 4 A graphical model of the evolution of a rural landscape in eastern
Östergötland, Sweden (after S. O. Lindquist, 1968, 48)

Öland and Gotland proved to have counterparts in vast areas of prehistoric fields, mapped by G. Hatt in the heaths of Jutland in the 1930–40s.[6] In Sweden G. Nordholm was the first geographer to find prehistoric and medieval fields near Lund in 1937.[7] The interest of geographers in these physical remnants of past cultural landscapes was greatly inspired by German research in the early 1950s.[8] Systematic reconnaissance by the Department of Human Geography at the University of Stockholm, organised by D. Hannerberg in the 1950s and early 1960s, revealed a wealth of 'fossil field' localities previously unknown in Sweden. Efforts were concentrated on Öster- and Västergötland. The old field-patterns preserved on the ground could assist in testing long-debated hypotheses on the origin and development of different types of field and settlement structures. Historical geography joined with archaeology in the common demand for intensive field work on selected localities. Independently of each other, S.-O. Lindquist in Östergötland (Eastern Sweden) and O. Rønneseth in Jaeren (Western Norway) mapped and analysed a number of localities and gave a convincing geographical interpretation of these deserted cultural landscapes, the spatial organisation of farms, fields and fences.[9] Excavations were made to answer specific questions. Both came to the conclusion that there had been no total break in continuity of settlements and cultivation during the iron-age. Before or at the beginning of the medieval period (in Scandinavia c. AD 1000) new farming techniques and systems spread to these parts of Europe, causing changes in the structure and organisation of farms and fields. Lindquist summarised his findings in a generalised scheme of landscape evolution claimed as valid for east-middle Sweden during the first millennium of our calendar (Fig 4).

Important results of Lindquist's work were:

(a) the certain identification, exact mapping and dating (c. AD 650–700) of prehistoric, planned and fenced building sites (*tomt* or toft) of a small nucleated settlement (Halleby, east of Linköping). This is the oldest reference material for the retrogressive study of village tofts, taking their starting-point in the cadastral plans of the seventeenth to eighteenth centuries.

(b) the exact mapping and dating of prehistoric arable fields, the first ones in the east-middle Swedish *solskifte*-area. In Skåne, D. Hannerberg had already mapped and analysed a system of 'fossil fields' in the 1950s, demonstrating a reparcelling into typical medieval strips of previous 'celtic' fields.[10] At the same time K. Scharlau and M. Born had made similar observations in the German 'Mittelgebirge'.

(c) the identification of a two-field arrangement of the arable land. This statement has bearing on the dating of the east Swedish two-field rotation system, generally practised until the last century and well documented in medieval sources. It also has relevance in the discussion on the formation of village communities and nucleated settlements. In Västergötland Lindquist and others have mapped a deserted village which will possibly help to date the introduction of two-field rotation and later a three-field rotation, and in Närke U. Sporrong has C[14]-dated a stone fence separating the two fields of a village. Much more work has to be done to secure the dating of the phases of diffusion of these fundamental agrarian innovations.

In Jaeren, one of the oldest agricultural areas of Norway, Rønneseth in a number of papers since 1955 has reconsidered the old established ideas of iron-age landscape evolution. Jaeren is extremely rich in remnants of iron-age settlement, fields and fences, although present day intensive cultivation rapidly destroys many of the relict features (Fig 5). Combined with historical evidence they led Rønneseth to three fundamental conclusions:

(a) Many of the deserted farms had been continuously inhabited and cultivated from early iron-age well into medieval times.

(b) Between AD 600/650 and 1350 (probably around 1100) there had been a change in agrarian economy and technique, which led to the concentration of crop growing on a more restricted area around the farm, an area which was heavily manured by compost (humus layer up to 1.5m thick) and sown every year. There was also a shift towards greater livestock production. Parts of the previous arable fields were changed to meadows.

(c) Contrary to the general view, that Norway had never been influenced by the process of village community formation, Rønneseth traced a development in Jaeren which was very much like the one postulated for middle Europe and parts of Scandinavia in the same period.

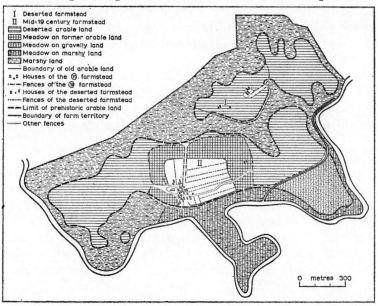

I   Deserted farmstead
II   Mid-19 century farmstead
▭   Deserted arable land
▦   Meadow on former arable land
▦   Meadow on gravelly land
▦   Meadow on marshy land
▩   Marshy land
——   Boundary of old arable land
◻,◻ Houses of the ⑲. farmstead
·—·— Fences of the ⑲ farmstead
▪,ᴵ Houses of the deserted farmstead
····· Fences of the deserted farmstead
▬▬ Limit of prehistoric arable land
——   Boundary of farm territory
······· Other fences

0   metres   300

Fig 5   Relict cultivation and settlement features in Njaerheim, Jaeren
(after O. Rønneseth, 1966, 30)

The works cited represent the type of intensified field-work on selected localities using a combination of methods (micro-analysis), including archaeological ones, which in the present state of knowledge are very necessary for geographers tackling specified problems and testing the more refined hypotheses put forward in modern historical geography. A very costly, beautifully documented, archaeological excavation like that of the Vallhager early iron-age settlement on Gotland, on the other hand, had very little to contribute to historical geography.[11] From an historical-geographical point of view an archaeologist like B. Ambrosiani obtained more valuable results in his macro-scale analysis of prehistoric settlement, based on the overwhelmingly rich wealth of prehistoric cemeteries in the eastern Lake Mälar region.[12] It considerably broadened our knowledge of early settlement geography in the politico-historical core area of the realm. His results differed in part from those of Lindquist, indicating contrasts between the northern and southern parts of eastern Sweden. As will be discussed later, D. Hannerberg has succeeded with the morphometric method that he has developed in his retrogressive analysis of village tofts and fields in meeting up with the results based on the field examination of prehistoric remnants.

As a result of a number of studies in the last decade we have gained a remarkably clear picture of the distribution, physical structure and spatial organisation of the oldest stratum of the agrarian cultural landscape in Scandinavia.

The regression phase of the late Middle Ages

In 1962 S. Helmfrid summed up our knowledge of the regression of settlement and arable land in late medieval times in Scandinavia and related it to the very fruitful historical-geographical discussion in Germany on this topic in the 1950s. Regional differences in the intensity and effect of the late medieval regression phase in agrarian settlement in Scandinavia remain relatively uncertain. The problems were discussed at a Symposium of Scandinavian historians in Bergen in 1964 and reports on recent research were published in the programme of this meeting.[13] To fill the gap in empirical knowledge historians organised an inter-Scandinavian 'deserted farm committee' in 1969, which has so far had three Scandinavian meetings, in Copenhagen in 1969, in Växjö in 1970, and in Joensuu in 1971.

Structural change and estate formation during the sixteenth and seventeenth centuries

Another field of co-operation between historians and historical geographers bearing upon the evolution of agrarian landscapes is the problems connected with the structural changes of agrarian society and economy in the sixteenth to seventeenth centuries in the countries around the Baltic. The process of estate formation, centred in the German lands south of the Baltic, spread over the Scandinavian countries. In 1965 S. Helmfrid made a survey of existing knowledge and sketched a programme for research at the Visby Symposium for Historical Sciences.[14] The most detailed geographical analysis of a large Scandinavian estate so far published is the study of D. Torbrand on Johannishus in Blekinge.[15]

The phases of land clearance and colonisation

It is a basic task of historical geography to map out the space-time process of land clearance and colonisation, which involved a more or less continuous growth of the settled and cultivated area in northern Europe through a period of more than 1,300 years. In Sweden it came to an end in the northern-most parts of inner Norrland around 1950, while in Finland the process of retreat has started only in recent years. In Norway, because of government subsidies to agriculture, land clearance in mountainous areas still takes place. The big phases of colonisation are well known in their spatial outlines from a great number of studies. But there have been relatively few detailed studies aiming to elucidate the local and regional course of the process of land clearance and settlement founda-tion. Nonetheless, a great deal of the last phase of large-scale land occupance from the sixteenth century onwards can be subject to exact study in historical records.

The colonisation of Iceland by Norwegian farmers and fishermen during the Viking age is uniquely well documented for this early period, but it still awaits the detailed and com-prehensive historical-geographical analysis it deserves. Finland has been settled since the late Iron Age. The extent of per-manently settled areas at the end of the Middle Ages and the spread of colonisation northwards since then have been mapped by E. Jutikkala.[16]

The medieval colonisation of the forested regions of south Sweden has been studied by historians and place-name philo-logists, but only recently has it attracted the attention of historical geography.[17] The colonisation of inner north Sweden, which occurred mainly from the eighteenth century onwards, has been extensively studied by geographers at Uppsala. Based upon the pioneering works of J. Frödin on seasonal chalet

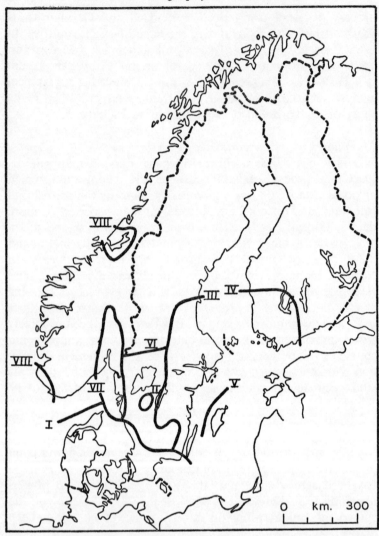

Fig 6   Border zones of particular relevance to the regional differentiation
        of rural landscapes in Scandinavia
   I   The old Swedish-Danish frontier (until 1658)
   II   The Falbygden area of Västergötland
   III   The extension of the eastern Swedish 'solskifte' area
   IV   The old-settled parts of Finland with villages and 'solskifte'
   V   Gotland
   VI   Southern border of 'Norrland terrain'
   VII–VIII Old-settled agricultural centres of Norway

settlements and G. Enequist on old permanent settlements, a number of their students have examined the historical geography of Norrland. The earlier studies were summarised by G. Enequist in 1959.[18] S. Rudberg traced the growth of farm settlements in Lapland in 50-year periods from 1750 to 1950 in a series of maps.[19] The well documented and detailed mapping and analysis of the colonisation of Pite lappmark by E. Bylund is in many respects the most important of this group of studies.[20] Bylund followed step by step, family by family, the phases of land clearance and colonisation. He laid the foundation for a very promising line of theoretical work on the mechanism and spatial structure of colonisation processes (see below, p. 87). Bylund identified two distinct phases in the course of colonisation—first, when a few remote settlers from the coast founded the first settlements inland far apart from each other, and secondly when descendants of the first settlers spread over the area, founding new settlements in successive phases of 'inner colonisation'.

This type of thorough reconstruction is extremely laborious but fundamentally important. Only with the aid of genealogical studies ('genealogical-topographical method') did F. Hultblad succeed in tracing the process of colonisation by nomad Lapps in Jokkmokk from 1780 to 1910.[21]

The morphogenetic analysis of open-field landscapes

There exists as yet no survey of the regional differentiation of rural landscapes in Scandinavia, not even for one of the countries. Nevertheless the basic pattern of existing regional differences is discernible. The map (Fig 6) is an attempt to show this, with the aid of some clearly defined and relevant boundaries of markedly different origin and character. An immense amount of work has to be done to develop this sketch into a map of agrarian landscape regions, and it must still be regarded as experimental. Only for Denmark do we have as yet, thanks to the work of F. Hastrup, a complete survey of the pre-enclosure type of each village.[22] Something similar has been compiled only for small parts of Sweden. There is sufficient evidence, in fact, to cover most of Scandinavia.

The traditional patterns of settlement and open-fields, differing in many ways from region to region, were a result of perhaps a thousand years of evolution. As has already been stated, it is well known that the old-settled plains of southern Scandinavia had a well-established agrarian settlement pattern in the first centuries AD. Innovations which caused changes and reorganisation at different points of time have spread from south to north and from west to east, mostly originating in continental Europe and/or in the British Isles. In the High Middle Ages this traditional rural landscape had already reached maturity; it remained—while under the continuous influence of the forces which had created it—practically unchanged in its structure until the land reforms of the eighteenth and nineteenth centuries, when it was left untouched by estate-formation. The morphogenetic analysis of this landscape, taking its point of departure in the village maps of the seventeenth and eighteenth centuries, must look upon it as one coherent space-time complex extending over a thousand years and spatially over the borders of northern Europe.

This space-time complex is the main object of agrarian historical-geographical research and in itself a basic source to social, economic and technological history. Recent studies have confirmed that the administrative division and spatial organisation of rural society in Scandinavia were well established at the end of prehistoric times. As to the original principles of the spatial administrative system, geographers have arrived at new views which differ from those put forward by earlier research.[23]

The most spectacular progress in analysing the morphogenetic structure of the old agrarian landscapes has been obtained fairly recently. In many aspects it bears the imprint of the pioneering methodological and theoretical work of D. Hannerberg. His methodological contribution, which is undoubtedly the most original Swedish contribution to historical geography, if not to human geography as a whole, will be treated later. First some problems, results and prospects will be discussed.

In the 1950s two Swedish geographers, S. Göransson and S. Helmfrid, inspired by the results achieved by the new morphogenetic methods developed in Germany by W. Müller-Wille and others, devoted their theses to the analysis of the genetic

compound of the traditional east Swedish *solskifte* landscape.[24]

Göransson and Helmfrid tried by the morphogenetic
approach to discern the model form of the different 'layers'
of landscape evolution. Both tried to knit together the traditional Scandinavian approach to research on these topics, little
known abroad, and the modern continental approach to
research then little known in Scandinavia. This process of
integration between different 'national schools' was considerably furthered by the Vadstena Symposium in 1960.[25] The
study of maps and documents from the morphogenetic point
of view revealed the complexity of forms and also a wealth of
problems within this superficially uniform area. The studies
provided insights into the genetic macro-structure and clear
indications of the main phases of landscape evolution. The
analysis of large villages with complex patterns of fields and
settlement and the special observation of the many deviations
from a regular *solskifte* model raised questions about the
structure of pre-*solskifte* landscape. The medieval transformation of villages by *solskifte* had not been so efficient and
radical as had been supposed. Hannerberg showed that regularities in village layout which had long been assumed to be
results of *solskifte* regulation could originate from much earlier
regulations.

Hannerberg had become interested in the 1940s in the
genetic problems inherent in the obviously planned and geometrically regular layout of villages as portrayed in seventeenth and eighteenth century cadastral plans in Närke, the
historical geography of which had been the subject of his
thesis in 1941. His assiduous thirty years' research on the
ideas and techniques behind the advanced physical planning
of villages in the old rural society was triggered off by the
relation between population and food production in the old
subsistence economy. As a fundamental variable for a quantitative economic history the area of arable land at different
points in time aroused his special interest. To derive reliable
quantitative data for cereal and animal production (and above
all of acreage) from historical records Hannerberg had to
clarify both the meaning of the figures given in the sources
available—mostly maps and taxation lists of various age and

F

origin—and also the size of the locally variant old measures used in sixteenth- and seventeenth-century Sweden.

Unlike his predecessors in this field of research, Hannerberg did not retire before the seemingly undecipherable chaos of local measures. Step by step he succeeded in unveiling systematic and explainable connexions between different systems of measures, changes in the system caused by the introduction of new basic measures of length and relationships between their geometrical size. New contributions to the chronology of measures were made as well. In a pioneering work Hannerberg had arrived in 1946 at two important results. First, the series of *utsädestal* (seed list, in barrels) noted for each farm in seventeenth-century taxation lists did not really mean the quantity sown on each farm, not even the area sown. They were, in the area of investigation, merely inherited taxation values of the farms, coinciding with the medieval land taxation units of *markland*. Secondly, the identification of the size of measures used for the layout of fields and farms in different periods, which opened up a way to identifying the different chronological strata of fields and tofts within the village.[26]

As a sequel to these results Hannerberg started a series of map and field analyses of relicts mainly in middle Sweden. About 1955 a number of papers proved the value of this approach, providing unexpected, and in part amazing, results. Hannerberg demonstrated the enormous amount of information about the thousand years of evolution inherent in old cadastral plans and measurable field relicts. The dating of the clearance of different fields within villages allowed in principle identification of the arable area of these villages at distinct points in time, for instance at the time of the introduction of the *solskifte*. The pattern of the *solskifte* morphometrically analysed clearly indicated the period of introduction of this system. Comparative studies of villages in the old Danish province of Skåne, with its well-preserved patterns of *bolskifte*, also gave fruitful insights into the structure of the *solskifte* villages of middle Sweden.[27] In an analysis of Veberöd, near Lund, Hannerberg exactly determined the normative size of the mansus-unit, the *bol*, assessed to the village in the Viking age. Applying the morphometric method in two villages in Skåne H. Andersson discovered a type of systematic land division, which he called *kedjeskifte,* with clear relations to both *bolskifte* and *solskifte.* In this form, the normal *bol*-parcels of equal width were split up into broad strips of unequal size, and intermingled.[28]

Since the end of the 1950s Hannerberg has again concentrated his efforts on middle Swedish villages, above all in Närke. The *bol*-conception has also been applied in middle Sweden in pre-*solskifte* farm- and village-assessment.[29] In a combination of inductive and deductive methods Hannerberg concluded:

(*a*) that there must have been a *bol*-assessment in middle Sweden long before the *solskifte* was introduced.

(*b*) that the medieval 'marklands'-assessment was not based on contemporary taxation of farm-size, but mainly formally converted older value assessments, which dated back to prehistoric time

(*c*) that the prehistoric taxation units formed the base of the regional administrative divisions, which were mathematically built up

(*d*) that it was a fundamental task to decipher and determine geometrically the exact normative size of the mansus-unit in its great variation through time and space

(*e*) that the assessed size of the farms was documented in the size of the building toft long before the *solskifte* regulation. The normative size of the mansus played a fundamental role not only for fiscal purposes but for the physical planning of farms and villages. There is evidence of a clear planning principle, the mansus assessment being evidenced in the size of the building toft and the arable area standing in a definite size relation to the area of the toft.

During recent years Hannerberg has step by step widened our knowledge of mansus sizes, their connexion with the systems of geometrical measures and their general chronology. Thus in principle he revealed a way of determining the size of arable land for farms and villages in the prehistoric or early historic period when the farms were first assessed in land taxation. In favourable cases this arable land and the building toft to which it belonged can be identified in the map and on the ground. In 1966 Hannerberg outlined the many-sided problems and exciting perspectives into the central questions of economic and social history which historical geography was able to give.[30]

Intensive field work, combining all available field techniques including excavation, carried out by U. Sporrong in different parts of the Lake Mälar region in the last five years confirm on important points the results achieved by Hannerberg.[31] Sporrong's work also throws new light upon the time-space spread of early evolution in the agrarian landscape of this central part of Sweden.

To be successful and yield significant results quantitative micro-analysis must be rooted in a combined data basis derived from pre-enclosure cadastral plans, relevant taxation values and other quantitative data from historical records as well as from field measurements and datings. Unfortunately this combination of sources is not available for a majority of villages. Research will have to concentrate on the most promising localities. Reliable large-scale maps are a *sine qua non* for such studies.

The most exact large-scale (1:250) map of a well-dated medieval village field pattern constructed so far was published by A. Steensberg as a first main result of fifteen years of field work in the deserted village of Borup on Själland.[32] It will be an important source reference in Denmark, hitherto lacking large-scale cadastral plans for the period before land consolidation and village dissolution. The main sources for the study of old Danish field systems and land-parcelling are the taxation assessment minutes of the Matrikkel 1688, containing parcel by parcel length, breadth and area of the fields, and they enabled R. Hansen and A. Steensberg to reconstruct field maps of a couple of villages.[33]

Another interesting and intensively studied feature of the old agrarian landscape in southern Scandinavia was the highly developed system of inter-village field communities, called *vångalag*. If villages co-ordinated their two- or three-field rotation with that of the neighbouring villages, fences between adjacent fields could be saved. This type of co-ordination had gone farthest on the plain in south-western Skåne, where hundreds of villages were linked to each other in a series of *vångalag.* The most complete survey of knowledge about this type of phenomenon was published by F. Hastrup in 1970.[34]

The analysis of rural landscapes and their evolution demands the combined evaluation of very different types of source material. It demands a combination of methods and thus a co-operation of specialists. It is a special responsibility of the historical geographer to make syntheses and models of development in its total aspects. With the well known work of B. H. Slicher van Bath, *Agrarian History of Western Europe AD 500–1850,* as a background, Hannerberg has just provided a general survey of results achieved so far and of problems for further research in Scandinavia.[35] As an integrated evaluation of research in the last 30–40 years, this promises to be a major inspiration for further work, and sets Swedish research in a European context as well as providing a survey of the source materials. The first volume is centred on the problems that arise in combining the different groups of sources in an analysis of the quantitative questions of old agrarian economy. The second part is centred on problems, methods and results from morphogenetic and morphometric studies of old rural landscapes.

Historical population geography

Population development plays a decisive role in the evolution of a rural economy and landscape. Sweden and Finland are especially well equipped for the historical study of population geography and many research workers from other countries have found here the detailed population records needed for testing demographic models over a longer time-span. The population registers, unique in their length and detail, make the old Swedish-Finnish realm a key area for historical population geography. The emphasis of Swedish historical-geographical concern in this field has been laid on the critical examination of the demographic records. On the basis laid down by Hannerberg in his thesis on Närke published in 1941 and in subsequent works, N. Friberg has devoted a series of works to the problems of early population records prior to the start of the official statistical service in 1749 (*Tabellverket*). His main concern was to find methods for critical control of population registers to ensure the calculation of exact population figures. Interesting results were established on the relation between production and population development in seventeenth-century Dalarna. Many challenging problems await more attention. In the nineteenth century Sweden went through a demographic transition, the radical dissolution of villages, inner colonisation, emigration and early industrialisation. The period of rapid population growth from 1820 to 1870 has so far been astonishingly neglected by historical geography, although the geographical analysis of early population records has proceeded far in Finland.[36]

In this essay the author has confined himself to treating only the main stream of historical geographical work in Scandinavia in the past and present, which is concerned with the pre-industrial rural society and open-field landscape. As a result, a great number of works on the historical geography of the last one hundred years, and studies on urban and industrial historical geography, have deliberately been excluded from the review. No doubt these fields of historical geography will call for new and growing attention in years to come. Geographers concerned with modern society and its evolution will meet in this field of research with geographers interested in the dissolution of pre-industrial rural landscapes. Considerable knowledge about early phases of industrialisation has already been accumulated in works from the 1940–50s by F. Hjulström, G. Arpi, G. Ericsson, O. Nordström and others. The space-time changes in rural population in Sweden have been thoroughly studied by K. Norborg,[37] the townscape of early industrial times in Sweden by L. Améen,[38] and the growth of urban settlements in Norway since 1830 by H. Myklebost.[39] J. Chr. Hansen has devoted a number of studies to the evolution of Norwegian industrial urban settlements. The work by the American geographer, R. L. Morrill, on the process of urbanisation in a southern Swedish region is also noteworthy for its methodological and theoretical implications.[40] The reconstruction from historical records of past phases of evolution served Morrill's aim of testing a model of evolution over a longer period of time, in intervals of twenty years, refining his model step by step to make better predictions.

METHODOLOGICAL PROGRESS

The last fifteen years of field work carried through within the programme of the Department of Human Geography at Stockholm University have brought substantial progress in field work techniques. The contribution of S.-O. Lindquist should be mentioned first. He succeeded in classifying functionally two different types of 'field walls' as remnants of former stone fences. They are distinct features of lost villages and make the reconstruction of the land-use pattern and physical organisation of the former settlement possible. The finding of possible ways of dating field-walls was also important; beneath the walls Lindquist consistently found charcoal, which he assumed to be formed at the original field clearance by fire. The systematic mapping of morphological features like field-walls and cattle paths made possible the exact localisation of the former building sites of farms, invisible on the ground. Before Lindquist, it appears that only G. Niemeier in W. Germany had tried to date early fields by the radio-carbon method.

Lindquist also initiated a systematic evaluation of the phosphate-method, developed in the 1920–30s by O. Arrhenius, which has been further explored and exploited by U. Sporrong. The method of mapping variations in the phosphate content of the soil has been extensively used as a means of identifying prehistoric settlement sites in Sweden, and recent refinements aim at a more systematic control of the possibilities of his method. A denser network of samples for analysis, for example, showed great differences in phosphate contents over distances of only a few metres. These differences within the building site of the village coincided with presumed differences in age between the individual farm building plots within the village[41] and phosphate mapping can thus be used together with other methods to establish or confirm relative chronology (Fig 7).

Another scientific method refined for the use of historical geographers is pollen-analysis. This technique, developed early in this century by L. von Post and others, has been widely used to trace the cultivation of crops through time ever since the German botanist F. Firbas succeeded in separating grain pollens from wild grass pollens in the 1930s. Scandinavian geologists and botanists like J. Iversen, K. Faegri, S. Florin, and M. Fries, contributed substantially to the quantitative and qualitative development of the method.[42] In co-operation with M. Fries, S. Helmfrid used pollen-analysis in order to trace the history of the cultural landscape in Östergötland with special reference to the problems of continuity in late prehistoric and historic times, introducing the method in Scandinavian historical geography.

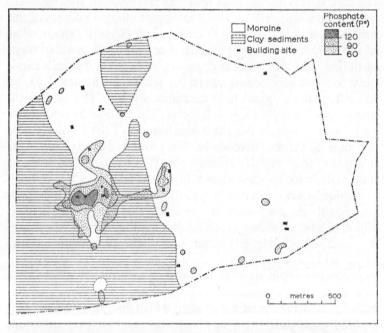

Fig 7 Prehistoric settlement sites and variations in the phosphate content of the soils around Berga, Närke (after U. Sporrong, 1971, 120)

Technically more advanced methods have been tentatively applied on historical-geographical problems in Scandinavia in a very limited number of cases as yet. The possibilities of air-photo interpretation had been clearly shown by British archaeologists over forty years ago. N. R. Jeansson gave a number of examples showing that air-photo interpretation could broaden our evidence of old deserted villages and fields,[43] but it is only in limited areas of the forested Scandinavian countries that air photos can provide new information on features invisible on the ground. Robert M. Newcomb has discussed possible applications of remote sensing techniques for the same purpose.[44]

The application of statistical methods to historical data has important methodological implications. Historical data are seldom 'complete'. The problem of applying sample techniques to overcome incompleteness of quantitative data sources from the past was investigated by B. Johnsson.[45] Using the practically complete seed-lists as an auxiliary variable, Johnsson obtained a highly convincing estimate of the total area of arable land in the province of Västmanland c. 1640–1650 on the basis of a stratified sample from a very incomplete set of contemporary maps.

The most original Scandinavian contribution to the methodology of historical geography is Hannerberg's metrology or morphometric analysis. Hannerberg published a first synthesis of his research on field measures in 1955.[46] Since then the idea has been further developed and the empirical knowledge has grown substantially. Further research has thrown new light upon variations of measures in time and space as well as upon their geometrical relationships. The 'module test' technique introduced by S. R. Broadbent was developed into a standard technique for determining modules in field measures.[47] A comprehensive methodological textbook aiming at a new summing up of morphometric theory and practice is in preparation. Parts of it have been published in the report series of Hannerberg's current research project.[48]

As against the expectations in the early stages of morphometric analysis, it has become apparent that the technique can produce results only when it can be founded on a great number of measurements and an interpretation of the whole system of length and areal measures used in the particular planning phase. Only in a comprehensive analysis can a statistically significant decision be made between a great number of possible combinations. It has also proved impossible to use the simple metrological identification of the basic unit of measure employed in the layout of single fields or building plots for absolute dating. The spread in time and space of different measures is too complicated and still too little known in detail. On the other hand, analysis of the areal measures gave extremely interesting results. Hannerberg proved the systematic connexion between areal measures used for field planning on the one hand and the cubic measures for grain on the other and explained the systems of length, square and cubic measures based on common units of length within peasant society. He thus identified among medieval and earlier measures a series of sets of connected measures which he called 'consequent agrarian measure systems'. A famous and well-known model system of this kind was the Roman one: Roman foot (29·574cm); *iugerum* (240 × 120 = 28,800 sq. feet = 2,519m²); *modius* (4 × 12 × 12 = 576 cubic inches = $\frac{1}{3}$ cubic foot); 8 *modii* were sown on a *iugerum*.

A measure reform in Sweden in the seventeenth century, aiming at regulation of the confusing regionally different measuring systems used in the country, constructed the following set of measures, used until the introduction of the metric system: Swedish *ell* (59·4cm); *tunnland* (14,000 sq. ells = 4·937m²): *tunna* (barrel) of 3 *skäppor* (bushels) with a diagonal of 24 inches and a height of 8 inches (146·21 = Swedish barrel). One *tunna* of rye was sown on one *tunnland* of arable land. Hannerberg has identified medieval and prehistoric measure systems related to the examples given.

N. Sahlgren, in a thesis inspired by Hannerberg, identified the geometrical construction of cubic measures for grain in their dependence on the basic length measures.[49] Elucidating the general geometrical models and the principles of construction of cubic measures, Sahlgren could show the systematic relationship between a great number of different cubic measures seemingly unrelated to each other. With the geometrical model known, the normative size can be exactly determined.

MODELS IN HISTORICAL GEOGRAPHY

It has already been stated that all models of space-time systems have historical-geographical implications. The aim of simulation models in geography, to explain and predict dynamic processes, claims a time dimension and the empirical base has to rest on historical evidence. Historical geography has served modern geography empirically. But model techniques have proved rewarding for historical geography itself too.

In a sense historical geography has always worked with model concepts.

1. Historical geography using historical evidence has to test the validity of theoretical concepts and models, claiming generality and predictive capacity.[50]
2. Historical geography develops simulation models to explain empirically known historical-geographical processes. The model conditions must include historical factors, which may be relevant only for the particular situation.[51] Generalisation may be very misleading. The work of Morrill, mentioned earlier in this essay, combines the two aspects of model work.
3. The third concept of model work—to trace models which have once guided the human planning of environments and the systems of social organisation in old societies— is implicit in all historical-geographical work. The concept of genetic layers in the evolution of agrarian landcapes may be taken as an example. The early fiscal system of normative farm sizes and regularly planned village communities, the administrative model, is likewise another type of theoretical model with manifest consequences in geographical reality. Most explicitly Hannerberg has formulated problems of this type.

A well-defined and still the most developed field of historical geographical model building has grown out of the study of colonisation. E. Bylund in his thesis on Pite lappmark used a theoretical approach—a Hägerstrand type of Monte Carlo simulation model of the spread of new settlement in an unpopulated area.[52] This theoretical discussion was developed further in a paper in 1960.[53] The exact mapping of the phases of colonisation, every new settlement being registered as a point by Bylund, has been used for the empirical testing of theoretical colonisation models by G. Olsson and others. Olsson tried to fit this empirical example to some mathematical functions as a means of describing in a general way the point patterns generated in the two distinct phases of colonisation. The attempt had little success,[54] but, nevertheless, Olsson contributed to the development of a theory of colonisation. In a more recent paper, Bylund has elucidated a characteristic feature in the

colonisation process he had mapped, and proposed a demographic model[55] in which the first few settlements were created
within a short period and where one generation later the sons
of settlers were ready to clear fields and build new farms of
their own. The effect of generation waves was levelled out
only after some generations.

S.-O. Lindquist in his study of iron-age settlement evolution
in Östergötland referred to the two-stage model of colonisation, trying to identify with the aid of a theoretical discussion
these same two phases in the settlement patterns of the early
and late iron age. Although the technical performance of analysis
included some errors, and the level of explanation from a historian's point of view may be questionable, Lindquist's was
a pioneer work introducing chorological techniques and model
simulation to deepen our knowledge of a pre-historic process.[56]
The techniques used involved a construction of an index of
territorial form, and the nearest neighbour test of settlement
distribution.

For historical geography as for human geography as a
whole the further development of theoretical models is very
promising. It is highly questionable, however, whether the
types of models employed as yet will provide any meaningful
'explanations' of historical processes. They can certainly reach
acceptable precision in quantitative description. A plea for
behavioural and stochastic models in human geography is relevant indeed in historical geography. The evolution of agrarian
landscapes can be looked upon as the result of a long series
of planning decisions either by individual owners of real
estate or by collective groups of part-owners in villages or by
authorities in different levels. From time to time fundamental
re-planning has taken place. How far can we reconstruct the
process of decision-making, identify the planning ideas in the
minds of the actors, and how far can we simulate the decision
process with its personal and random elements? Looking
backwards in search of the genesis of landscape features we
tend to seek regularities and their rational causes. If we look
more closely at the decision-making process in the situation
when a village needs to be reorganised, we must admit that a
number of uncertainties have a decisive influence upon the
actual outcome of discussions and decisions. Full conformity

to normative models for planning can be expected only in an authoritarian decision-making framework. Once the decision is taken, one out of many possible plans is put into practice, and later replanning has to find its starting-point in this situation. The actual cultural landscape is the outcome of myriad decisions, each of which could have directed the further evolution, within limits, in other directions as well. Can we hope to simulate in a realistic way historical decision-making in landscape planning? This would give a truly dynamic aspect to the morphogenetic element of cultural landscapes.

The rapid methodological development of human geography promises a great expansion of historical-geographical research. Sooner or later the interest of geographers as well as other social scientists will return on a larger scale to the questions of genesis and evolution in lasting perspectives. Historical data will be handled more effectively when we succeed in organising them with the aid of modern data-processing techniques.

The new system for registration of property which is being introduced in Scandinavian countries opens up wide perspectives in this connexion. All property will be registered with co-ordinates in a data bank. Official data series referable to houses and property (such as building data and census data) will be co-ordinated with this register. All historical-geographical data now stored in different archives can, theoretically, be organised in co-ordination with the property register, making possible a computer handling of search and analysis. Plans are being discussed at the Department of Human Geography in Stockholm to examine further the possibilities for organising a historical-geographical data bank.

5

Historical Geography in Britain

By *ALAN R. H. BAKER*

FROM THE STANDPOINT of the 1970s it is now clear that a fail-
ing of British historical geography during the last twenty-five
years or so has been its distinctiveness as an academic
discipline in managing to survive almost entirely on the
enthusiasms and insights generated by its own practitioners
without drawing much on concepts and methods developed
in other fields. From the point of view of the development
of the subject this was unfortunate but at least it makes it
possible in this essay to treat British historical geography
largely as a discrete field of study, more or less insulated from
the general evolution of the humanities and social sciences
during the period under review.

This essay on progress in historical geography in Britain
since 1946 adopts the view that *il faut reculer pour mieux
sauter* and will first review the nature of historical geography
in Britain in the late 1940s and early 1950s. It will then
attempt to examine the fundamental progress made within
the subject during the subsequent fifteen or so years before
briefly assessing its position and purposes today.

HISTORICAL GEOGRAPHY AND THE 'OLD' GEOGRAPHY IN BRITAIN c. 1950

A cluster of methodological writings on the nature of historical geography appeared around about 1950, allowing us to
establish the existing attitudes towards the subject. While it
was possible for one reviewer of N. J. G. Pounds' *A Historical*

and Political Geography of Europe to write in 1948 that the content of <u>historical geography</u> had long been a subject for controversy,[1] it is equally the case that the general view of the subject which was held at that time, as <u>the description of the geography of an area at some past time,</u> had deep roots. It was, of course, the view outlined by Hettner and elaborated by him in many subsequent studies. This working definition of the subject was accepted by J. F. Unstead in 1907, by Sir Halford Mackinder in 1928 and in 1932 by the anonymous author of a paper asking 'What is Historical Geography?'.[2] It was this position which was consolidated by a number of writers immediately after World War II.

The generally accepted view of historical geography during this period was that of <u>the reconstruction of past geographies.</u>[3] S. W. Wooldridge and W. G. East asserted that historical geography 'has for its main task the reconstruction of past geographies'[4] and H. C. Darby (1953) pointed out that the term 'historical geography' had come to be increasingly identified with <u>an approach in which the data were historical but in which the method was geographical.</u>[5] While geography itself was seen as cutting through time at the present period, historical geography cut through it at some preceding period. J. B. <u>Mitchell</u>, in her fundamental and systematic textbook *Historical Geography,* saw the subject, simply stated, as a geographical study of any period in the past for which a more or less ordered and dated sequence was established in human affairs.[6]

This, then, was the principal view of historical geography in Britain during the late 1940s and early 1950s. At the same time, two other themes were being stressed: the first concerned the relevance of studies of past geographies to an understanding of the present geography, and the second emphasised the all-pervading importance of the genetic approach in geography. Delimiting the frontier between historical geography and geography was seen to be difficult, for two reasons: firstly, the geography of the present is but a thin layer that is continually becoming history, 'all geography is historical geography, either actual or potential'; second, the characteristics of different regions are the result not only of physical but also of human factors in time.[7] Considerable stress was therefore put on the elaboration of 'vertical themes' of landscape change, with man as the principal instrument of landscape change in historic times.[8] The *ultimate,* if not the *immediate,* purpose of historical geography was seen by Wooldridge and East as the examination of processes which have operated in the past for the light which they shed on the world about us.[9] Darby traced his vertical themes of landscape change—clearing the wood, draining the marsh, reclaiming the heath, the changing arable, landscape gardens, towns and seats of industry—through from their beginnings to the then present day.[10] Seemingly, historical geography was in the service of geography, although A. G. Ogilvie suggested to 'the small band of historical geographers' in Britain a technique which he thought would make their researches of more immediate service to regional geography. While admitting that the proper and primary purpose of historical geography was to disclose the special adaptation of man to his environment at a given period in the past, Oglivie suggested that due weight could only be given in regional geography to the influences of the past if historical geographers applied themselves not selectively but simultaneously to the entire human imprint within a selected area, so that its elements could be classified tentatively as belonging to successive stages in time. The links between historical geography and geography were also seen to be close because of the imperative need to recognise the time element in geography. An historical approach was seen to be always necessary because it was the genetic approach. The close bondage of past and present thus doubly tied historical geography closely to geography.[11]

Such a tie was, for Mitchell, only one of two reasons for studying historical geography, the other being its intrinsic interest. The historical geographer *qua* historical geographer was not concerned with the survival of geographical patterns or with the evolution of geographical patterns in time, but with the establishment and study of their design at any one time, emphasising especially those features of place most characteristic of that particular time. The value of his work *qua* geographer, on the other hand, lay in the fact that understanding features in the present geography demands study of the geography of the period of their establishment and

development. In addition—and perhaps more significantly—
Mitchell argued that study of the evolution of landscape
elements might throw light on the general principles that
determine their geographical pattern, principles that the
human geographer, no less than the physical geographer, was,
in her view, ultimately striving to establish.[12] Such optimism
and—as it turned out—far-sightedness was in marked contrast to the narrowly pessimistic views expressed by J. M.
Houston in his treatment of the relation of geography to
history.[13]

One other methodological discussion published during this
period requires separate mention. In 1951 W. Kirk wrote on
historical geography and the concept of the behavioural
environment.[14] H. C. Brookfield has recently referred to Kirk's
paper as significant in being the earliest in geography to
separate the perceived environment as a distinct surface and
to frame it in terms of Gestalt psychology.[15] Kirk's views were
published in a relatively inaccessible journal and have only
recently been restated more publicly.[16] Concern with man as
an agent of environmental change, with the sequence of occupance of environments and with the physical relics of human
action—in other words, the generally accepted concerns of
historical geographers—Kirk saw as belonging to a phenomenal environment. Concern with the changing knowledge of
man's natural environment, of socio-economic processes and
of changing environmental values he envisaged as part of a
behavioural environment. Kirk saw facts of the phenomenal
environment entering the behavioural environment of man,
but only in so far as they are perceived by human beings with
motives, preferences, modes of thinking, and traditions drawn
from their social and cultural context. The same empirical
data may arrange themselves into different patterns and have
different meanings to people of different cultures, or at different stages in the history of a particular culture, just as a landscape may differ in the eyes of different observers. Kirk's main
purpose was to warn against the danger of attempting to
explain the actions of one community in terms of the values
and behavioural environment of another, different culture. For
historical geographers this meant not only reconstructing the
phenomenal environments of the past but also recreating the

G

behavioural environments of the communities whose spatial actions they were trying to interpret. Admittedly Kirk's paper did not inaugurate a new line of work—historians and historical geographers had long produced studies in perceptual geography—but it did make explicit a view of the world that was implicit in the writings of a number of others.[17] What Kirk did was to identify some of the psychological underpinnings of that work.

Each of these views of historical geography finds exemplification in substantive research work. The cross-sectional approach was seen *par excellence* in the publication in 1952 of the first book in the series on the Domesday Geography of England,[18] although Darby had published his first partial reconstruction of the Domesday geography of an area, East Anglia, as long ago as 1934.[19] Other notable period reconstructions, partial or complete, were of the charcoal iron industry in England in the early eighteenth century, of the agriculture of Oxfordshire at the end of the eighteenth century, of agriculture in England and Wales in 1801, of land use in the London area in 1800 and of the economic geography of Craven in the early nineteenth century.[20] Paradoxically, however, there were surprisingly few straightforward attempts to describe the geography of an area at some past time. There were, in fact, more studies elaborating 'vertical themes' of landscape change. Darby's book on the draining of the Fens had appeared before the War but in the immediate post-War period, in addition to his overview of the changing English landscape, there appeared his studies of woodland clearance in England and in Europe.[21] Other notable studies included that of medieval rural settlement and colonisation in Germany, of heathland reclamation in the Belgian Kempenland, of land clearance and drainage in Finland and of movements of population in England and Wales.[22] Even more studies of the period exhibited a genetic approach, a concern with the historical element in geography. Numerous studies were concerned with 'growth' and 'development' of geographical phenomena, such as the evolution of the jewellery and gun quarters in Birmingham, the development of roads in the Surrey and Sussex Weald and the development of the Northamptonshire iron industry from 1851 to 1930.[23]

Studies in historical perceptual geography were relatively few. Even before the War, J. N. L. Baker had produced a study of the geography of Daniel Defoe and E. G. R. Taylor had written essays on the geography of England in the six-teenth century as observed and recorded by John Leland and William Camden.[24] The 1950s saw some further explorations in this field, with Darby's review of some early ideas on the agricultural regions of England and his examination of the regional geography of Thomas Hardy's Wessex.[25] T. H. Elkins delved into an English traveller's perception of the Siegerland and F. V. Emery into the English topographer's view of the regions of the country.[26] Intrinsically interesting though each of these studies was, they did not in sum amount to the con-sistently analytical examination of the behavioural environ-ment which Kirk advocated. Nonetheless, they did constitute a direct if informal contribution towards our knowledge of man's changing perception of his environment. By contrast, it is difficult—if not impossible—to cite examples of empirical studies in historical geography published during this period which aimed explicitly at the induction of general principles determining geographical patterns of human activity.

METHODOLOGICAL EXPLORATIONS AND EMPIRICAL INVESTIGATIONS WITHIN THE TRADITIONAL FRAMEWORK

The 1950s and early 1960s may be seen as essentially a period of consolidation rather than of innovation in the practice of historical geography in Britain. Considerable progress was made, but in familiar fields. Advances there clearly were, but along already established fronts: few—if any—new salients were opened up. Much of the methodological jungle of histori-cal geography was explored and cleared by Darby in his general overview of the subject produced as part of a sympo-sium on approaches to history and in a paper exploring the problem of geographical description.[27] The first of these two publications devoted fourteen pages to 'Geographies of the past', five pages to 'Changing landscapes', five pages to 'The past in the present' and four pages to 'Geographical history'. The balance of this particular essay, together with its fourfold classification of the subject matter of historical geography,

thus confirmed the overriding importance in historical geography of the reconstruction of past geographies and of studies
of geographical changes through time. At the same time, much
of Darby's concern was with the limitations of the cross-
sectional method, which was seen as being essentially descriptive. As soon as historical geographers sought to explain as
well as to describe, problems and dangers were encountered.
An examination was made of writings in historical geography,
not only in British historical geography, to discover what
sorts of solutions had pragmatically been offered to Whittlesey's puzzle of writing incontestable geography that also
incorporates the chains of event necessary to understand fully
the geography of the present day. At least six possible kinds of
solution were identified—sequent occupance, introductory
narrative, parenthesis, footnote, retrospective cross-section and
use of the present tense—while at the same time recognising
that variants and combinations of these six methods provided
challenges to literary skill and ingenuity. During the 1960s
many workers took up these challenges and adopted one or
other of the methods so usefully elucidated by Darby.

Of the various approaches examined by Darby, that which
had been adopted by J. O. M. Broek in his work on the Santa
Clara Valley in California[28] seems to have offered him most
attraction and he has outlined a similar approach which is
being adopted for a new study of the historical geography of
England.[29] Broek's method of utilising cross-sections separated
by studies of the social and economic forces that led to
successive changes in the landscape serves, in Darby's view,
'to furnish a genetic explanation of each landscape but also to
provide connecting links between the successive views. It is a
most interesting methodological approach'.[30] A few studies
have explicitly adopted this approach since Darby drew
attention to it. J. L. M. Gulley's unpublished account of the
Weald began with a reconstruction of its geography in the
early seventeenth century and then traced back the antecedents
of this scene, including two further cross-sections, one in the
early fourteenth century and another in the late eleventh century.[31] A. Harris' study of the rural landscape of the East
Riding of Yorkshire 1700–1850 included a discussion of 'The
old order' (the rural landscapes in the early eighteenth cen-

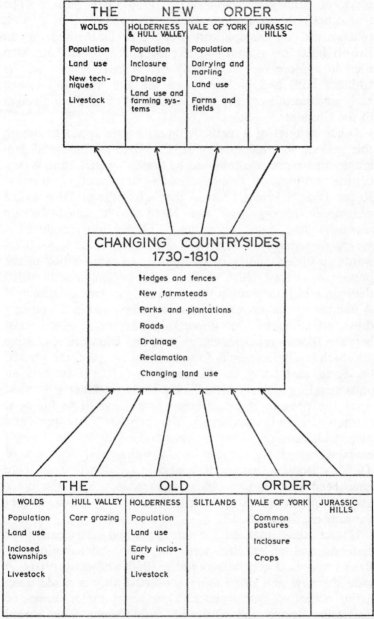

Fig 8 The methodological framework of A. Harris, *The Rural Landscape of the East Riding of Yorkshire 1700–1850* (London, 1961)

tury), of 'Changing countrysides, 1730–1810' and of 'The
new order' (the rural landscape in the 1850s).³² Harris' book
remains the best exemplification of the Broek methodology in
British historical geography (Fig 8). The approach was also
used in a more restricted study of the field systems of the
Chiltern Hills and of Kent from the late thirteenth to the
early seventeenth century and in a study of land-use changes
in the Chilterns.³³

Other writings of a methodological nature appeared during
this period. A brief note by H. C. Prince on historical geography in France was followed by Gulley's penetrating survey
of the writings of France's leading historical geographer,
Roger Dion.³⁴ Prince claimed that what Roger Dion called
géographie rétrospective and Marc Bloch called *histoire
régressive* had much in common. Gulley also produced a
survey of writings in historical geography which worked towards an understanding of the past by an examination of the
present, or at least which studied late or present conditions for
the light which they could throw on early or past conditions.³⁵
A number of studies adopted this procedure and in the process
drew attention to the important differences which exist
between Bloch's retrogressive method and Dion's retrospective
approach.³⁶ The former is focused upon the past, the present
or recent past being considered in so far as it furthers an
understanding of earlier conditions, while the latter is focused
upon the present, the past being considered in so far as it
furthers an understanding of the present.³⁷ Another—and
more wide-ranging—study of ideas and methods was Gulley's
examination of the conception, adoption and rejection of
Turner's frontier thesis.³⁸ It is also interesting to note there
have been few studies which have made use of the other
major methodological approach advocated by Bloch, that of
the comparative method.³⁹

If the consolidation, classification and clarification of
methods and approaches were important contributions by
British historical geographers in the 1950s and early 1960s, so
were the new and often more concerted attacks made upon
major bodies of source materials and upon major themes of
landscape change and economic development. This period
certainly saw much more use being made by historical

geographers of a variety of documents compiled for taxation purposes. For example, the Hundred Rolls and various Lay Subsidies have been used as indicators of regional prosperity in medieval England,[40] as have the land taxes as indicators of regional variations in agricultural prosperity in the nineteenth century.[41] One of the quite distinctive features of this period in English historical geography, in fact, was its emphasis on attempting geographical interpretations from an individual historical source or from groups of source materials. This, after all, was the basic tenet underpinning the whole of the series of Domesday Geographies. Thus one can point to specific analyses undertaken during this period of sources such as medieval tax assessments, the acreage returns of 1801, the Tithe Surveys, the parish registers, the Census returns, the Factory Inspectors' returns, agricultural statistics and trade directories.[42] This particular view—that the approach of the historical geographer towards a given theme is largely determined by the material available—was perhaps stretched to its logical conclusion in D. Thomas' study of agriculture in Wales during the Napoleonic wars.[43] That the problem was approached through the sources was demonstrated in his discrete, as opposed to integrated, discussion of the statistical, cartographic and literary evidence. Such an approach, although useful from an experimental point of view, is open to some serious limitations and no further studies have been similarly presented. Much more conventional—but perhaps also more successful—were the integrated analyses of wide varieties of sources demonstrated in such excellent works as Harris' study of the rural landscape of the East Riding of Yorkshire, D. Grigg's examination of the Agricultural Revolution in south Lincolnshire and M. Williams' study of the draining of the Somerset Levels.[44] On a different theme but adopting an integrative approach were E. A. Wrigley's analysis of regional industrial growth and population change in north-west Europe during the nineteenth century and P. Hall's work on the industries of London since 1861.[45] Attempts to master historical sources—instead of becoming their slaves —were a distinctive feature of British historical geography during this period.

Sources have been examined for the light which they throw

upon problems of landscape change and economic development. Some old problems were thoroughly investigated during this period, some new problems brought to the surface. It is extremely difficult to select those substantive issues in which most progress has been made. R. A. Donkin has done much to elucidate the role of the Cistercians in the making of the English landscape and G. R. J. Jones has opened the way for a new examination of the evolution of patterns of rural settlement in Britain.[46] A considerable amount of work has been done by historical geographers on the regional varieties of field systems for the middle ages onwards and on historical population geography.[47] Perhaps one of the most striking contributions of the period, achieved by an interdisciplinary team of enquirers, was the demonstration that many of the Broads of Norfolk were man-made.[48] All of these efforts and many others were contributing towards an increasing understanding of the historical geography of Britain. Even so, Darby was able to comment in 1960 that as far as the sources were concerned one could but say 'so little done, so much to do'.[49]

It is worth stressing that most of this work was couched in the orthodox 'cross-sectional—vertical theme—historical element in geography' framework and that it employed the traditional methods of historical and geographical analysis. It is not the purpose of this essay to offer a critical assessment of this substantive work. Some new emphases, however, were apparent and are more pertinent to the present essay's theme. Ogilvie's suggestion for the dating of all elements within a cultural landscape was tested in two very different situations. E. M. Yates dated the man-made features in the landscape of a small area of Sussex and J. W. Watson carried out a similar exercise in relation to Halifax, Nova Scotia.[50] Watson went further, treating relict features not only as objects produced by continuing processes of change, considering them 'indicators of the ever-moving frontiers of the past which make up the ecology of the present'. Studies of relict features have been a marked and persistent characteristic of British historical geography, and individual sets of features—such as strip lynchets, ridge-and-furrow, field boundaries, moated settlements, pits and ponds—have received considerable study, both as phenomena to be explained by retrospective enquiry and as sources of evidence for retrogressive studies. Morpho-genetic analysis of town plans has been particularly fruitful.[51]

In one sense, studies of relict features serve to illustrate the essentially idiographic approach of much British historical geography during this period. One can point to few explicit attempts in this period to follow Mitchell's suggestion that historical geographers should endeavour to throw light upon general principles of the evolution of spatial activity. The exceptions, however, are worth noting. H. Carter, for example, examined the relevance of the concept of an urban hierarchy in historical geography by studying the development of such a hierarchy in north-east Wales.[52] D. W. Harvey examined some general principles of the development of patterns of agricultural land use by studying locational change in the Kentish hop industry.[53] These two papers, together with the work by Thomas on crop combination regions and on the diffusion of an agricultural innovation (1961) and P. Hall's locational analysis of the clothing trades in London 1861–1951 were certainly among the first to employ statistical analyses and theoretical concepts in British studies in historical geography.[54]

Explicit studies of man's changing knowledge of his environ-ment, in particular of his changing literary and cartographic expression of that knowledge, were still few. Prince wrote on the geographical imagination, Mead on Pehr Kalm's percep-tion of the Chilterns, Emery on Gower in the 1690s as seen by Edward Lhuyd and some of his Glamorgan correspondents and G. M. Lewis on the changing emphasis in the description of the natural environment of the American Great Plains area, a change from the concept of the Great American Desert to that of the Great Plains.[55]

HISTORICAL GEOGRAPHY AND THE 'NEW' GEOGRAPHY IN BRITAIN c. 1970

That a new model-based paradigm has been replacing the old predominantly classificatory geographical tradition is now a commonplace.[56] But in their survey of quantification and the development of theory in human geography, W. J. Campbell and P. A. Wood stress two further points necessary to put this paradigm shift into perspective: first, the adoption of a theoretical approach has clearly gone further in some branches of human geography than in others. Cultural and historical geography, they claim, seem less ready for the development of theory, although their subject matter poses some questions which cast doubts upon the general applicability of theories being developed in other systematic branches of geography. For example, historical studies raise the whole question of comparisons between different cultures and modes of perception. Secondly, analogy with other disciplines suggests that it is quite normal for different modes of thought or traditions of enquiry to co-exist for long periods of evolutionary transition. Rarely, as change occurs, are all links with earlier traditions completely severed and often ideas or viewpoints which have been long discarded are taken up again as new methods or information renew their significance. Both of these points are relevant to an appreciation of the position and purpose of British historical geography today.[57]

It is certainly the case that some excellent studies are still being published within the 'cross-section—vertical theme—historical element in geography' framework and that similarly conceived and executed studies are likely to constitute a considerable part of the output of British historical geographers for some years to come. In the reconstruction of geographies of past periods one may cite such good examples as D. M. Smith's study of the British hosiery industry at the middle of the nineteenth century, W. R. Wightman's description of the pattern of vegetation in the Vale of Pickering area c. 1300 and K. L. Wallwork's examination of the calico printing industry of Lancastria in the 1840s.[58] Recent scholarly studies of man as an agent of landscape change have included P. F. Brandon's account of medieval clearances in the East Sussex Weald, H. D. Clout's study of the retreat of the wasteland of the Pays de Bray and M. J. Mortimore's examination of landownership and urban growth in Bradford 1850–1950.[59] In addition, substantive contributions continue to be made in the field of historical population geography.[60] Similarly, the fascination of relict features remains: ridge-and-furrow and strip lynchets, for example, continue to be mapped and described,[61] and the best recent study of relict features is undoubtedly that by C. T. Smith, W. M. Denevan and P. Hamilton of the ancient ridged fields in the region of Lake Titicaca.[62] There has, then, been considerable continuity in the study of British historical geography throughout the entire period since 1946.

Such continuity is discernible not only in substantive research publications but also in methodological writings. Only strictly orthodox viewpoints, for example, were elucidated in R. A. Butlin's review of the relevance of historical geography to local studies in Ireland.[63] Similarly Prince's report on the Historical Geography section of the 1964 London meeting of the International Geographical Union was inevitably written within the framework of the three orthodox themes selected for discussion: relict features, past geographies and changing geographies.[64] On another occasion, Prince opened a discussion meeting of the Agrarian Landscape Research Group of the Institute of British Geographers by providing a rationale for the study of relict features.[65] D. J. Robinson has elaborated upon the relevance of studies of the past to an understanding of the present in his plea for cultural and historical perspective in area studies.[66] Some useful overviews of the subject or parts of the subject have also been written. R. A. French produced an account of the principal interests and sources of Russian historical geographers and P. J. Perry a survey and review of Darby's contribution to historical geography.[67] Although Perry's assessment contained inaccuracies—such as over-emphasising the influence of F. Debenham on Darby's career—it nonetheless usefully demonstrated that his approach may best be described not as one of conservative cross-sectionalism but as methodological pragmatism, in that the approach adopted should essentially depend upon the nature of the problem being studied and of the source materials available for study. Perry pointed out that many now widely accepted and well known aspects of Darby's scholarship represented a new and radical approach when he first adopted and advocated them. Indeed, much of his methodological thinking was stimulated by the problems and shortcomings of the orthodox cross-sectional approach.

Taking the pulse of the world's geographers in 1964, Prince discovered an appreciation of the value of an historical

approach to an extent and degree not apparent at previous
I.G.U. Congresses. 'Not only in breadth but also in precision
and refinement, historical reasoning would seem to be gaining
ground.'[68] If more human geographers were becoming increasingly interested in dynamic studies, in studies of change
through time, it is also the case that more historical geographers in Britain were becoming aware of the need to study
change more precisely and more perceptually. Smith's survey
of trends and prospects in historical geography constituted a
more critical than hitherto assessment of the traditional concerns of the subject—the operation of the historical factor in
geography, the evolution of changing landscapes and the
reconstruction of past geographies.[69] At the same time he
argued that the abandonment of doctrinaire attitudes towards
the nature and content of historical geography opened the way
for a much more flexible approach to the organisation of work
and its presentation. Darby's methodological pragmatism has
now itself become so common as to be orthodox.[70] Smith's
own inclinations were to stress the need to study geographical
changes through time, to study in particular the processes by
which geographical change through time may take place. He
also drew attention in this essay to the possibility of refining
explanation in historical geography by the application of
statistical methods and theoretical concepts of locational
analysis. These two points Smith took up again in his *An
Historical Geography of Western Europe Before 1800*. A discussion in the preface explains why Smith rejected all of the
three traditional views of historical geography as a framework
for his book and adopted instead his theme of 'geographical
change', a term which comprehends changes in the use of
resources and of position as a response to social, economic
and technological conditions, but which also is concerned with
the processes involved in bringing about new spatial distributions: colonisation and settlement, migrations, the spread of
innovations, the relationships of towns to the regions they
serve and the regional effects of urban growth; the localisation
of agriculture and industry; and the processes involved in the
concentration or dispersal of settlement, commercial activity
and industry. The organisation of Smith's book reflected his
belief that many of the new ideas, theories and models relating

to spatial patterns and processes are applicable in principle to historical situations. 'Before 1800, statistical data are hard to come by,' he wrote, 'and there are as yet few studies in this vein but it may be that the approach and concepts of location analysis will open up new lines of research and new methods of integrating the knowledge about the past as well as the present.' Smith admitted that, although historical geography might be on the threshold of a new major task, it was one which was only occasionally hinted at in his book.[71] It has, none the less, been hailed by an American reviewer as a step in the right direction.[72]

A considerable step further was undoubtedly taken in Harvey's survey of studies of the evolution of spatial patterns of human activity.[73] Harvey, like Smith, was concerned with bridging the gap between the scholarly studies of the specialist historical geographers and the analytical techniques of human geographers concerned with contemporary distributions. His essay was based on two principles: first, that the development of cultural forms over space is not a haphazard process and principles of spatial evolution can be developed; secondly, that no simple monolithic principle holds the key to explana-

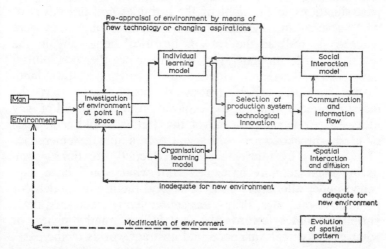

Fig 9 A synoptic model system to show one mode of approach to the evolution of spatial patterns in human geography (after D. Harvey, 1967, 596)

tion nor, even, do few principles combined offer an adequate explanation of the tremendous complexity of change in the real world. Harvey's emphasis was on our relative ignorance of the nature of the processes shaping the evolution of spatial patterns in human geography and he strongly advocated building explicit models of development over space and time, demonstrating, with reference to one of Carl Sauer's statements, that many of the generally expressed ideas on spatial evolution can be given formal expression (Fig 9).

Other methodological writings have given support to this new emphasis within studies in British historical geography. L. W. Hepple argued that historical geography has a twofold contribution to make towards geographical studies: first, to extend geographical models back into the past and build models of change over time; secondly, to develop what he termed the 'historical language' band of the epistemological spectrum.[74] That an eclectic attitude towards historical geography has now become firmly established as the new orthodoxy is seen in a recent discussion on 'the future of the past' in which to the traditional concerns and techniques of the historical geographer are added new approaches and methods (see also Fig 10).[75] In addition to emphasising the study of past situations in the light of the attitudes and objectives of past societies and the extent to which these objectives were realised, as well as the role of historical geography in the search for order in geography, a number of other possibilities have been outlined: the simulation of changing abstract landscapes, against which real-world counterparts may be measured and appraised; the exploration of the spread of new ideas or new techniques and of the decline of old economies or of the breakdown of old social orders and the emergence of new ones by fabricating counterfactual situations—comparing what actually happened with what would have happened under alternative conditions; and the use of models for postdictive purposes. Prince has subsequently elaborated these various attitudes towards the past into a lengthy review of what he calls 'real, imagined and abstract worlds of the past', thus making explicit an organisational framework which has always been implicit in studies in historical geography and which might come to be accepted as the new orthodoxy.[76]

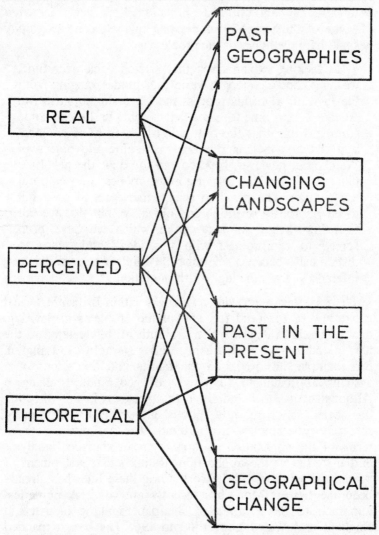

Fig 10 Some approaches to historical geography

Another examination of the basic problem confronting historical geographers today, that of integrating traditional empirical
techniques which must eventually reach out for a theoretical
framework and the theoretical analysis which must in turn
reach out to embrace the complexities of the real world, was

both cautionary and optimistic in its tone.[77] Harvey's dissection of some of the temporal modes of explanation in geography has laid bare the bones of the problem:

'In seeking explanations that stretch back over time, we may choose among a variety of modes ranging from the logically rigorous process model to simple narrative. At the present time it seems that nothing useful can come from insisting that the only admissible form of explanation is that which is rigorously scientific and objective. We should, however, be prepared to admit the problems inherent in using less rigorous modes of temporal explanation. The problem is not, therefore, that we fail to be rigorously scientific and objective, but that we fail to acknowledge the respects in which we have been forced to compromise with this ideal, and hence to distinguish between permissible and non-permissible inferences, given the logic of the situation'.[78]

There is, then, a growing awareness within British historical geography of the need for, and of the problems in devising, new research strategies which are authentically related to the new paradigms of both history and geography. J. Langton, for example, has reviewed the merits and limitations of a systems approach to the study of geographical change.[79] Although it has to be admitted that progress in this direction has been slow, recently published writings and current research programmes give grounds for optimism, both in terms of the application of more rigorous statistical analyses and in terms of the application, testing and development of spatial theory. Some early work along these lines has already been mentioned. More has recently appeared. A numerical approach to the location of the paper-making industry in England and Wales from 1860 to 1965 has been expanded into a general theory of industrial location.[80] Carter extended his study of Welsh towns within the framework of the central place model, enabling both a critical revision of studies of the development of city systems and a presentation of a conceptual scheme of the growth of the Welsh city system.[81] Wrigley's model devised to analyse London's importance in changing English society and economy in the seventeenth and eighteenth centuries is a pioneer study in hypothetical historical geography.[82] Other advances have been of a more constrained nature, limited to the use of specific statistical analyses of sets of historical data. Thomas has used linear regression procedures in an examination of the relationship between climate and cropping in the early nineteenth century in Wales, and was able to demonstrate that with one of the three crops studied the correlation coefficient with distance from a cultural base line was higher than that with rainfall, and with another crop, the correlation and coefficients were very close.[83] Association analysis of data derived from nineteenth century trade directories of East Anglian towns produced what with hindsight seemed obvious results, but 'this is surely encouraging, for when new methods or more rigorous forms of study can be introduced and are found to substantiate intuitive findings and stimulate new ones, then rapid progress can be made'.[84] Analysis of data from the 1851 Census enumerators' manuscript returns, using a SYMAP V computergraphics programme, has produced maps of social group surfaces, indicating a definite tendency towards segregation of social classes within the new town of Goole in 1851.[85] Characteristics of the pattern and size continuum of some rural settlements of the south-western Paris Basin in the nineteenth century have been classified by nearest-neighbour and rank-size analysis.[86] A study of marriage distances in rural Dorset during the nineteenth century employed multiple regression analysis of data derived from marriage registers to demonstrate the substantial and rapid breakdown of rural isolation in the last two decades of the nineteenth century and its causes.[87] F. W. Carter's study of the medieval Serbian oecumene employed connectivity analysis, eigenvalues and measurement of accessibility to demonstrate that Stefan Dusaan's choice of capital does not theoretically appear to have been the best and that the possible area of the medieval Serbian oecumene seems to have extended further west than has hitherto been realised.[88] Each of these studies represents only a modest gain, but there is no mistaking the direction of the advance. Furthermore, some current research programmes in historical geography—such as componential analysis of medieval manorial court rolls and analysis of the Tithe Survey by nearest neighbour techniques

H

to produce, via SYMAP proximal map electives, maps drawn by computer of land use and cropping patterns on a county scale[89]—are likely to extend the advance considerably.

Statistical and theoretical considerations are, then, entering increasingly into studies by British historical geographers. It is not possible to argue that this is equally the case with explicitly behavioural and perceptual considerations. J. H. Paterson produced a fascinating study of Scotland through the eyes of Sir Walter Scott, D. Lowenthal and H. C. Prince delved into English landscape tastes, and G. M. Lewis attempted to isolate the factors which have influenced man's ideas about the Cis-Rocky Mountain West in the United States.[90] R. L. Heathcote's inquiry into land appraisal and settlement in the semi-arid pastoral country along the Queensland-New South Wales border sought to establish the perceived environment of initial settlement and of the several stages of settlement, including the effects of climatic hazard and economic disaster on perception. He used land rents as indicators of contemporary ideas on land values and employed these as his principal quantitative measure to set alongside his careful culling of the qualitative material.[91] 'Probably no historical geographer has yet made more specific use of environmental perception in his reconstruction.[92] But rigorously analytical perception studies have not yet been widely adopted in British historical geography, perhaps because of the difficulty of obtaining information on, or even reliable surrogates for, the decision-making process in historic times. Again, although the approach of the historical geographer towards a given theme may be influenced by the intellectual climate within which he is operating, it is nonetheless largely conditioned by the source materials available.

6

Historical Geography in the USSR

By R. A. FRENCH

THE REVIVAL OF INTEREST

THE STUDY OF geography in the Soviet Union is undertaken on a very large scale, whether measured by the numbers of geographers involved, or by volume of publication, or by the range of topics. Unfortunately this generalisation, which applies as much to each branch of geography as it does to the subject as a whole, is scarcely valid where historical geography is concerned. Almost alone among the many aspects of geographical investigation, historical geography in the USSR is characterised by comparative paucity of work. Such neglect is not for lack of precedent. It may well be true that more work in the field was accomplished in pre-Revolutionary Russia than in any other country at that period, save possibly Germany.[1] But with the Revolution came an almost total cessation of historical geographical work. The historian Yatsunskiy, writing in 1941, admitted that historical geography 'has been studied by us very little, much less than in bourgeois countries.'[2]

The article, 'The scope and aims of historical geography', in which Yatsunskiy made the statement, was a plea for the development of the subject, to lift it from the status of a minor aid to history in establishing locations of the past to become an independent field of study. Yatsunskiy's concepts of historical geography were clearly influenced by pre-Revolutionary work in Russia, not only by the many historians concerned with tracing the location of historical events and features, but also and particularly by historians such as Got'ye and Zamyslovskiy, who produced geographical 'cross-sections' in past periods,

111

and by geographers such as Voyeykov, who analysed the man-made changes in the landscape. At the same time, he was much impressed by work in western countries, notably *An Historical Geography of England before 1800*.[3] Yatsunskiy advocated studies, which 'give a series of characteristics of the economic and political geography of a given country at a corresponding moment of time.'[4] These characteristics should include, first the natural landscape of the period in question, which he termed historical physical geography; secondly, population in its ethnic, distributional, and migrational aspects (the historical geography of population); thirdly, the geography of production and economic links (historical economic geography); and finally, the location of internal and external political boundaries and of historical events (historical-political geography). Of these four elements, which 'must be studied not in isolation, but in their interrelations and causations',[5] the first was of minor significance. 'As the natural landscape in itself has changed comparatively little over the historical period of the development of mankind, so obviously historical geography has comparatively little need to concern itself with the geography of natural conditions. It concentrates its attention chiefly on the geography of man.'[6] As an ardent Marxist-Leninist, Yatsunskiy naturally insisted that the periodisation of historical geography should correspond with that of Marxist historical studies and that the subject should consider 'the social level of the development of the economy.'[7] *An Historical Geography of England,* although praised as the best example of work in the field by bourgeois geographers, suffered from a typically bourgeois approach, in that no mention was made of the class struggle.

The discipline, which Yatsunskiy envisaged, had a right to its own place in the field of knowledge. 'Historians usually consider historical geography an auxiliary science . . . The traditional opinion of historians is unquestionably out-of-date. Historical geography is, without doubt, developing into a separate branch of historical science.'[8] It was important not to confuse historical geography with the history of geography and geographical knowledge, although the two fields of study were related and could assist each other. More than once Yatsunskiy insisted that, 'historical geography studies the concrete geography of past historical epochs.'[9] He had need to stress the distinction, which has been frequently blurred in Soviet writings. As late as 1967, the geographer M. I. Belov, surveying Soviet research in historical geography, included within its scope the history of exploration, the history of geographical thought, the history of cartography, and even the work of publishing sources, such as travellers' diaries.[10] Yatsunskiy himself divided his work between both areas of investigation. His principal publication, *Historical Geography: the history of its origin and development in the fourteenth to eighteenth centuries,* was concerned with the progress of historical geographical concepts from Petrarch to d'Anville.[11]

The 1941 article by Yatsunskiy can be regarded as the foundation stone of recent historical geographical study in the USSR, the trigger for a revival of interest and research. Certainly the editorial board of *The Marxist Historian* considered it to be of the greatest importance, for it took the highly unusual step of adding an editorial comment to the article:

> From the editors. One must note the importance of the questions raised in the article by comrade V. Yatsunskiy. The state of affairs in historical geography in our scientific research establishments and higher educational institutions is completely unsatisfactory.
>
> The editors of the journal consider that the Committee for Higher Educational Affairs must undertake the necessary measures to change the existing situation in the matter of the study of historical geography in higher educational institutions. Our historical scientific research establishments must, of course, introduce the working out of problems of historical geography into their plans.[12]

This exhortation may well have had an effect. Certainly Yatsunskiy continued his proselytizing efforts. In 1950 he once more urged the importance of investigations along the lines he had earlier suggested[13] and at the same time stressed its essential role in the training of economic geographers.[14] The year 1956 saw him claiming a key place for historical geography in works of regional economic geography.[15] The historian was supported in his views by a geographer, Yu. G.

Saushkin, who as early as 1940 had complained that historical textbooks almost wholly ignored the role of the geographical setting. Saushkin did not advocate historical geography as such, but such an approach was implicit in his demand for the study of 'the cultural landscape', that is, 'natural complexes, in which man has strongly altered the natural environment and established to a significant degree a new environment.'[16]

Both Yatsunskiy and Saushkin saw difficulties in the way of progress in historical geography, in that individuals were rarely trained in the techniques of both history and geography. As Yatsunskiy pointed out, 'The specialist in historical geography must not only know history, but also have training in the sphere of geography',[17] dual qualifications which he himself did possess. Perhaps, however, the greatest difficulties lay in other directions, not overtly acknowledged by the Soviet writers. Since the Revolution, the whole climate of geographical research has been dominated by the necessity for applied studies. One has only to consider the frequency with which the word 'tasks' is used in geographical writings, or examine the resolutions for future research taken at congresses of the All-Union Geographical Society, to understand that the overwhelming majority of Soviet geographers consider it their duty to gear their work to the contemporary needs of society and its developing economy. Little place is seen for work that looks back into the past. The enthusiasts for historical geography have always found it necessary to justify themselves, by stressing that, in the words of S. V. Kirikov, 'for the deep understanding of the present and prevision of the future, one must thoroughly know the past',[18] or again, more recently, of R. L. Yugay, 'Indeed, any forecast is built on the basis of analysing the conditions at the present and in the past.'[19]

As great a difficulty lay in the division of geography into physical and economic branches, with little enough contact or interaction between them. This division, with the arguments for and against it, culminated in the bitter controversy of the 1960s over Anuchin's doctoral thesis, which propounded a 'unified' geography. The controversy is well enough known in Western writings to obviate the need for restatement here.[20]

Nevertheless there is no doubt that the ideas of the 'monists' like Anuchin provide a more favourable framework in which historical geography might develop, in that their ideas emphasise the interaction of the natural and the human in the environment. 'The geographical environment . . . is the part of external nature that is being changed by purposeful human activity and saturated with the results of man's labour.'[21] Conversely, the rigid separation of geography into physical and economic disciplines raises problems for historical geography, as Saushkin, a strong supporter of Anuchin, realised:

> Physical geographers are little related to historical and economic sciences, the study of which is essential for the cognisance of the history of the development of the cultural landscape in connexion with the history of society; economic geographers are little tempted to cognisance of the natural environment and of the laws of development of natural landscapes.[22]

HISTORICAL PHYSICAL GEOGRAPHY

The broad partition of Soviet geography has tended to be reflected within the narrower field of historical geography. On the one hand are those who, like Yatsunskiy, stress the human element and history, on the other are the physical geographers, who see the scope of the subject as limited to changes in physical conditions during historic time—if not, indeed, even longer. To the latter, all other matters are the concern solely of historians. Naturally even the most extreme proponents of this view recognise that man has been one element in bringing about physical changes, but they study only the end-product of man-made changes. The process of human activity causing the changes, with its guiding economic and social factors, lies entirely outside their field of vision. For many of this group of geographers, the term historical geography is interchangeable with palaeogeography. The eminent physical geographer S. V. Kalesnik, in drawing up a classification of geographical sciences, puts historical geography as a sub-division of physical geography under the general heading of 'the group of natural sciences', as opposed to 'the group of social sciences', which includes the history of geography and

economic geography.[23] He defines its content as the palaeogeography of historical times, as distinct from palaeogeography
proper, which is the study of landscapes in the geological past.
Another no less eminent physical geographer, K. K. Markov,
does not make even this distinction, seeing the synonyms
palaeogeography and historical geography as concerned with
a continuous process of development of the physical environment to the present. Man's role does not emerge at all in
Markov's own work.[24] Markov at least, unlike some others
of the same opinion, is careful to distinguish his concept as
historical 'earth science' (*zemlevedeniye*), in contrast to the
historical 'geography' (*geografiya*) of the historians.

Another member of this group, V. S. Zhekulin, is less
extreme in outlook. For him, historical geography must be
separated from what he calls general palaeogeography, 'not
so much by the distinctiveness of the natural conditions of
the quaternary period, as by the appearance of such a powerful factor in changing the face of the landscape as human
society.'[25] Zhekulin stresses heavily the very large role of man
as a factor and criticises authors who ignore it. Nevertheless,
the objects of study are exclusively features of the physical
environment, falling into three groups: hydromorphic (lakes,
swamps, flood-plains, deltas, estuarine marshes, glaciers),
lithogenic (karst, gullies, stream-channel elements, shorelines)
and biogenic (soils, vegetation, fauna, biocenoses). The aims
of work on these features should be 'the study of the history
of development and change of individual landscape-forming
factors; the establishment of the main stages of development
of present landscapes, as a result of the interaction of natural
and historical factors.'[26] But although historical geography is
intermediate between the natural and social sciences, its
closest links are with the former and indeed it overlaps with
palaeogeography. Zhekulin is emphatic that historical geography as he sees it, 'has nothing in common with a historical
geography assigned to the cycle of historical sciences. The
latter deals with the geography of countries and individual
regions in past epochs. Its competence principally includes
such questions as the distribution of population, structure of
towns, communications, etc.'[27] Here perhaps, the bisection of
geography is seen at its most depressingly inflexible. Of course,

a huge volume of work on physical changes of the quaternary period has been undertaken in the USSR, although few of the people concerned would think of themselves as historical geographers, by any definition of the term. Gully erosion alone has a vast Soviet literature; one might cite as an example, which does use the historical approach to some extent, the Academy of Sciences volume on agricultural erosion.[28]

HISTORICAL BIOGEOGRAPHY

The restricted view of historical geography held by Kalesnik, Zhekulin and others, is obviously confined to physical geographers, but it is not held by all working on physical aspects of geography. Not surprisingly, biogeographers tend to give far greater weight and attention to human and historical factors, because these have so very markedly modified the biological world. Thus Semenova-Tyan-Shanskaya, examining changes in the vegetation of the forest-steppe, not only made use of eighteenth-century cartographic material to compile a map of forests at that time, but also related subsequent changes in forest cover to the advancing frontier of Russian settlement and the spread of arable. However, the process of settlement and ploughing-up is merely mentioned briefly and is not examined or analysed at all.[29] Although the map of eighteenth-century forests is a product of the historical method, Semenova-Tyan-Shanskaya's purpose is simply the comparison of that map with the present-day map of forests.

The historical geography of cultivated plants is, of course, closely tied to the development of society. This is a sphere of study in which the Soviet Union, in the person of Academician Vavilov, has long made a contribution of world-wide significance. In recent times, Vavilov's work on the early diffusion of cultivated plants has been continued by his colleague, Ye. N. Sinskaya, whose major opus *The Historical Geography of Cultivated Flora* appeared posthumously in 1969.[30] Terrestial in its scope, the book is a little thin on recent work in the field by Western authors, but covers thoroughly areas within the USSR that are poorly known to those outside the country. The adoption and spread of crops in historic times has received much attention in the Soviet Union from agrarian historians, for example Mordvinkina on the history of oat cultivation in Russia.[31]

Two soil geographers, A. V. Gedymin[32] and A. S. Fat'yanov,[33] have engaged in extremely interesting work in historical geography, as a necessary preliminary to the study of contemporary soils. Both used the cadastres of the late fifteenth to seventeenth centuries and the maps of the eighteenth-century General Survey (*General'noye Mezhevaniye*) to analyse changes in forest cover and the spread of arable, Gedymin in Ryazan' *Oblast'* and Fat'yanov in Gor'kiy *Oblast'*. Through intensive field-work, Gedymin successfully developed techniques of relating accurately the eighteenth century cartography to the present-day ground. He sought to examine whether qualitative variations in soil were principally the result of long-term cultivation, but demonstrated clearly that the variations were more closely connected to variations in parent material. He also demonstrated that in the process of Russian settlement and ploughing-up of new arable, there was conscious selection of the best areas first. Nevertheless, the longer an area has been under the plough, the greater the effect on the soil and further work by Gedymin on chernozems has shown that certain chemical changes in the soil can be quantitatively related to the length of time that cultivation has taken place.[34] Gedymin's work exemplifies well the way in which Soviet historical geographical studies are given unmistakable contemporary relevance.

Of all Soviet work on the biogeography of the past, perhaps the most deserving of attention is that of S. V. Kirikov. His long years of research in Soviet archives resulted in an impressive series of publications during the last two decades, on the changing distribution of fauna. Particular interest attaches to the investigations of Kirikov, not only because they have a strong claim to be the most profoundly scholarly of all Soviet work in historical geography, but even more because little enough has been done in this field anywhere—and almost nothing by geographers. He himself acknowledges the rarity of this kind of study: ' "The obtaining of many explanations from historical documents still faces zoology"—these words of A. F. Middendorf (1869) remain in full force even now and one must be surprised how little work has been done in this field.'[35] Outside the USSR Kirikov's work is almost unknown by geographers, although better known by zoologists and ornithologists.[36] It is based on thorough use of documentary evidence, including *inter alia* medieval chronicles, sources relating to hunting such as the archives of the Ober-Jägermeister's office, records of taxes and rents paid in furs (notably the archives of the Siberian Department) and the manuscript surveyors' notebooks, compiled for the General Survey.

As Kirikov points out:

> Changes of natural conditions, arising as a result of the economic activity of man, were one of the principal causes of changes taking place in the distribution and number of commercially valuable animals. But at the same time great influence has been displayed by excessive exploitation and also by the disturbance introduced by people and domestic animals into the habitats of wild animals and birds.[37]

Therefore much of his attention has been focused on fur-bearing animals, for so very long one of the principal sources of wealth to the Russian state and for which the quantity of documentary evidence is very large.[38] Since changes in habitat through human activity were at least as important as the direct effect of hunting, Kirikov examines closely the spread of settlement and different types of agricultural exploitation, as they affected fauna. He also considers climatic variation to some extent, extracting any records of weather conditions from his sources.[39] His studies of changes in the distribution of individual species, such as the black hamster and lynx, and of fauna in general in specific regions, such as the Moscow area[40] and southern Urals,[41] culminated in comprehensive surveys of fish, birds and mammals in the steppe and forest-steppe,[42] the forest and forest-tundra,[43] and finally the USSR as a whole.[44] From the frequency of references and locations given in documents, Kirikov establishes limits of distribution of species at different periods, some conception of the commonness or rarity of species and also the reasons for change. There is no quantitative analysis, but this is scarcely possible by the nature of the evidence.

LANDSCAPE AND ETHNOS

Among Soviet historical geographers, who place their emphasis on physical rather than on human or economic aspects —they themselves would say on geographical rather than historical—L. N. Gumilev stands out for individuality of thought and for his unique attempt to establish an entirely new concept of historical geography. This concept he develops in a long series of articles under the general title of 'Landscape and Ethnos'.[45] Gumilev is basically concerned with the examination of man-environment relationships through time, but his essentially physical approach is revealed in his definition of historical geography—'the science of post-glacial landscape in its dynamic state, for which the ethnos is the indicator.'[46] 'Ethnos' he uses in its Greek meaning of 'species' and defines as a human group or community, distinct from any others. Various criteria may be used to distinguish an ethnos—language, customs or culture, ideology 'or religion in old epochs', and origin.[47] Not all of these are applicable in every case, but 'a permanent, essential characteristic of an ethnic group is the personal recognition of each individual: "we are such and all other people are something else".'[48] Such a group, in Gumilev's view, is not so much related to the environment as part of it. In this respect the ethnos may be one of two types, those 'entering into the biocenosis, inscribing themselves into the landscape and limited in their increase by the biocenosis' and those 'intensively multiplying, settling beyond the limits of their biotopes and changing their primary biocenosis.'[49] One might suppose that the Australian aborigines and the nineteenth-century English represented extremes of the two types.

From this, Gumilev argues, it follows that changes in an ethnos are related to changes in the environment and by historical study of the ethnos, physical changes can be discovered or confirmed and, in particular, climatic cycles. 'The use of the timetable of political history in the given context gives an absolute chronology for geological processes of the contemporary epoch.'[50] This thesis he explores at length in the context of the arid and semi-arid zones of the USSR, the desert and steppe during the millenia when they were occupied by generally nomadic peoples. He attempts to establish a series of climatic cycles, when the normal trend of cyclonic tracks lay well to the north, or well to the south, or in an inter-mediate position. The different paths gave rise to greater or lesser aridity in the forest, steppe and desert zones at varying periods and to these differences of moisture the rise and fall of ethnic groups can be related. Gumilev has compiled charts of these relations between cyclonic tracks, precipitation and the flourishing of different cultures for the pre-historic period[51] and for the middle ages.[52] His theories are worked out on the basis of considerable research on the Huns[53] and on the Khazar culture of the lower Volga-Caspian-Caucasus region in the fifth to thirteenth centuries AD, making great use of archaeological evidence.[54] Gumilev attributes the rise of the Khazar people to a period of increased moisture supply in the north and west Caspian area[55] and their decline to increased precipitation further north in the Volga catchment area of the forest zone, which brought about a rise of the Caspian sea level and the drowning of the principal areas of Khazar settlement.[56]

Within the compass of his own research—the nomadic peoples of the steppe and desert—Gumilev builds up a well-argued case, on the foundation of much solid historical, archaeological and palaeogeographical evidence. He is less convincing in his efforts to make his concepts universal in application. He recognizes the difficulty—'the interaction between the ethnic group and the landscape is seen every-where, but with different degrees of clarity'—and confesses that 'the most suitable material for us will be the Eurasian steppe and its nomadic population', because 'they [Hunnic, Turkic and Mongol nomads] were an inseparable part of the landscape, together with the vegetation and fauna.'[57] It is cer-tainly very hard to see Gumilev's theories in the context of settled, developed, and above all urban, societies, or in areas without the very fine heat-moisture balance of the steppe and semi-desert. One might have trouble applying his concepts to the north European plain. It is equally difficult to follow his argument that the ethnos which does change its environment, does so only once, in a period of intensive activity at the start of its life-cycle, and thereafter maintains a stable ethnos—environment relationship. 'It is essential to take into account that peoples accomplish the adaptation of the landscape to their needs only once during the period of existence of each people.'[58] Taken to its logical conclusion, this would suggest that Gumilev thought that the post-Enclosure English were a different ethnos from the pre-Enclosure English. Most historical geographers, both within and outside the Soviet Union, tend to see the process of environmental adaptation as a continuous one, related in large measure to technological developments. Yet again, the evidence he adduces from other parts of the world seems often thin, highly selective and at times quaintly inaccurate. English readers will be slightly taken aback to learn that the English speak two languages, 'English in the south and Norwegian in Northumberland.'[59]

In the USSR Gumilev's views are not universally accepted, partly perhaps on the grounds described, partly perhaps because they contain a strong undercurrent of determinism. Marxism firmly rejects geographical determinism, although it recognises that physical conditions can and do influence man's economic activity and the march of historical events. Even Stalin admitted:

> There is no argument that the geographical environment is one of the permanent and inevitable conditions of the development of society and that it, of course, influences the development of society—it hastens or retards the progress of development of society. But its influence is not a determining influence, since the changes and development of society take place incomparably faster than the changes and development of the geographical environment.[60]

Nevertheless, all too often Soviet geographers and historians, in their anxiety to avoid the Scylla of determinism, have been drawn into the Charybdis of discounting physical influences entirely. Moreover Marxism, while conceding the influence of environment on economic activity, rejects any such influence on the way in which society develops. This issue is only partially avoided by Gumilev in his use of the ethnos and in his rather vague statement that 'in contradistinction to class, ethnos does not define the relationship of the collective to production.'[61] Undoubtedly many Soviet geographers would

reject Gumilev's belief that 'migrations and processes of ethno-
genesis are, without any doubt, conditioned by elements of the
landscape and correspond to climatic fluctuations.'[62] But
although his concepts are open to much argument, one cannot
deny that they are thought-provoking and perhaps the most
wide-ranging of all Soviet writings on historical geography. On
the local scale, they are a real contribution to the historical
geography of the steppe.

HISTORICAL ECONOMIC GEOGRAPHY

In the USSR the umbrella of economic geography is wide,
covering the whole field usually known in Western writings as
human geography. It also covers historical geography, at least
as Yatsunskiy envisaged it, concentrating 'chiefly on the geography of man.' But economic geographers have played only
a small part in the revival, which Yatsunskiy initiated. For
them, as much as for the physical geographers, the need to
undertake applied work has been paramount, especially in
relation to planning. As a consequence, studies of the past are
no more than a handful of more or less unrelated topics,
investigated by varying techniques, all of which are long
familiar in English and American geography. One of the best,
Kharitonychev's monograph on the Volga right bank area
near Gor'kiy,[63] traces the process of landscape change, in an
approach not altogether dissimilar to that of Hoskins on the
English landscape.[64] The principal themes of Kharitonychev,
followed from earliest times to the Revolution, are the spread
and development of settlement, the development of agriculture
and its counterpart, the clearing of the forest, and the growth
of gully erosion. These themes are examined in relation to one
another in the framework of four long, but unequal periods—
up to the sixteenth century, the sixteenth and seventeenth
centuries, the eighteenth and early nineteenth centuries, the
late nineteenth and early twentieth centuries. As well as considerable documentary evidence, Kharitonychev makes some
limited use of place-names and pollen-analysis.

Possibly only one work from a geographer's pen might be
considered as a 'cross-section' geography of a particular period,
that of Vorob'yeva on the economic geography of southern

East Siberia in the first half of the eighteenth century.[65]
It is a rather brief account, seeking principally to sub-divide
the study area into regions on the basis of economic activity.
This would appear to be the kind of work envisaged by
Saushkin for historical economic geography, when he defined
it as 'the science of past territorial associations of productive
forces and of the past development of the territorial division
of social labour.'[66] The historical geography of population and
settlement has been illuminated by several local studies.
Pokshishevskiy has written several accounts of pre-Revolutionary internal migrations, for example to the southern part
of the Russian Far East,[67] and also of the economic development of St Petersburg.[68] Vitov has analysed the distribution,
locations and patterns of settlement in the Lake Onega region,
particularly in relation to landownership.[69] Both Pokshishevskiy and Vitov stress the role of socio-economic factors. Vitov,
dealing with an area of Russian and Karelian settlement,
strongly opposes the Meitzen emphasis on ethnic factors. Conceding that, in the analysis of village form, 'the role of ethnic
tradition must, indisputably, be considered', he believes that
'all these differences in pattern are far more easily and
logically explained by peculiarities of the economy and,
in particular, of the nature and degree of development of
communications.'[70]

The small volume of work by geographers is not unexpected
in view of the common attitude that these are matters for the
historian and it is the historians who have provided the bulk
of work of value to the historical geographer. It is true that
they, as much as the geographers, have ignored the 'cross-
section' approach, which Yatsunskiy advocated. The only
significant work of this nature is Tikhomirov's *Russia in the
Sixteenth Century,* which examines, major region by major
region, landownership, the economy (especially agricultural
practices) and urbanisation.[71] The method is largely descriptive and static; with the exception of the foundation of new
towns, the processes of change then active are only most
briefly mentioned. Nor are natural conditions dealt with at
all.

The development through time of individual aspects of the
economy has been the subject of a very considerable literature.

For example, in the history of industry, valuable contributions have been made by Academician Strumilin on the metallurgical industry[72] and by Pazhitnov on the textile industry.[73] Agricultural development has attracted many investigators, of whom one might cite as examples, Shunkov,[74] Rubinshteyn[75] and Kochin.[76] The economic development of towns and trade has also interested many, represented by the collection of contributions, *The Towns of Feudal Russia*.[77] Almost all the abundant work in these fields is not historical geography, nor is it claimed to be by the authors concerned; almost all lies well beyond the vague frontier with economic history. Hardly ever is there consideration of environmental factors, hardly ever are the topics treated in any spatial sense. One exception is Shunkov, who does concern himself with the geographical distribution of arable farming in seventeenth-century Siberia.[78] Much of the work by historians, which does lay claim to be historical geography, follows the pre-Revolutionary tradition of tracing past geographical locations, especially of trade routes. Bernshteyn-Kogan on the Dnepr route[79] and Sverdlov on the Volga route[80] in Kievan times are among the more recent followers of a long tradition of research, dating back to the early nineteenth century. Historical geography of this type is still very much the 'auxiliary science of history.' On occasion the term historical geography has been applied to what is little more than straightforward historical chronology, notably in Lappo's article on the towns of Moscow *Oblast'*.[81]

Of course, in the USSR as elsewhere, economic history is at times very close to historical geography. Two Soviet historical scholars in particular have produced invaluable work along this disciplinary border, both based on a thorough knowledge of the documentary evidence. The late M. A. Tsvetkov used the vast store of archival material on forests to unravel the process and consequences of forest clearance and the development of forest husbandry and reafforestation in European Russia from 1700 to the Revolution.[82] More recently, V. P. Zagorovskiy has traced the history of establishment and precise geographical alignment of the Belgorod *cherta*, the greatest of the Russian defensive lines through the forest-steppe.[83] Perhaps a little curiously, the frontier as a theme has not figured largely in Soviet history, which has never produced

I

its Turner, although population changes, colonisation and
settlement have been the subjects of a number of investigations, for example Rashin on the dynamics of nineteenth-
century population,[84] Aleksandrov on the seventeenth- and
early eighteenth-century settlement of the Yenisey region,[85]
and Preobrazhenskiy on the colonisation of the western Urals
at the same period.[86]

THE FADING REVIVAL

The volume of work, which followed Yatsunskiy's plea for a
revival of the subject in the early 1940s, was only modest. By
the late 1960s even this limited degree of interest seemed to
be petering out. Yugay in 1970 acknowledged: 'In justice one
must remark that since then [1940] geographers have not
achieved significant results in resolving problems, linked with
the reconstruction of the geography of past historical epochs.'[87]
Some of the persons involved have turned their attention elsewhere, outside the field. Sadly, many of the key figures, such
as Sinskaya and Tsvetkov, have died. Yatsunskiy, the main-
spring of the revival, died in 1966 and it would seem that without his enthusiasm and inspiration, the tempo of research has
begun to slacken. Yet others are now very near their retirement. Of the geographers, cited in this chapter, Gumilev
almost alone is still regularly publishing work in the sphere of
historical geography.

The limited amount and the rather disparate nature of what
has been accomplished, makes it difficult to speak of a Soviet
'school' of historical geography. Certain underlying premises,
such as the frequent separation of the physical and economic,
the emphasis on contemporary relevance and the Marxist
interpretations of historical development are essentially, if not
exclusively, Soviet. But in general, there has been a handful
of individuals, pursuing individual lines of research, nearly
always on rather traditional lines. Sinskaya followed an
approach worked out in the 1920s and 1930s by Vavilov;
Bernshteyn-Kogan's work on 'the road from the Varangians
to the Greeks' is in the direct line of descent from Khodakov-
skiy and Spitsyn in the last century. There has been little that
is new in subject matter, except to some extent the work of

Kirikov on fauna, there has been little that is new in methodology, except to some extent the concepts of Gumilev on the ethnos. The methods of the 'new' geography and the use of quantitative analysis and models were slow to be adopted by Soviet geography in general; the 1960s saw great strides made in utilising the new techniques, but as yet they have not touched historical geography. Concepts of west European and North American historical geography, such as sequent occupance, diffusion, the retrospective method, and perception, have been wholly ignored in the Soviet Union. It is a little depressing that Belov's definition of historical geography in 1967, 'the study of the geographical side of the historical process',[88] should echo precisely the definition propounded by Yatsunskiy in 1941.[89]

However the prospect for the coming decade may well be less bleak. The most recent publication on the content and objectives of historical geography, by Yugay in 1970, seems to foreshadow, albeit very faintly, a new interest in perception. Yugay acknowledges the revival of the last three decades; 'As far as historical geography is concerned, until recent times it still basically served historical science, being its subsidiary discipline, but recently (since 1940) it has attracted attention among geographers also. They found a place for it in their system of sciences, giving it a particular geographical character.'[90] He also acknowledges Yatsunskiy's role. Yatsunskiy however had insisted that 'historical geography does not study the geographical concepts of people of the past.'[91] Yugay, on the contrary, believes such perceptions are of vital relevance to historical geography: 'The history of the development of mental concepts of the surrounding environment . . . cannot be torn from the history of that environment's development.'[92] Yugay does not pursue his ideas very far, seeing in the history of geography, and especially of exploration, merely a source of facts for historical geography. He does not appear to make much connexion between a people's perception of their environment and their exploitation and adaptation of it, other than to comment: 'scholars will be able to show the development of one or another landscape in historical times and express change in geographical concepts about it, change which was evoked by changes taking place in the landscape,

either with or without the action of anthropogenic factors.'[93]
But at the same time Gumilev would seem to be moving
in a similar direction, in a recent article on 'Landscape
and Ethnos.' Basing his case on a consideration of ancient
Tibetan maps, he argues the need to comprehend the concepts
of a different ethnos in order to make proper use of the
evidence deriving from that ethnos.[94] The suggestions of Yugay
and Gumilev are little enough evidence of a new direction, but
they might well be straws in the wind of the 1970s.

Certainly the 1960s have seen a considerable debate in
Soviet philosophy and geography on questions of the man-
society-environment relationships. Much of the discussion
has been highly philosophical, much has been devoted to the
choice of term for a sphere of study comprising the complex
man-nature interaction. Trusov proposed the adoption of
Vernadskiy's 'noosphere', a materalist derivation from Le
Roy, as opposed to de Chardin's spiritual concept.[95] Other
terms include anthroposphere, sociosphere, technosphere and
noology. The dialectic complexities of the argument are
focused on the relationships of the present and historical
geography as such is not mentioned, but the movement in
Soviet geography towards a more integrated examination of
the human-physical relationships in the geographical environment must surely provide a methodological framework, into
which historical geography can fit more comfortably in the
future than in the past.

7

Historical Geography in North America

By *ANDREW HILL CLARK*

INTRODUCTION

THIS ESSAY WAS invited as a survey of accomplishments and directions in historical geography, and by historical geographers, in the United States and Canada during the past twenty-five years. Clearly the terms of reference are broad, permissive and elastic. If one were to discuss only scholars who explicitly list themselves, the courses they teach, or the contributions they publish, under the rubric 'historical geography', the inventory would be small and the comment relatively brief. If one were to include all the humanistic, natural or social studies which have a substantial content of relevance to historical geographers, the list of work and workers would be unmanageably comprehensive. Some clear criteria for selection are needed.

Negatively one must eschew any effort at encyclopedism based on 'fairness' or territorial representativeness; citations can cover, at best, but a small part of the literature and relatively few scholars. In practical terms attention will be largely (although by no means exclusively) confined to North American residents who have devoted their attention to the territory of the two countries. Because the writer was chiefly responsible for a similar assessment in the 1950s[1] very little attention will be given to the earlier parts of the quarter century and there will be a focus on the most recent years. Again, since R. C. Harris made a quite comprehensive study of historical geography in Canada only five years ago[2] (part of a belated Canadian centennial-year self-assessment of the Canadian Association of Geographers) the Canadian scene will receive rather cursory treatment. Within these guidelines the sole criteria for mention will be suitability to illustrative purpose and familiarity (often accidental and frequently of friends or former students) to the writer. This is neither a catalogue nor an honour roll and the relative virtue of works or scholars included or omitted is not at issue. Nevertheless, it is hoped that the chief kinds and directions of work are clearly indicated.

THE PHILOSOPHY AND METHODOLOGY OF NORTH AMERICAN HISTORICAL GEOGRAPHY

As to what could or should be considered historical geography we can refer to a good many critical essays for help.[3] Within the broad purview of history and geography at both the most intellectually sophisticated and more popular levels, historical geographers and geographical historians are concerned with the past character of the world of man and with how that character has changed through time. In theory, historical and geographical interests, concerned respectively with the time and place co-ordinates of phenomena, are fully comprehensive and without categorical limitations. Thus, in the broadest view, history and geography have no exclusive subject matter; there are, indeed, no peculiarly 'geographical' or 'historical' 'facts' or 'factors'. All phenomena clearly are embraced in various groupings by one or more of the categorically defined disciplines, and the practitioners of such fields usually have to be concerned more or less about place and time and thus, must have some geographical or historical interests. It is perfectly true that categorical limitations clearly mark the history and geography of a great many scholars who claim one or another of the two labels. But, again in the broad view, however arbitrarily they may limit themselves in time and space, it is as geographers and historians that they accept the general assignment of interest in location in the space of the earth's surface—the world of man—and in changes in that world through time.

Those who work the history-geography borderlands are,

thus, concerned simultaneously with co-ordinates of both place and time and the 'purest' kind of geographical history or historical geography presumably would be concerned simply and only with changes through time in, or past characteristics of, locational or spatial characteristics or relationships. Indeed, there are studies so abstract and austere that they do little more than this and there is increasing interest in them. But we may regard it as fortunate that students of man and his physical, social, political, economic, intellectual, aesthetic and other worlds, who operate with an historical-geographical bias, are rarely so narrowly focused. We have suggested that economists, sociologists or political scientists, for example, usually must be historians and geographers as well; likewise, the latter contantly make use of the information and methodology that the economist, or botanist, for example, might claim for his own and usually must have competence in one or more of the categorically defined disciplines. Abstraction for analysis of locational or chronological characteristics usually will have little value or interest until the generalised model, that may be the positive result of such analysis, is re-inserted in context. Although this may be seen more clearly in connexion with the historian's theories of social, economic and political change, in the writer's view of the intellectual and social missions of geography it applies equally to geographers.

Perhaps the most critical question for historical geographers today is the place of the regional historical study. Assuming for the moment that it has value, it would seem to be ideally suited to the interests and training of the history-geography hyphenates. It is a kind of study that has catered to a very wide and well-sustained popular and intellectual interest and that, properly taught, provides a superb framework for regional geography lecture courses which, otherwise, often become encyclopedically or abstractionally tedious. However, of more interest at the moment may be the degree to which it provides the indispensable contextual matrix from which more theoretical generalising concepts can emerge. If much contemporary statistical or mathematical work in geography fails to find an audience or to establish general relevance, that well may be charged to its failure to relate in an interpretative way to the general and specific characteristics of particular regions.

Almost all scholars constantly search for broad generalisations (models, theory) in their work and to disparage such a search would be sheer know-nothingism. However, it is equally true that to disparage the ordering of information in substantial, broad empirical studies of regional change (and, perhaps the derivation of at least first-order generalisations therefrom) would be but another kind of intellectual obscurantism and one with rather chilly implications. Many of us believe that it is in the study of the geography of the past, particularly as it has changed through time, that much of modern human and economic geography finds not only its roots but much of its fundamental framework of exposition and analysis. And for very practical, if no other, reasons each of us can hope to obtain some mastery of information and interpretation for only limited parts of the world of man (and for only limited periods of time). If we assume that there are degrees of spatial order in the world of man, we must further accept that, by understanding them, perhaps through developing special geometries of the human condition, we shall perhaps make more sense of that world. But we must never forget that making such sense is our full and only purpose. We must never let any kind of methodology, or any specific theoretical assumptions, crowd out the history or geography in their comprehensive senses. If we do, we turn ourselves into second-string apprentices of one or another categorically defined discipline which may have found clearer purposes or directions of its own. The 'world knowledge' functions of both history and geography remain absolutely vital to the intellectual health of mankind; we believe, too, that such knowledge is of great importance to his social, economic and political well-being.

Fortunately, in this view, comprehensive empirical studies by regional historical geographers are still prominent in this genre of scholarship in North America. Happily, more and more of the scholars involved are making the fullest relevant or possible use of locational and behavioural theory, statistical procedures and new computational facilities. But, with the best of them, the traditional skill in the recording, exposition and analysis of the geographies of nature and culture, and in the use and interpretation of primary historical sources, remain of fundamental importance. It is from such a firm foundation that the new tools may display their often formidable power for the checking of intuitive hypotheses, the clarification of implicit models and the development of alternative explanations.[4]

REGIONAL HISTORICAL GEOGRAPHY

Most regional studies have strong topical biases of one sort or another and, since the best topical studies are firmly rooted in regions, the arbitrary quality of classification appears at once in noting a few kinds of regional interest. Examples of such work focused outside of the United States include James Parsons' studies of Colombia, Dan Stanislawski's of Portugal, Robert West's of Middle America, and Carl Sauer's of the Caribbean.[5] Rather more topical in its emphasis on population was Canute Vandermeer's study of Cebu,[6] one of a good many of its kind. Fred Kniffen's cultural group, trained at Baton Rouge, produced several domestic regional monographs, notably those of Gary Dunbar and Peter Wacker; perhaps Kniffen's own regional history of Louisiana should be included.[7] Apart from the writer's three regional books,[8] Madison seminars and dissertations helped to generate such volumes by Andrew Burghardt, Paul English, James Gibson, Cole Harris, Terry Jordan, James Lemon, and Roy Merrens, among others.[9] Perhaps the best single recent example of the genre was Donald Meinig's prize-winning *The Great Columbia Plain,* a magnificent study which was preceded by one on South Australia and to which he has recently added two more shorter regional accounts.[10] Erich Isaac's studies of Kent Island in Chesapeake Bay[11]—although very much above the average in quality—may serve as one example of other domestic American contributions. Since the days of Alfred Meyer's concern with the Kankakee Swamp and Marvin Kaatz's study of the Black Swamp, the Lake Plains have received less historical attention, but one topical study with strong regional bias in that direction was that of Douglas McManis (1964) on the 'prairie peninsula' area.[12] In and of

Canada, apart from Harris, we might note that Warkentin's *Western Interior of Canada* foreshadowed his currently intensifying interest in the 'prairie' region and that Eric Ross's *Beyond the River and the Bay* is a most successful study of early Manitoba modelled on Ralph Brown's *Mirror for Americans* . . .[13] In both countries more localised regional studies, of widely ranging quality, have been common vehicles for masters' and doctors' degrees.

As was suggested, most of the regional studies had strong topical biases. To use examples from the group out of Madison best known to me, Harris was interested in the cadastral reflection and general geographical imprint of a land-tenurial structure, Hilliard was seeking answers to the question of the antebellum South's degree of self-reliance in different kinds of food, Jordan was comparing the agricultural impact of two contrasting groups of immigrants to Texas (German and native southern), Lemon was mainly concerned with socio-economic structure and function, Mitchell with the temporal and locational gradients of the strength of the non-subsistent sector of the farming enterprise, and Ward with the shifting locations of economic functions and immigrant residence within large nineteenth-century cities.[14] A tendency of many who begin with a sharper regional focus to become more topically oriented with time is a clear trend as Ward's book well illustrates.[15]

URBAN INTERESTS

A city is, of course, a very special and concentrated example of a region and the current popularity of urban studies has contributed a number of individual city studies many of which are clearly historical. Indeed it is in city studies, where urban geographers and urban historians often become almost indistinguishable in their interests, that the distinction between geographical history and historical geography may be at its foggiest. One of the relatively pioneering studies by historians —Richard Wade's *The Urban Frontier*—has been heralded as a fine contribution to historical urban geography; Wade also has co-operated with geographer Harold Mayer in a lively pictorial history of Chicago.[16] Thus the succession of outstanding nominal historians with deep concerns in matters of geographical interest, which may be said to have begun in American historiography with Frederick Jackson Turner, continues. Another likely candidate for the roster would be Sam Bass Warner—in his non-polemical phases at least—on whom many historical urban geographers have depended.[17] Much of the material in *The Growth of Seaport Cities, 1790-1825*[18] is of prime geographical concern, emphasising again our debt to historians. Planners too, notably John W. Reps, have contributed useful information and ideas.[19]

It is perhaps more usual than not for urban geographers interested in the present to concern themselves with some depth of time, but generally this is more appropriately discussed under the rubric of 'changing geographies' below. However, there have been several explicitly historical studies both of individual cities, as that of Peter Goheen, and more general treatments like those of Jacob Spelt, Andrew Burghardt, Howard Nelson and Alan Pred.[20] The last-named scholar is very much part of the new wave of theorists and statisticians and in many ways his study ties in more (as he undoubtedly meant it to do) with the work of students of contemporary urban and industrial problems than with those of many historical geographers. Goheen unearthed a massive array of data for the computer to resolve and in both theory and techniques he speaks with a most modern voice, but to the degree that any city, like Toronto, is properly thought of as a regional entity on its own, he too is a regional historical geographer. For earlier periods and for broader perspectives, with more traditional methodologies of research and description there has been a wide variety of urban-focused historical studies by geographers of which those by Burghardt, Nelson and Spelt are representative.

GENERAL TOPICAL STUDIES

Of course there has been a considerable variety of topical historical research that has had little if anything to do with the phenomena of urbanisation. Galloway's continued interest in the development of Brazil's sugar industry[21] has had many counterparts. Two rather different kinds of transporation interest are represented by Andrew Burghardt on the evolution of a transportation network in the Niagara peninsula and Alan Grey on the decision-making in the route location for the Union Pacific Railroad.[22] Much more characteristic of European than North American historical geography have been Norman Pound's many Old World studies.[23] Herbert Whitney made some interesting experiments in the unearthing and use of sources in a population study of colonial Rhode Island and the indefatigable Wilbur Zelinsky has had a strong historical thread running through his very wide-ranging interests and prolific production in population and cultural geography.[24] Hildegard Binder Johnson, one of our most scholarly and industrious historical geographers, has tackled such a wide variety of topics that her work almost defies classification.[25] Louis De Vorsey continues his work on colonial Indian frontiers and Kenneth Thompson is exploring what might be called historical medical geography.[26]

CURRENT FASHIONS IN METHODS AND MODELS

Inevitably there is an increasing amount of empirical statistical research and more mathematically oriented theoretical interest among geographical students of the past which is by no means restricted to urban interests. Regretfully, too much of it appears to be the result of the existence of accessible information for testing or elaborating very general theory and too little is devoted to the development of specific models by which the evolution of particular socio-economic, political, and general regional entities may be better understood. Many methodological proposals such as that of Forrest Pitts have proved to be of rather limited interest.[27] From any point of view some of the best of such work has been done by Richard Morrill.[28] There has been no specifically North American attempt to fit historical geography *per se* into a theoretical quantitative framework comparable to Harvey's 1967 'Models of the Evolution of Spatial Patterns in Human Geography'[29] although an essay by Leslie Curry (unhappily incomprehensible to most of the historical/cultural scholars) has some interesting implications for an historical approach.[30] Exemplary of increasing quantitative activity, if at a relatively elementary methodological level, are the countless regression models in use, such as those developed by Michael Conzen in his study of nineteenth-century Wisconsin farming.[31] Assessment of the few statistical contributions to historical geography thus far suggests that it would be salutary if model makers in that genre would commit themselves, as Conzen did, to long and rigorous development and testing in a context with which they had taken pains thoroughly to familiarise themselves. Literally, for an historical geographer reaching for useful generalisations there is no substitute for his 'laboratory' regions, which he must know thoroughly in historical and geographical breadth and depth, and where all theory applicable to them may be tested within them. To arbitrarily restrict oneself to very limited categories of information about such regions may lead to a logically disastrous kind of special pleading. This is an advocacy not of encyclopedism but of enough breadth to encompass a wide range of conceivably relevant variables. The current fad among many of the newest wave of geographers to depreciate information can only prove to be intellectually debilitating.

CHANGING GEOGRAPHIES AND GEOGRAPHICAL CHANGE

Since the writer has shown some scepticism in the past about cross-sectional approaches to the geography of either past or present and has suggested the value of thinking of all geography as a constantly changing entity, and of historical geography as 'the changing geography of the past',[32] he would emphasise that there is, currently, as always, a great deal of study of geographical change which is not explicitly intended by its writers to be, or recognised by its readers as, historical geography. John Weaver's crop-livestock studies of the mid-fifties were excellent examples of this genre.[33] Another good example is the Hewes-Schmieding study of changing patterns of crop failure on the Great Plains; indeed much of Hewes' individual work, although often more explicitly historical, could be classified here.[34] Gary Dunbar, along with his interests in the historical geography of the American southeast, and in individual unsung geographers of the past, took a flier at a geography of change while on a tour of duty in Africa.[35]

John Fraser Hart and Wilbur Zelinsky have each contributed many studies of change in American rural and population geography over longer or shorter periods.[36] Richard Hough examined the effect of the decline of the raw silk industry on parts of Japan.[37] John Jakle, responsible on his own for a fine topical historical study of salt on the Ohio Valley frontier, also joined with James Wheeler in one of the many studies of urban change.[38] Also focused on change, but of incidental historical interest, are the Robert Lewis and Richard Rowland report on seventy years of urbanisation in the USSR and Katzman's attempt to correlate ethnic composition of regional populations with economic performance.[39] To round out this highly eclectic listing we might include some of James Vance's studies of change in cities here rather than as specifically historical.[40]

'CULTURAL' GEOGRAPHY AND GEOGRAPHERS

The writer did not know in 1954, and still does not, quite how to relate the cultural-environmental interests, with their often strong anthropological overtones, which have derived especially from the Sauer era at the University of California at Berkeley, to the rest of the variegated body of historical-geographical work. As has been indicated, Carl Sauer himself and a number of his students have contributed regional monographs to what the writer considers to be the very heart of historical geography although these tended to be concentrated in Ibero-American areas. But many, and perhaps most, of Berkeley cultural students of the postwar period, including such as Homer Aschmann, William Denevan, Marvin Mikesell, Erhard Rostlund, Frederick Simoons, David Sopher and Philip Wagner, several 'second generation' men (as Isaac who studied with George Carter, and William Thomas with Joseph Spencer), and a great many others of no Berkeley connexion, have worked chiefly in this stream of geographical culture history, parallel to but often quite distinct from the work of the more historiographically focused historical geographers.[41] It is interesting that Carl Sauer himself used the adjective 'historical' in a clear and prominent way only in his presidential address to the Association of American Geographers in

1941 and not at all in this period so far as the writer is aware, even though, in his recent *Early Spanish Main* and *Northern Mists* we have two of his most important explicitly historical book-length publications.[42] But, in general, it is on the inter- play of culture and nature, on the distribution and diffusion of various facets of culture, and on man's role in the altera- tion of his own material environment, that attention is focused.[43] The ancillary training of the members of this group has tended to be in physical and biotic geography and in anthropology rather than in social, economic and political history. This has proved of great advantage in most of what the cultural geographers actually have done, although at times, as their interests have become more explicitly historical, difficulties have arisen through lack of documentary skills or of contextual historical information.

Some scattered recent examples of this same general type by other than those scholars already named are Karl Butzer's first-rate *Environment and Archaeology: An Introduction to Pleistocene Geography*[44] and studies by John Bergman, Robert Fuson and Stanley Ross.[45] Although clearly different in direc- tion from the 'historical' historical geographers, a reasonably close liaison between the latter and the 'cultural' group is maintained. Both the writer and Fred Kniffen, who have each had many explicitly 'historical' students, were both also students of Sauer and also have guided 'cultural' dissertations in the Berkeley tradition at Madison and Baton Rouge; reci- procally, many of the 'cultural' group, as Mikesell at Chicago, have encouraged candidly 'historical' research.

MORPHOLOGICAL INTERESTS

Kniffen himself has been perhaps the major American scholar concerned with what we might call morphological aspects of the cultural landscape, beginning with covered bridges and county fairgrounds and ending with an immensely detailed and comprehensive description and interpretation of the diffusion and location of American house types. Yet, as the variety of his own and his students' work shows, his historical and cultural interests are quite catholic.[46] His influence is clear in the work of Peter Wacker who, with Richard Pillsbury, has

attacked the problem of the evolution of Middle Atlantic
street patterns and who joined with R. J. Trindell in a study
of the earliest New Jersey house types.[47]

Edward Price, another Sauer student with broad historical
and cultural interests, has shared some of Kniffen's interests.[48]
Despite the warm reception of their work by scholars in a
variety of disciplines, what has been referred to elsewhere as
the 'chimney-pot' type of morphological interest has had little
other geographical following in the United States or Canada.
Of course, cultural impress on the land takes many forms
other than house types, street patterns, vegetation alteration,
and the like. The cadastral pattern with its reflection in fences,
fields and roads and general arrangement of settlement is very
much in point and we are fortunate in having fine historical
studies by two geographers, William Pattison and Norman
Thrower, of the American rectangular survey system.[49]

ENVIRONMENT AND PERCEPTION

Those of the 'cultural' brotherhood who have been most
explicitly interested in environmental quality and the substantial changes wrought by man in his own environmental context recently have had the good fortune to find themselves
much in fashion and enjoying better than usual audiences. As
the pieces in *Man's Role in Changing the Face of the Earth*[50]
suggest, much of such interest is implicitly historical, although
space does not permit a general discussion of that literature
here. However, one related sector of it (that of environmental
perception) would seem to deserve special mention because of
the current attention being focused upon it. Indeed one of
the more perplexing questions in research on past geographies
has been our own assessment of the perceptions of the environment that were contemporary with the period under study.
It was a problem that concerned Ralph Brown very much in
his *Historical Geography of the United States*[51] and has been
widely explored by writers of regional historical studies.

Perhaps no one has been more concerned with the intellectual problems raised than David Lowenthal,[52] and perhaps no
North American area has been more critically affected by its
occupiers' perception of it than the Great Plains. Martyn

Bowden includes the latter area in general terms in relation to the western interior of the U.S. during much of the nineteenth century.[53] Specifically on the Great Plains, Malcolm Lewis has been most active[54] and of major importance is Walter Kollmorgen's presidential address to the Association of American Geographers where, in considering differing nineteenth-century perceptions of the plains, he reaffirmed some of Walter Prescott Webb's major theses.[55] Herman Friis of the National Archives, whose interests and scholarly publications in historical geography range widely in time, topic and region, has contributed a perception estimate based on the papers of scientific explorers.[56]

HISTORICAL GEOGRAPHY IN CANADA

Richard Colebrook Harris' 1966 account of Canadian historical geography is almost entirely restricted to work done on Canadian topics, although he made no restrictions as to the residence of the authors, and it includes some studies by outsiders in French and German as well as English.[57] In the writer's judgement he includes most of the serious historical-geographical work done in Canada to that time. Several interesting and important monographs and papers have appeared since, some of which have been referred to above. In the very issue of the *Canadian Geographer* in which Harris' article appeared, there was a sharply perceptive comment on the exploration and settlement of the western interior plains by J. G. Nelson.[58] What may now be considered the 'Old Guard' of historical geographers of Canada, including Andrew Burghardt, Louis Gentilcore, Gordon Merrill, W. H. Parker, Richard Ruggles, Jacob Spelt, Wreford Watson and the writer, are well represented. Most encouraging is the size of the new wave following along with, and subsequent to, Harris: Frank Innes, Eric Ross, and J. D. Wood. (John Warkentin seems to belong to both camps). In all, Harris turned up nearly sixty theses and dissertations concerned with Canada's past and its development and, to the writer's knowledge, several of the master's theses listed have been or are being followed by doctoral dissertations also with an historical bias.

Perhaps the key to Harris' whole review, and a pertinent

K

observation it is, is contained in the first sentence: 'In considering the place of historical geography in Canada, it is well to remember that the land has always dominated much of the writing about this country.' Also of much interest is his enumeration of themes in Canadian historical geography which deserve more exploration. Under 'occupation of the land' he lists: 1, the impact of man on the natural environment; 2, European-Indian contacts; 3, distribution of the land; 4, modification of European systems of agriculture; 5, the transfer of the ethnic group; and 6, attitudes towards knowledge of the new world. Other main headings included 'technological change and resource utilization', 'urban growth and urbanisation', and 'regional development'.

CONCLUSION

We might have used headings of the kind employed by Clifford Darby, Helmut Jäger, Hugh Prince or C. T. Smith in their surveys of historical geography in general (but chiefly of the United Kingdom or continental Europe)[59] to arrange our comments for these two North American countries and, indeed, one of the initial false starts on this essay was so patterned. But, although most attempts at classification tend to become procrustean operations, this one seemed to be insupportably so; the kinds of work accomplished in the United States and Canada demanded an organisation peculiar to themselves. We might also have been much more generous in citations. Some well known, consistently productive, historical and cultural geographers have not been cited at all—most notably, perhaps, Jan O. M. Broek whose Santa Clara study of the thirties must always have a prominent place among the classics of the genre;[60] Loyal Durand, Merle Prunty or Halleck Raup, whose interests and scholarly efforts have never flagged.[61] Moreover, the students of George Carter at Johns Hopkins, and of Joseph Spencer and his colleagues at U.C.L.A., deserve more attention.[62] But within the limits of space available the writer believes the categories chosen to be valid and the works cited, all personally familiar to the writer, to be fairly representative of their categories, although for a full, fair inventory one would have to consult sources like Harris on Canada, Douglas

McManis's *Bibliography of the Historical Geography of the United States* (second edition in preparation),[63] and standard international bibliographies, like *Current Geographical Publications* (which, however, does a poor job of classifying material in historical geography).

With Ralph Brown's death and Carl Sauer's apparent shift away from a more historiographic bias, that emphasis in the history-geography borderlands appeared to suffer something of an eclipse in the late forties and to recover only slowly in the fifties. But, within the last decade in particular, a firmly 'historical' historical geography has been moving briskly again (perhaps even more so in Canada than in the United States). Despite the upheaval in methodology that the quantifiers have generated in the social, historical and natural sciences, historical geography may have gained more, and lost less, than many other traditional geographical fields of interest. Indeed it appears to be that the new methodologies are often peculiarly suitable to the study of the changing geographies of the past.

8

Historical Geography in Australia and New Zealand

By R. L. HEATHCOTE and M. McCASKILL

SINCE THE AUTHORS accepted the invitation to write this chapter, two reviews have appeared on recent work in historical geography on both sides of the Tasman Sea.[1] These valuable studies say little about the early development of historical geography in Australia and New Zealand and the present essay will therefore devote some attention to the antecedents of recent studies.

Australia and New Zealand were both explored and settled during the great outflow of European enterprise in the eighteenth and nineteenth centuries. In both countries the decades between 1840 and 1880 were especially formative in the making of their cultural landscapes and the patterns of settlement and economy. The establishment of settlement in empty or sparsely occupied lands, the interaction of alien society and novel environment and the rapid sequence of geographic changes have provided geographers in both countries with a host of challenging problems. Because of the timing of settlement there is a wealth of archival sources to document its processes. Literate explorers and pioneers, officials and businessmen both literate and numerate, left a wealth of maps, sketches, paintings, photographs, diaries, statistical compendiums, newspapers, voluminous parliamentary papers and royal commissions—all grist for the historical geographers' mill. Because of the heavy involvement of officialdom in early locational decisions and the nineteenth-century penchant for paperwork it is often possible to identify causes and motivations for the early patterns of society on the land, whereas these often can only be surmised from indirect evidence in Europe, Asia and eastern North America.

In the early development of academic geography Australia and New Zealand proceeded virtually independently. Although several New Zealand graduates took up early positions in Australian university geography departments, there was little intellectual interchange across the Tasman until the 1960s. Each country seems to have drawn its inspiration, techniques and staff directly from North America or the United Kingdom. Despite the similarity in the timing of European settlement in Australia and New Zealand and the general similarity of the source materials, it is only within the past few years that persons with research experience in the one country have worked on similar problems in the other.

Further, the fundamental difference in size of the two nations needs to be remembered. Within Australia the mere size of the continent, with university centres five hundred or more miles apart and the separation of source materials in the archives of the six states rather than a national repository, have served to isolate the few historical geographers from each other. In New Zealand on the other hand, size was much less of a problem.

HISTORICAL GEOGRAPHY IN AUSTRALIA—THE ANTECEDENTS

The process of discovery and exploration of the patterns of land and water was one major theme for a century following first permanent European settlement in 1788. The geographers were in fact explorers—official naval and military surveyors, private sealers, whalers, pastoralists, miners, and adventurers. Most of the official findings were published, first in local newspapers and official gazettes, then in European journals—particularly the proceedings of the various geographical societies, and finally in book form. At least one official explorer produced a text for local schools in the contemporary question-and-answer 'capes and bays' idiom, based on his own and his predecessor's explorations, but he apparently was the exception, as one hundred years after first settlement complaints were still being made that many schools were using British texts and as a result learning British and not Australian geography.[2]

In spite of this early practical interest, geography was a late starter as a fully-fledged discipline in Australian universities. The first post, held by Griffith Taylor, was established as an associate professorship at the University of Sydney in 1920 and no further establishments were made until the 1950s. Teaching in geography was undertaken in the interim at some of the other universities, but not beyond second or third year of undergraduate study, and usually as part of courses in geology or economics. The 1950s saw the establishment of full chairs at all but one university (Adelaide 1959, Tasmania 1956, Melbourne 1959, New England 1959, Queensland 1958, and the Commonwealth-sponsored Australian National University 1951 and 1962). The exception was Western Australia, where the chair was not created until 1964, by which time the second round of chairs at the new universities had been set up (Flinders 1965, Macquarie 1966, Monash 1962, New South Wales 1967, Newcastle 1963). Such dates speak for themselves, although they mask the rapid expansion of fourth (honours) year BA theses and some MA theses in the early 1950s, and the research work of professional geographers attached to other departments such as geology, economics and history.

Before 1945 historical geography was undertaken by a variety of researchers, not all of them geographers by title or training. The initial interest in exploration and discovery was followed by general concern for the continent's resources to which many disciplines contributed. Thus Griffith Taylor, the first professor, was British by birth, by training a geologist, by inclination and experience an explorer of desert and icecap, and by his publications variously a climatologist, physiographer, and ethnographer, as well as a geographer. He saw the continental environment as placing several constraints on the possibilities for land settlement. The patterns of geology— as affecting fuels, raw materials, soils and underground water supplies, and climate, particularly aridity—as affecting the areas open to agricultural and pastoral land use, were for him the major themes of geographical study.[3] A contemporary, Grenfell Price, placed more emphasis on individual actions as formative influences, but also saw climate—in this case humidity—as a constraint for European settlement in the north of Australia as well as other tropical areas.[4]

A further logical theme stemming from the history of the continent was the interest in the processes of European and later Anglo-Australian land settlement. Prior to 1945, most work had been by economic historians who saw land settlement as the end-product of the inter-relationships through time of the traditional trilogy of land, labour and capital, set in a changing political context. Land settlement was seen as the means by which an area was brought into economic commercial production.[5] Only one historian, S. H. Roberts, concerned himself with the patterns generated by the settlement processes but he stressed the patterns of land tenure and ownership rather than the visual impacts of these on the landscape. Nonetheless his two works were and still are masterpieces in their own right and have recently been reprinted basically unchanged.[6] His lead was not followed, although as part of a survey of the British Dominions a study of the 'geography behind the history' of Australia appeared about the same time.[7]

For the geographers, Grenfell Price examined some misconceptions of the environment of South Australia as they affected its early history, while his colleague Fenner examined the spread of settlement in the state by means of the first sequence of population dot maps to appear in Australia.[8] Some ten thousand miles away, at the same time, the German geographer Rühl was preparing for publication a sequence of dot distribution maps of crop and livestock statistics, as a basis for a study of the evolving economic geography of eastern Australia.[9] The method used in this latter study—cross-sections of data at significant dates linked by explanatory narrative—was to inspire Jan Broek's Santa Clara Valley study.[10] Andrews had produced a preliminary study of the evolution of rural settlement prior to 1945, but the results of his Cambridge thesis on settlement in the wheat lands did not appear until 1966.[11]

Of more immediate impact, both in the information provided and the method used, was *Land Utilisation in Australia,* the combined effort of the professors of agriculture and

commerce at Melbourne University.[12] In this volume the traditional concern for the economics of land settlement was
blended with an explanatory description of the patterns of
actual land use an an 'evolutionary sequence', in which the
documentation of the impacts of technical innovation and
scientific research was paralleled by consideration of the
sequence of economic forces and the 'natural factors controlling
the use of land'. Here was the first blend of history, economics,
and geography on the continental scale and Chapter II—'The
historical survey of settlement' was the first continental-wide
venture in historical geography in Australia.

AUSTRALIAN HISTORICAL GEOGRAPHY SINCE 1945

Since 1945, studies in historical geography in Australia have
received several stimuli, some originating outside geography,
others within. From outside has come the historian's concept
of the frontier of settlement and the ecologist's concern for
environmental modification, while from within has come the
recognition of technological change, the constraints of institutional policies and concern for the behavioural patterns of the
resource managers. In addition there has been an intermittent
inflow of ideas and people from the United Kingdom and to
a lesser extent the United States.

Themes
Historians first transferred F. J. Turner's 'frontier' hypothesis to Australian conditions, and saw sufficient similarities
to justify comparative studies of the formative influences of
the stresses at the frontier of settlement.[13] Only two geographers, one a visiting American (D. W. Meinig), used the
concept as the main theme for their studies but both were
major works and the concept, if much modified, is implicit
in much other work on rural land settlement.[14]
The modification of the continental ecology by land settlement had been recognised from the early years of the
colonies,[15] but the theme has come under renewed scrutiny
recently. Ecologists have examined the effect of the clearance
of native vegetation and of continued cropping on soil
fertility,[16] while Grenfell Price has surveyed the broader

picture for flora and fauna and Jennings has made a preliminary survey of man as a geological agent.[17] The current general public and scientific interest in conservation of the environment is likely to provide a further stimulus to detailed historical studies of past as well as current changes in Australian ecosystems.

After 1945 there was also a revival of anthropological studies in Australia, and attempts have been made to reconstruct the pattern of Aboriginal cultures and economies at the time of first contact with the European invaders.[18] Of these, only one was by a geographer (Lawrence), but all the studies were concerned with the spatial patterns and associations. Not until 1969, however, did the first attempt to reconstruct a rounded picture of Aboriginal Australia appear[19] and it is an illustration of the rapidity with which archaeological discoveries are currently being made, that significant revision of long-held hypotheses is forecast in this volume—not only hypotheses on the nature of Aboriginal cultures, but also their role in the wider history of man on earth.

The impact of European land settlement on the continent and its indigenous inhabitants was achieved in part by considerable technological innovations, and recognition of their role has been a particular feature of geographical enquiries since 1945. The mechanisation of land clearance and cultivation techniques was early seen as a major factor in changing use of the land[20] and the significance to the spread of grain fields at the expense of savannah woodland and mallee scrub, in a society where hand labour was scarce and expensive, was re-emphasised by Andrews and Meinig.[21] Reduction of the friction of distance by transport innovations on land and water enabled the Australian interior to become an economic producer for the European market;[22] developments in mining and earth-moving machinery have opened up new mineral fields and are bringing considerable landscape changes,[23] while preliminary work has begun to document the sequential changes in energy supply available for manufacturing processes and the results in urban industrial intensification.[24]

The spread of settlement and technological innovations, however, have not taken place in a vacuum, but within the constraints not merely of the physical environment but also

of institutional policies by which the patterns of land settlement were supposedly controlled. Recognition of the importance of these policies, their origin (often outside Australia),
and their application in Australia, has become a major
research field for historical geographers. The official land
survey and settlement policies and the rural cadastral and
tenurial patterns which resulted (deliberately or accidentally)
have been examined for New South Wales, Queensland, South
Australia, and Victoria,[25] and there have been some equivalent
studies in the urban context.[26] One feature stressed in both
types of studies has been the continuity of formal land survey
patterns, settlement sites and structures, long after their
original rationale has disappeared.[27] Thus the speed by which
functional patterns of Australian population, land use, and
production have changed has not been paralleled by the
relatively inflexible institutional framework for that settlement, and the results are a youthful landscape (in terms of
absolute time scales) littered with the relics of outmoded land
settlement systems.

The explanations for these relics has led researchers into
examination of the original motivations of official and private
decision makers. Historians have begun to revise long-held
penal-colony explanations for the initial settlement in Australia in favour of commercial and strategic motives based on
contemporary assessment of marine resources and trade routes
to the Pacific.[28] Geographers have limited their attention to
the contrasts between official and private knowledge and
motivations in land settlement, and the gaps between intended and actual outcomes.[29] The landscape influence of
individual decision makers has as yet received only limited
attention.[30]

Sources

Despite the fact that many of the voluminous official and
private primary sources are still being collected and cata-
logued,[31] most of the studies of rural land settlement done by
geographers have made careful comparisons of official records
of land survey and ownership with such independent property
and business records as have been available.[32] The official
record has provided the framework and sequence of events,

the detailed local explanations for which have often come from the independent sources. Of particular value here, however, have been the royal commissions, and perhaps the best example of their use for a specific purpose was Cain's study of the impact of the 1896–1905 drought in western New South Wales, where the evidence to the commission of pastoral station managers could be checked against the business records of their properties.[33]

Despite such studies, however, many sources remain untapped. The various state lands departments and archives still have most of the basic facts of land settlement relatively untouched, the detailed sequence of population change throughout the continent lies in the census files awaiting systematic enquiry, the evolving functions of the central places are arrayed in untouched splendour in the state libraries' shelves of business directories and gazetteers, and only Meinig has made any serious attempt to survey systematically the local newspaper sources over a specific period of time.[34]

Economic historians have produced valuable national compilations of production and capital investment to demonstrate the changing flow of capital through the national and state economies over time—seeing this flow as a major explanatory factor in the sequence of economic development in Australia.[35] In few other countries have the national 'balance sheets' of capital flows been made available so readily but the historical geographers have not yet grasped the significance of this particular source.

Techniques

One of the features of the period since 1945 has been the proliferation of regional histories. Some have resulted from centennial festivities and with local residents as authors have produced collections of interesting but unsifted local facts and fancies.[36] Occasionally, however, a professional historian has been called in[37] or has seen his particular research problem in a specific location,[38] and the result is a superior thematic blend of official and local sources. These latter studies make up a mosaic, which partially covers the more intensively settled eastern and south eastern Australia. Western Australia and Northern Territory are relative blanks.[39] But the coverage of such studies is uneven, techniques are not always comparable, and most of them have been criticised for either ignoring or glossing over the role of urban centres in the processes of land settlement.[40]

For their part, historical geographers have shied away from the synthesis of change through time implied in regional histories. Their interest in areas appears to have been less for the sake of the area itself, but more because it happened to have been the stage whereon a particular sequence of events or process was played out. Thus, Perry studied the Nineteen Counties of New South Wales as the testing ground for the frontier hypothesis because these were the first contiguous areas occupied from the hearth at Sydney; Allen and Heathcote pegged out rational but nonetheless arbitrary portions of the interior plains to test particular hypotheses of pastoral settlement; Langford-Smith chose the Murrumbidgee area for his study of the evolution of an irrigation settlement; and Williams used the convenient political unit of South Australia to test some definitions of the term 'settlement'.[41] Perhaps the nearest to a true regional study was Powell's study of western Victoria.[42] Here, the land settlement and appraisal was examined through time as a learning system for the evaluation of, and adaptation to, local resources.

To portray change through time, a variety of methods have been adopted. The study of one landscape component as it changes through time—the vertical technique—has been used in studies of the spread of the wheatlands, the spread of sugar production, a sequence of land drainage, and the evolution of a mining town.[43] Some studies have made use of cross-sectional techniques; Williams has summarised rural settlement in South Australia at 1840 and 1855 and Powell has reconstructed the woodland of Victoria from official sources at 1869.[44] For the urban areas, Solomon reviewed Hobart's form and function in 1845 and Walsh went a step further and produced an 'historic present' survey of Sydney in 1803, using only sources available at the time and couching his description as far as possible in the contemporary literary style.[45]

In retrospective vein, an incisive overview of the past influences on the current landscapes of 'bush and city' has been made by Spate,[46] but detailed use of the technique has been limited to a survey of relict architectural styles in Tasmanian country towns,[47] an explanation of relict rural settlement types in New South Wales,[48] and the pattern of home building materials in south eastern Australia.[49]

Methods

Innovation in methodology has been basically in two fields, first the development of models by which hypothetical sequences can be simulated and tested against 'reality', and secondly, an increasing concern for the decision-making process as a significant factor in explanation of that reality.

Most of the land settlement studies mentioned above, and especially the studies of the frontier hypothesis, have implied explicitly or implicitly a Toynbean model of challenge and response. This assumed inputs of settlers with a common European cultural and technological background confronted with similar environmental challenges, and set in similar political contexts (policies which encouraged intensive land settlement by independent, often family, producers). Given the similarities of inputs and the challenges faced, the outputs should show similar responses and the contrasts reflect local variations in the nature of the challenge. That the contemporary settlers were aware of the similarities with other nineteenth-century areas of European settlement has been indicated in the context of irrigation technology,[50] and that unconsciously they were pursuing similar responses has been suggested for pastoral resource use.[51]

Von Thünen's theory has been used by Rose to explain, by means of an 'isolated continent', the initial and continued functional dominance of Australia's metropolitan centres—based upon several external (oceanic) and internal (rail) transport links as opposed to a hypothetical single external (rocket) and internal (hovercraft) transport system.[52]

Christaller's central place theories have been tested for contemporary New South Wales country towns,[53] but an historical approach has not yet appeared, although Meinig's consideration of the patterns of wheat townships' growth in South Australia came close to it.[54] A local variant on central place theory, Daly's 'dispersed city' hypothesis, has been derived from study of the evolution of one of the major non-metropolitan urban complexes in Australia.[55]

One type of model which has already appeared, but which seems assured of future importance, is the identification of resource use systems and their spatial patterns. Thus, Powell produced a model of the spatial evolution of early pastoral properties in Victoria, and a schema of their seasonal activities[56] and Higman suggested six types of sugar production systems had evolved in New South Wales.[57]

Concern for the decision-making process is not new, but was recognised in early studies of South Australian settlement where opinions and perceptions seem to have been as numerous as the original settlers.[58] In recent studies, however, it has been more to the forefront of research. Documentation of the often wide differences between official and private perceptions of land resources and motivations for land settlement have been at the core of the work of Heathcote, Meinig, and Powell, mentioned above. The contemporary 'climates of opinion' have been used to illustrate the rationalistic evaluation, by latitudinal analogy, of southern Australian resources well before they were actually discovered,[59] and not only literature but art history and semantics have provided useful clues to the Man-Nature relationship through time.[60]

HISTORICAL GEOGRAPHY IN NEW ZEALAND—THE ANTECEDENTS

Concern for historical themes has been a persistent feature of geographical study in New Zealand since the formal establishment of the discipline in the University of Canterbury in 1937. The first head of department, George Jobberns, had been trained as a geologist and had strong sympathy for the Davisian genetic approach to landform study as developed in the prolific writings on the landforms of New Zealand by Sir Charles Cotton. During a visit to the United States in 1939 Jobberns became attracted to the philosophy of Carl Sauer and the Berkeley school of geography. He recruited two able young Berkeley graduates, Robert Bowman and Andrew H. Clark, as visiting lecturers to Canterbury between 1940 and 1942. Kenneth B. Cumberland had arrived from London in 1938 with a background of research in agricultural geography, and was immediately impressed at the scale and rapidity of the transformation that had occurred in the New Zealand landscape in scarcely a century of European settlement. Thus the beginnings of academic geography were forged in a productive convergence of the indigenous experience of Jobberns and the techniques and outlook of the London and Berkeley schools of the late 1930s.

At the time of geography's formal establishment in New Zealand historical retrospection was favoured by the preparations for the celebration of the centennial of organised British settlement in 1840. The Historical Branch of the Department of Internal Affairs had begun preparation of a national atlas which was to be a cartographic record of the century of European settlement, and the high quality photographic series *Making New Zealand; Pictorial Surveys of a Century,* published by this branch, gave some simple vivid historical geography for the general citizen.

In the late 1930s there was much public concern at the destructive consequences of European occupation especially of the hill and mountain lands. These had not shared in the 'grassland revolution' that had made the North Island lowlands a prosperous overseas farm of the United Kingdom. Farm abandonment, spectacular soil erosion, depletion of forest resources and destructive lowland flooding were immediate problems inviting geographical appraisal in an historical context.

Geography had a rapid development in New Zealand during the 1940s. The first five honours students graduated from Canterbury in 1941. Departments were established at Auckland and at Dunedin (University of Otago) in 1946 and full courses were offered at the Victoria University of Wellington in 1952 after the appointment of K. M. Buchanan to the foundation chair. Chairs were established in 1964 at Palmerston North (Massey), and at Hamilton (Waikato) in 1965.

The relevance of an historical approach to New Zealand geography was acknowledged by two of its founders, Jobberns and Cumberland, in the first issue of *New Zealand Geographer,* published in 1945. Jobberns wrote:

A hundred years ago this habitat had been little altered

from its primitive condition by the small population of Polynesian stock. Within this hundred years our people have changed the face of the country. They came here from Britain transplanting their culture, tradition or habit of living and set out on the gigantic task of transforming the new land in the image of the land they had left . . . We can describe it as we see it now, but we cannot interpret the contemporary scene unless we see how it has come out of the past. This historical background is essential.[61]

Cumberland noted that some eighty years earlier George P. Marsh, in *The Earth as Modified by Human Action*, had described New Zealand as a 'theatre where man is engaged, on a great scale, in transforming the face of nature':

It is this transformation which has more strongly characterised the country as a whole and more sharply differentiated its parts. This transformation has also bequeathed to New Zealanders of this, and future generations, a host of formidable and serious problems; . . . . problems which without exception characterise all those lands that have in the past four and a half centuries felt the violent impact of an insurgent European culture; problems such as derive more immediately from the destruction of bush, the depletion of indigenous grasses, the decimation of native fauna, and the denudation of the very soil.[62]

Given the context of the time it is not surprising that historical geography in New Zealand began with an evolutionary emphasis—with a concern for change rather than point-of-time reconstructions—and with a preoccupation with rural rather than urban landscapes.

New Zealand's first academic geographers were handicapped by a dearth of reliable studies in local or regional history. Academic historians had concentrated largely on political and constitutional issues and local history had been left by default to enthusiastic amateurs who were more concerned with personalities than landscapes and relied on the memories of pioneers rather than documentation. There were, however, a few valuable studies touching on geographical themes.

Acland's *Early Canterbury Runs*,[63] was a carefully researched account of the pastoral occupation of the tussock grassland of Canterbury and a record of each change of ownership on several hundred properties. Condliffe's *New Zealand in the Making*[64] defined the main sequence of the country's economic history and provided Cumberland with the skeleton for the 'five periods of cultural activity' in his pioneer paper 'From natural to cultural vegetation' in 1941.[65] Naturalists, in the nineteenth-century tradition of the self-trained observer, had left valuable records of the introduction and dispersal of alien plants and animals and had for a few areas documented changes they witnessed in the vegetation following settlement.[66] The most outstanding contribution in this vein was Guthrie-Smith's *Tutira: The Story of a New Zealand Sheep Station*, first published in 1921, and now firmly established as a classic of New Zealand writing.[67] It deserves wider recognition as a classic of historical geography.

The book is essentially a landscape history of a 60,000 acre sheep station in the hill country of Hawke's Bay, North Island. The author became part-owner of the station while still a minor in 1882 and farmed the property, though progressively selling all but 2,000 acres, until his death in 1940. Guthrie-Smith was an extraordinarily acute observer of the landscape, the flora and fauna and its changes. Beginning with an account of the physical features, including micro-relief forms caused by soil erosion, the author goes on to describe the Maori occupation, their settlement sites, eel weirs and trails, and the destruction of much of the primitive forest by native fires. The middle chapters describe the purchase and lease by station owners in 1873 and the author's own heartbreaking experiences in the thirty-year task of converting the bracken-fern into productive grassland. There is a remarkable chapter on ' the chartographers of the station' dealing with the role of pigs, cattle, sheep, mounted shepherds and pack-horse teams in scoring the surface of the station with a network of stock paths, wind-blows, sleeping shelves and 'sheep viaducts'. The later half of the book deals with the origins, invasion routes and dispersals of the naturalised alien plants, birds and animals and is illustrated with maps at the macro- and micro-scales. The conclusion aptly summarises the theme of

L

man-land relations as pursued by geographers in all parts of the world which experienced the out-thrust of European settlement in the nineteenth century:

> [the author] cannot too strongly emphasise the fact that there is nothing very exceptional in the little bit of land about which he has written. Taking chapter by chapter, every sheep station in Hawke's Bay has been moulded by a great rainfall; possesses legends and relics of a splendid aboriginal race; has been clothed with forest, flax, and fern; has been subdued by pioneers in desperate straits for cash and credit; has been overrun by an alien vegetation and alien beasts; has righted its equilibrium; has had its surface mapped by stock, its rivers affected by scour, and, lastly, has been, or is in process of being subdivided into smaller holdings.[68]

Tutira is the sort of historical geography that could not have been written from documents, but only from the observations of an intelligent participant in changes that took place over half a century. That a well-to-do Scottish landowner should have despatched his son to New Zealand was a singular stroke of good fortune for New Zealand geography, literature and natural history. There is no comparable study for any area in Australia, a country thirty times the size of New Zealand.

NEW ZEALAND HISTORICAL GEOGRAPHY SINCE 1945

In a recent review of work published in New Zealand in the past twenty-five years, Peter Perry points out that historical geography there has been written in much the same manner as elsewhere in the English-speaking world,[69] but that methodological debate on how it should be written has been muted.[70] In 1955 Cumberland, apparently accepting Hartshorne's 1939 standpoint in *The Nature of Geography,* argued against incorporating studies of 'geographical change through time' within the fields of historical geography. Nevertheless, much of Cumberland's earlier work in the 1940s on soil erosion and vegetation change and his later work in the 1960s emphasised processes of change rather than past distributions and period 'reconstructions'.

Change was certainly the dominant concern of A. H. Clark's *Invasion of New Zealand by People, Plants and Animals,* 1949, a book which remains the only published monograph in New Zealand historical geography.[71] This was an impressive result from a mere two years residence and research in the country. Limitations of time and wartime difficulties of travel confined Clark to the South Island where land use history and plant and animal introductions had been better documented than the North Island. Clark's technique, after summarising the general course of settlement in the island, was to select each of the alien invaders—people, domestic animals, crops, trees and animal pests, to plot and describe their distribution in 1941, then to trace their evolution and interaction with other elements from the time of their introduction. In a sense Clark applies to a larger area the themes so successfully pursued in a small area by Guthrie-Smith, although the different approaches of the naturalist and geographer are readily apparent. Understandably Clark was preoccupied with the nineteenth-century 'entry phase' of the invading elements and their dispersals up till the late nineteenth century, but rather surprisingly, Clark's distribution maps virtually all apply to the period about 1940. These, together with his descriptions, now have historical value as 'cross-sectional' documents of the South Island thirty years ago, but the mapping of distributions at say 1860 and 1890 would have provided more valuable illustration of his themes. Time, and the difficulties of determining the boundaries of statistical areas for the nineteenth century, no doubt deterred Clark from producing maps of distributional change of crops and livestock, but at the time he was writing there was reasonable expectation that some of this information would appear in the historical section of the national atlas.

The atlas was deferred during World War II and, although revived shortly afterwards with the appointment of an enthusiastic team of graduate historians and geographers, it eventually succumbed to official apathy. A much less ambitious publication, *A Descriptive Atlas of New Zealand,* containing mainly contemporary material finally appeared in 1959 under the editorship of A. H. McLintock, and rapidly sold out two large editions. Some of the historical material prepared for the original atlas (comprising maps on early whaling, sealing and missionary enterprise, land purchases and the military geography of the Maori Wars), appeared in the official three volume *Encyclopedia of New Zealand,* also published under McLintock's editorship in 1966. Unfortunately the small-scale reduction and scattered distribution of the maps throughout some 2,600 pages reduce their value as a cartographic representation of New Zealand's historical geography.

Past geographies

Between 1949 and 1962 six cross-sectional reconstructions were published by Cumberland and Hargreaves in *Geographical Review* and *New Zealand Geographer.*[72] These cover the country as a whole from the early phase of its Polynesian occupation about AD 1250 to the late Victorian New Zealand of 1881. Together these six studies give an excellent introductory account of its rapidly changing geography in a depth of comparative detail that has not yet been done for any comparable area in Australia nor for that continent as a whole. Although avowedly 'cross-sectional' in aim—five of the six articles conclude with a region by region summary—the authors do not ignore the processes and characteristics of changes operating immediately before the selected date. The illustrations in this series reflect the variety of sources available for different periods—the cumulative archaeological record of moa hunter sites in the 1250 paper, the informed guesswork of Cumberland's maps of Maori population distribution in 1780 and 1838, the scanty 'presence or absence' data on early European commercial enterprise in 1838, the landscape paintings and rudimentary official statistics for 1853, and the much fuller statistical record and photographic sources available for 1867 and 1881. The last ninety years of the development of New Zealand landscape await similar reconstructions—the census years of 1911 and 1936 would be at least two significant periods worthy of study—but the volume of available source material becomes progressively more embarrassing nearer the present and the intellectual rewards for the labour invested in 'reconstruction' type of historical geography at present appear rather slight with so many unsolved explanatory and developmental problems awaiting attention.

Cross-sectional studies have also appeared for smaller areas of the country and for single elements of its geography. Hill has described the Wairarapa—the nuclear area of New Zealand sheep farming—in its formative years, 1844–53.[73] Johnston and Forrest have reconstructed from early surveyors' maps and notebooks the distribution of grassland, swamp and forest vegetation in coastal Canterbury and Otago at the foundation of European settlement.[74] McCaskill reconstructed the Maori geography of the South Island west coast,[75] Hargreaves produced several cross-sectional accounts of Maori agriculture in the North Island during the nineteenth century,[76] while two accounts have appeared of cities at the turn of the century.[77] Armstrong's 'Auckland by Gaslight' is written in the historic present tense, a literary contrivance introduced in Ralph Brown's *Mirror for Americans*. More significantly, Clark's Dunedin and Armstrong's Auckland demonstrated the possibility of deriving quantitative evidence on land use and property values for New Zealand urban areas from valuation assessments that had survived wartime paper drives.

Geographical change

It is noteworthy that since 1962 no 'cross-sectional' study in historical geography has appeared from New Zealand despite its vigorous advocacy in the 1950s in the University of Auckland. By contrast the themes of geographical change and the treatment of geographical problems in a developmental context have retained their popularity, perhaps because change has so obviously been a feature of the New Zealand scene.

Nowhere has this been more apparent than in the goldfield regions where the sudden irruption of thousands of miners and their technology resulted in the virtually instantaneous creation of new geographies in the wilderness. Regional studies of the goldfield areas have been made by Forrest[78] and McCaskill,[79] both focusing on the course of population movements and their resultant spatial patterns. A study of the small West Coast goldmining town of Ross by P. R. May, an historian who also received geographical training, is the best New Zealand example of the sequent occupance theme applied to a small area and has an outstanding series of photographs, mine plans and sketches.[80] Sequential studies of geographic change have appeared for Auckland city by Pownall,[81] the North Island Bay of Plenty littoral by Dinsdale,[82] and the rural areas of Wellington Province, North Island by Franklin.[83] The latter is notable for its emphasis on the emergent colonial society in contrast to the more common preoccupation of New Zealand geographers with the landscape and economic activities. Ten short articles by Jobberns and McCaskill in *An Encyclopedia of New Zealand* deal with the sequential historical geography of the ten provincial districts, organised around population maps of the 1874, 1911 and 1956 censuses.[84]

Compared with other non-Asian and non-African areas colonised by European settlers in the nineteenth century, New Zealand has a large indigenous minority. Unlike the Australian aborigine, who was virtually eliminated or relegated to remote, harsh environments, the Maori strongly influenced the sequence and spatial pattern of European settlement during the nineteenth century. Much of the North Island had to be won for the Europeans by formal military campaigns, subsequent guerilla warfare, and, following the peace, by lengthy land-sales negotiations over several decades. To date, little work has been done on the geographical aspects of Maori and pakeha interaction, but there are a few suggestive beginnings. Lewthwaite has a carefully documented review of the contemporary estimates of Maori population totals, their distribution and changes under indirect European influences in the period 1770–1850.[85] Cunningham, in one of the few New Zealand contributions to historical political geography, analyses the locational factors in the Maori-pakeha conflict, 1858–1885, and suggests reasons for the spatial pattern of Maori nationalism and insurgency.[86] Murton has studied the complicated pattern of the transfer of Maori land to European settlers in Poverty Bay following the Maori Wars.[87] In an unpublished MA thesis of the University of Auckland (1969), Dorothy Urlich has described the 'geography of disruption' among the North Island Maori following the introduction of firearms at a few coastal points, their diffusion throughout the island and the population migrations that were set in train by the differential patterns of firepower among the tribes.

Problems of agricultural origins and change have attracted

several workers, notably Hargreaves, who has documented early mission farming in northern New Zealand, the foundations of Taranaki farming, and the regional diversity of farm fences up to 1880.[88] Forrest has dealt with the conflict between the theoretical notions of the planners of the 1848 Otago settlement and the geographic realities of terrain, vegetation and distance.[89] As was common in several other Australasian settlements of the time a von-Thünen-like zonation of farm size and farm enterprise was provided in the subdivision of land for urban, 'suburban', 'rural' and pasturage areas. Insight into the details of pioneering in a bushland farm is provided in Johnston's graphical analysis of the annual cycle of activities on a 100-acre Taranaki small holding at four dates between 1876 and 1900.[90] The method derives from W. R. Mead's work in Finland, but its application to New Zealand is notable in that few farm diaries from the bushland pioneers have survived, or indeed may ever have been kept. Much work remains to be done on the precise mapping at medium and large scales of the spread of the agricultural and pastoral frontiers.

Although the records are available in land titles registries, the returns for arduous clerical work come slowly. The problem is complicated because the ten provincial administrations each used different methods of land allocation and registration before the abolition of the provinces in 1876. The detailed advance of the agricultural frontier across the Canterbury Plains has been mapped by Cant from cadastral records and revealed an orderly relationship between date of initial land purchase, and vegetation, soil texture, and distance from Christchurch.[91] The role of land legislation and government sponsorship in settling the bushlands of Wellington Province is described by Heerdegen, while in a rather broader survey, Duncan has reviewed the impact of land legislation on the spread of settlement throughout the country in the late nineteenth century.[92]

In contrast to the attention given to the evolution of the rural landscape there are few historical studies of geographic change in the urban scene or in industry, transport, or demography. Significant exceptions are Pownall's work on the surface growth of towns and Rimmer's study of seaports, both of whom develop schematic models of processes of geographic change.[93] Plans showing past land use and the built-up portions of New Zealand towns at successive dates are disappointingly few, but Pownall has combined the evidence for eight towns, developed schematic models and showed how they could be accommodated by modifications of Hoyt's wedge theory of urban growth. Rimmer developed the Taafe, Morrill and Gould model of the expansion of a transport network in an under-developed country, to account for changes in the hierarchical ranking of New Zealand seaports in the period 1853–1960. Rimmer later applied the model to Australia and added a fifth stage to the idealised sequence. Analysis of changing industrial distributions are handicapped by lack of statistics on a close-areal mesh but evolutionary studies have been made by Linge of Auckland city and of the country as a whole.[94]

Contributors to New Zealand historical geography have been content on the whole with empirical description and with solving problems of localised extent. A great deal of the historical work has been done by writers who would not claim the formal label of historical geographers but who have been attracted to the field in search of the origins of some contemporary problem or pattern. Of the writers who have spent the greater part of their professional lives in New Zealand, Hargreaves alone has worked exclusively on historical problems. Theorising has largely been avoided, but there have been two notable exceptions.

Cumberland, maintaining his early interest in the themes of 'Man in Nature', challenged Holloway's hypothesis that climatic change in the thirteenth century could be a significant factor in explaining anomalies in South Island forest and grassland patterns.[95] His lengthy essay calls on a wide range of physical and cultural evidence in pointing to anthropogenic fires as sufficient explanation for the pattern anomalies. Rose, as noted previously, argues that metropolitan 'primacy' rather than the rank-size distribution of city size, should be the 'normal' condition in areas of pioneer settlement.[96] This paper, together with Pownall's 'Surface growth and towns', is one of the few historical papers by New Zealand geographers to start with a problem drawn from the general body of geographic theory. However, to the extent that this is a shortcoming, New Zealand and Australian writers have probably been no less errant than their overseas colleagues.

ASSESSMENT AND PROSPECT

Despite differences in emphasis, historical geography in Australian and New Zealand has shown a common preoccupation with the patterns and processes of land settlement, particularly with rural land settlement. This emphasis is shared with historical geography as it has been practised in the other New World lands settled by Europeans and their descendants since the eighteenth century. In all these cases writers have been concerned with relatively short periods of major human modification of the landscape and have had at their disposal an abundance of records. In New Zealand there has perhaps been a greater emphasis on the man-land relations theme and perhaps a greater identity of aim and style among writers in the field. In Australia there has been rather more consideration of land-use technologies, the geometric patterns of land settlement and the behavioural aspects of the settlement process. In neither country has there been much consideration of the locational analysis theme in geography and even simple graphical models of the evolution of spatial structure over time are few.

Most of the traditional techniques of historical geography have been tried in the antipodes and have given rise to a few particularly successful and stimulating case studies. The literature of each country has been further enhanced by a notable monograph from the pen of a North American visitor.[97] In addition to the published material reviewed here, there is a considerable accumulation of historical geography —good, bad and indifferent—in the bachelors and masters theses housed in the libraries of the seventeen universities which have granted honours degrees in geography.

In assessing the contribution of historical geography to knowledge about the two countries we may claim substantial areal coverage of New Zealand (there is at least one published article on some aspect of historical geography for each major region of the country); there is fairly good coverage of South

Australia, New South Wales and western Victoria but rather slight attention to central and eastern Victoria, Tasmania, Queensland and West Australia. Thus, on the credit side, geographers 'down under' may claim some success both in exemplifying the themes of historical geography generally and in furthering our understanding of how particular parts of the earth have been shaped by man.

On the debit side, however, the late 1960s witnessed a decline in the standing of historical geography within the field of geography in both countries. Many early contributors of historical papers are now working in other fields and few new graduate students in either country have been attracted to historical theses. Two writers from New Zealand recognise a malaise when they speak of 'the dilemma of historical geography' and of the need for historical geography 'to catch up with the rest of geography'.[98] The theoretical and quantitative revolution of the late 1950s and 1960s has left scant mark as yet on the practice of historical geography in Australia and New Zealand although some of the contributors to theories of spatial change, such as Rose and Rimmer, were brief sojourners in the historical field. Solomon, a Tasmanian geographer, and now a member of the Federal Parliament, shortly before his electoral victory used correlation analysis to measure the degree of consistency in the areal pattern of Tasmanian voting habits over 50 years.[99] Perry fitted a regression line to the distances separating marriage partners in North Otago, New Zealand—an aplication of a technique he had earlier applied to nineteenth-century Dorset in England.[100] Two papers, however, scarcely constitute a revolution and most geographers versed in techniques of statistical inference and computer classification have sought contemporary problems and present-day data. The rich ore bodies of official statistical data published in both countries since the 1850s have hitherto been worked selectively by 'pick and shovel' methods. Although there are formidable problems in the comparability of areal units over time, this ore awaits more economical working by computer mapping and the testing of hypotheses by statistical inference.

Innovations seldom diffuse evenly over space or through communities and while the winds of change have blown gustily through most branches of our discipline, historical geographers seem to have remained sheltered in their archival basements, painstakingly poring over their maps and documents, or have surfaced to become caught up with the eddies of contemporary issues and the study of short-run processes. Except at highly generalised levels, the development of theories and models of spatial change through time is a difficult task, and if historical geography is the last branch of our discipline to absorb the theoretical and quantitative revolution it may yet gain from the tempering of early excesses elsewhere. A major task for historically aware geographers in the 1970s will be to build on the empirical work of their predecessors by posing new questions of old material or asking old questions with more refined tools. In Australia and New Zealand in 1970 at least, the pity is that there are so few young pioneers equipped and eager to take up these tasks.

9

Historical Geography in Latin America

By D. J. ROBINSON

ONE MIGHT forgive the cynic's assuming that in a continent so dramatically involved in contemporary geographical change as Latin America there can be little future for those engaged in the study of the past. Indeed, evidence to support such an assumption would not be difficult to obtain, either from the range of contributions offered by Latin American geographers to international congresses, or from the topics of interest emerging from the pages of Latin American geographical journals and the lecture courses offered by the various centres of geographical study. Increasingly within Latin America there is likely to be a preoccupation with the present and a concern for the future, not primarily because the present or immediate future have suddenly achieved greater real significance, but rather because the intellectual climate of opinion within influential centres outside Latin America has, for the past decade at least, laid more emphasis on those aspects of the subject. Given the lag in information diffusion, what Europe and North America do today, Latin America will be doing in ten years' time. It is important, therefore, to note the effects of such lag phenomena on the techniques, objects, areas, and personnel involved in geographical study in Latin America.

INDIGENOUS IMPEDIMENTS AND IMPERFECTIONS

In assessing the status of historical geography it will be necessary to pass some judgement on geography as a whole, since

for many Latin Americans the two are so intimately inter-
woven as to be virtually indistinguishable. Geography is not
a well-developed subject in Latin American universities.[1]
In the eyes of the academic community it is often thought to
combine a lack of scientific rigour and literary elegance that
reduces its potential impact in the face of competition from
disciplines such as geology, anthropology, and history, to name
but three. Given the literary tradition of Latin America, where
it often appears that what matters is not what is said but the
way it is said, it is unfortunate that geography has, as yet,
neither produced nor attracted a literary stylist.[2] An equally
important limitation on the development of the subject has
been the dualism existing within geography, a marked dichotomy between the pedagogic aspects of the subject and interest
in extending the frontiers of knowledge. In the majority of
Latin American universities the primary role of geography
departments is the preparation of secondary school teachers,
with a characteristic predominance of female students.[3] Curri-
cula reflect the requirements of the students. Geography often
embraces not only global history, but also an outline of mathematics and the physical evolution of the universe. At the
other extreme the students' attention is rigidly confined to
masses of undigestible information relating to the physical
and human landscape of the relevant country.[4] There are, of
course, some notable exceptions to this generalisation.[5]

Until recently, especially in institutions in which the subject
has been associated with faculties of Philosophy and Letters,
or Humanities, geography has been partner in an unscholarly
alliance with history or anthropology.[6] Too often in such
circumstances the historical explanation of change, and the
investigation of transformation in societies and the like have
reduced the geographical component of the course to the im-
potence of poor description of places. It almost seems as
though the closer the institutional links, the fewer, and weaker,
and the less productive is interaction.

Additional problems that face the Latin American geographer who wishes to engage in research rather than merely
teach, are a chronic shortage of financial assistance, poor to
non-existent physical facilities such as libraries, and the need
for so many university teachers to find at least one other

means of paid employment in order to keep pace with a spiraling cost of living on a fixed state salary. This means, for example, that a teacher cannot afford to engage in research until he has built up a satisfactory alternative income, either from further teaching or the addictive pastime of writing textbooks. The sacrifice of material comfort for intellectual satisfaction is uncommon. This situation is exacerbated by the rigidity of the academic hierarchy, which effectively equates intellect with age, promoting frustration that leads either to the waste of youthful vigour and possible innovative ability, or else the migration of geographers to greener pastures overseas.[7] Even with the frequent closure of universities by student action, there is little time for research.

Significant though advances may be in geographical theory and practice in the United States or Europe, if details of them can only be acquired with scarce dollars, and then in neither Spanish nor Portuguese, their impact is both delayed and inevitably diminished. In the face of such enormous difficulties the visitor can only be impressed by the devotion and perseverence of many Latin American geographers, members of the small but durable band of part-time, virtually amateur investigators. An interesting feature of geographical research has been the establishment of private or semi-autonomous institutions separate from the universities.[8]

In terms of fields of research that are cultivated by geographers in Latin America there has been for many years an imbalance in favour of the physical side of the subject. A majority would argue that geography is essentially a natural science.[9] In part this view stems from the early association of geography—through the tradition of Humboldt, Sapper and others—with natural scientists, reflecting the links between the formative period of geography in Latin America and the scientific rediscovery of the continent during the nineteenth century.[10] In opting for the physical side a geographer could also steer clear of problems in which social opinions, moral attitudes and political views were involved, as well as becoming peripheral members of the international community of physical scientists, and perhaps gain access to the nationally respected circle of *peritos*.[11]

In contrast to the bias towards natural science, the facilities for the study of geographies of the past have been woefully neglected. Whereas his colleagues could relatively easily explore river valleys and map soils etc., the geographer interested in the past had to face many more obstacles. First there was, and in part still is, the difficulty of obtaining information. As the Latin American historians have long experienced, archives too often possessed more than a passing resemblance to geological deposits, needing sampling, ordering in sequence, classifying, dating, preserving, and not least interpreting. During the nineteenth century, when historical preoccupation centred on national origins, heroic personalities, and general narratives based on few facts, national archives were quite unusable, if they existed at all. It has been only during the last twenty years that any systematic search in primary documents in Latin American archives has been possible on any reasonable scale.[12] Added to the Latin American difficulties was the impracticability of visiting the major colonial repositories that existed in European centres such as Seville and Lisbon. Frequently, therefore, the geographer would have to be satisfied with a description of what was present when he visited a region under study, together with a few desultory comments on earlier periods gained from local lore or accounts of historians who had in all probability never stirred from their desks.

Lest it be thought that many geographers took the time or trouble to carry out detailed field studies, it should be noted that field work in human geography meant little more than a stroll round the settlement or site concerned, with swift recourse to the opinion of the local sage. The notion of attempting to dig out ownership records of estates, mines, and houses, would scarcely have entered their heads, given the strict social code of behaviour common to most of Latin America. Hospitality would never be refused a traveller, but as to questioning the host, or enquiring into his past, such familiarity could only come with time, the commodity the researcher so often had the least of. With a notebook, an observant eye and no little imagination, the geographer could quite adequately describe what he saw, but all too often he had, and still has, little success in investigating origins or explaining evolution. For the brash visitor, of course, who was usually prepared to work in the sun, and ask awkward questions, the story was quite different.

INTELLECTUAL COLONIALISM

Despite their frequent and often eloquent protestations to the contrary, Latin American social scientists, including geographers, have inherited, although in modified forms, their intellectual expertise from European and North American innovators.[13] In geography the tradition was established early with the work of the colonial chroniclers and cosmographers: Oviedo, Las Casas, Fernão Cardim, Vazquez de Espinoza— the list is long. Throughout the colonial period successive generations of explorers reduced fables to fact and began the process of establishing the physical and cultural lineaments of the landscape.[14] This process of episodic contact with European geographic thought and practices has continued to the present day. In many Latin American countries links have been established with German, French, and United States universities. In terms of historical and cultural studies such contacts have been few in number but significant in their influence. The most important are outlined below.

French geographers established close and continuing relations with the University of São Paulo, Brazil, from the first visit of Pierre Deffontaines in 1934. A succession of visitors who both taught courses as well as engaged in research included Monbeig, de Martonne, Dion, Gourou, Ruellan, Papy, and Prost.[15] Stimulated by their French colleagues, who unlike their North American counterparts took up often long-term residence in Brazil, a group of Brazilian geographers were introduced to the art of French regional geography. Emphasis was placed in successive studies on a rigorous description of the physical and cultural landscapes.[16] However, in contrast to Monbeig's studies of the evolution of coffee cultivation in São Paulo state, and with the exception of Lino de Mattos' study of the evolution of vine growing in São Paulo, the primary objective of Brazilian students has been to establish detailed but static pictures of various parts of the country at different dates.[17] In Argentina French influence has similarly affected research in historical and human geography at the University of Cuyo, Mendoza. A recent publication describing trends in Argentine geography reflects in its bibliography the predominance of French influence.[18] In the recent past the resident Frenchman Gaignard has made major contributions to the analysis of agricultural evolution within the pampa region.[19] Elsewhere in Latin America French researchers have carried forward the banner of the region.[20]

German geographers have been second only to the French in influencing the course of research into the historical geography of Latin America followed by Latin American students. In Colombia, Chile, Argentina, Mexico, and Brazil Germans have been active.[21] Especially important as centres of German influence were the Argentine universities of Tucumán and Córdoba. Schmieder, Wilhelmy, and Rohmeder all played decisive roles in promoting their chosen fields of historical research.[22] In Mexico, Venezuela, and Brazil, Pfeifer, Otremba, and Waibel respectively added to the study of Latin America's past.[23]

In spite of the fact that perhaps the best-known work in English on Latin America is Preston James' *Latin America* (4th edn 1969), his influence on succeeding American and Brazilian students has been less than might perhaps be expected. While his own contributions on settlements, land-use patterns and population distributions within Brazil especially were models of careful description and analysis, his students turned, perhaps understandably, to research on topics connected with problems of development.[24] In contrast to the paucity of James' students engaged in research on historical aspects of Latin America, the interest of Carl Sauer in the region triggered-off a spate of research monographs prepared by his Berkeley students. Sauer's personal involvement in the region came through his repeated visits to Middle America, beginning in the late twenties.[25] His dual skills of perceptive observation and inspired interpretation find a fitting monument not only in his own series of monographs,[26] but also in the numerous issues of *Ibero-Americana,* that he founded with Kroeber in 1932, as well as in the several issues of the *University of California Publications in Geography*. They bear witness to his inspiration as a teacher in the broadest sense of that term.[27]

M

Partly due no doubt to Sauer's personal interests, as well as the research focus of Berkeley at that time, few of his own early studies come much closer to the present than the sixteenth century. It is as if he regarded the prospect of ploughing through vast quantities of documentary evidence with some trepidation, as though it might restrict a bold interpretation. While his students certainly continued to dig profitably into regional and national archives in search of fresh evidence,[28] Sauer himself, fortunately for geography as a whole perhaps, moved back into the prehistoric period, and then out of Middle America in his investigations into agricultural origins. More recently he has returned to the Caribbean to reconstruct a contact situation with a minimum of documentation, but with an incredibly detailed knowledge of the area, a temporary move before searching out more hazardous waters to the north.[29]

For all his undoubted personal brilliance and the formative role that he played in creating what has been termed the 'Berkeley school',[30] Sauer had little influence on Latin Americans. Even within the restricted area of northern Latin America where he practised his art, few Latin Americans know of his work, or have attempted to follow his many avenues of research. Unlike French and German geographers, however, Sauer continually posed questions, many of which have still to be answered. His powerful intellect was better employed in generating hypotheses than in searching for proof.

These then have been the three principal components of the intellectual colonialism that has shaped the study of the past by geographers in Latin America. One other name deserves mention, if only because in his publications is to be found the unmistakable imprint of the teaching of one of England's most prominent historical geographers, H. C. Darby. In a series of studies, Patricio Randle, of the University of Buenos Aires, has summarised the contents of a seminar conducted by Darby at University College London, on aspects of the theory and methods of historical geography.[31] Though the main work would have been improved by the use of more relevant Latin American examples, Randle's presentation of the ideas and practices of the European school of historical geography must be counted as a major step forward. At least now no Latin

American can plead ignorance. The only fields of study not covered in Randle's work are those concerned with perception and the use of abstract models, both of which have been so elegantly integrated into historical geography since Randle studied in Europe.[32]

The dominant feature of the methodologies exported by the European and North American centres described above was the difference between the Berkeley school of investigation who derived their approaches within the Latin American setting in the main, and the Europeans who were far more rigid in the application of methods and approaches essentially based on European experience. Few French researchers asked whether there was any purpose in isolating regions within Brazil, or debated at what scale regions made good geographical sense. Equally little comment is to be found in the published literature relating to the suitability of examining in great detail small areas of the agricultural landscape.

SCALES, AREAS AND THEMES OF RESEARCH

Although the content of many studies concerned with Latin American historical geography make any classification or categorisation difficult, it is possible to identify several major themes. Each is examined and exemplified below.

A theme that has apparently fallen out of fashion lately, but which has received much attention in Latin America is that of the reconstruction of the primitive landscape, the landscape before the hand of man had affected it. In both Venezuela and north-west Argentina, German scholars have attempted this task with slight success.[33] The key problem remains that of determining not when man arrived on the scene but the extent to which he may have affected such items as the vegetation, before any evidence of 'cultural' activities are to be found. Particularly suspect are vegetational distributions based on exceedingly flimsy evidence for Holocene climatic conditions. Better known is Sauer's attempt to identify and describe the 'personality' of Mexico.[34] In 1941 Sauer maintained that the 'dominant traits' of that country owed their origin to a formative period before the middle of the sixteenth century, predicting that the invasion by the modern western world would remain partial and relatively unimportant. Such views, however well versed Sauer may have been in the pre-Hispanic history of Mexico, lacked the necessary comparative historical knowledge, particularly of the critical centuries between 1600 and 1900, to make them worthy of the praise heaped upon the study. The fact of the matter was that Sauer used such undefinable terms, eg 'dominant traits', to make any detailed critical analysis of the study almost impossible. No mention is made either of the population decline of the late sixteenth century or of the agricultural revolution that took place during the seventeenth century. Yet since Chevalier's work, we know just how much modern Mexico owes to the seventeenth century.[35] Again, in 1941 Sauer was not to know that the pace of change would increase rapidly, that population would expand, that urbanisation would reconcentrate the people over wide areas, that agrarian reform, regional development and planned growth would alter the face of so many parts of the land. Sauer's 'formative period' became no more than one phase in terms of the evolution of the total Mexican 'personality', if such a thing exists.

Allied closely to the notion of primitive landscapes are studies that have attempted to estimate the impact of human activity on specific areas, and in special conditions. Schmieder pursued this theme for many years in his study of the origin of the vegetation on the *pampa* of Argentina.[36] He argued that the deciduous broadleaf *monte* scrub woodland had, prior to the migrations of Indians into the region, been far more extensive in its natural state. However, in a case similar to that of deciding on the origins of savanna-forest margins in Brazil and elsewhere, the evidence was very poor. To what extent Indians had repeatedly burnt the area, or the water table had fluctuated could not, and still have not been satisfactorily answered.[37] A similar study by Rohmeder on vegetational changes in the Tucumán region likewise suffers from very weak inferential arguments.[38]

Several studies of lake level changes during the last two centuries are based on much stronger documentary foundations. Bockh, in Venezuela, has neatly correlated fluctuations in Lake Valencia's height with the changing agricultural activities of the basin surrounding the lake.[39] Zamorano, in a quite distinctive ecological situation, has explained the disappearance of several large shallow lakes in western Argentina, around which *balsa* raft fishermen used to live, by an analysis of the river diversion and drainage carried out during the eighteenth and nineteenth centuries.[40] Several students of Sauer have also analysed the changing relationship between ecological and cultural phenomena, especially woodland and open savanna regions.[41] For the majority of Latin Americans interest in the remote past has tended to concentrate on patterns of settlement during the pre-Hispanic period,[42] rather than on relict agricultural features,[43] and former patterns of land-use.[44] It should be mentioned that many foreign workers in Latin America have found it easier to come by air photos than have their resident colleagues.

Another well-defined group of studies has analysed the evolutionary aspects of rural landscapes. Classic studies in Chile have monitored, with the aid of excellent primary documentation, the changing pace of fragmentation and disintegration among large estates in the central valley.[45] Others have examined the complexities of irrigation water allocation in the Chilean *Norte Chico*, and the changing regional economy from the end of the colonial period through until the modern era.[46] Elsewhere excellent analyses have been carried out into the coffee and sugar industry in Brazil,[47] and the developments in Argentine agricultural colonies have received much attention.[48] Marginality in Córdoban farms, and the role of company activity in promoting agricultural enterprises during the nineteenth century have also been studied.[49] The differing agricultural appraisals of contrasting ethnic groups with widely varied backgrounds is also worthy of note.[50] It would not be unfair to say that, with the exception of one or two studies, the most significant difference between Latin American students' investigations and those of the foreign visitors was the emphasis that the latter placed on obtaining as much information as possible on the function of the farming units, rather than be satisfied with formal aspects. Some may regret that Ardissone could not obtain a place in the geographical lexicon for 'tesigeography', the geography of ownership.[51]

In contrast to the static studies of agricultural change within farm units, are those whose focus has been the spatial dynamism of the phenomena. Some have ambitiously attempted to view the combination of land-use changes, population spread and immigration as a single complex frontier study.[52] Another has more successfully analysed the retreat of the forest margin under the pressure of agricultural colonisation.[53] The evolution of the Brazilian coffee frontier has attracted many studies which have mapped the fluctuation of the western edge of the crop under the influence of capital availability, climatic hazards, and the provision of suitable transportation networks.[54] The story of São Paulo was repeated in Colombia as Parsons has so thoroughly documented.[55] Butland has recently published a highly generalised but most useful map showing frontiers of various dates.[56] The comparability of many areas with similar geographical characteristics has gone largely unnoticed in Latin American historical geography, as has the unsatisfactory Bolton frontier thesis.[57]

It is often demonstrable that the advance and retreat of frontiers are closely related to modifications in accessibility within the region. Several studies have analysed the changing pattern of communications within Latin America. One of the earliest was concerned with the identification of an historic Mexican routeway,[58] others have traced the sequence of land communication networks in great detail,[59] the search for most suitable routeways,[60] and the expansion of roads and rails into pioneer zones.[61] A profitable field of research might well link together the evolution of transportation networks with a study of marketing systems.

Urban historical geography has received a considerable measure of attention in Latin America. Studies have been made of the foundation of Spanish towns in the early colonial period,[62] their instability and multiple site transfers,[63] and the provenance of their regular planned form.[64] One of the earliest studies undertaken by Deffontaines was his analysis of the evolution of the Brazilian system of urban settlements, a subject which has more recently benefited from an excellent study of colonial towns by Azevedo.[65] Azevedo's group research project on São Paulo's evolution has produced one of the most competent studies yet to appear from a Latin American university.[66] Several other authors have adopted a case study approach in monitoring urban and regional growth.[67] From several recent studies it has become clear that the customary view of the *pampa* as an area of rural settlement has now to be modified to take into account the extent of urban settlements founded in that area.[68] The scale of Wilhelmy's study of the urban settlement history of the entire continent is comparable only with work undertaken by leading historians.[69] Wilhelmy is exceptional in so far as he pays much more attention than any others to the interrelationships of the urban settlements.

One of the most popular themes in Latin American historical geography is the development of regional identities during past periods. In several cases the regional frameworks are political,[70] but in others geographical regions can be distinguished whose identity may have depended upon isolation, a distinctive regional economy, a phase of specialised settlement, or a particular combination of population elements.[71] In none of these regional studies are any unusual methods of presentation utilised. For the majority the choice is between a series of cross-sectional descriptions, or else thematic treatment with comments on significant data sources at specific junctures. Few of them explain their choice of method or the reasons for selecting certain themes at the expense of others. Several of the contributions of the Berkeley geographers are superb pieces of geographical reconstruction, particularly those of R. C. West.

A notable feature of most of the work consulted is the relatively small area selected for investigation. With a few important exceptions most of the researches are conducted within at least a national boundary, in the case of Latin American contributions more often within one of the major administrative districts. It is also relevant to perhaps comment on those periods of the past in which little geographical study has been undertaken. There can be little doubt now, following the work of the historians, that the seventeenth century was in many ways as formative a period in new world historical geography as the sixteenth or eighteenth. It was between 1600 and 1700 that the urban settlements adjusted themselves to their regional hinterlands. At the same time beginnings were made in converting labour resources into more permanent elements of the social system. Yet few geographers have ventured into these byways.[72] Equally surprising, particularly in view of the abundance of relatively reliable statistical data, is the paucity of studies of the late eighteenth century. With detailed censuses, mission records, and a proliferation of birth, marriage and death records geographers might have been expected to emulate the work of the historical demographers.[73] As far as the nineteenth century is concerned, the geographical

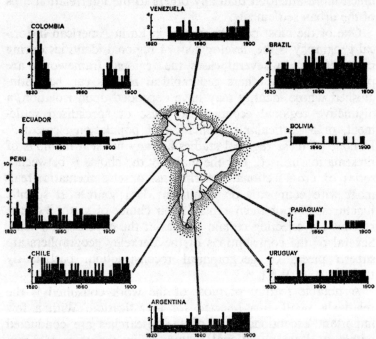

Fig 11 Availability of Reports from British Consuls in South America, 1820–1900

literature scarcely realises that the wars for independence had been fought, and that fundamental processes of change were under way.[74] Of the multitude of new sources that become available during the nineteenth century, such as customs house records, consular reports and travellers' accounts little is heard (Fig 11). Agricultural censuses of the early years of the present century await their analysts, and rooms full of company records await the enterprising student.

COMPETITION FROM ALLIED DISCIPLINES

One explanation for the relatively underdeveloped state of historical geography in Latin America might be found in the vigour of its associated disciplines. With anthropology, sociology, history, and economics quite capable of examining spatial aspects of historical development, the threat of encroachment is always present. Indeed, if, as has already been noted, several disciplines are brought together in joint university degrees, most social scientists might be thought to have the minimum geographical qualifications for research. More significant, however, than poaching, is the lack of any dynamism in the geographical research at present being undertaken. Space permits only a brief glimpse of some of the more interesting and often exciting hypotheses that are widely discussed in social science circles, usually, alas, in private research centres such as El Colegio in Mexico or the Di Tella Institute in Buenos Aires. Many of the models could so easily be adapted to shed light upon geographical problems concerned with the past as well as the present.

The first practice that Latin American historical geographers, and many of the foreign visitors, could profitably adopt is the use of the deductive hypothesis. While many new methods have been introduced in European historical geography over the last ten years, in Latin America traditional approaches endure. While historians use computers to reconstruct population data of the late eighteenth century,[75] geographers complain of a lack of statistical information.[76] Whereas timid distribution maps are being drawn up for insignificant geographical studies, historians are formulating stimulating notions of centrifugal-centripetal processes of urban evolution, applicable to any town on the continent.[77] Geographers have been content to simply describe the arrival of European man in the New World, while the anthropologists have been generating process-response models of culture conquest and the like.[78] If by now the Latin American historical geographers have accepted the fact that the frontier concept is of restricted value, given the widely dispersed clusters of population, they should now be attempting to test Friedmann's centre-periphery model against various historical realities.[79] Likewise all who subscribe to the idea of the significance of technological change should be recalibrating and attempting to apply Germani's modernization model.[80] Sarfatti's small book analysing on Weberian lines the Spanish bureaucratic-patrimonial system in Latin America should keep many a geographical seminar occupied until the small hours.[81] In fact, the great hope is that geographers in Latin America will look over their inter-disciplinary fences more often.

If one singular defect of Latin American historical geography had to be isolated it would probably be the lack of competent systematic studies based on sound research. If, for example, the work of geographers interested in agriculture had to be compared with similar work completed by historians, the contrasts would be seen to be remarkable. In Venezuela, the historian Brito-Figueroa has said more about the evolution of agriculture during the colonial period than any geographer has yet said about modern agriculture.[82] Out of a complex muddle of primary documentation he has reconstructed not only where agriculture was carried out during the eighteenth century, but also how the systems operated, where the labour, capital and entrepreneurs came from, and how the whole complex evolved. It is now known, for example, that the *llanos* cattle ranching areas were not isolated regional economic units, but closely integrated into the northern farming and marketing systems. Like West in Colombia and Borah in Mexico, Brito-Figueroa took the trouble to find out the facts.[83]

In Mexico and Argentina the story is similar. In a classic French thesis, Chevalier has revolutionised concepts concerning the evolution of the great hacienda. His work has had repercussions well into the late nineteenth century.[84] This single monograph must be worth more than a hundred of his compatriots' geographical articles written on little more than the basis of a bus trip or a weekend field excursion. The same could be said of the work of Scobie on agricultural evolution in the Argentine *pampa*. At last details have been provided of the mechanisms, both social and technological, that explain the phenomenal landscape changes that affected the Plate estuary during the period 1860 and 1910.[85] Social history reminds one of that giant of Brazilian letters Gilberto Freyre, who, as Azevedo has pointed out, has written some of the best historical geography ever likely to appear on Brazil.[86] In *Nordeste* one can find synthesis to match even the greatest of the French regional essayists.[87]

The tradition of historical scholarship is nowhere better exemplified in Latin American studies than in a monumental analysis of the transport linkages that held the empire together.[88] As Stein has said, the demographic analyses of the Berkeley school, although fundamental to the study of New World evolution, are little more than 'scattered vantage points overlooking a vast cañon of unexplored or partially explored human experience.'[89] In history, as in economics, stimulating debates continue: was the seventeenth century a period of economic depression, as Borah suggested,[90] or has Lynch's thesis more to support it in maintaining the reverse?[91] How does the economic and social evidence fit the ecological clues first noted by Cook?[92] Of much wider concern are the general economic models put forward by Frank[93] and Furtado.[94] What do geographers studying the past in Latin America make of Frank's surplus-expropriation chain, and the effects of scale on the 'economic constellations' that are said to have long characterised Latin American development?[95] Again the historical geographer must have something to say in the debate over 'stability' and 'instability' in the area's evolution.[96] Are there particular geographical aspects of the break-up of Gran Colombia, and the fragmentation of the Central American republics? What can be said about the onset of modernisation or the beginnings of urbanisation? Since other disciplines are prepared to accept dichotomies such as rural and urban, is there any assistance that historical geographers can afford in analysing more meticulously the raw data?[97]

Historical geographers need have no hesitation in entering into debate on the major issues of the day that clearly transcend subject boundaries; that way the subject has the hope, without losing any of its individual appeal, of being transformed into a more challenging and exciting experience. The time has come, at least within the Latin American context, for carrying the banner into the camps of other social sciences.

Historical geographers should heed the Spanish proverb: *el comer y el rascar, todo es empezar*: appetite comes with eating.

AN OUTLINE FOR THE FUTURE

With so many fields untilled, and workers so scarce, the task of writing an historical geography of Latin America must wait. All that is attempted here is an outline, necessarily tentative, of some of the components of such a future study. One of the first requirements will be a useful temporal framework in which processes of change and cross-sectional studies may be fitted. Elsewhere a twofold temporal division has been suggested,[98] but it may be better to consider three major phases of development: pre-European; colonial; and transitional. Some might wish to subdivide the last period into two, in order to place more emphasis on a modern phase from around the year 1914. If such a further subdivision were accepted, the main cross-sections, the summary views, would be around the years 1500, 1810 and 1914. The major processes affecting each of these time periods would be:

(a) A phase extending back from the end of the fifteenth century characterised by endogenous processes of development within aboriginal America. Its main characteristics would be the differential cultural development leading to the patterns encountered by European man.

(b) The evolution of Spanish and Portuguese colonial systems, including demographic, economic, political and social processes of differentiation. A further characteristic of this period would be the variety of adjustment made by colonial powers and aboriginal peoples in different locations and at different times.

(c) The penetration into the former colonial territories, gradually emerging as nation states, of non-Iberian values and North European modernising technology. This third period would, like the second, be experiencing differential adaptation as the modernising processes confront traditional situations.

(d) The acceleration of modernisation, rapid population growth and urbanisation. The post-1914 period would include the differential adaptation of all pre-existing institutions in society and economy to varying levels of economic development that had either been attained, or were thought desirable.

Within such a chronological framework it would be possible to isolate for detailed analysis a wide range of systematic subjects. Here only population will be used as an illustration. Setting aside the task of obtaining data on the population distribution and total numbers at the three critical dates, some of the main proceses of change can be identified.[99] First, the changing ethnic structure of the population, from few whites with many Indians, through phases of few whites with reduced Indians, more whites with reduced Indians and Negroes, to a social/racial stratification by the end of the colonial period with significant numbers of mestizos. Second, one might wish to study the changing impact of disease or improved medical care on selected groups of the population through time, such as *mita* labour gangs, mission village populations, Indian reserve groups, rural farming communities, and urban migrants. Third, it would be possible to study the roles of specialised occupations (*caciques, mayordomos,* agricultural advisors) in, say, phases of cultural adjustment. It should be clear from the types of analyses proposed that no period other than the immediate present is excluded from the outline. Historical geography, like culture history, may only be a second away in time.

Leaving there the crude outline, awaiting as it does many detailed systematic and regional studies, what of the perceived world of the past in Latin America? In that uncharted sea landfalls have been few. The colour of Argentine landscapes have been analysed,[100] the symbolism of the colonial urban design noted, [101] the poverty of sixteenth-century explorers' ecological lexicons reported.[102] Yet much more remains to be done. Only recently have the early colonial questionnaires been subjected to detailed scrutiny;[103] we still need to assess the variable meanings attached to words such as *sabana, campaña, sertão* and *vecino*. The problems of interpreting technical terms relating to distance, area, value and capacity are formidable. From the codices, through the rough sixteenth-century soldiers' impressions of their New World, via the social rituals of coffee houses in the nineteenth century, to the opinions and impressions of the Birmingham business man, much has still to be deciphered.

Eldorados have multiplied, Cipango transformed from carib sea to Spanish Main; a Latin America has been identified, a Bolivia created, a *tierra del fuego* tamed. How could any historical geographer not wish to enjoy the fruits of study in such a land?

10

Historical Geography in Africa

By KWAMINA B. DICKSON

GEOGRAPHY IS A well established discipline in most of the universities of Africa, and in many cases geography departments were among the earliest to be established. Nevertheless, schools of thought or strong methodological bias in geography in African universities cannot be said to exist; for one thing, the mixed backgrounds of teaching staffs in the departments and, in some cases, the need felt to study seriously all shades of opinion from whatever source have together precluded the hardening of attitudes into definite schools of thought. Certainly differences do exist in the degree of emphasis laid on teaching the various aspects of the subject, but these occur only within a general context of methodological permissiveness.

PROGRESS IN HISTORICAL GEOGRAPHY IN AFRICA

In spite of the permissive attitude towards the teaching of geography generally, there is one viewpoint in the subject which is given little attention, and that is historical geography. Perhaps this state of affairs reflects the situation in Western Europe, where teachers of geography in many African universities received their initial training, and where for a long time historical geography was a rather diffuse concept, defined in markedly different ways, and appeared, for a part of geography, to be unusually eclectic. A recent survey showed that in all African university institutions, which number about sixty, there are not more than five which offer a course specifically entitled historical geography.[1]

Among the reasons advanced for not including historical

geography in the syllabus were that the subject is not relevant to national needs, especially to economic development; that there was hardly any literature to support a course in historical geography of Africa – if there are going to be courses in historical geography in African universities they should be on Africa; and that, compared with the other specialisms, historical geography was a difficult one to teach. Also, most of the graduates in geography were destined to teach in secondary schools where historical geography was not included in the syllabus. Finally, the historical perspective was usually present in either regional or in systematic geography courses. This last point was made in two ways: as a definite reason for regarding a special course in historical geography as unnecessary, and in the sense that although there was no special course in historical geography a certain amount of it was necessarily taught.

The survey also asked for definitions of historical geography. There were three kinds of reaction to this request: a positive definition was attempted, not necessarily because historical geography was taught in the department; no definition was offered since the discipline was not taught, and, thirdly, the other courses taught were enumerated. From the point of view of the probe into the status of historical geography, the listing of courses offered, not necessarily *instead* of this discipline but as an act of supplying additional information, is as important as the positive definitions given. Thus, according to some respondents, historical geography is not taught, but—as additional information—human geography, economic geography or political geography is taught. This is surely an implied statement of what historical geography is not.

Here are some of the positive definitions offered. Historical geography is:

(1) A study of past societies in their spatial dimension.
(2) A study of relationships between man and his environment in the past as well as changes in his relationships in time.
(3) Human geography of past periods including evolution, development in time.

(4) The study of geographical change through time.
(5) A study of past landscapes with particular reference to man's role in altering the 'natural' landscape.
(6) That branch of geography which emphasises the time dimension in the spatial arrangement, differentiation and organisation of natural and man-made phenomena.

The remaining definitions are essentially variants of the six recorded. In only one or two cases could the other definitions be considered to be extensions of those listed here. For example, one definition starts off essentially as in (2), that is, a study of relationships between man and his environment, but adds 'and the resultant changes in physical and biological systems arising from man's presence'. It must be emphasised that these definitions were generally offered from departments which do not teach courses in historical geography and were therefore described as tentative. It was not unusual for a respondent to add that the scope of historical geography was probably wider than is implied in the definition given.

In only two cases were reasons given for 'recommending the study of historical geography', and they were 'the importance of a dynamic or evolutionary view of geographical situations and problems in the past or present', and 'the value of a study of the history of present day geographical and developmental problems'. Also, historical geography is useful because it is basic to social and economic history. (It may be added that although this last point was made by a professional historian who specialised in 'Histoire de la population et géographie humaine', it is not unusual for professional geographers to do the same.)

The impression should not be created that there is a general hostility to the discipline. Indeed, there seems to be considerable sympathy towards it, and courses in it would be offered if suitable teachers were available. Some universities already have a tentative syllabus ready for the consideration of whoever might offer to teach the subject. Instances of the subject being taught and then dropped are rare. They have occurred through the loss of the services of the teacher or a shift of the teacher's interest not, one might suspect, so much on methodological grounds, as on account of the enormous task involved in putting together the necessary materials to make the teaching of the subject intellectually satisfying. The geography department of the University of Ghana, Legon, is one of the very few that offer well-rounded courses in the historical geography of Africa, that of Western Europe also being taught for contrast.

It can be seen that it would be premature to speak of progress in historical geography in Africa, except with special reference to the very few geography departments in African universities which are actively engaged in teaching and perhaps research in the subject. It should on the other hand be noted that a few of the works published by geographers in African universities, who disclaim any expertise in the subject, could justifiably be called historical geography. Even when they are not wholly cast in the mould of historical geography, many of the publications from the geography departments in Africa contain sections which are of great historical geographical interest.

Thus, since progress in historical geography in Africa generally does not exist, the rest of the essay will be devoted to exploring the possibilities of fruitful research into the historical geography of Africa, which is what needs to be taught most in African universities.

POSSIBILITY OF AN HISTORICAL GEOGRAPHY OF AFRICA

No more than the merest indication of an outline can be given here. But it will first be necessary to be clear about the kind of historical geography in mind. As a discipline, historical geography does not concern itself, on methodological grounds, with the history of navigation, the development of cultural techniques, the evolution of maps and other tools of the geographer, or the history of geographical thought. Historical geography is none of these, nor is it many of the other things it is often said to be, for example, a background to history.

Historical geography is human (cultural) geography itself, for the latter cannot be studied and the processes responsible for its contemporary features understood except through time. But human geography, as it is to be understood in the African context and indeed generally, does not limit itself to the study of a given set of phenomena related to the ever-changing patterns of interaction of culture with environment and often taken to be the *correct* subject matter for geographical study in Europe or the United States of America. Mines, homes, workshops, etc are to be understood as generic terms; their physical forms will often not be those to which the Western geographer is accustomed. It is important to recognise local features for what they are and to investigate their functions, which may be of greater fundamental importance than that of the more familiar features or physical forms. Again, human geography, in Africa at any rate, must be given a much wider definition than the study of 'man's record upon the landscape'.[2] The historical geographer in Africa *should* be interested in 'energy, customs, or beliefs of man'.

Another preliminary point that should be settled is that of the level of detail at which the historical geography of Africa may be studied under the present circumstances. This point relates to the question of the strategy to be adopted in studying an aspect of the geography of an area which has received little attention. Should we begin by tackling limited, isolated problems, examining them in detail and eventually pulling all the loose strands together? Or should we first of all put down all that is known about the subject and the broad relationships already ascertained in order to shape a preliminary hypothesis which will guide the further recognition of problems and collection of data? In a sense these questions are academic, for any problem in geography or in any other discipline will have to be placed in a context of sorts, and the snowballing effect of attempting to block out the context will generally lead to what is suggested in the second question. Once this broad framework is organised around one theme or another, it should be easier to go into specific problems in depth and with insight.

PRE-COLONIAL TIMES

It is becoming increasingly clear that Africa in the past did not consist of a series of cultural islands isolated from one another. There were movements of people, materials and ideas over vast distances at certain periods in Africa's history, and these made for a certain degree of similarity in cultures over large areas of the continent. Nor was Africa as a whole isolated:

> Africa, when seen in perspective, was a full partner in the development of the Old World, participating in a continual process of cultural give and take that began long before European occupation. Neither isolation nor stagnation tell the tale. It is as incorrect to think of Africa as having been for centuries isolated from the rest of the world as it is to regard the vast area south of the Sahara as the 'darkest Africa', whose peoples slumbered on until awakened by the coming of the dynamic civilisations of Europe.[3]

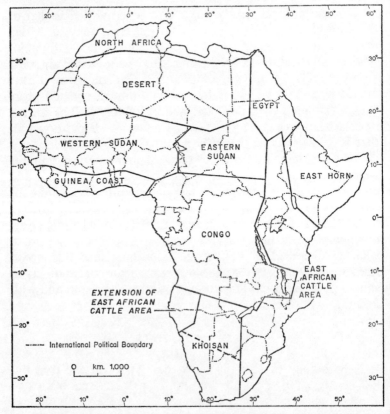

Fig 12 Culture areas of Africa (after M. J. Herskovits, 1967, 57)

Cultural diffusion and the resultant spatial variations in culture and how they developed from a base line are two of the critical themes in the historical geography of Africa. It is for this reason that Herskovits suggested a broad division of Africa into culture areas on the basis of ecological and institutional factors (Fig 12). As Herskovits stresses, the culture area concept is a purely analytical tool and, cutting across contemporary political boundaries as it does, should not be invested with any geopolitical significance. The concept can be applied in the investigation of, for example, the key question of why some parts of Africa were more receptive of innovative ideas and developed faster, economically, than others, or why a society, known to be in the front line of innovators in the past, is now stagnating. An historical geography that restricts itself to observing physical changes in the cultural landscape will achieve little in the endeavour to understand the changing dynamics of spatial organisation in Africa.

However differently the base line culture areas of Africa are delimited, the question of how they acquired or developed new cultural techniques, eg agriculture and the knowledge of iron working, can be studied. Herskovits' division already assumes the adoption and practice of cultivation because he is more interested in the much later impact of the European presence. But when Murdock pushes his datum line further back into time, his objective being to trace the culture history of African peoples from earliest times,[4] he necessarily comes up against another major theme in the historical geography of Africa, the origins and spread of agriculture on the continent. The issue of agricultural hearths or centres of dispersal will continue to be debated for a long time to come;[5] nevertheless, the importance of the early adoption of agriculture and the extensive use of fire as an agricultural implement in subsequent developments in various parts of the continent cannot be overlooked. Organised settlement, the beginnings of centralised political systems which among other things tended to guarantee population increase,[6] and a more effective utilisation of resources were some of the characteristics of the early agricultural societies.

Before the spread of agriculture, which was originally confined to Africa north of the equator, the climate of the continent had been oscillating at long intervals, with a general tendency towards increasing dryness. The Sahara desert was, during early neolithic times, a wetter place, covered by a mixture of grass and trees, and its progressive desiccation which reached a climax in the first or second millennium BC was of great significance to Africa as a whole. North Africa became more fully integrated into the Mediterranean culture complex, although its links with the areas to the south were not completely severed, because of the caravan trails that went across the Sahara. Additionally, the negroid inhabitants of the Sahara fled in all directions. For West Africa in particular the arrival of the Saharan refugees was important, for they were bearers of neolithic culture and were to enrich life in the Western Sudan.

A reconstruction of the original climatic climax vegetation formations is not at all easy, but there is sufficient indication to show that extensive areas of the continent now covered with parkland or savanna vegetation were originally clothed in some form of forest vegetation. A study of the destruction of the original vegetation and the new problems of living created by the change in the physical ecological relationships is one of the major tasks of the historical geographer in Africa. The process of vegetation destruction necessarily continues, and its nature (magnitude and rate) and effects still constitute problems.

Some time in the first or second century AD, the knowledge of iron working spread widely over Africa north of the equator, although it is possible that it was also known through Indonesians on the east coast of southern Africa. It is no accident that most of these innovations first came to Africa north of the equator; this was the portion of the continent closest to other inhabited areas. In its effects the adoption of iron technology was far more revolutionary than the spread of agriculture. The Nile Valley (Meroe in the Sudan) and North Africa are said to be the sources of iron technology, which quickly spread from there to West Africa. In Africa, iron did not immediately replace stone as an agricultural implement, but it became the most decisive factor in cultural diffusion, politics and trade. With the aid of the iron spear the Bantu, perhaps experiencing overpopulation in their home areas, were able to spread from the eastern end of West Africa or southern Congo eastwards to the lands bordering the Indian Ocean and southwards from the Congo or East Africa to South Africa. Southern Africa was now translated in a single leap from a Palaeolithic to an Iron Age. Then followed a long period of adjustment as the Bantu societies searched for suitable habitats and struggled among themselves in the process. The Southern African Bantu had acquired the art of rearing cattle and were now also agriculturists.

The Iron Age in Africa was also marked by the emergence of strong centralised kingdoms or states, and it was within these that towns and cities flourished in consequence of trading, the successful organisation and prosecution of which was ensured by the centralised governmental systems. The location of the first Western Sudanese kingdom of Ghana at the southern edge of the Sahara at the termini of trans-Saharan trade routes was deliberate; equally significant was the emergence of this kingdom around the fifth century AD, not long after the camel became the established means of crossing the Sahara desert.

In this sketchy and generalised account of culture history, no mention has been made of the contribution of non-African peoples. Indonesians, Arabs, and Chinese, for example, contributed much to cultural development in East Africa, including Mozambique. The Arabs deserve special attention. They not only traded, like the others, with the East African coast but also made it their home and left their stamp on the cultural geography of East Africa. For example, the concentration of population in a long line of towns on the East African coast is the result of a process that began with Arab settlement and gathered momentum through time, in spite of severe reverses during the period of Portuguese occupation. Arabs from North Africa were also active in West Africa (the Western Sudan) where they introduced a number of crops, created an awareness of certain wild plants, eg cotton, as a natural resource, and introduced Islam whose impact on human geography is yet to be fully investigated. In West Africa the Mande of the Western Sudan, benefiting from contact with the Arabs, were to become the most important group of entrepreneurs and means of cultural diffusion in and after the medieval period. Their sphere of operations was much greater than that of the

Hausa, who in post-medieval times were equally foot-loose and brought the eastern third of the Guinea coast into firm contact with the Western Sudan.

No account of the pre-Colonial times would be complete without mention of the Europeans who came to trade in Africa. The Portuguese were the first to gain a sure foothold on the continent. In West Africa they focused their attention on the coast of Ghana, then called the Gold Coast, and built a number of trading forts and castles. They settled similarly on the coast of modern Angola and East Africa, including Mozambique, with consequences that are only too obvious today. The Dutch, English, French, etc joined the Portuguese, who were supplanted in West and East Africa in the seventeenth century. In West Africa the establishment of Europeans on the coast, coupled with the economic decline of the Western Sudan, caused a major reversal of the orientation of the Guinea forest states from northwards to the Western Sudan to southwards to the Atlantic coast. This reversal is a theme that features prominently in the geography of West Africa.

One important result of the activities of the Europeans and the Arabs before them was the alarming and unprecedented increase in the scale of the export slave trade. The presence of many empty and economically negative areas in East Africa and West Africa (eg the Middle Belt of West Africa),[7] the shifts of population, the development of attitudes that disdained agriculture and the creation of undying hostility between peoples are but a few of the consequences of the export slave trade.

North Africa and the Nile Valley also deserve mention. North Africa, the Maghreb, developed differently. The Phoenicians who founded Carthage at the north-eastern tip of modern Tunisia in the early ninth century BC and were known in North Africa as Carthaginians, and the Romans who succeeded them after 146 BC, laid the foundations for the cultural geography of North Africa. Among other things, the evolution of Mediterranean agriculture began with the Carthaginians; in the case of the Romans it might be claimed that their greatest contribution was the introduction of true urban life. After a dark age in which the Vandals destroyed Roman North Africa came a period that was to add greatly to the complexity of cultural life in North Africa. In the seventh century AD came moslem Arabs who built to some extent on the Roman foundations. But the second major Arab invasion, the Hilalian invasion of the eleventh century, was markedly different in character. These 'cattle Arabs' introduced the tent and converted cultivated land to pasture. Subsequent influences from Mediterranean Europe were to complicate the picture even more but without erasing the earlier features. The geography of North Africa cannot be understood without reference to the region's spatial relations.

Egypt had a much older civilisation which was a compound of native ingenuity and foreign influences. By the time of the Empire or the New Kingdom, Egypt had reached a stage in its cultural life whose basic features were to remain essentially unchanged for centuries. The Greek and the Roman occupations were among the most significant events in post-Empire times; for example, the rapid colonisation of the Nile delta and its emergence as the centre of gravity in the economic life of Egypt occurred during the time of the Greeks and the Romans. The next major event, as in North Africa, was the arrival of the Arabs from the seventh century onwards and the Turks in the sixteenth century.

South of the Egyptians in the Nile Valley were the Nubians, whose cultural development was in many ways patterned upon that of the Egyptians. The Nile Valley was like a loosely sealed tube, open at the Mediterranean end only, and the Egyptians served as the medium through which outside influence filtered southwards to the Nubians. This is not to deny the importance of cultural influences from Ethiopia, another area whose role in the culture history of Africa cannot be overlooked. At this lower end of the Nile Valley occurred a remarkable synthesis which resulted in the flourishing of Sudanese cultures. As in Egypt, Islam was to introduce new determinants, and one of the major problems in the cultural geography of contemporary Republic of the Sudan is the division of the country into two generalised culture areas, the moslem north on the one hand and the Christian and the pagan south on the other. No geography of the Republic of the Sudan can ignore this fact, which is parent to a host of development problems.

South Africa stands on its own. The arrival of the Dutch

at the Cape in the sixteenth century, later to be joined by French Huguenots, and the English, led to developments that were not paralleled anywhere in Africa. The systematic displacement of the Bantu by the Boer, fortified by an intolerant Calvinist doctrine, and then by the English was to be the one organising principle of the country's cultural geography and was to provoke a northward return of the Bantu, which had serious consequences for Rhodesia and Zambia. A puzzling feature of the geography of these two countries is the apparent stagnation in economic life before European settlement; a puzzle because of the cultural traditions of a people which included the Zimbabwe civilisation. The devastating invasions by the returning Bantu from South Africa in the nineteenth century undoubtedly provide a major part of the answer.

COLONIAL AND POST-COLONIAL TIMES

What has gone before provides a background against which to view the events of the colonial period during which the British, the Germans and the Portuguese principally carved up Africa and shared it among themselves. The partition of Africa among the European powers was sanctioned by the Treaty of Berlin signed in 1885, and it sought to regularise claims which had been made by the European powers following the penetration of the continent by explorers, Christian missionaries and trading agents.

Colonialism ushered Africa into a new phase of development. Political boundaries were drawn which ignored existing ethnic and cultural affinities (see Fig 12), slave trading was eventually abolished, new towns were built, roads and railways were constructed. The story is too well known to be narrated here, but a number of points must nevertheless be kept in mind. For example, the generally exploitative intention of colonialism and the neglect of areas within a country which did not offer prospects for immediate returns to investment; the injudicious interference, out of ignorance, with local political structures and values and the consequences for present day development; and the extent to which the cultural innovations during the colonial period could be assimilated by the Africans.

Post-colonial Africa is in the process of adjusting to conditions created partly by colonialism, and finding solutions to problems of regional development, problems that scarcely arose in colonial times. Various political, not economic, ideologies have been adopted or experimented with in the effort to build a state in which all the different cultural groups function as a unit.

Ghana will serve as an illustration.[8] The period immediately preceding the colonial era was one in which an economy had developed based largely on trade and mining. Agricultural products were also exported, but cultivation was not a basis for the acquisition of wealth. In the middle of the nineteenth century the pattern of population distribution, which crystallised much earlier, was essentially as it is today, showing two densely populated areas in the north-eastern and north-western corners of northern Ghana. These were succeeded southward by an enormous stretch of sparsely populated land which swept across the country in a broad arc from south of Wa to northern Krakye district, taking in the Afram Plains (Fig 13). The Akan Closed Forest contained areas of high population concentration in Asante, the mining areas of the Western Region, and the Fante areas of the Central Region immediately inland from the coast. But the Eastern Region, unlike today, was sparsely populated. The coastline was dotted with numerous towns, large and small, important among which were Axim, Elmina, Cape Coast, Saltpond, Accra, Prampram, Ada and Keta. These coastal towns had developed as a result of the trading activities of the Europeans on the coast.

Northern Ghana was not behind the rest of the country in economic development, for it was engaged in a lively middle-man trade between Asante and the Western Sudan. Salaga, Wa, Bole, and Yendi were among the flourishing towns. Linking up the country from north to south were roads (pathways) which centred on Kumasi, the capital of Asante. Politically and economically Asante dominated the country, and the convergence of the trade routes, as today, on Kumasi was the result of a deliberate policy of the Asante Court which took shape during the eighteenth century (Fig 14); and many of the broad features of geography described for about the

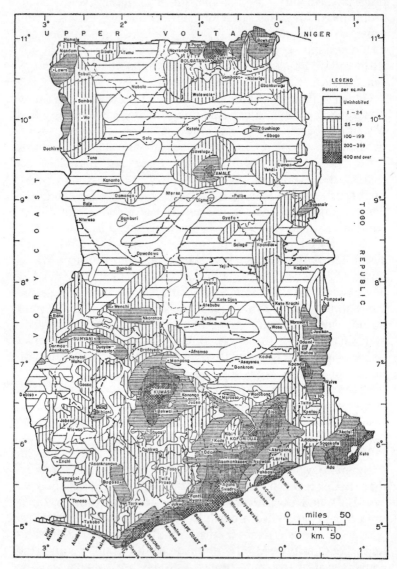

Fig 13 Distribution of population in Ghana (based on the 1960 Census
of Population)

mid-nineteenth century were attributable to the activities of the Asante.

By about 1870 the British were more involved in the affairs of the country than ever before and had overshadowed the Dutch, then their only rivals, who left the country two years later. In 1873–4 the British brought in the crack Black Watch Regiment which, aided by troops from southern Ghana and Sierra Leone, defeated the Asante and sacked Kumasi. For over two decades afterwards the British failed to serve as an effective substitute for the Asante Court which had hitherto pumped life along the great arteries of commerce to almost every corner of the land and maintained peace, even if by harsh means. Consequently there was chaos in the land as tribal wars erupted with distressing frequency. It must not be forgotten that all these events had their effects on patterns of settlement and economic life generally.

In the early 1880s the Germans also began their operations in Togoland, of which the Volta Region formed part, and down to the end of the century they and the British competed vigorously for supremacy in northern Ghana. The contest affected the status and subsequent development of such towns as Atebubu, Salaga, the river port town of Kete Krakye and Kintampo. For example, the British practically succeeded in killing the trade at Kete Krakye, which was in German hands, and the town never recovered subsequently. It lost its central place functions in a large area which no longer had a flourishing market to which agricultural produce could be sent. Again, the Germans burnt Salaga, then the pivot of economic life in northern Ghana, and although the British deliberately rebuilt it in the 1890s to be a counterpoise to the economic superiority of towns controlled by the Germans to the east, Salaga was never the same, and the large surrounding area dependent on it economically became impoverished.

By 1902 it was clear that the British had won the contest for political control in northern Ghana. Asante was also annexed to the British Crown in that year, so that the British, who already controlled southern Ghana (the colony) became the dominant power in what is now Ghana, except a narrow eastern strip of land which belonged to German Togoland.

The contrasting effects of the British and German brands

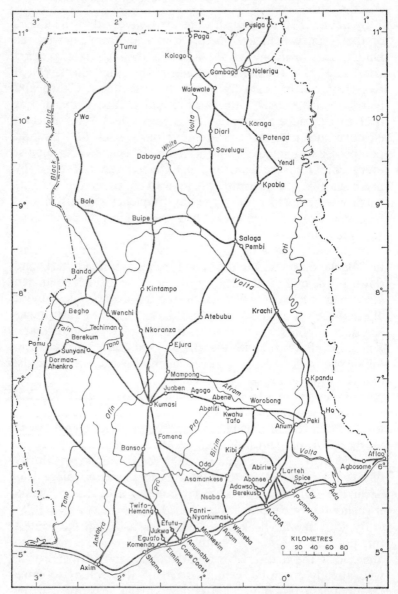

Fig 14 Major trade routes in Ghana in the eighteenth century

of colonialism are a subject matter of prime importance. The Germans were involved more positively in the affairs of their colonies, and before they were driven out of Togoland during World War I and their territory shared between the British and the French, they had done enough to set a pattern for the future development, or lack of it, in the Volta Region. The British were also directly involved, but nowhere near the extent to which the Germans were. Thinking of the British and the Germans together, the spread and effects of innovations from the coast, the thinning out of the new ideas in the interior, north of Asante, the impact of spatially selective development, and the deliberate plan by the British to make northern Ghana a reservoir of labour for the south should be considered in detail. Thus there is now the problem of imbalance in regional development which must be overcome in the interests of nation building.

These are but a few of the numerous themes that could be investigated with great profit. Without knowledge of these it is hard to see how the significant in the contemporary scene could be recognised, rational and accurate explanations provided—and it is essential that explanations be accurate, and on the basis of these make forecasts or formulate problems correctly. For example, many attempts in post-colonial times to develop northern Ghana have failed simply because the reasons for the existence of the problem were not carefully assessed. Apathy in some of the areas selected for development was wrongly taken to be a sign of primitiveness rather than a protest against a ruling family which was imposed arbitrarily by the British and through which the planners tried to reach the people. Sparsely populated areas were often declared to be of low environmental quality and ignored, when the same areas used to support a thriving agricultural population, which was decimated by slave trading, and could be brought once more into productive use if the right sort of incentives were forthcoming.

SOURCE MATERIALS

An apparent lack of source materials is one of the reasons why historical geography is not taught in many universities in Africa. But the problem is not so much the scarcity of source materials, which on the contrary are plentiful, as their being widely scattered in a number of countries. The problem of bringing them together is a real one; but it would probably be true to say that in any country enough exists to give a useful indication of the outlines of its historical geography.

This is not the place to review the strengths and weaknesses of source materials on the historical geography of Africa.[9] Nevertheless a few things might be said in general terms. It is not only the written sources and maps that should be relied on. Oral tradition is another source that should be tapped, but with great care; oral tradition is dangerous material in the hands of the incautious.[10] Also, the results of researches by professionals in other disciplines, eg archaelogists, biologists, theologians, historians, linguists, and anthropologists, are invaluable. The African past is a subject that has fascinated scholars from a great variety of disciplines, and historians and anthropologists in particular range widely over the field and produce works which elsewhere would be labelled differently. All these source materials must be supplemented with extensive field work.

The question of how much detail is contained in the source materials is one that cannot be answered for every country. Yet it would not be wrong to say that most of the materials available for the centuries preceding the nineteenth are seriously deficient in statistical data on the basis of which quantitative analyses could be made. This does not in any way destroy the possibility of writing on those earlier centuries, for what is more important is a knowledge of cultural changes and effects which can readily be obtained without the aid of detailed statistical data. A series of cross-sectional maps of agricultural production reaching far back into time would of course be invaluable; nevertheless such maps (or statistics showing trends) would be no more than precise descriptions (assuming the statistical data are themselves reliable) of situations which may already be known from written verbal accounts.

A great deal will also depend on the scale of the problem and the level of generalisation in terms of which the problem is to be discussed. If the problem is of continental proportions and therefore demands explanations of broad contrasts in cultural geography, then a fuller version of the sketchy indication of culture history given above will suffice. In other words, the necessarily few references relating to this essay and the many more that could be added should support reasonable statements about the main outlines of historical geography. More detailed information will be required when the problems are limited in scale and have to be dissected more finely.

Works on Africa specifically bearing the title of historical geography are few, and not all of them may be regarded as true historical geographies, although the information they contain is essential for the work of the historical geographer. Examples are C. P. Lucas' series on the *Historical Geography of the British Colonies* (Oxford, 1890–1913), and *Historical Geography of the Gold Coast* (London 1929) by J. W. de Graft Johnson.

HISTORICAL GEOGRAPHY OF AFRICA AND MODELS IN HUMAN GEOGRAPHY

Historical geographers are exhorted to formulate or test existing theories in human geography. The historical geography of Africa is concerned with culture groups, regarded as spatial entities, whose characteristics are usually not included in the assumptions built into the current models in human geography. This does not imply that such models should be ignored; on the contrary, they should be carefully considered by the historical geographer working on Africa but not necessarily as analytical tools to resolve problems. They should rather be studied with a view to building into them, if possible, new assumptions about the African situation and thus making them more widely applicable. A warning is necesary: it would be dangerous to lift a phenomenon out of its spatial-cultural context in Africa and use it to illustrate a theory developed within a different cultural context. Phenomena may have certain forms and physical characteristics in common which impart a seeming uniformity to them wherever they are. But these characteristics will probably be viewed differently in, say, North Africa and West Africa and must therefore be reduced to a common denominator defined in terms of function before

o

meaningful comparisons can be made. The appraisal of functions can only be done within the relevant spatial-cultural context.

So far the little that has been written on Africa of a specifically historical-geographical nature has not put forward theories. The stage reached is that of collecting data, classifying and analysing them with an eye to process relationships, or simply working to know the extent of the problem. A number of detailed intra-cultural studies must be available before law-like generalisations can be made. In the meantime it would be helping geographers in general to text existing models when the situations which they purport to apply to in Africa have been more thoroughly investigated.

CONCLUSION

Historical geography is relatively new in most African universities. But the subject has immense possibilities in Africa. Although the written sources needed for a study of the historical geography of Africa or parts of it are extremely diverse and are scattered in the archives of several countries, it should still be possible to obtain enough to rapidly sketch a reasonable outline of its historical geography. Emphasis will have to be placed on the spatially varying patterns of culture history which alone will account for the variations in ways of life on the continent.

Much has been done by historians, anthropologists, archaeologists and others to uncover the past of Africa and to understand the nature of differential cultural development. The gap left by geographers in this general effort to study the influence of the past on the present in Africa is a big one, for there is still much that is not known about spatial variations in modes of living and the processes that accounted for them. In this effort the geographer must apply modern scientific methods in the hope of leading to the formulation of new analytical concepts or the reshaping of existing ones. But this culminating stage in the application of scientific method must be based on patient enquiry into the basic elements of historical geography, and this for the moment should be the preoccupation of researchers into the historical geography of Africa.

Notes and References

Chapter 1   *Rethinking Historical Geography*

1   Chang, K. C. *Rethinking Archaeology* (New York, 1967) ; Leach, E. R. 'Rethinking anthropology', *London School of Economics Monographs On Social Anthropology,* 22 (1961) 1–27 ; Lynd, S. 'Historical past and existentialist present' being 87–101 of Roszak, T. (ed) *The Dissenting Academy* (Harmondsworth, Middlesex, 1969)

2   Chorley, R. J. and Haggett, P. (eds) *Models in Geography* (London, 1967). An especially thoughtful review of this book was 'First choose your paradigm', *The Times Literary Supplement,* 11 July 1968, 736

3   Wheatley, P. 'Great expectations', *The Bloomsbury Geographer,* 1 (1968), 2–9

4   Cooke, R. U. and Johnson, J. H. (eds) *Trends in Geography* (Oxford, 1969)

5   Smith, C. T. *An Historical Geography of Western Europe Before 1800* (London, 1967) vi ; Harvey, D. 'Models of the evolution of spatial patterns in human geography' being 549–608 of Chorley and Haggett, *Models* ; Hepple, L. W. 'Epistemology, model-building and historical geography', *Geographical Articles,* 10 (1967), 42–8

6   Newcomb, R. M. 'Twelve working approaches to historical geography', *Yearbook of the Association of Pacific Coast Geographers,* 31 (1961), 27–50

7   Harvey, D. *Explanation in Geography* (London, 1969) 407–32

8   Baker, A. R. H., Butlin, R. A., Phillips, A. D. M. and Prince, H. C. 'The future of the past', *Area,* no 4 (1969), 46–51

9   Prince, H. C. 'Progress in historical geography' in Cooke and Johnson, *Trends,* 110–22 and 'Real, imagined and abstract

worlds of the past', *Progress in Geography,* 3 (1971), 1–86

10 Baker, A. R. H., Hamshere, J. D. and Langton, J. (eds) *Geographical Interpretations of Historical Sources. Readings in Historical Geography* (Newton Abbot, 1970) 13–25 ; Patten, J. H. C. 'The past and geography reconsidered', *Area,* no 3 (1970), 37–9 ; Baker, A. R. H. 'Today's studies of yesterday's geographies', *Geographical Magazine,* 43 (1970–71), 452–3

11 Bowden, M. J. in *Economic Geography,* 46 (1970), 202–3

12 Koelsch, W. A. in *Economic Geography,* 46 (1970), 201–202

13 Harris, R. C. 'Reflections on the fertility of the historical geographical mule', *University of Toronto Department of Geography Discussion Paper Series,* no 10 (1970)

14 Koroscil, P. M. 'Historical geography: a resurrection', *Journal of Geography,* 70 (1971), 415–20

15 Baker, A. R. H. *Historical Geography: an Introduction* (forthcoming)

16 Darby, H. C. 'Historical geography' being 127–56 of Finberg, H. P. R. (ed) *Approaches to History. A Symposium* (London, 1962)

17 Smith, C. T. 'Historical geography: current trends and prospects' being 118–43 of Chorley, R. J. and Haggett, P. *Frontiers in Geographical Teaching* (London, 1965). The quotation is on page 128. More recently another writer claimed 'the principal task of the historical geographer is to attempt to reconstruct, as accurately as possible, some or all aspects of the geography of a region as it was in the past': Butlin, R. A. 'Historical geography and local studies in Ireland', *Geographical Viewpoint,* 1 (1966), 141–54

18 Baker, Hamshere and Langton, *Geographical Interpretations,* 13–14 ; Harvey, *Models,* 550, 563–4 ; King, L. J. 'Approaches to location analysis: an overview', *East Lakes Geographer,* 2 (1966), 1–15, especially 15 ; Pred, A. 'Postscript' being 299–334 of Hägerstrand, T. *Innovation Diffusion as a Special Process* (Chicago, 1967), especially 305 ; Prince, *Trends,* 111 ; Prince, *Progress in Geography,* 3, 6–12

19 Harvey, *Explanation in Geography,* 422

20 Prince, *Progress in Geography,* 3, 22–24

21 *Research in Economic and Social History* (London, 1971) 17

22 Prince, *Progress in Geography,* 3, 23

23 *Research in History,* 123

24 Berkhofer, R. F. *A Behavioural Approach to Historical Analysis* (Toronto, 1969) 271–3

25 *Research in History,* 123

26 Klein, M. 'Bibliography of writings on historiography and the writing of history' being 213–47 of Gottschalk, L. (ed) *Generalization in the Writing of History* (Chicago, 1963)

27 Aydelotte, W. O. 'Notes on the problem of historical generalization' being Gottschalk, *Generalization in the Writing of History*, 145–77

28 Leach, 'Rethinking anthropology', especially 2

29 Chang, *Rethinking Archaeology*; Clarke, D. L. *Analytical Archaeology* (London, 1968)

30 A useful introduction is Mackenzie, N. (ed) *A Guide to the Social Sciences* (London, 1966)

31 Darby, H. C. 'On the relations of geography and history', *Transactions and Papers of the Institute of British Geographers,* 19 (1953), 1–11; 'The problem of geographical description', *Transactions and Papers of the Institute of British Geographers,* 30 (1962), 1–14

32 Berkhofer, *Behavioural Approach to Historical Analysis,* 236

33 Wheatley, P. personal communication 22 June 1970

34 Lewis, I. M. (ed) *History and Social Anthropology* (London, 1968) xii–xiv

35 Evans-Pritchard, E. E. *Anthropology and History* (Manchester, 1961); Mikesell, M. W. 'Geographic perspectives in the anthropology', *Annals of the Association of American Geographers,* 57 (1967), 617–34

36 Lewis, *History and Social Anthropology*

37 *Research in Social Anthropology* (London, 1968) 30

38 *Research in Social Anthropology,* 13

39 See, for example, Moore, W. E. *Social Change* (Englewood Cliffs, 1963)

40 Berkhofer, *Behavioural Approach to Historical Analysis,* 231–2

41 Berkhofer, *Behavioural Approach to Historical Analysis,* 232. A similar point has been made in Harvey, *Explanation in Geography,* 431 and in Hepple, *Geographical Articles,* 10, 46

42 Langton, J. 'System theory and the study of change in human geography', *Progress in Geography,* 4 (1972)—in the press

43 Baker, Hamshere and Langton, *Geographical Interpretations,* 18–19; Hays, S. P. 'The use of archives for historical statistical inquiry', *Journal of the National Archives,* 1 (1969), 7–15

44 *Research in History,* 8

45 Aydelotte, W. O. 'Quantification in history', *American Historical Review,* 71 (1966), 803–25; Cochran, T. C. 'Economic history, old and new', *American Historical Review,* 74 (1969), 1561–72; Hunt, E. H. 'The new economic history: Professor

Fogel's study of American railways', *History,* 53 (1968), 3–18 ; Rashevsky, N. *Looking at History through Mathematics* (London, 1968) ; Rowney, D. K. and Graham, J. Q. (eds) *Quantitative History* (New York, 1969) ; Shorter, E. *The Historian and the Computer* (Englewood Cliffs, 1971)

46 *Research in History,* 9
47 See G. Olsson's review of Berry, B. J. L. and Marble, D. F. (eds) *Spatial Analysis. A Reader in Statistical Geography* (Englewood Cliffs, 1968) in *Journal of Regional Science,* 8 (1968), 253–5 for a spirited criticism of the use of statistical analysis for purely descriptive purposes and of the idea that geography can be equated with applied geometry
48 Olsson, G. 'Complementary models: a study of colonization maps', *Geografiska Annaler,* 50 (1968), 115–32, especially 130–1
49 King, L. J. 'The analysis of spatial form and its relation to geographic theory', *Annals of the Association of American Geographers,* 59 (1969), 573–95, especially 587–9
50 Harvey, *Models,* 588
51 Harvey, 587–8 ; Pred, *Innovation Diffusion,* 310–24
52 Rashevsky, *Looking at History,* 8
53 Harvey, *Explanation in Geography,* 428
54 Sewell, W. H. 'Marc Bloch and the logic of comparative history', *History and Theory,* 6 (1967), 208–18 ; Gould, J. D. 'Hypothetical history', *Economic History Review,* 22 (1969), 195-207
55 Harvey, *Models,* 577–82
56 Smith, D. M. *Industrial Location. An Economic Geographical Analysis* (New York, 1971) 270–1
57 Plackett, R. L. 'Current trends in statistical inference', *Journal of the Royal Statistical Society,* Series A 129 (1966), 249–67. See also Harvey, *Explanation in Geography,* 249–52 ; King, L. J. *Statistical Analysis in Geography* (Englewood Cliffs, 1969), 84–5
58 Leach, 'Rethinking anthropology', 7–8
59 *Research in Social Anthropology,* 11
60 Aydelotte, *Generalization in the writing of History,* 166
61 Harvey, D. personal communication August 1970
62 Kaplan, A. *The Conduct of Inquiry* (San Francisco, 1964) 268
63 Prince, *Progress in Geography,* 3, 22–3
64 Samuelson, P. A. 'Dynamic process analysis' being 352–87 of Ellis, H. S. (ed) *A Survey of Contemporary Economics* (Philadelphia, 1948)
65 Langton, *Progress in Geography,* 4 (in the press)
66 Vance, J. E. *The Merchant's World. The Geography of Wholesaling* (Englewood Cliffs, 1970) 139

67 Hägerstrand, *Innovation Diffusion as a Spatial Process*, 1-241

68 Leach, 'Rethinking anthropology', 5

69 Blalock, H. M. *Theory Construction. From Verbal to Mathematical Formulations* (Englewood Cliffs, 1969) 3–5

70 Smith, D. M., *Industrial Location*, 21

71 Blalock, *Theory Construction*, 8

72 Desai, M. 'Some issues in econometric history', *Economic History Review*, 21 (1968), 1–16

73 Morrill, R. L. 'Migration and the spread and growth of urban settlement', *Lund Studies in Geography Series B*, 26 (1965) ; Pred, A. 'Behaviour and location. Foundations for a geographic and dynamic location theory', *Lund Studies in Geography Series B*, 27, 28 (1967, 1969)

74 Harvey, D. 'Behavioural postulates and the construction of theory in human geography', *University of Bristol Department of Geography Seminar Papers Series A*, 6 (1967)

75 Harris, *Toronto Geography Discussion Paper Series*, no 10, 28

76 Ward, D. *Cities and Immigrants. A Geography of Change in Nineteenth Century America* (London, 1971)

77 Lewis, *History and Social Anthropology*, xx

78 *Research in History*, 25–30

79 Blaut, J. M. 'Space and process', *Professional Geographer*, 13 no 4 (1961), 1–7. The quotation is from page 6

80 Hudson, J. C. 'A location theory for rural settlement', *Annals of the Association of American Geographers*, 59 (1969), 365–81 ; Semple, R. K. and Golledge, R. G. 'An analysis of entropy changes in a settlement pattern over time', *Economic Geography*, 46 (1970), 157–60; Sibley, D. 'Density gradients and urban growth', *Urban Studies*, 7 (1970), 294–7

81 Lewis, J. P. *Building Cycles and Britain's Growth* (London, 1965)

82 Doherty, J. M. 'Developments in behavioural geography', *London School of Economics Graduate School of Geography Discussion Papers*, no 35 (1969)

83 Olsson, G. 'Trends in spatial model building: an overview', *Geographical Analysis*, 1 (1969), 219–24

84 Hägerstrand, T. *What about People in Regional Science?* (Copenhagen, 1969) 2

85 *Relevance of Models for Social Anthropology*, xxxvi–vii

86 Chang, *Rethinking Archaeology*, 3–17

87 Berkhofer, *Behavioural Approach to Historical Analysis*

88 *Research in History*, 32–37

89 *Research in History*, 12–13

90 Catchpole, A. J. W., Moodie, D. W. and Kaye, B. 'Content analysis: a method for the identification of dates of first freezing and first breaking from descriptive accounts', *Professional Geographer,* 22 no 5 (1970), 252–7; Moodie, D. W. 'Content analysis: a method for historical geography', *Area,* no 3 (1971), 146–149

91 Harvey, *Models,* 593

92 Prince, *Trends,* 114

93 Patten, *Area,* no 3 (1970), 38; Prince, *Progress in Geography,* 3, 28–32

94 George, D. *England in Transition* (London, 1931; Harmondsworth, 1953) 29

95 Kirk, W. 'Historical geography and the concept of the behavioural environment', *Indian Geographical Journal,* Silver Jubilee vol (1952), 152–60

96 Prince, *Progress in Geography,* 3, 24–44

97 Chorley, R. J. 'The role and relations of physical geography', *Progress in Geography,* 3 (1971), 87–109. The quotation is from 97

98 Berkhofer, *Behavioural Approach to Historical Analysis,* 167

99 Vance, *The Merchant's World,* 140

100 Hepple, *Geographical Articles,* 10, 45

101 Patten, *Area,* no 3 (1970), 39

102 Marc Bloch's writings were, of course, voluminous. A useful review of his work is Davies, R. R. 'Marc Bloch', *History,* 52 (1967), 265–82

103 This viewpoint has been expressed before but has yet to be widely accepted: Smith, C. T., *Frontiers,* 140–1; Baker, Hamshere and Langton, *Geographical Interpretations,* 21

Chapter 2   Historical Geography in France

Acknowledgement: The author is indebted to the editor, Dr Alan Baker, for translating a draft of this chapter.

1 Expressed since the early nineteenth century in the stream of activity centred on the Geographical Society of Paris, founded in 1821, and notably demonstrated towards the end of the century in the work of Elisée Reclus (1830–1905), especially in the

Nouvelle Géographie Universelle, 19 vols (Paris, 1876–94)

2 Levêque, P. and Claval, P. 'La signification géographique de la colonisation grecque', *Revue de Géographie de Lyon,* 45 (1970), 179–200

3 Claval, P. *Essai sur l'évolution de la géographie humaine* (Paris, 1964), 103–147

4 An extensive bibliography of French work on historical agrarian geography will be found in Juillard, E., Meynier, A., de Planhol, X. and Sautter, G. *Structures agraires et paysages ruraux: un quart de siècle de recherches françaises* (Nancy, 1957)

5 Derruau, M. *La Grande Limagne auvergnate et bourbonnaise* (Clermont-Ferrand, 1949)

6 Chevalier, M. *La vie humaine dans les Pyrénées Ariégeoises* (Paris, 1956)

7 de Planhol, X. *De la plaine pamphylienne aux lacs pisidiens: nomadisme et vie paysanne* (Paris, 1958) 65–132

8 Lerat, S. *Les pays de l'Adour. Structures agraires et économie agricole* (Bordeaux, 1963) 33–166

9 Janin, B. *Une région alpine originale, le Val d'Aoste: tradition et renouveau* (Grenoble, 1968) 113–333

10 Daveau, S. *Les régions frontalières de la montagne jurassienne. Etude de géographie humaine* (Lyon, 1959) 37–106

11 Huetz de Lemps, A. *Vignobles et vins du Nord-Ouest de l'Espagne* (Bordeaux, 1967) 165–582

12 Lebeau, R. *La vie rurale dans les montagnes du Jura méridional* (Lyon, 1955) 275–488

13 Juillard, E. *La vie rurale dans la plaine de Basse Alsace* (Strasbourg, 1953)

14 Brunet, P. *Structure agraire et économie rurale des plateaux tertiaires entre la Seine et l'Oise* (Caen, 1960) 275–467

15 Brunet, R. *Les campagnes touloisaines. Etude géographique* (Toulouse, 1965) 275–430

16 Flatrès, P. *Géographie rurale de quatre contrées celtiques. Irlande, Galles, Cornwall et Man* (Rennes, 1957)

17 Fel, A. *Les hautes terres du Massif Central. Tradition paysanne et économie agricole* (Clermont-Ferrand, 1962)

18 Livet, R. *Habitat rural et structures agraires en Basse-Provence* (Gap, 1962)

19 Desplanques, H. *Campagnes ombriennes* (Paris, 1969)

20 A bibliography of works published before 1957 will be found in Juillard, E. *et al, Structures agraires.* More recent works are listed in Meynier, A. 'Les études de géographie agraire au Laboratoire de Géographie de Rennes', *Norois,* 9 (1962), 127–47

and Meynier, A. 'La genèse du parcellaire breton', *Norois*, 13 (1966), 595–610

21 Published in Juillard, E. *et al*, *Structures agraires*, 86–7

22 ibid 88

23 For an example, see Meynier, *Norois*, 13, map of Janzé at 1:50,000 between pages 606 and 607

24 Much of the work of J. Peltre is still unpublished, but accessible studies are: Peltre, J. 'Du XVIᵉ au XVIIIᵉ siècle: une génération de nouveaux villages en Lorraine', *Revue Géographique de l'Est*, 6 (1966), 3–28; 'Premiers enseignements d'une étude métrologique des terroirs lorrains', *Bulletin de l'Association de Géographes Français*, nos 352–3 (1967), 11–19; 'L'évolution des methodes d'arpentage en Lorraine du XVIᵉ au XVIIIᵉ siècle et ses conséquences sur la structure agraire' in Jäger, H., Krenzlin, A., and Uhlig, H. (editors) *Beiträge zur Genese der Siedlungs- und Agrarlandschaft in Europa* (Wiesbaden, 1968) 138–144

25 Caillemer, A. and Chevallier, R. *Atlas des centuriations romaines de Tunisie* (Paris, 1954); Caillemer, A. and Chevallier, R. 'Les centuriations de l'*Africa vetus*', *Annales Economies Sociétés Civilisation*s, 9 (1954), 433–60

26 Despois, J. 'L'Atlas des centuriations romaines de Tunisie: une question de méthode' *Annales Economies Sociétés Civilisations*, 12 (1957), 460–6; Caillemer, A. and Chevallier, R. 'Mise au point à propos de l'Atlas des centuriations romaines de Tunisie: quelques questions de méthode' *Annales Economies Sociétés Civilisations*, 13 (1958), 304–7. On the general problem of centuriations, see Chevallier, R. 'La centuriation et les problèmes de la colonisation romaine', *Etudes Rurales*, 3 (1961), 54–79

27 de Planhol, X. 'Anciens openfields méditerranéens et proche-orientaux' in *Colloque de géographie agraire organisé en l'honneur des 25 années d'enseignement de M. le Professeur Meynier à la Faculté des Lettres, Rennes, 23–24 novembre 1963* (Rennes, 1965) 9–34

28 Duby, G. *La société aux XIᵉ et XIIᵉ siècles dans la région maconnaise* (Paris, 1953); Duby, G. *L'économie rurale et la vie des campagnes dans l'Occident médiéval* (Paris, 1962)

29 Higounet, C. 'L'assolement triennal dans la plaine de France au XIIIᵉ siècle', *Comptes-Rendus de l'Académie des Inscriptions et Belles-Lettres*, (1956), 507–510; Higounet, C. *La grange de Vaulerent. Structure et exploitation d'un terroir cistercien de la plaine de France, XIIᵉ–XVᵉ siècles* (Paris, 1965); Fossier, R. *La terre et les hommes en Picardie jusqu'à la fin du XIIIᵉ siècle* (Paris, 1968) 335–42

30 Febvre, L. *La terre et l'évolution humaine* (Paris, 1922)

31 Notably that of Huntington, E. *Palestine and its Transformation* (Boston, 1911) and *Civilization and Climate* (New Haven, 1915), but also those in the synthesis, often without much foundation, of Brooks, C. E. P. *Climate through the Ages* (London, 2nd edn 1950)

32 de Planhol, X. 'Limites antique et actuelle des cultures arbustives méditerranéennes en Asie Mineure', *Bulletin de l'Association de Géographes Français,* nos 239–40 (1954), 665–73

33 Le Roy Ladurie, E. *Histoire du climat depuis l'an mil* (Paris, 1967). Earlier papers by the same author include: 'Histoire et climat', *Annales Economies Sociétés Civilisations,* 14 (1959), 3–34; 'Climat et récoltes aux XVIIᵉ et XVIIIᵉ siècles', *Annales Economies Sociétés Civilisations,* 15 (1960), 434–65; 'Aspects historiques de la nouvelle climatologie', *Revue Historique,* 235 (1961), 1–20

34 Le Roy Ladurie, E. *Les paysans du Languedoc* (Paris, 1962)

35 Demougeot, E. 'Variations climatiques et invasions', *Revue Historique,* 233 (1965), 1–22

36 de Planhol, X. 'Les nomades, la steppe et la forêt en Anatolie', *Geographische Zeitschrift,* 53 (1965), 101–116; de Planhol, X. 'Le déboisement de l'Iran', *Annales de Géographie,* 78 (1969), 625–35

37 de Planhol, X. *Les fondements géographiques de l'histoire de l'Islam* (Paris, 1968); Despois, J. 'Géographie et histoire en Afrique du Nord' being pp. 187–94 of *Eventail de l'histoire vivante. Hommage à Lucien Febvre* (Paris, 1953)

38 Tomas, F. 'Problèmes de démographie historique: le Forez au XVIIIᵉ siècle', *Cahiers d'Histoire,* 13 (1968), 381–99

39 Braudel, F. *La Méditerranée et le monde méditerranéen à l'époque de Philippe II* (Paris, 2nd edn 1966)

40 Lombard, M. *L'Islam dans sa première grandeur: VIIIᵉ au XIᵉ siècles* (Paris, 1971)

41 Mauny, R. *Tableau géographique de l'Ouest africain au Moyen-Age d'après les sources écrites, la tradition et l'archéologie* (Dakar, 1961)

42 Silbert, A. *Le Portugal méditerranéen à la fin de l'Ancien Régime, XVIIIᵉ au début du XIXᵉ siècle* (Paris, 1966)

43 Yacono, X. *La colonisation des plaines du Chélif* (Algiers, 1955–6); Roche, J. *La colonisation allemande et le Rio Grande do Sul* (Paris, 1959)

44 Poncet, J. *La colonisation et l'agriculture européenne en Tunisie depuis 1881* (Paris, 1961); Monbeig, P. *Pionniers et planteurs de Sao Paulo* (Paris, 1952)

45 Sclafert, T. *Cultures en Haute-Provence: déboisement et pâtur-ages au Moyen-Age* (Paris, 1961)

46 Nougier, L. R. *Les civilisations campigniennes en Europe occidentale* (Le Mans, 1950) ; Nougier, L. R. *Le peuplement préhistorique. Ses étapes entre Seine et Loire* (Toulouse, 1950)

47 Millotte, J. P. *Le Jura et les plaines de la Saône aux âges des métaux* (Paris, 1963)

48 Millotte, J. P. *Carte archéologique de la Lorraine (Ages du Bronze et du Fer)* (Paris, 1965). For later periods, see de Planhol, X. and Pérardel, A. 'La répartition géographique des vestiges archéologiques gallo-romains en Lorraine', *Revue Géographique de l'Est*, 9 (1969), 177–80 ; de Planhol, X. and Lacroix, J. 'Géographie et toponymie en Lorraine', *Revue Géographique de l'Est*, 3 (1963), 9–14

49 Fossier, *La terre et les hommes en Picardie*, 114, 119, 133 and 158–9

50 Broens, M. 'Le peuplement germanique de la Gaule entre la Méditerranée et l'Océan', *Annales du Midi*, 63 (1956), 17–32. For other, more local, examples of such cartographic analysis, see Higounet, C. 'L'arrière-pays de Bordeaux au XIIIᵉ siècle, esquisse cartographique', *Revue Historique de Bordeaux et du Département de la Gironde*, 4 (1955), 201–210 ; Higounet, C. 'Une carte agricole de l'Albigeois vers 1260', *Annales du Midi*, 65 (1958), 65–72 ; Higounet, C. 'La méthode cartographique en histoire', *Relazioni X Congresso Internationale di Scienze Storiche*, 7 (Rome, 1955), 104–106

51 Despois, J. *Le Djebel Amour* (Paris, 1957) ; Despois, J. 'Le Djebel Ousselat, les Ousseltiya et les Kooub', *Cahiers de Tunisie*, 7 (1959), 407–27

52 For example, Roblin, M. *Le terroir de Paris aux époques gallo-romaine et franque* (Paris, 1951)

53 Cavaillès, H. *La route française. Son histoire. Sa fonction. Etude de géographie humaine* (Paris, 1946)

54 Imberdis, F. *Le réseau routier de l'Auvergne au XVIIIᵉ siècle. Ses origines et son évolution* (Paris, 1967)

55 Markovitch, T. J. *L'industrie lanière à la fin du règne de Louis XIV et sous la Régence* (Leiden, 1968) ; Woronoff, D. 'Vers une géographie industrielle de la France d'Ancien Régime', *Annales Economies Sociétés Civilisations*, 95 (1970), 127–30

56 Mours, S. *Essai sommaire de géographie du protestantisme réformé français au XVIIᵉ siècle* (Paris, 1966)

57 Baratier, E., Duby, G. and Hildesheimer, E. (eds) *Atlas Historique. Provence, Comtat, Orange, Nice, Monaco* (Paris, 1969)

58 A bibliography and critique of Dion's writings will be found in Gulley, J. L. M. 'The practice of historical geography. A study of the writings of Professor Roger Dion', *Tijdschrift voor economische en sociale geografie,* 52 (1961), 169–83. Dion's publications since 1961 are listed in successive volumes of *l'Annuaire du Collège de France,* which includes each year a synopsis of Dion's course.

59 Dion, R. *Le Val de Loire* (Tours, 1934) ; Dion, R. *Essai sur la formation du paysage rural français* (Tours, 1934)

60 Dion, R. 'La part de la géographie et celle de l'histoire dans l'explication de l'habitat rural du Bassin Parisien', *Bulletin de la Société de Géographie de Lille,* (1946), 6–80

61 Dion, R. 'Le beau et bon pays nommé Champagne Pouilleuse', *L'Information Géographique,* 95 (1961), 209–14

62 Dion, R. *Les frontières de la France* (Paris, 1947)

63 Dion, R. 'Effets de l'insécurité sur le choix des sites d'habitat rural', *L'Information Géographique,* 10 (1946), 143–6

64 Dion, R. *Histoire de la vigne et du vin en France des origines au XIXe siècle* (Paris, 1959)

65 Dion, R. 'Querelle des anciens et des modernes sur les facteurs de la qualité du vin', *Annales de Géographie,* 61 (1952), 417–31

66 Dion, R. 'Vin de Chalon et vin d'Autun', *Bulletin de l'Association de Géographes Français,* nos 218–9 (1951), 125–33 ; Dion, R. 'Metropoles et vignobles en Gaule Romaine: l'exemple bourguignon', *Annales Economies Sociétés Civilisations,* 7 (1952), 1–12

67 Dion, R. 'Orléans et l'ancienne navigation de la Loire', *Annales de Géographie,* 47 (1938), 126–54

68 Many French geographers have, to varying degrees, ventured into the geography of viticulture. See for example, Enjalbert, H. 'Comment naissent les grands crus: Bordeaux, Porto, Cognac', *Annales Economies Sociétés Civilisations,* 8 (1953), 315–28 and 457–74 ; Galtier, G. 'La viticulture de l'Europe occidentale à la veille de la Révolution Française, d'après les "Notes de Voyage" de Thomas Jefferson', *Bulletin de la Société Languedocienne de Géographie,* 39 (1968), 43–86

69 Dion, R. 'Sur le problème des Cassitérides', *Latomus,* 48 (1952), 306–14. A recent synthesis of this topic is Ramin, J. *Le problème des Cassitérides et les sources de l'étain occidental depuis le temps protohistoriques jusqu'au début de notre ère* (Paris, 1965). For an approach similar to Dion's, see de Planhol, X. 'Geographica Pontica I–II', *Journal Asiatique,* 251 (1963), 293–309, which explains the discrepancies in ancient texts

relating to a mythical people, the *Khalybes,* alleged inventors of iron founding, by the fact that the name meant simply 'smiths' and had been given to all kinds of people.

70 Dion, R. 'Le Danube d'Hérodote', *Revue de Philologie, de Littérature et d'Histoire Anciennes,* 94 (1968), 7–41

71 Dion, R. 'Pythéas explorateur', *Revue de Philologie, de Littérature et d'Histoire Anciennes,* 92 (1966), 191–216

72 Dion, R. *Les anthropophages de l'Odyssée: Cyclopes et Lestrygons* (Paris, 1969)

Chapter 3 Historical Geography in Germany, Austria, and Switzerland

Acknowledgement: The author is indebted to Dr K. A. Sinnhuber for translating this chapter from its original German

1 Baker, A. R. H. 'A note on the retrogressive and retrospective approaches in historical geography'. *Erdkunde,* 22 (1968), 244–45 ; Jäger, H. 'Reduktive und progressive Methoden in der deutschen Geographie', *Erdkunde,* 22 (1968), 245

2 Mager, F. *Der Wald in Altpreussen als Wirtschaftsraum,* 2 vol (Köln/Graz, 1960)

3 'Geomer' means a section of the geosphere (earth shell) regardless of size and by what kind of boundaries it is delimited

4 Mortensen, H. and G. *Die Besiedlung des nordöstlichen Ostpreussens bis zum Beginn des 17. Jahrhunderts. I Die preusisch-deutsche Siedlung am Westrand der grossen Wildnis um 1400 II Die Wildnis im östlichen Preussen, ihr Zustand um 1400 und ihre frühere Besiedlung* (Leipzig, 1937, 1938)

5 Müller-Wille, W. 'Langstreifenflur und Drubbel', *Deutsches Archiv f. Landes- und Volksforschung,* 8 (1944), 9–44
   Müller-Wille, W. 'Blöcke, Streifen, Hufen', *Berichte z. deutschen Landeskunde,* 29 (1962), 296–306

6 Winkler, E. 'Fünfzig Jahre schweizerische Kulturlandschaftsgeschichtsforschung', *Zeitschr. f. Schweizerische Geschichte,* 24 (1944), 107–128

7 Mortensen, H. 'Die Arbeitsmethoden der deutschen Flurforschung und ihre Beweiskraft', *Berichte z. deutschen Landeskunde,* 29 (1962), 205–14

8 Uhlig. H. 'Old hamlets with infield and outfield systems in Western and Central Europe', *Geografiska Annaler,* 43 (1961), 285–312

9 Krenzlin, A. and Reusch, L. *Die Entstehung der Gewannflur nach Untersuchungen im nördlichen Unterfranken.* (Frankfurt, 1961)

10 Bachmann, H. 'Zur Methodik der Auswertung der Siedlungs- und Flurkarte für die siedlungsgeschichtliche Forschung', *Zeitschrift f. Agrargeschischte u. Agrarsoziologie*, 8 (1960), 1–13

11 Rippel, J. K. 'Eine statistische Methode zur Untersuchung von Flur- und Ortsentwicklung', *Geografiska Annaler*, 43 (1961), 252–63

12 Mortensen, H. 'Die "quasinatürliche" Oberflächenformung als Forschungsproblem', *Wissenschaftl. Zeitsch. d. Ernst-Moritz-Arndt-Univ. Greifswald*, 4 (1954/55), 625–28

13 Käubler, R. 'Junggeschichtliche Veränderungen des Landschafts-bildes im mittelsächsischen Lössgebiet', *Wissenschaftl. Veröffentl. d. Deutschen Museums f. Länderkunde, NF* 5 (1938), 71–97
Jäger, H. 'Historische Geographie im Felde', in: *Methodisches Handbuch für Heimatforschung in Niedersachsen* (ed. H. Jäger), (Hildesheim, 1965), 409–26
Ewald, K. Ch. *Agrarmorphologische Untersuchungen im Sundgau (Oberelsass) unter besonderer Berücksichtigung der Wölbäcker* (Liestal, 1969)
Meibeyer, W. 'Über den Profilaufbau des Pflughorizontes in Wölbäckern', *Zeitschr. f. Agrargeschichte u. Agrarsoziologie*, 17 (1969), 161–70
Müller-Wille, *Eisenzeitliche Fluren in den festländischen Nordseegebieten* (Münster, 1965)

14 Semmel, A. and Machann, R. 'Historische Bodenerosion auf Wüstungsfluren deutscher Mittelgebirge', *Geographische Zeitschrift*, 59 (1970), 250–66

15 Guyan, W. U. 'Die ländliche Siedlung des Mittelalters in der Nordschweiz', *Geographica Helvetica*, 23 (1968), 57–71

16 Düsterloh, D. *Beiträge zur Kulturgeographie des Niederbergisch-märkischen Hügellandes* (Göttingen, 1967)

17 Krüger, H. 'Des Nürnberger Meisters Erhard Etzlaub älteste Strassenkarte von Deutschland', *Jahrbuch f. Fränkische Landes-forschung*, 18 (1958), 1–286
Denecke, D. *Methodische Untersuchungen zur historisch-geographischen Wegeforschung im Raum zwischen Solling und Harz. Ein Beitrag zur Rekonstruktion der mittelalterlichen Kul-turlandschaft* (Göttingen, 1969)

18 Fink, J. 'Die Veränderung der Böden in der Kulturlandschaft', *Mitt. d. Österreichischen Geogr. Ges.*, 105 (1963), 511-18

19 Firbas, F. *Waldgeschichte Mitteleuropas*, 2 vols (Jena, 1949, 52)

Krausch, D. 'Die Menzer Heide', *Jahrbuch f. Brandenburgische Landesgeschichte,* 13 (1962), 96–118

Rubner, H. 'Wald und Siedlung im Frühmittelalter am Beispiel d. Landschaften zwischen Alpen und Main' *Ber. z. deutschen Landeskunde,* 32 (1964), 114–27

Rubner, H. 'Siedlungsland und Wald im 6. Jahrhundert', *Bayerischer Geschichtsatlas* (München, 1969), map 8a

20 Bönisch, F. 'Die Fluren der Gemarkung Klein-Räschen', *Jahrb. für brandenburgische Landesgeschichte,* (1960), 101–17

21 Schmidt-Kraepelin, E. and Schneider, S. *Luftbildinterpretation in der Agrarlandschaft* (Bad Godesberg, 1966)

22 Neef, E. 'Über die Veränderlichkeit unserer geographischen Umwelt', *Ber. über d. Verhandl. d. sächs. Akad. d. Wissensch. Leipzig, Math.-Nat. Kl.,* 103.4 (1959), 1–19

Jäger, H. 'Zur Erforschung der mittelalterlichen Landesnatur', *Studi Medievali,* 3a S, IV (1963), 1–51

Glässer, E. 'Zur Frage der anthropogen bedingten Vegetation, vor allem in Mitteleuropa', *Die Erde,* 100 (1969), 37–45

Hard, G. 'Vegetation und Kulturlandschaft an der Dogger-Stufe des Metzer Landes', *Decheniana,* 119 (1968), 141-82

23 Flohn, H. 'Die Klimaschwankungen in historischer Zeit', in: v. Rudloff, H. *Die Schwankungen und Pendelungen des Klimas in Europa seit dem Beginn der regelmässigen Instrumenten-Beobachtungen 1670* (Braunschweig, 1967)

24 Fels, R. *Der wirtschaftende Mensch als Gestalter der Erde,* (2nd ed. Stuttgart, 1967)

25 Haarnagel, W. 'Die prähistorischen Siedlungsformen im Küstengebiet der Nordsee', *Beiträge zur Genese der Siedlungs- und Agrarlandschaft in Europa* (Wiesbaden, 1968), 67–84

Hafemann, D. *Die Niveauveränderungen an den Küsten Kretas seit dem Altertum* (Mainz, 1966)

Wilhelmy, H. 'Verschollene Städte im Indusdelta', *Geographische Zeitschr.,* 56 (1968), 256–94

Dongus, H. 'Die Entwicklung der östlichen Poebene seit frühgeschichtlicher Zeit', *Erdkunde,* 17 (1963), 205–22

26 Goehrke, C. 'Geographische Grundlagen der russischen Geschichte', *Jahrb. f. Geschichte Osteuropas,* 18 (1970), 161–204

27 Lautensach, H. 'Otto Schlüter's Bedeutung für die methodische Entwicklung der Geographie', *Petermanns Geogr. Mitt.,* 96 (1952), 219–231

Bobek, H. 'The Main Stages in Socioeconomic Evolution from a Geographic Point of View'. In: *Readings in Cultural Geography* (ed. P. L. Wagner and M. W. Mikesell), Chicago, 1962, 218–47

28 Grund, A. 'Die Veränderungen der Topographie im Wiener Wald und Wiener Becken', *Geogr. Abhandl.*, 8 (Leipzig, 1901)

Jäger, H. 'Wüstungforschung und Geographie', *Geogr. Zeitschrift*, 56 (1968), 165–180

Goehrke, C. *Die Wüstungen in der Moskauer Rus* (Wiesbaden, 1968)

Janssen, W. 'Burg und Siedlung als Problem der Rheinischen Wüstungsforschung', *Chateau Gaillard*, 3 (1969), 77–89

Fehring, G. P. 'Grabungen in Siedlungsbereichen des 3. bis 13. Jahrhunderts sowie an Töpferöfen der Wüstung Wülfingen am Kocher', *Chateau Gaillard*, 3 (1969), 48–60

Hütteroth, W. D. *Ländliche Siedlungen im südlichen Inneranatolien in den letzten vierhundert Jahren* (Göttingen, 1968)

29 Jäger, H., Krenzlin, A., Uhlig, H. (Editors) *Beiträge zur Genese der Siedlungs- und Agrarlandschaft in Europa* (Wiesbaden, 1968)

Uhlig, H. (Editor) *Flur und Flurformen* (Giessen, 1967)

30 Eitzen, G. 'Deutsche Hausforschung in den Jahren 1953–62', *Zeitschrift f. Agrargesch. u. Agrarsoziologie*, 11 (1963), 213—33

Krenzlin, A. 'Probleme geographischer Hausforschung', *Wissenschaftl. Zeitschr. d. Ernst-Moritz-Arndt-Univ.*, Math.-Nat. R. IV (1954/55), 629–41

Schröder, K.H. 'Einhaus und Gehöft in Südwestdeutschland', in: *Berichte zur deutsch. Landeskunde*, 31 (1963), 84–103

Weiss, R. *Häuser und Landschaften der Schweiz* (Erlenbach-Zürich, 1959)

31 Bobek, H. and Lichtenberger, E. *Wien. Bauliche Gestalt und Entwicklung seit der Mitte des 19. Jahrhunderts* (Graz/Köln, 1966)

Leister, I. 'Marburg', *Marburger Geogr. Schr.*, 30 (1967), 3–76

Keyser, E. *Städtegründungen und Städtebau in Nordwestdeutschland im Mittelalter* (Remagen, 1958)

Schöller, P. *Die deutschen Städte* (Wiesbaden, 1967)

32 Stewig, R. *Byzanz-Konstantinopel-Istanbul* (Kiel, 1964)

Wirth, E. 'Damaskus-Aleppo-Beirut', *Die Erde*, 97 (1966), 96–137

Wilhelmy, H. *Südamerika im Spiegel seiner Städte* (Hamburg, 1952)

33 Schwarz, G. *Allgemeine Siedlungsgeographie* (3rd ed. Berlin, 1966)

Krenzlin, A. and Reusch, L. *Die Entstehung der Gewannflur nach Untersuchungen im nördlichen Unterfranken* (Frankfurt, 1961)

34 Nitz, H.-J. 'Siedlungsgeographische Beiträge zum Problem der

fränkischen Staatskolonisation im süddeutschen Raum', *Zeitschr. f. Agrargesch. u. Agrarsoziologie,* 11 (1963), 34–62

Fehn, K. *Siedlungsgeschichtliche Grundlagen der Herrschafts- und Gesellschaftsentwicklung in Mittelschwaben* (Augsburg, 1966)

35 Born, M. 'Langstreifenfluren in Nordhessen?' *Zeitschr. f. Agrargeschichte und Agrarsoziologie,* 15 (1967), 105–33

36 Krenzlin, A. *Historische und wirtschaftliche Züge im Siedlungsformenbild des westlichen Ostdeutschland,* (Frankfurt, 1955)

Benthien, B. *Die historischen Flurformen des südwestlichen Mecklenburg* (Schwerin, 1960)

August, O. 'Untersuchungen an Königshufenfluren bei Merseburg', *Deutsche Akad. d. Wissensch. Berlin, Schr, d. Sekt. f. Vor- und Frühgeschichte,* 16 (1964), 375–94

37 Kuls, W. *Wirtschaftsflächen und Feldsysteme im westlichen Hintertaunus* (Frankfurt, 1951)

Herold, A. *Der zelgengebundene Anbau im Randgebiet des fränk. Gäulandes* (Würzburg, 1965)

Galluser, W. A. 'Die Dreizelgenflur im Laufener Jura und ihre heutige Verbreitung im Nahbereich von Basel', *Regio Basiliensis* (1959), 3–10

Sperling, W. and Zigrai, F. 'Siedlungs- und Agrargeographische Studien in der Gemarkung der Gemeinde Liptovská Teplička', *Geografický Časopis,* vol 22 (1970) 3–18

Otremba, E. *Atlas d. deutchen Agrarglandschaft* (Wiesbaden, 1962 ff)

38 Jäger, H. 'Der agrarlandschaftliche Umbau des 19. Jahrh.' In: *Unterfranken im 19. Jahrhundert* (Würzburg, 1965)

Borcherdt, Chr. 'Beiträge zur Kenntnis der bayerischen Agrarlandschaft im beginnenden 19. Jahrhundert', *Mitteilungen der geographischen Gesellschaft München,* 40 (1955) 121–143

Hahn, H. 'Eine Karte der Flächennutzung 1803–1820', *Erdkunde,* 21 (1967), 226–230

Pape, H. *Die Kulturlandschaft des Stadtkreises Münster um 1828 aufgrund der Katasterunterlagen* (Remagen, 1956)

39 Schröder, K. H. *Weinbau und Siedlung in Württemberg* (Remagen, 1953)

Winkelmann, R. *Die Entwicklung des Oberrheinischen Weinbaus* (Marburg, 1960)

Tisowsky, K. *Häcker und Bauern in den Weinbaugemeinden am Schwanberg* (Frankfurt, 1957)

Krausch, H.-D. 'Der frühere Weinbau in der Niederlausitz', *Jahrbuch f. Brandenburgische Landesgesch.,* 18 (1967), 12–55

Hahn, H. *Die deutschen Weinbaugebiete. Ihre historisch-geographische Entwicklung und Wirtschafts- und Sozialstruktur* (Bonn, 1956)

Morawetz, S. 'Der Rückgang des Weinbaus in der südwestlichen Steiermark von 1823/26 bis 1955', *Mitt. der österr. Geogr. Ges.-Wien.* 105 (1963), 187–209

40 Schlüter, O. *Die Siedlungsräume Mitteleuropas in Frühgeschichtlicher Zeit* (Remagen, 1952, 1953, 1958)

Mager, F. *Der Wald in Altpreusen als Wirtschaftsraum*, 2 vols (Köln/Graz, 1960)

Rubner, H. 'Wald und Siedlung im Frühmittelalter am Beispiel Der Landschaften zwischen Alpen und Main', *Ber. z. deutschen Landeskunde*, 32 (1964), 114–27

Rubner, H. 'Siedlungsland und Wald im 6. Jahrhundert', *Bayerischer Geschichtsatlas* (München, 1969), map 8a

Krausch, H. D. 'Der frühere Weinbau in der Nieder lausitz', *Jahrbuch f. Brandenburgische Landegesch.*, 18 (1967), 12–55

Krausch, H. D. 'Die Menzer Heide', *Jahrbuch f. Brandenburgische Landesgeschichte*, 13 (1962), 96–118

Jäger, H. 'Alte Kiefernbestände im fränkischen Laubholzgebiet', *Jahrb. f. fränk. Landesforsch.*, 26 (1966), 217–37

Tichy, F. *Die Land- und Waldwirtschaftsformationen des Kleinen Odenwaldes* (Heidelberg, 1958)

Hendinger, H. 'Wandlungen der Waldbesitzstruktur und der Forstwirtschaft in Franken durch machtpolitische und wirtschaftliche Einflüsse in Napoleonischer Zeit', *Forstwissensch. Zentralblatt*, 85 (1966), 65–128

Jäger, H. 'Der Wald im nördlichen Süddeutschland und seine historisch-geographische Bedingtheit', *Mélanges de Géographie* (Gembloux, 1968), 597–613

Troll, C. 'Die Stellung des Waldes in den deutschen Kultur- und Wirtschaftslandschaften', in: *Die Bedeutung des Waldes in der Raumordnung, Schr. d. deutschen Forstwirtschaftsrates* (1962), 3–30

Abrahamczik, W. 'Die Almen und Wälder im steirischen Teil des Dachstein-Stockes in ihrer historischen Entwicklung', *Centralblatt für das gesamte Forstwesen*, 79 (Wien, 1962), 17–104

41 Overbeck, H. *Die gewerblich-industriellen Wirkkräfte im Werden der Stadt Heidelberg.* In Overbeck H. *Kulturlandschaftsforschung und Landeskunde* (Heidelberg, 1965) 240–8

Mertins, G. *Die Kulturlandschaft des westlichen Ruhrgebietes.* (Giessen, 1964)

Ritter, G. *Velbert, Heiligenhaus, Tönisheide* (Ratingen, 1965)

42 Hahn, H., Krings, W., Zorn, W. 'Historische Wirtschaftskarte der Rheinlande um 1820', *Erdkunde*, 24 (1970), 169–180

43 Historische Raumforschung 1–7, *Forschungs- und Sitzungsberichte d. Akademie f. Raumforschung und Landespanung*, 6, 10, 15, 21, 30, 31, 48, 50 (1956–69)

44 Huttenlocher, F. 'Die ehemaligen Territorien des deutschen Reiches in ihrer kulturlandschaftlichen Bedeutung', *Erdkunde*, 11 (1957), 95–106

Metz, F. 'Bistum und Hochstift Speyer', *Geographische Zeitschrift*, 54 (1966), 72–96

Overbeck, H. *Kulturlandschaftsforschung und Landeskunde*, (see reference 41)

Pfeifer, G. 'Die Rhein-Neckar-Lande im Wandel historisch-geographischer Situationen'. In *Heidelberg und die Rhein-Neckar-Lande* (Wiesbaden, 1966)

Schöller, P. 'Die Bedeutung einer alten Territorialgranze für die heutige Verflochtenheit des bergisch-märkischen Industriegebiets', *Petermanns Geogr. Mitt.*, 97 (1953), 187–192

Fricke, W. 'Die Beeinflussung der sozialräumlichen Struktur durch Nassauische Territorien', *Nassauische Annalen*, 71 (1960), 174–84

Lamping, H. *Zur Relevanz administrativer Zentren und Einheiten für die Entwicklung zentraler Orte und ihrer Bereiche* (Würzburg, 1970)

45 Schulten, A. *Iberische Landeskunde* (2 vol, Strasbourg/Kehl, 1955, 57)

46 Philippson, A. *Die Griechischen Landschaften* (Lehmann, H. and Kirsten, E. [eds] 4 vols, Frankfurt 1951–59)

47 Mortensen, H. and G., see reference 4

Oberbeck, G. *Die mittelalterliche Kulturlandschaft des Gebietes um Gifhorn* (Bremen-Horn, 1957)

Herzog, F. *Das Osnabrücker Land im 18. und 19. Jahrhundert* (Oldenburg, 1938)

48 Mager, F. *Entwicklungsgeschichte der Kulturlandschaft des Herzogtums Schleswig in Historischer Zeit* (vol 1 Breslau, 1930, vol 2 Kiel, 1937)

Guyan, W. U. 'Beiträge zur Kulturlandschaftsgeschichte des Durachtals'. In *Das Durachtal* (Schaffhausen, 1968), 27–54

Winkler, E. 'Fünfzig Jahre Schweizerische Kulturlandschafts-geschichtsforschung', *Zeitschr. f. Schweizerische Gesch.*, 24 (1944), 107–28

Jäger, H. 'Zur Geschichte der deutschen Kulturlandschaften', *Geogr. Zeitschr.*, 51 (1963), 90–143

Hütteroth, see reference no 28

49 Pfeifer, G. *Atlantische Welt. Probleme der Gestaltung neuweltlicher Kulturlandschaften* (Würzburg, 1966)
Tichy, F. 'Die Entwicklung der Agrarlandschaften seit der vorkolumbinischen Zeit'. In: *Das Mexiko-Projekt der Deutschen Forschungsgemeinschaft* (Wiesbaden, 1968), 145–52
Rostankowski, P. *Siedlungsentwicklung und Siedlungsformen in den Ländern der russischen Kosakenheere* (Berlin, 1969)

50 Engelhard, K. *Die Entwicklung der Kulturlandschaft des nördlichen Waldeck seit dem späten Mittelalter* (Giessen, 1967)
Röll, W. *Die kulturlandschaftliche Entwicklung des Fuldaer Landes seit der Frühneuzeit* (Giessen, 1966)
Marten, H.-R. *Die Entwicklung der Kulturlandschaft im alten Amt Aerzen des Landkreises Hameln-Pyrmont* (Göttingen, 1969)
Fliedner, D. *Die Kulturlandschaft der Hamme-Wümme-Niederung* (Göttingen, 1970)

51 Franz, G. *Historische Kartographie. Forschung u. Bibliographie* 2. ed. Hannover, 1962). Since published: Alter, W. (Editor) *Pfalzatlas* (Speyer, 1963 ff); Amann, H. and Meynen, E. (eds) *Geschichtlicher Atlas für das Land an der Saar* (Saarbrücken, 1965 ff)
Mortensen, H., Mortensen, G., Wenskus, R. *Historisch-geographischer Atlas des Preussenlandes* (Wiesbaden, 1968 ff)
Franz, G. 'Historische Kartographie' (annotated bibliography), *Blätter für Deutsche Landesgeschichte,* 105 (1969), 175–85 and 106 (1970), 175–80

Chapter 4 Historical Geography in Scandinavia

1 Jäger, H. *Historische Geographie* (Braunschweig, 1969) ; Baker, A., Butlin, R., Philips, A. D. M., and Prince, H. C. 'The future of the past', *Area,* no 4 (1969), 46–51

2 Wührer, K. 'Die agrargeschichtliche Forschung in Skandinavien seit 1945', *Zeitschrift für Agrargeschichte und Agrarsoziologie,* 5 (1957), 198–220 ;
Jäger, H. 'Neuere Arbeiten zur Genese Schwedischer Kulturlandschaften.' *Göttingische Gelehrte Anzeigen,* 217 (1965), 295–311

3 Fink, T. *Udskiftningen i Sønderjylland indtil 1770* (Copenhagen, 1941)

4 Helmfrid, S. 'The Storskifte, Enskifte and Laga skifte in Sweden

—General Features', *Geografiska Annaler,* 43 (1961), 111–29

5 Helmfrid, S. Östergötland "Västanstång". Studien über die ältere Agrarlandschaft und ihre Genese', *Geografiska Annaler,* 44 (1962), 1–277

6 Hatt, G. *Oldtidsagre* (Copenhagen, 1949)

7 Nordholm, G. 'Forntida och medeltida åkrar i Kungsmarken', *Skånes naturskyddsförenings årsskrift,* 24 (1937), 84–103

8 Mortensen, H. and Scharlau, K. 'Der siedlungskundliche Wert der Kartierung von Wüstungsfluren.' *Nachrichten der Akademei der Wissenchaften in Göttingen, Phil.-Hist. Klasse,* 8 (1499), 303–31

9 Lindquist, S.-O. *Det förhistoriska kulturlandskapet i östra Östergötland* (Stockholm, 1968) ;
Rønneseth, O. *Frühgeschichtliche Siedlungs- und Wirtschaftsformen,* (Neumünster, 1966)

10 Hannerberg, D. 'Die Parzellierung vorgeschichtlicher Kammerfluren und deren spätere Neuparzellierung durch "Bolskifte" und "Solskifte" ', *Zeitschrift für Agrargeschichte und Agrarsoziologie,* 6 (1959), 101–58

11 Stenberger, M. and Klindt-Jensen, O. *Vallhagar—A Migration Period Settlement on Gotland, Sweden* (Copenhagen and Stockholm, 1955)

12 Ambrosiani, B. *Fornlämningar och bebyggelse* (Uppsala, 1964)

13 *Ødegårder og ny bosetning i de nordiske land i sermiddelalderen* (Bergen, 1964)

14 Helmfrid, S. *Gutsbildung und Agrarlandschaft in Schweden im 16.-17. Jahrhundert. Visbysymposiet för historiska vetenskaper* (Stockholm, 1965)

15 Torbrand, D. *Johannishus fideikommiss intill 1735* (Uppsala, 1963)

16 Jutikkala, E. *Suomi, a General Handbook on the Geography of Finland, Fennia,* 72 (1952)

17 Thor, L. 'De administrativa gränsdragningarna i södra delen av Kalmar län intill 1500-talets mitt', *Forskningsprojektet Administrativa Rumsliga System, Meddelande, no* 22 (1969)—stencil

18 Enequist, G. *Geographical Changes of Rural Settlement in Northwestern Sweden since 1523* (Uppsala, 1959)

19 Rudberg, S. *Ödemarkerna och den perifera bebyggelsen i inre Nordsverige* (Uppsala, 1957)

20 Bylund, E. *Koloniseringen av Pite lappmark t.o.m. år 1867* (Uppsala, 1956)

21 Hultblad, F. *Övergang från nomadism till agrar bosättning i Jokkmokks socken* (Lund, 1969)

22 Hastrup, F. *Danske landsbytyper* (Copenhagen, 1968)

23 Sporrong, U. 'Kulturlandskapsutveckling och administrativ indelning', *Ymer*, 89 (1969), 31–43

24 Göransson, S. 'Field and village on the island of Öland', *Geografiska Annaler*, 40 (1958), 101–58

25 Helmfrid, S. (ed) 'Morphogenesis of the agrarian landscape', *Geografiska Annaler* 43 (1961), 1–328

26 Hannerberg, D. 'Tunnland, öresland, utsäde och tegskifte', *Gothia*, 6 (1946)

27 The well-known features of *bolskifte* and *solskifte* are described in many texts, see for instance Hannerberg, D. 'Solskifte and older methods of partitioning arable land in Central Sweden during the Middle Ages', *Annales de l'Est*, 21 (1959), 245–59

28 Andersson, H. *Parzellierung und Gemengelage* (Lund, 1959)

29 Hannerberg, D. 'Byamål och tomtreglering i Mellansverige före solskiftet', *Ymer*, 79 (1959), 161–93

30 Hannerberg, D. 'Bytomt och samhällsplanering', *Ymer*, 86 (1966), 55–83

31 Sporrong, U. *Kolonisation, bebyggelseutveckling och administration. Studier över det agrara kulturlandskapets utveckling under vikingatiden och tidig medeltid med exempel från Uppland och Närke* (Lund, 1971)

32 Steensberg, A. *Atlas over Borups agre 1000–1200 e. Kr.* (Copenhagen, 1968);
Steensberg, A. 'Village fields from A.D. 1000–1200 mapped and investigated in a Danish wold', *VIIIth Congress of Anthropological and Ethnological sciences*, (Tokyo, 1968), 159–60

33 Hansen, R. and Steensberg, A. *Jordfordeling og Udskiftning* (Copenhagen, 1951)

34 Hastrup, F. 'Danske vangelag i nordisk perspektiv', *Kulturgeografi*, no 114 (1970), 65–100

35 Hannerberg, D. 'Part I: Åkerareal, produktion, konsumtionsramar' (stencil, 1970)

36 Jutikkala, E. 'Finland's population movement in the eighteenth century'. In *Population in History*, ed. by D. V. Glass and D. E. C. Eversley, et op. cit.

37 Norborg, K. *Jordbruksbefolkningen i Sverige* (Lund, 1968)

38 Améen, L. *Stadsbebyggelse och domänstruktur* (Lund, 1964)

39 Myklebost, H. 'Norges tettbygde steder 1875–1950', *Ad Novas*, no 14 (1960)

40 Morrill, R. *Migration and the Spread and Growth of Urban Settlement* (Lund, 1965)

41 Sporrong, U. 'Phosphatkartierung und Siedlungsanalyse', *Geografiska Annaler*, 50 (1968), 62–74

42 Fries, M. 'Vegetationsutveckling och odlingshistoria i Varn-hemstrakten', *Acta Phytogeographica Suecica,* 39 (1958)

43 Jeansson, N. R. in *Svensk Geografisk Arsbok* (1961 and 1963)

44 Newcomb, R. M. 'An example of the applicability of remote sensing in historical geography', *Geoforum,* 1 (1970), 89–92

45 Johnsson, B. *Åkerns omfattning vid 1600-talets mitt enligt de geometriska jordeböckerna* (Stockholm, 1965)

46 Hannerberg, D. *Die älteren skandinavischen Ackermasse. Ein Versuch zu einer zusammenfassenden Theorie* (Lund, 1955)

47 Broadbent, S. R. 'Quantum hypotheses', *Biometrica,* vol 42 (1955), 45–57 and 'Examination of a quantum hypothesis based on a single set of data', *Biometrica,* 43 (1956), 32–44

48 *Forskningsprojektet Administrativa Rumsliga System. Meddelande 1, Kulturgeografiska institutionen, Universitetet i Stockholm 1967* and in continuation (stencil)

49 Sahlgren, N. 'Äldre svenska spannmålsmått', *Meddelanden från Kulturgeografiska institutionen vid Stockholms universitet,* no B 12, (Stockholm, 1968)

50 Morrill, *Migration,* and Olsson, G. 'Complementary models: a study of colonisation maps', *Geografiska Annaler,* 50 (1968), 115–32

51 Lindquist, *Förhistoriska kulturlandskapet,* and Bylund, E. *Koloniseringen av Pite lappmark intill år 1867* (Uppsala, 1956)

52 Bylund, *Koloniseringen av Pite lappmark*

53 Bylund, E. 'Theoretical considerations regarding the distribution of settlement in inner north Sweden', *Geografiska Annaler,* 42 (1960), 225–31

54 Olsson, *Geografiska Annaler,* 50, 115–32

55 Bylund, E. 'Generationsvågor och bebyggelsespridning', *Ymer,* 88 (1968), 64–71

56 See a review by Helmfrid, S. 'Nya metoder inom bebyggelse-forskningen', *Svensk Historisk Tidskrift,* II: 32 (1969), 101–8

Chapter 5   *Historical Geography in Britain*

Acknowledgements. A draft of this essay was read on 2 June 1970 before a memorably informal gathering of some of the author's Cambridge colleagues (Professor H. C. Darby, Dr E. A. Wrigley, Dr D. R. Stoddart, Mr J. Langton, Mr H. S. A. Fox and Mr R. M. Smith). He is indebted to them for their helpful comments made in the course of discussion. He is also grateful to Mr F. V. Emery, Dr A. Harris, Mr H. C. Prince and Professor P. Wheatley who kindly read and offered criticisms of drafts of the essay during its preparation.

1 E. M. J. C's review in *Geographical Journal*, 112 (1948), 95–6

⨯ 2 Baker, J. N. L. 'The development of historical geography in Britain during the last hundred years', *Advancement of Science* 8 (1952), 406–12

3 See, for example, the letter by W. H. Parker in *Geographical Journal*, 119 (1953), 369–70, written in defence of J. N. L. Baker's chapter in H. C. Darby (ed), *An Historical Geography of England before 1800* (Cambridge, 1936), which had been criticised in Spate, O. H. K. 'Toynbee and Huntington: a study in determinism', *Geographical Journal*, 118 (1952), 406–24. Spate asserted that the view of historical geography simply as the reconstruction of past human geographies carried with it the risk of a tendency to merely empirical description, and cites Baker's chapter as an example of 'no more than economic history plus maps . . . overlooking political sequences and distributions'

⨯ 4 Wooldridge, S. W. and East, W. G. *The Spirit and Purpose of Geography* (London, 1951) 81. Chapter 5 is a discussion on 'Historical geography'

5 Darby, H. C. 'On the relations of history and geography', *Transactions and Papers of the Institute of British Geographers* 19 (1953), 1-11

6 Mitchell, J. B. *Historical Geography* (London, 1954) 12

7 Darby, *Transactions and Papers of the Institute of British Geographers*, 19, 6 and Darby, H. C. *The Theory and Practice of Geography. An Inaugural Lecture delivered at Liverpool on 7 February 1946* (London, 1947) 19–20

8 Darby, *Transactions and Papers of the Institute of British Geographers*, 19, 6–9

9 Wooldridge and East, *The Spirit and Purpose of Geography*, 81

10 Darby, H. C. 'The changing English landscape', *Geographical Journal*, 117 (1951), 377–94

11 Ogilvie, A. G. 'The time-element in geography', *Transactions and Papers of the Institute of British Geographers*, 18 (1952), 1–16

12 Mitchell, *Historical Geography*, 14

13 Houston, J. M. *A Social Geography of Europe* (London, 1953), 39–46

14 Kirk, W. 'Historical geography and the concept of the behavioural environment', *Indian Geographical Journal*, Silver Jubilee vol (1951), 152–60

15 Brookfield, H. C. 'On the environment as perceived', *Progress in Geography*, 1 (1969), 51–80

16 Kirk, W. 'Problems of geography', *Geography* 48 (1963), 357–72

17 Brookfield, *Progress in Geography*, 1, 54–6; Sauer, C. O. 'Foreword to historical geography', *Annals of the Association of American Geographers*, 31 (1941), 1–24; Wright, J. K. 'Terrae Incognitae: the place of the imagination in geography', *Annals of the Association of American Geographers*, 37 (1947), 1–15; Berkhofer, R. F. *A Behavioral Approach to Historical Analysis* (New York, 1969), 146–68

18 Darby, H. C. *The Domesday Geography of Eastern England* (Cambridge, 1952)

19 Darby, H. C. 'Domesday woodland in East Anglia', *Antiquity*, 8 (1934), 185–99

20 Johnson, B. L. C. 'The charcoal iron industry in the early eighteenth century', *Geographical Journal*, 117 (1961), 167–77; Lambert, A. M. 'The agriculture of Oxfordshire at the end of the eighteenth century', *Agricultural History*, 29 (1955), 31–8; Henderson, H. C. K. 'Agriculture in England and Wales in 1801', *Geographical Journal*, 118 (1952), 338–45; Bull, G. B. G. 'Thomas Milne's land utilization map of the London area in 1800', *Geographical Journal*, 122 (1956), 25–30; Lawton, R. 'The economic geography of Craven in the early nineteenth century', *Transactions and Papers of the Institute of British Geographers*, 20 (1954), 93–111

21 Darby, H. C. *The Draining of the Fens* (Cambridge, 1940); *Geographical Journal*, 117; 'Man and the landscape in England', *Journal of the Town Planning Institute*, 39 (1953), 74–80; 'The clearing of the English woodlands', *Geography*, 36 (1951), 71–83; 'The clearing of the woodland in Europe', in Thomas, W. L. (ed) *Man's Role in Changing the Face of the Earth* (Chicago, 1956), 183–216

22 Dickinson, R. E. 'Rural settlements in the German lands', *Annals of the Association of American Geographers*, 39 (1949), 239–63; Monkhouse, F. J. *The Belgian Kempenland* (Liverpool, 1949) 36–92; Mead, W. R. *Farming in Finland* (London, 1953) 43–82; Darby, H. C. 'The movement of population to and from Cambridgeshire between 1851 to 1861', *Geographical Journal*, 101 (1943), 118–26; Constant, A. 'The geographical background of inter-village population movements in Northamptonshire and Huntingdonshire, 1754–1943', *Geography*, 33 (1948), 78–88; Smith, C. T. 'The movement of population in

England and Wales in 1851 and 1861', *Geographical Journal*, 117 (1951), 200–10

23 Wise, M. J. 'On the evolution of the jewellry and gun quarters in Birmingham', *Transactions and Papers of the Institute of British Geographers*, 15 (1949), 58–72 ; Fuller, G. J. 'The development of roads in the Surrey and Sussex Weald and coastlands between 1700 and 1900', *Transactions and Papers of the Institute of British Geographers*, 19 (1953), 37–49 ; Beaver, S. H. 'The development of the Northamptonshire iron industry, 1851–1930', in Stamp, L. D. and Wooldridge, S. W. (eds) *London Essays in Geography* (London, 1951), 33–58

24 Baker, J. N. L. 'The geography of Daniel Defoe', *Scottish Geographical Magazine*, 47 (1931), 257–69 ; Taylor, E. G. R. 'Leland's England' and 'Camden's England', in Darby, *An Historical Geography of England before 1800*, 330–53 and 354–86

25 Darby, H. C. 'Some early ideas on the agricultural regions of England', *Agricultural History Review*, 2 (1954), 30–47 and 'The regional geography of Thomas Hardy's Wessex', *Geographical Review*, 38 (1948), 426–43

26 Elkins, T. H. 'An English traveller in the Siegerland', *Geographical Journal*, 122 (1956), 306–16 ; Emery, F. V. 'English regional studies from Aubrey to Defoe', *Geographical Journal*, 124 (1958), 315–25

27 Darby, H. C. 'Historical geography', in Finberg, H. P. R. (ed) *Approaches to History* (London, 1962), 127–56 ; 'The problem of geographical description', *Transactions of the Institute of British Geographers*, 30 (1962), 1–14

28 Broek, J. O. M. *The Santa Clara Valley, California* (Utrecht, 1932)

29 Darby, H. C. 'An Historical Geography of England: twenty years after', *Geographical Journal*, 126 (1960), 147–59

30 Darby, *Geographical Journal*, 126, 149

31 Gulley, J. L. M. *The Wealden Landscape in the Early Seventeenth Century and its Antecedents* (Unpublished Ph.D. thesis, University of London, 1960)

32 Harris, A. *The Rural Landscape of the East Riding of Yorkshire 1700–1850* (London, 1961)

33 Roden, D. and Baker, A. R. H. 'Field systems of the Chiltern Hills and of parts of Kent from the late thirteenth to the early seventeenth century', *Transactions of the Institute of British Geographers*, 38 (1966), 73–88 ; Coppock, J. T. 'Land use changes in the Chilterns, 1931–51', *Transactions and Papers of*

the Institute of British Geographers, 20 (1954), 113–40

34 Prince, H. C. 'Historical geography in France', *Geographical Journal,* 124 (1958), 137–9

35 Gulley, J. L. M. 'The retrospective approach in historical geography', *Erdkunde,* 15 (1961), 306–9

36 Eyre, S. R. 'The upward limit of enclosure on the East Moor of north Derbyshire', *Transactions and Papers of the Institute of British Geographers,* 23 (1957), 61–74; Gulley, *The Wealden Landscape;* Baker, A. R. H. 'The field system of an East Kent parish (Deal)', *Archaeologia Cantiana,* 78 (1963), 96–117; Baker, A. R. H. 'Open fields and partible inheritance on a Kent manor', *Economic History Review,* 17 (1964–5), 1–23; Baker, A. R. H. 'Field systems in the Vale of Holmesdale', *Agricultural History Review,* 14 (1966), 1–24; Sheppard, J. A. 'The pre-enclosure field and settlement patterns in an English township (Wheldrake, near York)', *Geografiska Annaler,* 48 (1966), 59–77

37 Baker, A. R. H. 'A note on the retrogressive and restrospective approaches in historical geography', *Erdkunde,* 22 (1968), 243–4

38 Gulley, J. L. M. 'The Turnerian frontier: a study in the migration of ideas', *Tijdschrift voor Economische en Sociale Geografie,* 50 (1959), 65–72 and 81–91

39 Perhaps the most interesting was a study produced by a British historical geographer who had migrated to the United States: D. Ward, 'A comparative historical geography of streetcar suburbs in Boston, Massachusetts and Leeds, England 1850–1920', *Annals of the Association of American Geographers,* 54 (1964), 477–489; see also Roden and Baker, *Transactions and Papers of the Institute of British Geographers,* 38 (1966)

40 Harley, J. B. 'Population trends and agricultural developments from the Warwickshire Hundred Rolls of 1279', *Economic History Review,* 11 (1958–9), 8–18; Glasscock, R. E. 'The distribution of wealth in East Anglia in the early fourteenth century', *Transactions and Papers of the Institute of British Geographers,* 32 (1963), 113–23; Sheail, J. 'Men and their money in Tudor England', *Geographical Magazine,* 42 (1970), 876–84

41 Grigg, D. B. 'Changing regional values during the Agricultural Revolution in South Lincolnshire', *Transactions and Papers of the Institute of British Geographers,* 30 (1962), 91–103

42 For a selection of papers, see: Baker, A. R. H., Hamshere, J. D. and Langton, J. *Geographical Interpretations of Historical Sources. Readings in Historical Geography* (Newton Abbot, 1970)

43 Thomas, D. *Agriculture in Wales during the Napoleonic Wars* (Cardiff, 1963)

44 Harris, *Rural Landscape of the East Riding of Yorkshire* ; Grigg, D. *The Agricultural Revolution in South Lincolnshire* (Cambridge, 1966) ; Williams, M. *The Draining of the Somerset Levels* (Cambridge, 1966)

45 Wrigley, E. A. *Industrial growth and population change* (Cambridge, 1961) ; Hall, P. *The Industries of London since 1861* (London, 1962)

46 eg Donkin, R. A. 'The Cistercian order in medieval England: some conclusions', *Transactions and Papers of the Institute of British Geographers,* 33 (1963), 181–98 ; Jones, G. R. J. 'Early territorial organisation in England and Wales', *Geografiska Annaler,* 43 (1961), 174–81

47 Baker, A. R. H. and Butlin, R. A. (eds) *Studies of Field Systems in the British Isles* (Cambridge, forthcoming) ; Wrigley, E. A. *Population and History* (London, 1969)

48 Lambert, J. M., Jennings, J. N., Smith, C. T., Green, C., and Hutchinson, J. N. 'The making of the Broads: a reconsideration of their origin in the light of new evidence', *Royal Geographical Society Research Series,* 3 (1960)

49 Darby, *Geographical Journal,* 126, 155

50 Yates, E. M. 'History in a map', *Geographical Journal,* 126 (1960), 32–49 ; Watson, J. W. 'Relict geography in an urban community: Halifax, Nova Scotia', in Miller, R. and Watson, J. W. (eds) *Geographical Essays in Memory of Alan G. Ogilvie* (London, 1959), 110–43

51 Conzen, M. R. G. 'Alnwick, Northumberland. A study in town-plan analysis', *Institute of British Geographers Publications,* no 27 (1960) ; Ward, D. 'The pre-urban cadaster and the urban pattern of Leeds', *Annals of the Association of American Geographers,* 52 (1962), 150–66

52 Carter, H. 'The urban hierarchy and historical geography: a consideration with reference to north-east Wales', *Geographical Studies,* 3 (1956), 85–101

53 Harvey, D. W. 'Locational change in the Kentish hop industry and the analysis of land use patterns', *Transactions and Papers of the Institute of British Geographers,* 33 (1963), 123–44

54 Thomas, D. 'The statistical and cartographic treatment of the acreage returns of 1801', *Geographical Studies,* 5 (1958), 15–25 and 'The acreage returns of 1801 for the Welsh borderland', *Transactions and Papers of the Institute of British Geographers,* 26 (1959), 169–183 ; Hall, P. 'The location of the clothing trades in London, 1861–1951', *Transactions and Papers of the Institute of British Geographers,* 28 (1960), 155–78

55 Prince, H. C. 'The geographical imagination', *Landscape*, 9 (1962), 22–5; Mead, W. R. 'Pehr Kalm in the Chilterns', *Acta Geographica*, 17 (1962), 1–33; Emery, F. V. 'Edward Lhuyd and some of his Glamorgan correspondents: a view of Gower in the 1960s', *Transactions of the Honourable Society of Cymmrodorion*, (Session 1965, Part I), 59–114; Lewis, G. M. 'Changing emphases in the description of the natural environment of the American Great Plains area', *Transactions and Papers of the Institute of British Geographers*, 30 (1962), 75–90

56 Haggett, P. and Chorley, R. J. 'Models, paradigms and the new geography', in Chorley, R. J. and Haggett, P. (eds) *Models in Geography* (London, 1967) 19–41

57 Campbell, W. J. and Wood, P. A. 'Quantification and the development of theory in human geography', in Cooke, R. U. and Johnson, J. H. (eds) *Trends in Geography. An Introductory Survey* (London, 1969) 81–9

58 Smith, D. M. 'The British hosiery industry at the middle of the nineteenth century: an historical study in economic geography' *Transactions and Papers of the Institute of British Geographers*, 32 (1963), 125–42; Wightman, W. R. 'The pattern of vegetation in the Vale of Pickering area c. 1300', *Transactions of the Institute of British Geographers*, 45 (1968), 125–42; Wallwork, K. L. 'The calico printing industry of Lancastria in the 1840s', *Transactions of the Institute of British Geographers*, 45 (1968), 143–56

59 Brandon, P. F. 'Medieval clearances in the East Sussex Weald', *Transactions of the Institute of British Geographers*, 48 (1969), 135–53; Clout, H. D. 'The retreat of the wasteland of the Pays de Bray', *Transactions of the Institute of British Geographers*, 47 (1969), 171–89; Mortimore, M. J. 'Landowernship and urban growth in Bradford and its environs in the West Riding conurbation', *Transactions of the Institute of British Geographers*, 46 (1969), 105–19

60 eg Johnson, J. H. 'Harvest migration from nineteenth century Ireland', *Transactions of the Institute of British Geographers*, 41 (1967), 97–112; Lawton, R. 'Population changes in England and Wales in the later nineteenth century: a analysis of trends by Registration Districts', *Transactions of the Institute of British Geographers*, 44 (1968), 55–74

61 Harrison, M. J., Mead, W. R., and Pannett, D. J. 'A Midland ridge-and-furrow map', *Geographical Journal*, 131 (1965), 366–9; Robinson, D. J., Salt, J. and Phillips, A. D. M. 'Strip lynchets

in the Peak District', *North Staffordshire Journal of Field Studies*, 9 (1968), 92–103

62 Smith, C. T., Denevan, W. M. and Hamilton, P. 'Ancient ridged fields in the region of Lake Titicaca', *Geographical Journal*, 134 (1968), 353–67

63 Butlin, R. A. 'Historical geography and local studies in Ireland', *Geographical Viewpoint*, 1 (1966), 141–54

64 Prince, H. C. 'Historical geography', being Report of Section VI, *20th International Geographical Congress Proceedings* (London, 1967) 164–72

65 Prince, H. C. 'Relict landscapes', *Area*, no 1 (1969), 29–31

66 Robinson, D. J. 'Cultural and historical perspective in area studies: the case of Latin America' in Cooke and Johnson, *Trends in Geography*, 253–67

67 French, R. A. 'Historical geography in the USSR', *Soviet Geography: Review and Translation*, 9 (1968), 551–61 ; Perry, P. J. 'H. C. Darby and historical geography: a survey and review', *Geographische Zeitschrift*, 57 (1969), 161–78

68 Prince, *20th International Geographical Congress Proceedings*, 164

69 Smith, C. T. 'Historical geography: current trends and prospects', in Chorley, R. J. and Haggett, P. (eds) *Frontiers in Geographical Teaching* (London, 1965), 118–43

70 Smith, *Frontiers in Geographical Teaching*, 134

71 Smith, C. T. *An Historical Geography of Europe before 1800* (London, 1967) v–x

72 Bowden, M. J. in *Economic Geography*, 46 (1970), 202–3

73 Harvey, D. W. 'Models of the evolution of spatial patterns in human geography', in Chorley and Haggett, *Models in Geography*, 549–608

74 Hepple, L. W. 'Epistemology, model-building and historical geography', *Geographical Articles*, 10 (1967), 42–8

75 Baker, A. R. H., Butlin, R. A., Phillips, A. D. M. and Prince, H. C. 'The future of the past', *Area*, no 4 (1969), 46–51. See also Baker, A. R. H. 'Today's studies of yesterday's geographies', *Geographical Magazine*, 43 (1970–71) 542–3

76 Prince, H. C. 'Progress in historical geography' in Cooke, R. U. and Johnson, J. H. (eds) *Trends in Geography. An Introductory Survey* (London, 1969) 110–22 and 'Real, imagined and abstract worlds of the past' *Progress in Geography*, 3 (1971), 1–86

77 Baker, A. R. H., Hamshere, J. D. and Langton, J. 'Introduction' in Baker, Hamshere and Langton (eds), *Geographical Interpretations of Historical Sources*, 13–25

78 Harvey, D. W. *Explanation in Geography* (London, 1969) 407–32. The quotation is taken from page 431

79 Langton, J. 'Systems theory and the study of change in human geography' *Progress in Geography*, 4 (1972—in the press)

80 Lewis, P. 'A numerical approach to the location of industry exemplified by the distribution of the paper-making industry in England and Wales from 1860 to 1965', *University of Hull Occasional Papers in Geography*, 13 (1969) and 'Measuring spatial interaction' *Geografiska Annaler*, 52 (1970) 22–39

81 Carter, H. 'Urban systems and town morphology', in Bowen, E. G., Carter, H. and Taylor, J. A. (eds) *Geography at Aberystwyth* (Cardiff, 1968) 219–34 and *The Growth of the Welsh City System. An Inaugural Lecture delivered at the University College of Wales Aberystwyth on 12 February 1969* (Cardiff, 1969)

82 Wrigley, E. A. 'A simple model of London's importance in changing English society and economy 1650–1750', *Past and Present*, 37 (1967), 44–70

83 Thomas, D. 'Climate and cropping in the early nineteenth century in Wales', in Taylor, J. A. (ed) *Weather and Agriculture* (Oxford, 1967), 201–12

84 Caroe, L. 'A multivariate grouping scheme: association analysis of East Anglian towns', in Bowen, Carter and Taylor (eds), *Geography at Aberystwyth*, 253–69

85 Porteous, J. D. 'The company town of Goole. An essay in urban genesis', *University of Hull Occasional Papers in Geography*, 12 (1969)

86 Baker, A. R. H. 'Reversal of the rank-size rule: some nineteenth century rural settlement sizes in France', *Professional Geographer*, 21 (1969), 386–92

87 Perry, P. J. 'Working class isolation and mobility in rural Dorset, 1837–1936: a study of marriage distances', *Transactions of the Institute of British Geographers*, 46 (1969), 115–35

88 Carter, F. W. 'An analysis of the medieval Serbian oecumene: a theoretical approach', *Geografiska Annaler*, 51 (1969), 39–56

89 Personal communications from R. M. Smith of University of Cambridge and R. P. Kain of University College London

90 Paterson, J. H. 'The novelist and his region: Scotland through the eyes of Sir Walter Scott', *Scottish Geographical Magazine*, 81 (1965), 146–52; Lowenthal, D. and Prince, H. C. 'English landscape tastes', *Geographical Review*, 55 (1965), 186–222; Lewis, G. M. 'Regional ideas and reality in the Cis-Rocky Mountain West', *Transactions of the Institute of British Geographers*, 38 (1966), 135–50

91 Heathcote, R. L. *Back of Bourke. A Study of Land Appraisal and Settlement in Semi-arid Australia* (Melbourne, 1965)
92 Brookfield, *Progress in Geography*, 1, 57

Chapter 6 Historical Geography in the USSR

1 French, R. A. 'Historical geography in the USSR', *Soviet Geography: Review and Translation*, 9 (1968), 551–3
2 Yatsunskiy, V. 'Predmet i zadachi istoricheskoy geografii', *Istorik Marksist*, no 5/93 (1941), 29
3 Darby, H. C. (ed) *An Historical Geography of England before 1800* (Cambridge, 1936)
4 Yatsunskiy, *Istorik Marksist*, no 5/93, 21
5 ibid
6 Yatsunskiy, V. K. 'Znacheniye istoricheskoy geografii v podgotovke ekonomiko-geografa', *Voprosy Geografii*, 18 (1950), 164
7 Yatsunskiy, V. K. 'Voprosy ekonomicheskogo rayonirovaniya v trudakh V. I. Lenina', *Voprosy Geografii*, 31 (1953), 29
8 Yatsunskiy, *Istorik Marksist*, no 5/93, 26
9 Yatsunskiy, *Voprosy Geografii*, 18, 164
10 Belov, M. I. 'Sovetskiye istoriko-geograficheskiye issledovaniya (nekotoryye itogi i perspektivy)', *Izvestiya Vsesoyuznogo Geograficheskogo Obshchestva*, 99 (1967), 399
11 Yatsunskiy, V. K. *Istoricheskaya Geografiya. Istoriya yeye Vozniknoveniya i Razvitiya v XIV–XVIII vekakh* (Moscow, 1955)
12 Yatsunskiy, *Istorik Marksist*, no 5/93, 29
13 Yatsunskiy, V. K. 'Istoricheskaya geografiya kak nauchnaya distsiplina', *Voprosy Geografii*, 20 (1950), 13–41
14 Yatsunskiy, *Voprosy Geografii*, 18, 163–8
15 Yatsunskiy, V. K. 'K voprosu o meste istoriko-geograficheskogo analiza v stranovedcheskikh rabotakh po ekonomicheskoy geografii', *Izvestiya Akademii Nauk. Seriya Geograficheskaya*, no 3 (1956), 109-15
16 Saushkin, Yu. G. 'Kul'turnyy landshaft', *Voprosy Geografii*, 1 (1946), 97
17 Yatsunskiy, *Istorik Marksist*, no 5/93, 28
18 Kirikov, S. V. *Izmeneniya Zhivotnogo Mira v Prirodnykh Zonakh SSSR (XIII–XIXvv.). Stepnaya zona i Lesostep'* (Moscow, 1959), 3

19 Yugay, R. L. 'O vzaimodeystvii istorii geografii i istoricheskoy geografii', *Izvestiya Akademii Nauk. Seriya Geograficheskaya*, no 2 (1970), 106

20 Hooson, D. J. M. 'Methodological clashes in Moscow', *Annals of the Association of American Geographers*, 52 (1962), 469–75

21 Anuchin, V. A. 'The problem of synthesis in geographic science', *Soviet Geography: Review and Translation*, 5 no 4 (1964), 41

22 Saushkin, *Voprosy Geografii*, 1, 105

23 Kalesnik, S. V. 'O klassifikatsii geograficheskikh nauk', *XIX Mezhdunarodnyy Geograficheskiy Kongress v Stokgol'me* (Moscow, 1961), 266–7

24 Markov, K. K. *Paleogeografiya* (Moscow, 1960)

25 Zhekulin, V. S. 'Nekotoryye mysli po povodu istoricheskoy geografii, *Izvestiya Vsesoyuznogo Geograficheskogo Obshchestva*, 97 (1965), 63 [Translated as: 'Some thoughts on the subject of historical geography', *Soviet Geography: Review and Translation*, 9 (1968), 570]

26 ibid, 63

27 ibid

28 Rikhter, G. D. (ed) *Sel'skokhozyaystvennaya Eroziya i Novyye Metody yeye Izucheniya* (Moscow, 1958)

29 Semenova-Tyan-Shanskaya, A. M. 'Izmeneniye rastitel'nogo pokrova lesostepi russkoy ravniny v XVI–XVIII vv. pod vliyaniyem deyatel'nosti cheloveka', *Botanicheskiy Zhurnal*, 42 (1957), 1400–1

30 Sinskaya, Ye. N. *Istoricheskaya Geografiya Kul'turnoy Flory* (Leningrad, 1969)

31 Mordvinkina, A. I. 'K istorii kul'tury ovsa v SSSR', *Materialy po Istorii Sel'skogo Khozyaystva i Krest'yanstva SSSR*, 4 (1960), 313–65

32 Gedymin, A. V. 'Opyt ispol'zovaniya materialov Russkogo mezhevaniya v geograficheskikh issledovaniyakh dlya sel'skokhozyaystvennykh tseley', *Voprosy Geografii*, 50 (1960), 147–71 [Translated as: 'The use of old Russian land survey data in geographic research for agricultural purposes', *Soviet Geography: Review and Translation*, 9 (1968), 602–24]

33 Fat'yanov, A. S. 'Opyt analiza istorii razvitiya pochvennogo pokrova Gor'kovskogo oblasti', *Pochvenno-geograficheskiye Issledovaniya i Ispol'zovaniye Aerofotos''yemki v Kartirovanii Pochv* (Moscow, 1959), 3–171

34 Gedymin, A. V., Pobedintseva, I. G. 'Opyt issledovaniya vliyaniya dlitel'noy raspashki na svoystva obyknovennykh chernozemov', *Pochvovedeniye*, no 5 (1964), 35–46

35 Kirikov, S. V. 'Istoricheskiye izmeneniya zhivotnogo mira nashey strany v XIII–XIX vv. (Soobshcheniye 4e)', *Izvestiya Akademii Nauk. Seriya Geograficheskaya*, no 1 (1958), 71

36 Kirikov, S. V. 'Les changements dans la distribution des oiseaux de la partie européene de l'Union Soviétique aux XVIIe–XIXe siècles', *Proceedings of the XIIth International Ornithological Congress, Helsinki 1958* (Helsinki, 1960), 404–21

37 Kirikov, S. V. *Promyslovyye Zhivotnyye, Prirodnaya Sreda i Chelovek* (Moscow, 1966), 310

38 Kirikov, S. V. 'Proshloye (XVI–XIX stoletiya) i sovremennoye razmeshcheniye promyslovykh zverey v SSSR', *XIX Mezhdunarodnyy Geograficheskiy Kongress v Stokgol'me* (Moscow, 1961), 220–4

39 Kirikov, *Izmeneniya Zhivotnogo Mira . . .* (1959), 127–9

40 Kirikov, S. V. 'Istoricheskiye izmeneniya zhivotnogo mira nashey strany v XIII–XIX vekakh. Soobshcheniye 2e. Izmeneniye yestyestvennykh ugodiy i zhivotnogo mira podmoskovnogo kraya v XIV–XVIII vekakh', *Izvestiya Akademii Nauk. Seriya Geograficheskaya*, no 4 (1953), 15–27

41 Kirikov, S. V. *Ptitsy i Mlekopitayushchiye v Usloviyakh Landshaftov Yuzhnoy Okonechnosti Urala* (Moscow, 1952)

42 Kirikov, *Izmeneniya Zhivotnogo Mira . . .* (1959)

43 Kirikov, S. V. *Izmeneniya Zhivotnogo Mira v Prirodnykh Zonakh SSSR (XIII–XIXvv.). Lesnaya Zona i Lesotundra* (Moscow, 1960)

44 Kirikov, *Promyslovyye Zhivotnyye . . .* (1966)

45 The first eight articles are available in English translation in *Soviet Geography: Review and Translation,* 5 no 6 (1964), 54–68 ; 7 no 2 (1966), 14–27 ; 7 no 2 (1966), 27–36 ; 7 no 10 (1966), 34–45 ; 9 no 1 (1968), 23–35 ; 9 no 1 (1968), 36–47 ; 9 no 7 (1968), 590–602 ; 11 no 7 (1970), 565–79

46 Gumilev, L. N. 'Po povodu predmeta istoricheskoy geografii (landschaft i etnos) III', *Vestnik Leningradskogo Universiteta*, no 18 (1965), 115

47 ibid, 114

48 ibid, 115

49 Gumilev, L. N. 'Ob antropogennom faktore landshaftoobrazovaniya (landshaft i etnos) VII', *Vestnik Leningradskogo Universiteta*, no 24 (1967), 106–7

50 Gumilev, L. N. 'Khazariya i Kaspiy (landshaft i etnos) I', *Vestnik Leningradskogo Universiteta*, no 6 (1964), 95

51 Gumilev, L. N. 'Geterokhronnost' uvlazhneniya Yevrazii v

drevnosti (landshaft i etnos) IV', *Vestnik Leningradskogo Universiteta,* no 6 (1966), 62–71

52 Gumilev, L. N. 'Geterokhronnost' uvlazhneniya Yevrazii v sredniye veka (landshaft i etnos) V', *Vestnik Leningradskogo Universiteta,* no 18 (1966), 81–90

53 Gumilev, L. N. *Khunny* (Moscow, 1960)

54 Gumilev, L. N. 'New data on the history of the Khazars', *Acta Archaeologica Academiae Scientiarum Hungaricae,* no 19 (1967), 61–103

55 Gumilev, L. N. 'Khazariya i Terek (landshaft i etnos) II', *Vestnik Leningradskogo Universiteta,* no 24 (1964), 78–88

56 Gumilev, *Vestnik Leningradskogo Universiteta,* no 6 (1964), 83–95

57 Gumilev, *Vestnik Leningradskogo Universiteta,* no 18 (1965), 117

58 ibid

59 ibid, 114

60 Stalin, I. V. *Istoriya VKP(b). Kratkiy kurs* (Moscow, 1936), 113

61 Gumilev, L. N. 'Etnos i landshaft. Istoricheskaya geografiya kak narodovedeniye', *Izvestiya Vsesoyuznogo Geograficheskogo Obshchestva,* 100 (1968), 195

62 Gumilev, *Vestnik Leningradskogo Universiteta,* no 18 (1965), 113

63 Kharitonychev, A. T. *Rol' Khozyaystvennoy Deyatel'nosti Cheloveka v Izmenenii Landshaftov Gor'kovskogo Pravoberezh'ya* (Gor'kiy, 1960)

64 Hoskins, W. G. *The Making of the English Landscape* (London, 1955)

65 Vorob'yeva, T. N. 'Formirovaniye territorial'nykh razlichiy v khozyaystve yuga vostochnoy Sibiri v pervoy polovine XVIIIv.', *Doklady Instituta Geografii Sibiri i Dal'nego Vostoka,* 10 (1965), 59–67

66 Saushkin, Yu. G. 'Sovremennoye sistema geograficheskikh nauk v SSSR', *Vestnik Moskovskogo Universiteta. Seriya V. Geografiya,* no 4 (1959), 9

67 Pokshishevskiy, V. V. 'K geografii dooktyabr'skikh kolonizatsionno-migratsionnykh protsessov v yuzhnoy chasti dal'nego vostoka', *Sibirskiy Geograficheskiy Sbornik,* 1 (1962), 85–92 [Translated as: 'On the geography of pre-Revolutionary colonization and migration processes in the southern part of the Soviet Far East', *Soviet Geography: Review and Translation,* 4 no 4 (1963), 17–31]

68 Pokshishevskiy, V. V. 'Territorial'noye formirovaniye promyshlennogo kompleksa Peterburga v XVIII–XIX vekakh', *Voprosy Geografii,* 20 (1950), 122–62

69 Vitov, M. V. *Istoriko-geograficheskiye Ocherki Zaonezh'ya XVI–XVIIvv.* (Moscow, 1962)
70 ibid, 158
71 Tikhomirov, M. N. *Rossiya v XVI Stoletii* (Moscow, 1962)
72 Strumilin, S. G. *Istoriya Chernoy Metallurgii v SSSR* (Moscow, 1954)
73 Pazhitnov, K. A. *Ocherki Istorii Tekstil'noy Promyshlennosti Dorevolyutsionnoy Rossii* (Moscow, 1958)
74 Shunkov, V. I. *Ocherki po Istorii Zemledeliya Sibiri (XVII vek)* (Moscow, 1956)
75 Rubinshteyn, N. L. *Sel'skoye Khozyaystvo Rossii vo Vtoroy Polovine XVIIIv.* (Moscow, 1957)
76 Kochin, G. Ye. *Sel'skoye Khozyaystvo na Rusi v Period Obrazovaniya Russkogo Tsentralizovannogo Gosudarstva. Konets XIII–nachalo XVIv.* (Moscow, 1965)
77 Druzhinin, N. M. et al (eds) *Goroda Feodal'noy Rossii* (Moscow, 1966)
78 Shunkov, V. I. 'Geograficheskoye razmeshcheniye sibirskogo zemledeliya v XVII veke', *Voprosy Geografii*, 20 (1950), 203–38
79 Bernshteyn-Kogan, S. V. 'Put' iz Varyag v Greki', *Voprosy Geografii*, 20 (1950), 239–70
80 Sverdlov, M. B. 'Tranzitnyye puti v vostochnoy Yevropy IX–XIvv.', *Izvestiya Vsesoyuznogo Geograficheskogo Obshchestva*, 101 (1969), 540–5
81 Lappo, G. M. 'Nekotoryye cherty istoricheskoy geografii gorodov Moskovskoy oblasti', *Voprosy Geografii*, 51 (1961), 27–51
82 Tsvetkov, M. A. *Izmeneniye Lesistosti Yevropeyskoy Rossii s Kontsa XVII Stoletiya po 1914 god* (Moscow, 1957)
83 Zagorovskiy, V. P. *Belgorodskaya Cherta* (Voronezh, 1969)
84 Rashin, A. G. *Naseleniye Rossii za 100 let* (Moscow, 1956)
85 Aleksandrov, V. A. *Russkoye Naseleniye Sibiri XVII–nachala XVIIIv.* (Moscow, 1964)
86 Preobrazhenskiy, A. A. *Ocherki Kolonizatsii Zapadnogo Urala v XVII–nachale XVIIIv.* (Moscow, 1956)
87 Yugay, *Izvestiya Akademii Nauk,* no 2 (1970), 105
88 Belov, *Izvestiya V.G.O.*, 99, 399
89 Yatsunskiy, *Istorik Marksist,* no 5/93, 21
90 Yugay, *Izvestiya Akademii Nauk,* no 2 (1970), 104
91 Yatsunskiy, *Istoricheskaya Geografiya* . . . , 3
92 Yugay, *Izvestiya Akademii Nauk,* no 2 (1970), 106
93 ibid, 108
94 Gumilev, L. N., Kuznetsov, B. I. 'Dve traditsii drevnetibetskoy

kartografii (landshaft i etnos VIII)', *Vestnik Leningradskogo Universiteta,* no 24 (1969), 88–101

95 Trusov, Yu. P. 'The concept of the noosphere', *Soviet Geography: Review and Translation,* 10 (1969), 220–37

Chapter 7 Historical Geography in North America

1 Clark, A. H. 'Historical geography' in James, P. E. and Jones, C. F. (eds) *American Geography: Inventory and Prospect* (Syracuse, 1954) 70–105

2 Harris, R. C. 'Historical geography in Canada', *Canadian Geographer,* 11 (1967), 235–50

3 Among the several critiques of work in historical geography in this period, some of the more useful have been: Darby, H. C. 'On the relations of geography and history', *Transactions of the Institute of British Geographers,* 19 (1953), 1–11 (which was reprinted in several successive editions of Taylor, T. G. (ed) *Geography in the Twentieth Century*); Darby, H. C. 'Historical geography' in Finberg, H. P. R. (ed) *Approaches to History* (London, 1962) 127–56; Smith, C. T. 'Historical geography: current trends and prospects' in Chorley, R. J. and Haggett, P. (eds) *Frontiers in Geographical Teaching* (London, 1965) 118-43; Merrens, H. R. 'Historical geography and early American history', *William and Mary Quarterly,* 3rd ser, 22 (1965), 529–48; Jäger, Helmut *Historische Geographie* (Braunschweig, 1969); and Prince, Hugh 'Progress in historical geography' in Cooke, R. U. and Johnson, J. H. (eds) *Trends in Geography* (London, 1969) 110–22

4 Some of my phraseology is borrowed from Morton Rothstein 'The cotton frontier of the antebellum South; a methodological battleground', *Agricultural History,* 44 (1970), 149–65

5 Parsons, J. J. *Antoquia's Corridor to the Sea: An Historical Geography of the Settlement of Uraba (Ibero-Americana,* no 49) (Berkeley, 1967) and, *idem Antioqueño Colonization in Western Colombia (Ibero-Americana,* no 32) (Berkeley, 1949; 2nd edition, 1969); Sauer, C. O. *The Early Spanish Main* (Berkeley, 1966); Stanislawski, D. *The Individuality of Portugal: A Study in Historical-Political Geography* (Austin, Texas, 1959) and *Landscapes of Bacchus: The Vine in Portugal* (Austin and London,

1970); West, R. C. *The Mining Community in Northern New Spain: The Parral Mining District* (*Ibero-Americana*, no 30) (Berkeley, 1949); and *idem, The Pacific Lowlands of Colombia: A Negroid Area of the American Tropics* (Baton Rouge, 1957)

6   Vandermeer, C. 'Population patterns on the island of Cebu, the Philippines: 1500–1900', *Annals of the Association of American Geographers*, 57 (1967), 315–37

7   Dunbar, G. *Historical Geography of the North Carolina Outer Banks* (Baton Rouge, La., 1958); Wacker, P. O. *The Musconet-cong Valley of New Jersey* (New Brunswick, N. J., 1967); and Kniffen, F. B. *Louisiana: its Land and People* (Baton Rouge, 1968)

8   Clark, A. H. *The Invasion of New Zealand by People, Plants and Animals: The South Island* (New Brunswick, N. J., 1949); *idem, Three Centuries and the Island: A Historical Geography of Settlement and Agriculture in Prince Edward Island, Canada* (Toronto, 1959); and *idem, Acadia: The Geography of Early Nova Scotia to 1760* (Madison, Wisconsin, 1968)

9   Burghardt, Andrew F. *Borderland. A Historical and Geographical Study of Burgenland, Austria* (Madison, 1962); English, Paul W. *City and Village in Iran. Settlement and Economy in the Kirman Basin* (Madison, 1966); Gibson, James R. *Feeding the Russian Fur Trade. Provisionment of the Okhotsk Seaboard and the Kamchatka Peninsula, 1639–1856* (Madison, 1969); Harris, R. Colebrook. *The Seigneurial System in Early Canada: A Geographical Study* (Madison, 1966); Jordan, Terry G. *German Seed in Texas Soil* (Austin, 1966); Lemon, James T. (In press at the Johns Hopkins University Press, Baltimore and tentatively titled:) *The Best Poor Man's Country. A Geographical View of Early Pennsylvania;* and Merrens, H. R. *Colonial North Carolina in the Eighteenth Century: A Study in Historical Geography* (Chapel Hill, 1964)

10   Meinig, D. W. *The Great Columbia Plain* (Seattle, 1963), *idem, Imperial Texas* (Austin, 1968), *idem, On the Margins of the Good Earth: The South Australian Wheat Frontier, 1869–1884* (Chigaco, 1962), and *idem, Southwest: Three Peoples in Geographical Change* (New York, 1971)

11   Isaac, Erich. 'Kent Island. Part I, The period of settlement' and 'Kent Island. Part II, settlements and landholding under the proprietary', *Maryland Historical Magazine*, 52 (1957), 93–119, 210–32

12   Meyer, Alfred H. 'Circulation and settlement patterns of the Calumet region of northwest Indiana and northeast Illinois:

the first stage of occupance—The Pottawatomie and the fur trader—1830', *Annals of the Association of American Geographers,* 44 (1954), 245–74 ; *idem,* '. . . The second stage of occupance—pioneer settlers and subsistence economy, 1830–1950', *ibid,* 46 (1956), 312-56 ; Kaatz Martin R. 'The Black Swamp: a study in historical geography', *ibid,* 45 (1955), 1–35 ; McManis, D. R. *The Initial Evaluation and Utilization of the Illinois Prairies, 1815–1840,* University of Chicago Department of Geography Research Series, no 94 (Chicago, 1964)

13 Warkentin, J. *The Western Interior of Canada: A Record of Geographical Discovery, 1612–1917* (Toronto, 1964) ; Ross, Eric *Beyond the River and the Bay* (Toronto, 1970) ; and Brown, R. H. *Mirror for Americans: Likeness of the Eastern Seaboard, 1810* (New York, 1943)

14 For the studies by Harris, Jordan and Lemon, see reference 9. Sam B. Hilliard's dissertation (a revised, as yet untitled, version is in press at the Southern Illinois University Press) was followed by 'Pork in the ante-bellum South: the geography of self-sufficiency', *Annals of the Association of American Geographers,* 59 (1969), 461–80 ; and 'Hog meat and cornpone: food habits in the ante-bellum South', *Proceedings, American Philosophical Society,* 113 (1969), 1–13. Robert D. Mitchell's dissertation, *The Upper Shenandoah Valley of Virginia During the Eighteenth Century* (Madison, 1969) was followed by 'The commercial nature of frontier settlement in the Shenandoah Valley of Virginia, *Proceedings, Association of American Geographers,* 1 (1969), 109–113. David Ward's dissertation, *Nineteenth Century Boston: A Study in the Role of Antecedent and Adjacent Conditions in the Spatial Aspects of Urban Growth* (Madison, 1963) has been followed by a number of papers relating to research growing out of that investigation of which three examples are: 'A comparative historical geography of streetcar suburbs in Boston, Massachusetts and Leeds, England: 1850–1920', *Annals of the Association of American Geographers,* 54 (1964), 477–89 ; 'The Industrial Revolution and the emergence of Boston's Central Business District', *Economic Geography,* 42 (1966), 152–71 ; and 'The emergence of central immigrant ghettoes in American cities, 1840–1920', *Annals of the Association of American Geographers,* 58 (1968), 343–59

15 Ward, D. *Cities and Immigrants* (New York, 1971)

16 Wade, R. C. *The Urban Frontier* (Chicago, 1967) ; and Wade, R. C. and Mayer, Harold M. *Growth of a Metropolis* (Chicago, 1969)

17 Warner, S. B. *Streetcar Suburbs: The Process of Growth in Boston, 1870–1900* (Cambridge, Mass., 1962) ; *idem The Private City: Philadelphia in Three Periods of Growth* (Philadelphia, 1968)

18 Edited by David T. Gilchrist (Charlottesville, Virginia, 1967)

19 Reps, John W. *The Making of Urban America: A History of City Planning in the United States* (Princeton, 1965) ; and (based on the foregoing), *idem, Town Planning in Frontier America* (Princeton, 1969)

20 Goheen, P. *Victorian Toronto, 1850–1900: Pattern and Process of Growth* (University of Chicago, Department of Geography Research Paper no 127) (Chicago, 1970) ; Spelt, J. *The Urban Development in South Central Ontario* (Assen, 1955) ; Burghardt, A. F. 'The location of river towns in the Central Lowland of the United States', *Annals of the Association of American Geographers*, 49 (1959), 305–23 ; Nelson, H. J. 'Walled cities of the U.S.A.', *ibid* vol 51 (1961), 1–22 ; and Pred, A. *The Spatial Dynamics of United States Urban Industrial Growth, 1800–1914: Interpretative and Theoretical Essays* (Cambridge, Mass. 1966)

21 Galloway, J. H. 'The sugar industry of Pernambuco during the nineteenth century', *Annals of the Association of American Geographers,* 58 (1968), 285–303

22 Burghardt, A. F. 'The origin and development of the road pattern of the Niagara Peninsula, Ontario, 1770–1851', *Annals of the Association of American Geographers*, 59 (1969), 417–40 ; Grey, A. H. 'Denver and the locating of the Union Pacific Railroad, 1862–1866', *The Rocky Mountain Social Science Journal*, 6 (1969), 52–9 ; and *idem*, 'The Union Pacific Railroad and South Pass', *Kansas Quarterly*, 2 (1970), 46–57

23 Two recent examples are Pounds, N. J. G. 'Northwestern Europe in the ninth century: its geography in the light of the polyptyques', *Annals of the Association of American Geographers,* 57 (1967), 439–61 ; and *idem*, 'The urbanization of the classical world', *ibid*, 59 (1969), 135–57

24 Whitney, Herbert. 'Estimating pre-census populations: a method suggested and applied to the towns of Rhode Island and Plymouth colonies in 1689', *Annals of the Association of American Geographers,* 55 (1965), 179–89. Wilbur Zelinsky's work offers an embarrassment of riches from the early 1950s to the late 1960s. Some examples are: 'An isochronic map of Georgia settlement, 1750–1850', *Georgia Historical Quarterly,* 35 (1951), 191–95 ; 'The log house in Georgia', *Geographical Review,* 43 (1953),

173–93 ; and 'Classical town names in the United States: the historical geography of an American idea', *Geographical Review*, 57 (1967), 463–95

25   Three of Mrs Johnson's papers illustrate her breadth of interest ; 'The location of German immigrants in the Middle West', *Annals of the Association of American Geographers*, 41 (1951), 1–41 ; 'Rational and ecological aspects of the quarter section: an example from Minnesota', *Geographical Review*, 47 (1957), 330–48 ; and 'French Canada and the Ohio Country: a study in early spatial relationship', *Canadian Geographer*, 3 (1958), 1–10

26   De Vorsey, Louis. *The Indian Boundary in the Southern Colonies, 1763–1775* (Chapel Hill, N.C., 1966) ; Thompson, Kenneth. 'Insalubrious California: perception and reality', *Annals of the Association of American Geographers*, 59 (1969), 50–64 ; and *idem* 'Irrigation as a menace to health in California: a nineteenth century view', *Geographical Review*, 59 (1969), 195–214

27   Pitts, F. R. 'A graph-theoretic approach to historical geography', *Professional Geographer*, 17 (1955), 15–20

28   eg Morrill, R. L. 'Migration and the spread and growth of urban settlement', *Lund Studies in Geography*, Series B, 26 (Lund, 1965)

29   Chorley, R. J. and Haggett, P. (eds) *Models in Geography* (London, 1967), 549–608

30   Curry, L. 'Quantitative geography, 1967', *Canadian Geographer*, 11 (1967), 265–79

31   Conzen, M. P. *Frontier Farming in an Urban Shadow* (Madison, 1971)

32   Clark, A. H. 'Geographical change: a theme for economic history', *Journal of Economic History*, 20 (1960), 607–13

33   Two of several papers generated by this research were: Weaver, John C. 'Crop combination regions for 1919 and 1929 in the Middle West', *Geographical Review*, 44 (1954), 560-72 ; and *idem* 'Changing patterns of cropland use in the Middle West', *Economic Geography*, 30 (1954), 1–47

34   Hewes, Leslie and Schmieding, Arthur C. 'Risk in the central Great Plains: geographical patterns of wheat failure in Nebraska, 1931–1952', *Geographical Review*, 46 (1956), 375–87 ; Hewes, L. 'Traverse across Kit Carson County Colorado, with notes on land use on the margin of the old Dust Bowl, 1939–40 and 1962', *Economic Geography*, 39 (1963), 332–40 ; and *idem* 'Causes of wheat failure in the Dry Farming Region, Central

Great Plains, 1939–1957', *Economic Geography*, 41 (1965), 313–30

35 Dunbar, G. 'African Ranches, Ltd, 1914–1931', *Annals of the Association of American Geographers*, 60 (1970), 102–23

36 Hart, J. F. 'Loss and abandonment of cleared farm land in the Eastern United States', *Annals of the Association of American Geographers*, 58 (1968), 417–40 ; Zelinsky, W. 'Changes in the geographic pattern of rural population in the United States, 1790–1960', *Geographical Review*, 52 (1962), 492–524

37 Hough, R. F. 'Impact of the decline of raw silk on two major cocoon producing regions in Japan', *Annals of the Association of American Geographers*, 58 (1968), 221–49

38 Jakle, J. A. 'Salt on the Ohio Valley frontier, 1770–1820', *Annals of the Association of American Geographers*, 59 (1969), 687–709 ; and Jakle, J. A. and Wheeler, J. O. 'The changing residential structure of the Dutch population in Kalamazoo, Michigan', *Annals of the Association of American Geographers*, 59 (1969), 441–60

39 Lewis, R. A. and Rowland, R. H. 'Urbanization in the USSR: 1897–1966', *Annals of the Association of American Geographers*, 59 (1969), 776–96 ; Katzman, M. T. 'Ethnic Geography and Regional Economies, 1880–1960', *Economic Geography*, 45 (1969), 45–52

40 Eg Vance, J. E. 'Emerging patterns of commercial structure in American cities', *Lund Studies in Geography*, Series B, 24 (1962) ; and *idem, Geography and Urban Evolution in the San Francisco Bay Area*. University of California Institute of Government Studies (Berkeley, 1964). Vance does have broad historical interests too, however, as witness: 'The Oregon Trail and the Union Pacific Railroad: a contrast in purpose', *Annals of the Association of American Geographers*, 51 (1961), 357–79 ; and 'Housing the worker: determinative and contingent ties in nineteenth century Birmingham', *Economic Geography*, 43 (1967), 95–127

41 Aschmann, H. *The Central Desert of Baja California* (Riverside, Calif., 1967) ; Denevan, W. M. *The Aboriginal Cultural Geography of the Llanos de Mojos of Bolivia (Ibero-Americana* no 48) (Berkeley and Los Angeles, 1968) ; Mikesell, M. *Northern Morocco: A Cultural Geography (University of California Publications in Geography*, 14) (Berkeley, 1961) ; Rostlund, E. 'The myth of a natural prairie belt in Alabama: an interpretation of historical records', *Annals of the Association of American Geographers*, vol 47 (1957), 392–411 ; *idem* 'The geographic

range of the historic bison in the Southeast', *ibid* vol 50 (1960), 395–407 ; Simoons, F. J. *Eat Not This Flesh: Food Avoidances in the Old World* (Madison, 1961) ; *idem, A Ceremonial Ox of India: The Mithan in Nature, Culture and History—With Notes on the Domestication of Common Cattle* (Madison, 1968) ; Sopher, D. E. *The Sea Nomads: A Study Based on the Literature of the Maritime Boat People of Southeast Asia, Memoirs of the National Museum* no 5 (Singapore, 1965) ; and Wagner, P. L. *Nicoya—A Cultural Geography* (*University of California Publications in Geography*, 12, no 3) (Berkeley, 1958)

42 *The Early Spanish Main* was cited in reference 5. *Northern Mists* was also published in Berkeley in 1968. The address was 'Foreword to historical geography', *Annals of the Association of American Geographers,* 31 (1941), 1–24

43 Sauer was one of the co-chairmen of a conference in Princeton, N.J., in 1955 which resulted in Thomas, W. L. ed *Man's Role in Changing the Face of the Earth* (Chicago, 1955) and which was conceived as in the tradition of George Perkins Marsh

44 Chicago, 1964

45 Bergman, J. F. 'The distribution of cacao cultivation in pre-Columbian North America', *Annals of the Association of American Geographers,* 59 (1969), 85–96 ; Fuson, R. H. 'The orientation of Mayan ceremonial centers', *Annals of the Association of American Geographers,* 59 (1969), 494–511 ; and Ross, S. H. 'Metallurgical beginnings: the case for copper in the prehistoric American southwest', *Annals of the Association of American Geographers,* 58 (1968), 360–70

46 Kniffen, F. B. 'The American agricultural fair: the pattern', *Annals of the Association of American Geographers.* 39 (1949), 264–82 ; *idem* 'The American agricultural fair: time and place', *Annals of the Association of American Geographers,* 41 (1951), 42–57 ; *idem* 'The American covered bridge', *Geographical Review,* 41 (1951), 114–23 ; and, *idem,* 'Folk housing: key to diffusion', *Annals of the Association of American Geographers,* 55 (1965), 549–77

47 Pillsbury, R. 'The urban street pattern as a culture indicator: Pennsylvania, 1682–1815', *Annals of the Association of American Geographers,* 60 (1970), 428–46 ; Wacker, P. O. 'Early street patterns in Pennsylvania and New Jersey: a comparison', *Proceedings, Association of American Geographers,* 3 (1970), 1–13 ; and *idem* and Trindell, R. T. 'The log house in New Jersey: origins and diffusion', *Keystone Folklore Quarterly,* 13 (Winter, 1969), 248–68

48 Price, E. T. 'The central courthouse square in the American county seat', *Geographical Review,* 58 (1968), 29–60

49 Pattison, W. D. *Beginnings of the American Rectangular Land Survey System,* (University of Chicago Department of Geography, Research Paper no 50) (Chicago, 1957); Thrower, N. J. W. *Original Land Subdivision: A Comparative Study of the Form and Effect of Contrasting Cadastral Surveys* (Chicago, 1966)

50 See reference 43

51 New York, 1948

52 Two examples of his continuing interest are: Lowenthal, D. 'Geography, experience and imagination: toward a geographical epistemology', *Annals of the Association of American Geographers,* 51 (1961), 241–60; and *idem* and Prince, H. C. 'English landscape tastes', *Geographical Review,* 55 (1965), 186–222

53 Bowden, M. J. 'The perception of the Western Interior of the United States, 1800–1870: a problem in historical geosophy', *Proceedings, Association of American Geographers,* 1 (1969), 16–21

54 Two of his many studies are: Lewis, G. M. 'Three centuries of desert concepts of the Cis-Rocky Mountain West', *Journal of the West,* 4 (1965), 457–68; and *idem* 'William Gilpin and the concept of the Great Plains Region', *Annals of the Association of American Geographers,* 56 (1966), 33–51

55 Kollmorgen, W. M. 'The woodsman's assaults on the domain of the cattleman', *Annals of the Association of American Geographers,* 59 (1969), 215–39; and Webb, W. P. *The Great Plains* (Boston, 1931)

56 Friis, H. R. 'The image of the American West at mid-century (1840–1860): a product of scientific geographical exploration by the United States government', in J. F. McDermott (ed) *The Frontier Re-examined* (Urbana, 1967) 49–63

57 See reference 2

58 Nelson, J. G. 'Man and landscape in the Western Plains of Canada', *Canadian Geographer,* 11 (1967), 251–64

59 See reference 3

60 Broek, J. O. M. *The Santa Clara Valley, California* (Utrecht, 1935)

61 Loyal Durand made the historical geography of the American dairy industry exhaustively his own in more than a dozen publications and Merle Prunty has been especially interested in agricultural land use in the American southeast over the past century and a half. Halleck Raup, for long the editor of *The*

Professional Geographer, and an early Sauer student at Berkeley, has been a steady contributor to our literature; particularly interesting to the writer was his 'Transformation of southern California to a cultivated land', *Annals of the Association of American Geographers,* 49 (1959), 58–79, one of a great many of his studies of the historical geography of that state

62 George Carter, a graduate student at Berkeley contemporary with the writer, Parsons, Stanislawski and West, for long headed the Isaiah Bowman Department of Geography at Johns Hopkins University and now is at Texas A. and M. University. His interests are chiefly in the antiquity of man in the New World and in pre-Columbian contacts between the New and Old Worlds. Joseph Spencer, an old 'China hand' and a Berkeley Ph.D. of the 1930s has maintained at the University of California at Los Angeles, with the help of another Berkeleyan, Henry Bruman, and others, the 'cultural' interests which have been subsiding at Berkeley since Sauer's retirement in the late 1950s

63 The first edition was published in 1965

Chapter 8 *Historical Geography in Australia and New Zealand*

1 Perry, P. 'Twenty five years of New Zealand historical geography', *New Zealand Geographer,* 25 (1969), 93–105; Williams, M. 'Places, periods and themes: a review and prospect of Australian historical geography: a review article', *Australian Geographer,* 11 (1970), 403–416

2 Mitchell, Sir T. L. *Australian Geography . . . Designed for the Use of Schools in New South Wales* (Sydney, 1850); Blair, D. *Cyclopaedia of Australiana* (Melbourne, 1881) viii

3 See his obituary in *Australian Geographical Studies,* 2 (1964), 1–9

4 Grenfell Price, A. 'White Settlers in the Tropics', *American Geographical Society Special Publication* 23 (New York, 1939) and *White Settlers and Native Peoples* (Melbourne, 1949)

5 Fitzpatrick, B. *The British Empire and Australia: an economic history 1834–1939* (Melbourne, 1941); Shann, E. *An Economic History of Australia* (Cambridge, 1930); Shaw, A. L. *The Economic Development of Australia* (Melbourne, 1944)

6 Roberts, S. H. *History of Australian Land Settlement 1788–1920* (Melbourne, 1924) and *The Squatting Age in Australia, 1835–1847* (Melbourne, 1935). Reprinted 1968 and 1964 respectively

7 Rogers, J. D. *A Historical Geography of the British Dominions, Volume 6 Australasia* (Oxford, 1925)

8 Grenfell Price, A. *The Foundation and Settlement of South Australia, 1829–1845* (Adelaide, 1924); Fenner, C. 'A geographical enquiry into the growth, distribution and movement of population in South Australia, 1836–1927', *Transactions Royal Society South Australia,* 53 (1929), 80–145

9 Rühl, A. 'Das Standortsproblem in der Landwirtschafts—Geographie. Das Neuland Ost-Australien'. *Institut für Meereskunde, Neue Serie B, Historisch Volkwirtschaftliche Reihe,* Heft 6 (Berlin, 1929)

10 Personal communication from Jan Broek confirmed a prior suggestion by Professor R. G. Ward.

11 Andrews, J. 'The settlement net and regional factor', *Australian Geographer,* 2 (1934), 33–48 and 'The emergence of the wheat belt in southeastern Australia to 1930', in Andrews, J. (ed) *Frontiers and Men: a volume in memory of Griffith Taylor 1880–1963* (Melbourne, 1966) 5–65

12 Wadham, S. M. and Wood, G. L. *Land Utilization in Australia* (Melbourne, 1939)

13 Alexander, F. *Moving frontiers: an American theme and its application to Australian history* (Melbourne, 1947); Allen, H. C. *Bush and Backwoods: a comparison of the frontier in Australia and the United States* (Michigan, 1959); Fitzpatrick, B. 'The big man's frontier and Australian farming', *Agricultural History,* 21 (1947), 8–12 and Sharp, P. F. 'Three frontiers: some comparative studies of Canadian, American and Australian settlement', *Pacific History Review,* 24 (1955), 369–77

14 Meinig, D. W. *On the Margins of the Good Earth: the South Australian wheat frontier, 1869–1884* (Chicago, 1962) and Perry, T. M. *Australia's First Frontier: the spread of settlement in New South Wales, 1788–1829* (Melbourne, 1963). The concept is implicit in Bauer, F. 'Historical Geographic Survey of Part of Northern Australia: Part 1—Introduction and the Eastern Gulf Region', *C.S.I.R.O. Div. Land Research Regional Study,* Report 59/2 (1959); Heathcote, R. L. *Back of Bourke: a study of land appraisal and settlement in semi-arid Australia* (Melbourne, 1965); Jay, L. J. 'Pioneer settlement on the Darling Downs, a Scottish contribution to Australian colonisation', *Scottish Geographical Magazine,* 73 (1957), 35–49; Powell, J. M. 'The squatting occupation of Victoria, 1834–60', *Australian Geographical Studies,* 7 (1969), 9–27 and Williams, M. 'The spread of settlement in South Australia' in Gale, F. and Lawton, G. H. (eds) *Settlement and Encounter: geographical studies presented to Sir Grenfell Price* (Melbourne, 1969) 1–50

15 Once the initial novelty wore off, the main function of the colonists was seen as replacing the 'useless' local flora and fauna by more commercially useful and aesthetically pleasing exotics. The results were being discussed in the latter half of the nineteenth century. See references and discussion in Heathcote, *Back of Bourke*, 25–9

16 Jacobs, M. R. 'History of use and abuse of wooded lands in Australia', *Australian Journal Science*, 20 (1957), 132–9 and Donald, C. M. 'The progress of Australian agriculture and the role of pastures in environmental change', *Australian Journal Science,* 27 (1962), 187–98

17 Grenfell Price, A. *The Western Invasions of the Pacific and its Continents: a survey of moving frontiers and changing landscapes, 1513–1958* (Melbourne, 1963) and 'The moving frontiers and changing landscapes of flora and fauna in Australia', in Andrews J. (ed) *Frontiers and Men: a volume in memory of Griffith Taylor 1880–1963* (Melbourne, 1966), 155–73 ; also Jennings, J. N. 'Man as a geological agent', *Australian Journal Science,* 28 (1965), 150–6

18 Lawrence, R. *Aboriginal Habitat and Economy* (Canberra, 1968), McCarthy, F. D. 'Habitat, economy and equipment of the Australian Aborigine', *Australian Journal Science,* 19 (1959), 88–96 and Tindale, N. B. 'Ecology of primitive man in Australia', in Keast, A. and Crocker, R. L. (eds) 'Biogeography and ecology in Australia', *Monographiae Biologicae,* 8 (The Hague, 1959) Chapter 3

19 Mulvaney, D. J. *The Prehistory of Australia* (London, 1969)

20 Wadham, S. M. and Wood, G. L. *Land Utilization in Australia* (Melbourne, 1939)

21 Andrews, *Frontiers and Men,* 5–65 ; Meinig, *On the Margins of the Good Earth.*

22 Blainey, G. *The Tyranny of Distance: how distance shaped Australia's history* (Melbourne, 1966) ; Meinig, D. W. 'A comparative historical geography of two railnets: Columbia Basin and South Australia', *Annals of the Association of American Geographers,* 52 (1962), 394–413 and Smith, R. H. T. 'The development and function of transport routes in southern New South Wales 1860–1930', *Australian Geographical Studies,* 2 (1964), 47–65

23 Blainey, G. *The Rush that Never Ended: a history of Australian mining* (Melbourne, 1963) ; Wilson, M. G. A. 'The changing Latrobe Valley. The impact of brown coal mining', *Australian Geographical Studies,* 1 (1963), 31–8

24 Walsh, G. P. 'The geography of manufacturing in Sydney, 1788–1851', *Bushiness Archives History*, 3 (1963), 20–52; Wilson, M. G. A. 'Town gas manufacturing in Australia, *Australian Geographical Studies*, 5, (1967), 97–112

25 For New South Wales see Heathcote, R. L. 'Changes in pastoral land tenure and ownership', *Australian Geographical Studies*, 3 (1965), 1–16; Jeans, D. N. 'The breakdown of Australia's first rectangular survey,' *Australian Geographical Studies*, 4 (1966), 119–28 and 'Territorial divisions and the location of towns in New South Wales 1826–1842', *Australian Geographer*, 10, (1967), 243–55. For Queensland see Camm, J. C. R. 'The Queensland Agricultural Purchase Act 1894 and Rural Settlement: a case study of Jimbour', *Australian Geographer*, 10 (1967), 263–74. For South Australia see Williams, M. 'Delimiting the spread of settlement: an examination of evidence in South Australia', *Economic Geography*, 42 (1966), 336–55 and 'The spread of settlement in South Australia' in Gale and Lawton, *Settlement and Encounter*, 1–50. For Victoria see Powell, J. M., *Australian Geographical Studies*, 7, 9–27, and 'The Victorian survey system 1837–1860', *New Zealand Geographer*, 26 (1970), 50–69

26 Jay, L. J. 'The foundation and early growth of Brisbane', *Geography*, 37 (1952), 166–78; Jeans, D. N. 'Town planning in New South Wales 1826–1842', *Australian Planning Institute Journal*, 3 (1965), 191–6; Williams, M. 'The parkland towns of Australia and New Zealand', *Geographical Review*, 56 (1966), 67–89 and 'Early town plans in South Australia', *Australian Planning Institute Journal*, 4 (1966), 45–51

27 Bird, J. 'The foundation of Australian seaport capitals', *Economic Geography*, 41 (1965), 283–99; Johnston, R. J. 'The Australian small town in the post-war period', *Australian Geographer*, 10 (1967), 215–9 and 'An outline of the development of Melbourne's street pattern', *Australian Geographer*, 10 (1968), 453–65; Robinson, K. W. 'Sydney, 1820–1952: a comparison of developments in the heart of the city', *Australian Geographer*, 6 (1952), 6–12 and 'Processes and patterns of urbanisation in Australia and New Zealand', *New Zealand Geographer*, 18 (1962), 32–49; Rose, A. J. 'Some boundaries and building materials in south-eastern Australia', in McCaskill, M. (ed) *Land and Livelihood: geographical essays in honour of George Jobberns* (Christchurch, 1962) 225–76; Williams, M. 'Gawler: the changing geography of a South Australian country town', *Australian Geographer*, 9 (1964), 195–206

28 Blainey, *The Tyranny of Distance*; Dallas, K. M. *Trading Posts*

R

or Penal Colonies: the commercial significance of Cook's New Holland route to the Pacific (Devonport, Tasmania, 1969); Young, J. M. R. *Australia's Pacific Frontier* (Melbourne, 1967)

29   Bauer, *C.S.I.R.O. Div. Land Research Regional Survey Report 59/2;* Heathcote, *Back of Bourke;* Meinig, D. W. 'Goyder's line of rainfall: the role of a geographic concept in South Australian land policy and agricultural settlement', *Agricultural History,* 35 (1961), 207–14; Powell, J. M. 'The Selection Acts of Western Victoria, 1860–1880' in Steel, R. W. and Lawton, R. (eds) *Liverpool Essays in Geography: a jubilee collection* (London, 1967) 293–314, also 'Gamblers by Act of Parliament: aspects of the first selection acts for Victoria', *Victorian History Magazine,* 39 (1968), 1–18 and 'Farming conditions in Victoria, 1857–1865: a prelude to selection', *Australian Geographer,* 10 (1968), 346–54

30   Ryan, B. 'Kameruka Estate, New South Wales, 1864–1964', *New Zealand Geographer,* 20 (1964), 103–21

31   Borchardt, D. H. 'Checklist of Royal Commissions, Select Committees of Parliament and Boards of Enquiry, Part 1, Commonwealth of Australia 1900–1950', in Stone, W. W. (ed) *Studies in Australian Bibliography No. 7,* (Cremorne N.S.W., 1958); Dillon, J. L. and McFarlane, G. C. (eds) *An Australasian Bibliography of Agricultural Economics 1788–1960* (Sydney, 1967); Tooley, R. V. 'The printed maps of Tasmania', *Map Collectors' Circle* no. 5 (1963), 'One hundred foreign maps of Australia 1773–1887', *ibid* no. 12 (1964), 'Early maps of Australia, the Dutch period', *ibid* no. 23 (1965), 'The printed maps of New South Wales 1773–1873', *ibid* no. 44 (1968), 1–49, and 'Printed maps of Australia', *ibid* no. 60 (1970), 1–40

32   Camm, *Australian Geographer,* vol 10, 263–274; Chapman, E. C. 'Pioneer settlement in Darwin's hinterland, 1911–1957', *Australian Geographer,* 7 (1958), 113–26; Coward, D. 'Free selecting on the Eumerella shore', *Journal Royal Australian Historical Society,* 55 (1969), 355–79; Heathcote, *Back of Bourke* and *Australian Geographical Studies,* 3, 1–16; Powell, *Victorian History Magazine,* 39, 1–18, *Australian Geographer,* 10, 346–54, 'Three squatting maps for Victoria', *Australian Geographer,* 10 (1968), 466–71 and *Australian Geographical Studies,* 7, 9–27; Williams in Gale and Lawton *Settlement and Encounter,* 1–50

33   Cain, N. 'Companies and squatting in the Western Division of New South Wales, 1896–1905', in Barnard, A. (ed) *The Simple Fleece* (Melbourne, 1962) 435–456

34   Meinig, *On the Margins of the Good Earth*

35 Butlin, N. G. *Australian Domestic Product, Investment and Foreign Borrowing, 1861-1938/9* (Cambridge, 1962) and *Investment in Australian Economic Development, 1861-1900* (Cambridge, 1964)

36 Two examples of such studies are: Bermingham, K. *Gateway to the southeast* (Millicent, South Australia, 1961); and Cameron, W. J. (ed) *The History of Bourke*, 2 vols. (Bourke, N.S.W., 1966 and 1968)

37 Gunson, N. *The Good Country: Cranbourne Shire* (Melbourne, 1968)

38 Bolton, G. C. *The Kimberley Pastoral Industry* (Perth, 1954) and *A Thousand Miles Away: a history of north Queensland to 1920* (Brisbane, 1963); Buxton, G. L. *The Riverina, 1861–1891: An Australian regional study* (Melbourne, 1967); Walker, R. B. *Old New England: a history of the Northern Tablelands of New South Wales, 1818–1900* (Sydney, 1966); Waterson, D. *Squatter, Selector and Storekeeper, a history of the Darling Downs, 1859–1893* (Sydney, 1968)

39 Williams, *Australian Geographer*, 11, 403–16, fig 1. Omitted from this map, however, is a study of the Western Australian wheat belt: Glynn, S. 'Government policy and agricultural development: Western Australia, 1900–1930' *Australian Economic History Review*, 7 (1967), 115–41

40 Bate, W. 'The urban sprinkle: country towns and Australian regional history', *Australian Economic History Review*, 10 (1970), 204–17

41 Perry, *Australia's First Frontier*; Allen, A. C. B. 'Marginal settlement—a case study of the Channel Country of southwest Queensland', *Australian Geographical Studies*, 6 (1968), 1–23; Heathcote, *Back of Bourke*; Langford-Smith, T. 'Murrumbidgee land settlement, 1817–1912' in Dury, G. H. and Logan, M. (eds) *Studies in Australian Geography* (London, 1968) 99–136; Williams in Gale and Lawton, *Settlement and Encounter*, 1–50

42 Powell, J. M. *The Public Lands of Australia Felix* (Melbourne, 1970)

43 Andrews, *Frontiers and Men*, 5–65; Higman, B. W. 'Sugar plantations and yeoman farming in New South Wales', *Annals of the Association of American Geographers*, 58 (1968), 697–720 and 'The regional impact of the sugar industry in New South Wales, 1870–1912', *Australian Geographical Studies*, 6 (1968), 43–58; Solomon, R. J. 'Broken Hill—the growth of settlement 1883–1958', *Australian Geographer*, 7 (1959), 181–192; Williams, M. 'The historical geography of an artificial drainage system:

the lower south-east of South Australia', *Australian Geographical Studies*, 2 (1964), 87–102

44 Williams, M. 'Two studies in historical geography of South Australia', in Dury, G. H. and Logan, M. (ed) *Studies in Australian Geography* (Melbourne, 1968) 71–98; Powell, J. M. 'Victoria's woodland cover in 1869: a bureaucratic venture in cartography', *New Zealand Geographer*, 23 (1967), 106–16

45 Solomon, R. J. 'Sprent's Hobart, circa 1845', *Papers Proceedings Royal Society Tasmania*, 101 (1967), 49–63; Walsh, G. P. 'The English Colony in New South Wales: A.D. 1803', *New Zealand Geographer*, 18 (1962), 149–69

46 Spate, O. H. K. 'Bush and city: some reflections on the Australian cultural landscape', *Australian Journal Science*, 18 (1956), 177–84

47 Solomon, R. J. and Goodhand, W. E. 'Past influences in present townscapes: some Tasmanian examples', *New Zealand Geographer*, 21 (1965), 113–32

48 Smailes, P. J. and Molyneaux, J. K. 'The evolution of an Australian rural settlement pattern: southern New England, N.S.W.', *Transactions Papers Institute British Geographers*, 36 (1965), 31–54

49 Rose, in McCaskill, *Land and Livelihood*, 255–76

50 Rutherford, J. 'Interplay of American and Australian ideas for development of water projects in Northern Victoria', *Annals of the Association of American Geographers*, 54 (1964), 88–106

51 Heathcote, R. L. 'The Pastoral Ethic: a comparative study of pastoral resource appraisals in Australia and America' in McGinnies, W. G. (ed) *Arid Lands in Perspective* (Tucson, 1969) 311–24

52 Rose, A. J. 'Dissent from Downunder: Metropolitan primacy as the normal state', *Pacific Viewpoint*, 7, (1966), 1–27

53 Daly, M. and Brown, J. 'Urban Settlement in Central Western N.S.W.', *N.S.W. Geographical Society*, Research Paper 8 (1964)

54 Meinig, *On the Margins of the Good Earth*, 197–201

55 Daly, M. 'The lower Hunter Valley urban complex and the dispersed city hypothesis', *Australian Geographer*, 10 (1968), 472–82 and 'The development of the urban pattern of Newcastle' *Australian Economic History Review*, 10 (1970), 190–203

56 Powell, *Australian Geographical Studies*, 7, 9–27 and 'A pioneer sheep station: the Clyde Company in Western Victoria, 1836–40'. *Australian Geographical Studies*, 6 (1968), 59–66

57 Higman, *Annals of the Association of American Geographers*, 58, 697–720.

58 Grenfell Price, A. *The Foundation and Settlement of South*

Australia, 1829–1845 ; Fenner, *Transactions Royal Society South Australia,* 53, 80–145

59 Perry, T. M. 'Climate and settlement in Australia 1700–1930: some theoretical considerations', in Andrews, J. (ed) *Frontiers and Men: a volume in memory of Griffith Taylor 1880–1963* (Melbourne, 1966) 138–154

60 See Baker, S. J. *The Australian Language* (Sydney, 1945); Green, H. M. *A History of Australian Literature* (Sydney, 1961); Smith, B. *European Vision and the South Pacific* (Oxford, 1960) and *Australian Painting 1788–1960* (London, 1962). A recent example is Moon, K. 'Perception and appraisal of the South Australian landscape 1836–1850' *Proceedings Royal Geographical Society Australasia (South Australian Branch),* 70 (1969), 41–64

61 Jobberns, G. 'Geography and national development', *New Zealand Geographer,* 1, (1945), 6

62 Cumberland, K. B. 'Foreword' *ibid,* 3

63 Acland, L. G. D. *The Early Canterbury Runs* (Christchurch, 1930, 1940). A good account of a single station was Burdon, R. M., *High Country: The Evolution of a New Zealand Sheep Station* (Auckland, 1938)

64 Condliffe, J. B. *New Zealand in the Making* (London, 1929)

65 Cumberland, K. B. 'A Century's Change: Natural to Cultural Vegetation in New Zealand', *Geographical Review,* 31 (1941), 529–54

66 Buchanan, J. 'Sketch of the botany of Otago', *Transactions and Proceedings New Zealand Institute,* 1 (1869) 181–211 ; Thomson, G. M. 'The rabbit pest', *New Zealand Journal of Science,* 2 (1884) 79–80 and *The Naturalisation of Plants and Animals in New Zealand* (Cambridge, 1922); Travers, W. T. L. 'On the changes effected in the natural features of a new country by the introduction of civilised races', *Transactions and Proceedings New Zealand Institute,* 2 (1869) 299–330; Walsh, P. 'The effect of deer on the New Zealand bush', *ibid,* 25 (1892) 435–8

67 Guthrie-Smith, H. *Tutira, the Story of a New Zealand Sheep Station* (Edinburgh and London, 1921, 1926, 1953, Christchurch, 1970)

68 Guthrie-Smith, *Tutira* (1953), 423

69 Perry, *New Zealand Geographer,* 25, 93–105.

70 Brief methodological statements have been made by Cumberland in 'American Geography: A Review and Commentary', *New Zealand Geographer,* 11 (1955), 184–5 and by McCaskill, M. 'The historical dimension in Geography' *Historical News,* no. 14 (University of Canterbury, 1967), 1–4. A. H. Clark described the technique employed in his book, *The Invasion of New Zealand*

by People, Plants and Animals in 'Field work in historical geography', *Professional Geographer,* 4 (1946), 13–23

71 Clark, A. H. *The Invasion of New Zealand by People, Plants and Animals. The South Island* (New Brunswick, 1949)

72 Cumberland, K. B. 'Moas and Men: New Zealand about AD 1250', *Geographical Review,* 52 (1962), 151–73 ; 'Aotearoa Maori: New Zealand about 1780', *Geographical Review,* 39 (1949), 401–24 ; 'A land despoiled: New Zealand about 1838', *New Zealand Geographer,* 6 (1950), 13–34 ; and ' "Jimmy Grants" and "Mihaneres": New Zealand about 1853', *Economic Geography,* 30 (1954), 70–89 ; Hargreaves, R. P. 'The Golden Age: New Zealand about 1867', *New Zealand Geographer,* 16 (1960), 1–32 ; Cumberland, K. B. and Hargreaves, R. P. 'Middle island ascendant: New Zealand in 1881', *New Zealand Geographer,* 11 (1955), 95–118

73 Hill, R. D. 'Pastoralism in the Wairarapa, 1844–53', in Watters, R. F. (ed) *Land and Society in New Zealand. Essays in Historical Geography* (Wellington, 1965) 25–49

74 Johnston, W. B. 'Locating the vegetation of early Canterbury', *Transactions Royal Society New Zealand (Botany* 1, 1961), 5–15 ; Forrest, J. 'Locating the vegetation of early coastal Otago', *Transactions Royal Society New Zealand,* 2 (1963), 49–58

75 McCaskill, M. 'The Poutini Coast: A geography of Maori settlement in Westland', *New Zealand Geographer,* 10 (1954), 134–50

76 All appear in the *Journal of the Polynesian Society ;* Hargreaves, R. P. 'The Maori Agriculture of the Auckland Province in the mid-nineteenth century', 68 (1959), 61–79 ; 'Maori agriculture after the wars', 69 (1960), 354–67 ; 'Maori flour mills of the Auckland Province, 1846–1860', 70 (1961), 227–32 ; 'Maori flour mills south of the Auckland Province, 1847–1860', 71 (1962), 101–4 ; 'Changing Maori agriculture in pre-Waitangi New Zealand', 72 (1963), 101–17

77 Armstrong, R. W. 'Auckland by gaslight: An urban geography of 1896', *New Zealand Geographer,* 15 (1959), 173–89 ; Clark, W. A. V. 'Dunedin at the turn of the century', *New Zealand Geographer,* 18 (1962), 93–115

78 Forrest, J. 'Population and settlement in the Otago goldfields, 1861–1870', *New Zealand Geographer,* 17 (1961), 64–86 ; 'Otago during the gold rushes' in Watters, R. F. (ed) *Land and Society in New Zealand. Essays in Historical Geography* (Wellington, 1965) 80–100

79 McCaskill, M. 'The goldrush population of Westland', *New Zealand Geographer*, 12 (1956), 32–50; 'Miner, Merchant and Mountain: A study in the political geography of gold rush Westland', *Proceedings 2nd New Zealand Geographers' Conference* (1958), 49–57; 'The South Island Goldfields in the 1860s. Some geographical aspects', in McCaskill *Land and Livelihood*, 143–69; 'Man and landscape in North Westland' in Eyre, S. R. and Jones, G. R. J. (eds) *Geography as Human Ecology* (London, 1966) 264–90

80 May, P. R. *Gold Town. Ross, Westland* (Christchurch, 1970). May's full length history of the West Coast gold rushes also has a strong geographic flavour: May, P. R. *The West Coast Gold Rushes* (Christchurch, 1962, 1967)

81 Pownall, L. L. 'Metropolitan Auckland 1740–1945', *New Zealand Geographer*, 6 (1950), 107–24

82 Dinsdale, E. 'Changing patterns of settlement in Tauranga County', *New Zealand Geographer*, 16 (1960), 170–89

83 Franklin, S. H. 'The village and the bush: Wellington Province, New Zealand', *Pacific Viewpoint*, 1 (1960), 143–81

84 McLintock, A. H. *An Encyclopedia of New Zealand*, 3 vols (Wellington, 1966), entries on Auckland, Taranaki, Hawkes Bay, Wellington, Marlborough, Nelson, Westland, Canterbury, Otago and Southland Provinces.

85 Lewthwaite, G. 'The population of Aotearoa: Its number and distribution', *New Zealand Geographer*, 6 (1950), 35–52

86 Cunningham, J. K. 'Maori-Pakeha conflict 1858–1885: A background to political geography', *New Zealand Geographer*, 12 (1956), 12–31

87 Murton, B. J. 'Changing patterns of land ownership in Poverty Bay', *New Zealand Geographer*, 22 (1966), 166–176

88 Hargreaves, R. P. 'Waimate—pioneer New Zealand farm', *Agricultural History*, 36, 38–45; 'Mission farming before 1830' *Proceedings 3rd New Zealand Geographers' Conference* (1961), 71–8; 'Pioneer farming in Taranaki 1841–1850', *New Zealand Geographer*, 19 (1963), 46–59; 'Farm fences in pioneer New Zealand', *New Zealand Geographer*, 20 (1965), 144–55

89 Forrest, J. 'Dunedin and the Otago Block: Geographical Aspects of a Wakefield Settlement', *New Zealand Geographer*, 20 (1964), 10–29

90 Johnston, W. B. 'Pioneering the bushland of lowland Taranaki: a case study', *New Zealand Geographer*, 17 (1961), 1–18. A regional treatment of Taranaki farming evolution over the same period is Burnett, J. 'The impact of dairying on the landscape of

lowland Taranaki' in Watters, R. F. (ed) *Land and Society in New Zealand* (Wellington, 1965) 101–19

91 Cant, R. G. 'The agricultural frontier in miniature: a micro-study on the Canterbury Plains, 1850–75', *New Zealand Geographer,* 24 (1968), 155–67

92 Heeredegen, R. G. 'Land for the landless', *New Zealand Geographer,* 23 (1967), 34–49 ; Duncan, J. S. 'The land for the people: land settlement and rural population movements, 1886–1906', in McCaskill, *Land and Livelihood,* 170–90

93 Pownall, L. L. 'Surface growth of New Zealand towns' *New Zealand Geographer,* 13 (1957), 99–116 ; Rimmer, P. J. 'The changing status of New Zealand seaports, 1853–1960', *Annals of the Association of American Geographers,* 57 (1967), 88–100

94 Linge, G. J. R. 'Manufacturing in Auckland: Its origins and growth, 1840–1936', *New Zealand Geographer,* 14 (1958), 47–64 ; 'Manufacturing in New Zealand, four years in a century of growth' in Watters, R. F. (ed) *Land and Society in New Zealand,* (Wellington, 1965) 139–59

95 Cumberland, K. B. ' "Climatic change" or cultural interference? New Zealand in Moahunter times', in McCaskill, M. (ed) *Land and Livelihood,* 88–142

96 Rose, A. J. *Pacific Viewpoint,* 7, 1–27

97 Clark, *The Invasion of New Zealand by People, Plants and Animals,* and Meinig, *On the Margins of the Good Earth*

98 Cant, R. G. 'The dilemma of historical geography' in Johnston, W. B. (ed) *Human Geography, Concepts and Case Studies* (Christchurch, 1969) 40–60, and Perry, *New Zealand Geographer,* 25, 93–105

99 Solomon, R. J. 'The geography of political affiliation in a federal state system: Tasmania 1913–1966', *Australian Geographical Studies,* 7 (1969), 28–40

100 Perry, P. 'Marriage—distance relationships in North Otago 1875–1914', *New Zealand Geographer,* 25 (1969), 36–43

Chapter 9 *Historical Geography in Latin America*

1 Parsons, J. J. 'The contribution of geography to Latin American studies', in Wagley, C. (ed) *Social Science Research on Latin America* (New York, 1964), 33–85 ; Watters, R. 'Geography as a social science: a more functional geography for Latin America', *The East Lakes Geographer,* 6 (1970), 5–25

2 Compare Hanke, L. 'Gilberto Freyre: social   historian',

Quarterly Journal of Inter-American Relations, 1 (1939), 24–44

3 Bassols Batalla, A. 'La investigación y la literatura geográfica en Mexico', *Revista Geográfica Panamericana,* 42 (1955), 169–197 ; Romero, E. 'La Geografía en nuestros días', *Boletín de la Sociedad Geográfica de Lima,* 82 (1964), 9–22 ; Daus, F. A. 'Informe sobre el estado de la geografía en la República Argentina', *Revista Geográfica Panamericana,* 40 (1953), 143–55

4 For a sample curriculum in Panamá see Rubio, A. 'Plan de Estudio de Geografia', *Revista Geográfica Panamericana,* 47 1957), 22–59. More general comments on Central America are to be found in Stouse, P. A. D. 'Geography in Central American Universities', *The Professional Geographer,* 11 (1959), 350–2

5 Ostuni, J. P. and Civit, M. E. F. de 'La Enseñanza de la Geografía', in Zamorano, M., Capitanelli, R. G. and Velasco, M. I. (eds) *La Geografía en la República Argentina* (Buenos Aires, 1968) 134–213

6 Sternberg, H. O'R. 'Geographic thought and development in Brazil', *The Professional Geographer,* 11 (1959), 16 ; Daus, F. A. *Que es la Geografía* (Buenos Aires, 1961) ; Geiger, P. 'The development of geography in Brazil', *The East Lakes Geographer,* 6 (1970), 56–62 ; Minkel, C. W. 'Geography in Central America : its status and prospects', *The East Lakes Geographer,* 6 (1970), 63–73 ; Velasco, M. I. 'Relaciones de la geografía con las ciencias humanas', in Zamorano, M. *et. al.* (eds) *La Geografía en la República Argentina* (Buenos Aires, 1968), 75–77 ; Monbeig, P. 'Os modos de pensar na Geografia Humana', *Boletim Paulista de Geografia,* 15 (1953), 45–56

7 Frustration is amply illustrated in Randle, P. H. *Hacia una nueva universidad?* (Buenos Aires, 1968) ; Sternberg's departure to the United States has robbed Brazil of one of its most competent students.

8 Such institutes as the Centro de Pesquisas de Geografia do Brasil in Rio de Janeiro ; the Instituto Geográfico de la Universidad de Chile, Santiago ; the Sociedad Argentina de Estudios Geográficos (Gaea) in Buenos Aires. For details of the activities of the Gaea see Daus, F. A. 'La Sociedad Argentina de Estudios Geográficos Gaea', *Revista Geográfica Panamericana,* 39 (1953), 121–2

9 Zamorano, M. 'Actualización de lo geográfico. Prejuicios y errores en Hispanoamérica', *Boletín de Estudios Geográficos* (Cuyo), 8 (1960), 141–59. The author notes that in the Gaea *Geografía de la República Argentina,* of the ten volumes published, all deal with physical geography, including three entirely devoted to geology.

10 Termer, F. 'Carlos Sapper, explorador de Centro América (1866–1945)', *Anales de la Sociedad de Geografía y Historia de Guatemala,* 29 (1956), 55–130; Ruíz, J. I. 'Caldas, primer geógrafo de Colombia', *Boletín de la Sociedad Geográfica de Colombia,* 24 (1966), 114–7; Muñoz, L. 'Notas sobre la influencia alemana en Colombia', *Boletín de la Sociedad Geográfica de Colombia,* 26 (1968), 90–7; Temple, E. D. 'Panorama geográfico del Peru en 1839', *Boletín de la Sociedad Geográfica de Lima,* 82 (1964), 23–52; Vila, P. and Carpio, R. *Codazzi-Humboldt-Caldas, precursores de la geografía moderna* (Caracas, 1960)

11 For an excellent analysis of the labours of an Argentine 'expert' see Pérez, M. 'Labor geográfico del Perito Moreno', *Boletín de Estudios Geográficos* (Cuyo), 2 (1950), 255–74

12 A sobering commentary on the fact that 'the Latin American by far prefers inventing history to studying it . . . on the other hand the Latin American barely tolerates history based on actual study' is provided by Villegas, D. C. 'History and Social Sciences in Latin America', in Diégues Júnior, M. and Wood, B. (eds) *Social Science in Latin America* (New York, 1967) 131; details of recent bibliographical aids for historical investigation may be found in Rodrigues, J. H. 'Brazilian historiography: present trends and research requirements', in Diégues Júnior, *Social Science in Latin America,* 226–8

13 Stabb, M. S. *In Quest of Identity: patterns in the Spanish American Essay of Ideas, 1890–1960* (Chapel Hill, 1967); Fernandes, F. 'The Social Sciences in Latin America', in Diégues Júnior, M. *Social Science Research in Latin America,* 20; Pereira, J. V. da C. 'A geografia no Brazil', in *As Ciências no Brasil,* 1 (São Paulo, 1955) 393; Ross, S. R. *Latin America in Transition* (New York, 1970), xiii deals with the problem of cultural imperialism; Hoy, D. R. 'Geographic research in development of Guatemala', *The East Lakes Geographer,* 6 (1970), 74–80;

14 Furlong, G. 'Bicentenario del primer geógrafo de la nación argentina: Pedro Andres García (1758–1958)', *Anales de la Academia Argentina de Geografía,* 2 (1958), 176–8; Wilson, I. H. 'Scientists in New Spain: the eighteenth century expeditions', *Journal of the West,* 1 (1962), 24–44; García, R. 'Historia das exploraçoes científicas', *Diccionario Histórico e Geográfico Brasileiro,* 1 (1922), 856–910

15 Sternberg, *The Professional Geographer,* 11 (1959), 13; Geiger, *The East Lakes Geographer,* 6 (1970), 56

16 Deffontaines, P. *Regioes e Paisagens do Estado de Sao Paulo*

(São Paulo, 1935); França, A. *A Ilha de São Sebastião: estudo de geografia humana* (São Paulo, 1954; Zarur, J. *A Baçia do Medio Sao Francisco* (Rio de Janeiro, 1946); Faissol, S. *O Mato Grosso de Goiás* (Rio de Janeiro, 1952); Monbeig, P. *Ensaios de Geografia Humana Brasileira* (São Paulo 1957)

17 Monbeig, P. *Pionniers et planteurs de São Paulo* (Paris, 1952); Lino de Mattos, D. (*Vinhedos e Viticultores de São Roque e Jundaia (São Paulo)* (São Paulo, 1958)

18 Zamorano, M. *La Geografía en la República Argentina* (Buenos Aires, 1968)

19 Gaignard, R. 'Un estudio de estructura agraria en la pampa seca: método y resultados', *Boletín de Estudios Geográficos:* (Cuyo), 13 (1966), 229–54

20 In Chile Jean Borde has significantly influenced historical geography, see Polisensky, J. V. 'Comentarios sobre la geografía histórica de Chile', *Ibero-Americana Pragensia* (Prague), 1 (1967), 64–87; in Venezuela Crist, R. E. *Étude géographique des Llanos du Vénézuela occidental* (Grenoble, 1937) betrays French influence

21 Parsons, *Social Science Research in Latin America*, 40; Muñoz, *Boletín de la Sociedad Geográfica de Colombia*, 26, 90–97

22 Schmieder, O. 'The historic geography of Tucumán', *University of California Publications in Geography*, 2 (1928), 359–386; Rohmeder, W. 'Paisaje natural y antropógeno en Tucumán', *Gaea*, 7 (1945), 293–315; Wilhelmy, H. *Siedlung in südamerikanishen Urwald* (Hamburg, 1949)

23 Pfeifer, G. 'Sinaloa und Sonara: Beiträge zur Landeskunde und Kultur-geographie des nordwestlichen Mexico', *Mitteilungen des Geographischer Gesellschaft Hamburg*, 46 (1939), 289–460, and 'The basin of Puebla-Tlaxcala in Mexico', *Revista Geográfica Panamericana*, 64 (1966), 85–107; Otremba, E. 'Entwicklung und Wandlung der Venezolanischen Kulturlandschaft unter der Herrschaft des Erdöles', *Erdkunde*, 8 (1954), 169–88; Waibel, L. 'European colonization in southern Brazil', *Geographical Review*, 40 (1950), 529–47

24 James' more historically orientated studies include: 'Rio de Janeiro and São Paulo', *Geographical Review*, 23 (1933), 271–98; 'The coffee lands of southeastern Brazil', *Geographical Review*, 22 (1932), 225–44; 'The Changing patterns of population in São Paulo State', *Geographical Review*, 28 (1938), 353–62

25 Sauer, C. O. *The Early Spanish Main* (Berkeley 1966) v–vi and Leighley, J. (ed) *Land and Life: a Selection from the Writings of Carl Ortwin Sauer* (Berkeley, 1963)

26 Sauer, C. O. 'The road to Cíbola', *Ibero-Americana*, 3 (1932);
'Aboriginal population of Northwestern Mexico', *Ibero-Ameri-cana*, 10 (1935); 'Colima of New Spain in the sixteenth century', *Ibero-Americana*, 29 (1948); *The Early Spanish Main* (Berkeley, 1966). For detailed publication list of Sauer up to 1962 see Leighly, *Land and Life*, 407–413

27 The number of contributions to the *University of California Publications in Geography* dealing with various aspects of Latin American cultural and historical geography make comprehensive references impossible here. The following selection illustrate the themes, areas and time periods included in the studies of Sauer's many pupils: West, R. C. 'The Mining Community in Northern New Spain: The Parral Mining District', *Ibero-Americana*, 30 (1949); Johannessen, C. L. 'Savannas of Interior Honduras', *Ibero-Americana*, 46 (1963); Harris, D. R. 'Plants, Animals, and Man in the Outer Leeward Islands, West Indies—an Ecological Study of Antigua, Barbuda and Anguilla', *University of California Publications in Geography*, 18 (1965), 1–184; Gordon, B. LeR. 'Human Geography and Ecology of the Sinú Country of Colombia', *Ibero-Americana*, 39 (1957); Denevan, W. M. 'The Aboriginal Cultural Geography of the Llanos de Mojos of Bolivia', *Ibero-Americana*, 48, (1966); Edwards, C. R. 'Aboriginal Watercraft on the Pacific Coast of South America', *Ibero-Americana*, 47 (1965)

28 For example Parsons, J. J. 'Antioqueño colonization in western Colombia', *Ibero-Americana*, 32 (1949); West, R. C. *Colonial placer mining in Colombia* (Baton Rouge, 1952) and *The Pacific Lowlands of Colombia, a negroid area of the American Tropics* (Baton Rouge, 1957)

29 Sauer, *The Early Spanish Main*

30 Chaunu, P. 'Une histoire hispano-américaniste pilote: en marge de l'oeuvre de l' École de Berkeley', *Révue Historique*, 124 (1961), 339–68 describes in great detail the interrelationship between geographers and other social scientists in Berkeley from the twenties, particularly in the field of historical demography

31 Randle, P. H. *Geografía histórica y Planeamiento* (Buenos Aires, 1966); *La Ciudad Pampeana: geografía historica* (Buenos Aires, 1969). It is of interest to note that before Randle's visit to Europe no mention has been made of an English 'school' of historical geography by English geographers. For example Steers, J. A. 'La orientación de la geografía en Oxford y Cambridge y las carreras a las cuales su estudio lleva', *Estuario* (Montevideo), 1 (1958), makes no mention of historical geography. Compare

the treatment of the past in James, P. 'Estructura conceptual de la geografía', *Revista Geográfica Panamericana,* 62 (1965), 5–28

32 Prince, H. C. 'Real, imagined and abstract worlds of the past', *Progress in Geography',* 3 (1971), 4–86

33 Hueck, K. *Urlandschaft, Raublandschaft und Kulturlandschaft in der Provinz Tucuman in N.W. Argentinien* (Bonn, 1953); Otremba, *Erdkunde,* 8 (1954), 169–88

34 Sauer, C. O. 'The personality of Mexico', *Geographical Review,* 31 (1941), 353–64. Compare Schmieder, O. 'The Brazilian culture hearth', *University of California Publications in Geography,* 3 (1929), 159–98

35 Chevalier, F. *La Formation des grands domaines au Méxique* (Paris, 1952)

36 Schmieder, O. 'The Pampa—a natural or culturally induced grassland?', *University of California Publications in Geography,* 2 (1927), 255–70; 'Alteration of the Argentine Pampa in the Colonial Period', *ibid,* 2 (1927), 303–21

37 Daus, F. A. 'La Transformación del paisaje natural en paisaje cultural antes de la Revolución de Mayo', *Gaea,* 11 (1961), 1–18; Greslebin, H. 'El paisaje primitivo de la pampa', *Revista de Educación* (La Plata), 6 (1958), 412–21

38 Rohmeder, W. 'Paisaje natural y antropógeno en Tucumán', *Gaea,* 7 (1945), 293–315. See a brief account of Rohmeder's work in Czajka, W. 'W. Rohmeder', *Die Erde,* (1952), 108–12

39 Bockh, A. *El desecamiento del Lago de Valencia* (Caracas, 1956)

40 Zamorano, M. 'Las desaparecidas balsas de Guanacache', *Boletín de Estudios Geográficos* (Cuyo), 2 (1950), 165–84

41 Johannessen, C. L. *Savannas of Interior Honduras;* Denevan, W. M. *Llanos de Mojos;* Sternberg, H. O'R. 'Man and Environmental change in South America', in Fittkau E. J. *et al.* (eds) *Biogeography and Ecology in South America,* 1 (The Hague, 1968), 413–45. Also of importance is Donkin, R. A. 'Pre-Columbian field implements and their distribution in the Highlands of Middle and South America', *Anthropos,* 65 (1970), 505–29

42 Andrés, S. S. de 'Poblaciones indígenas en el valle de Tafí, in *Geografia Una et Varia* (Machatschek-Festschrift) (Tucumán, 1951), 17–29; Ardissone, R. 'Esbozo de las instalaciones humanas en la provincia de Mendoza', *Gaea,* 9 (1955), 268–326; Cuesta, J. M. 'El distrito de Chirinos y sus aborígenes', *Boletín de la Sociedad Geográfica de Lima,* 87 (1968), 46–61. Compare these with Eidt, R. C. 'Aboriginal Chibcha settlement in Colombia', *Annals of the Association of American Geographers,* 49, (1959), 374–92

43 Smith, C. T., Denevan, W. M. and Hamilton, P. 'Ancient ridged fields in the region of Lake Titicaca', *Geographical Journal*, 134 1968), 353–66

44 Kelly, K. 'Land-use regions in the central and northern portions of the Inca Empire', *Annals of the Association of American Geographers*, 55 (1965), 327–38

45 Baraona, R., Aranda, X. and Santana, R. *Valle de Putaendo: estudio de estructura agraria* (Santiago, 1961); Borde, J. and Góngora, M. *Evolución de la propiedad rural en el Valle del Puangue* (Santiago, 1956) 2 vols; Góngora, M. 'Notas sobre la encomienda chilena tardía', *Boletín de la Academia Chilena de Geografía e Historia*, 61 (1959), 27–51

46 Aranda, X. 'Evolución de la agricultura en el Norte Chico, Valle de Huasco', *Informaciones Geográficas*, 16 (1969), 9–41; Monbeig, P. 'Notas relativas a evolução das paisagens rurais no Estado de Sãa Paulo', *Boletim Geográfico*, 16 (1944), 428–30; Prost, G. 'Dans le Nord-Est du Brésil: les pionniers du Cariris dans la Borborema semi-aride', *Les Cahiers D'Outre-Mer*, 20 (1967), 367–93 and 21 (1968), 78–102; Velasco, M. I., Ostuni, J. and Civit, M. E. F. de 'Estudio de geografía agraria de Carrizal y Ugarteche', *Boletín de Estudios Geográfico*s (Cuyo), 13 (1966), 1–97; Correa, V. F. 'Evolução dos procesos de aquisição de terras no Brasil', *Revista Geográfica Panamericana*, 23 (1958), 31–64; Becker, B. K. 'Changing land-use patterns in Brazil: the spread of cattle raising in Sao Paulo State', *Revista Geográfica Panamericana*, 71 (1969), 35–63; Andrés, S. S. de 'Reseña de la evolución del paisaje rural en la provincia de Tucumán', *Humanitas* (Tucumán), 13 (1966), 59–66; Monbeig, P. 'As estructuras agrárias da faixa pioneira paulista', in *Novos Estudos de Geografia Humana Brasileira* (São Paulo, 1957), 105–124

47 Valverde, O. *La Fazenda de cafe esclavista en el Brasil*, Cuadernos Geográficos No. 3 (Mérida, Venezuela 1965); Galloway, J. H. 'The sugar industry of Pernambuco during the nineteenth century', *Annals of the Association of American Geographers*, 58 (1968), 285–303

48 Giberti, H. C. E. *El desarrollo agrario argentino: estudio de la región pampeana* (Buenos Aires, 1964); Wilhelmy, H. *Siedlung in Südamerikanischen Urwald* (Hamburg, 1949)

49 Giagnoni, O. 'Cambio en la actividad económica de una hacienda marginal (Sierras de Bellavista)', *Informaciones Geográficas*, 8 (1958), 77–75; Crossley, C. C. 'La contribution britannique a la colonisation et au dévéloppement agricole en Argentine: étude

preliminaire', in *Les Problèmes Agraires des Amériques Latines* (Paris, 1967), 441–66

50 Roche, J. *La colonisation allemande et le Río Grande do Sul* (Paris, 1959) ; Gomes, A. 'O negro no Brasil em São Paulo: aspectos humanos', *Revista do Instituto de História e Geografia de São Paulo*, 48 (1958), 139–49 ; Krause, A. *Mennonite settlement in the Paraguayan Chaco* (Chicago, 1952 ; Lowenthal, D. 'Colonial experiments in French Guiana, 1760–1800', *Hispanic American Historical Review*, 32 (1952), 22–43 ; Ovalle, L. 'Ocupación y desarrollo de la Provincia de Aisén', *Informaciones Geográficas*, 4 (1954), 27–73 ; Parsons, J. J. 'Antioqueño Colonisation in western Colombia', *Ibero-Americana*, 32 (1949) ; Bowen, E. 'The Welsh colony in Patagonia 1865–1885: a study in historical geography', *Geographical Journal*, 132 (1966), 16–32

51 Ardissone, R. 'Esbozo de la tesigeografía o geografía de la propiedad', *Revista Geográfica Panamericana*, 9 (1952), 1–19. For details of Ardissone's links with historian Félix Outes see Daus, F. A. 'Romualdo Ardissone', *Boletín de Estudios Geográficos* (Cuyo), 8 (1961), 91–6

52 Jefferson, M. *Peopling the Argentine Pampa* (New York, 1926)

53 Berninger, O. *Wald und offenes Land in Süd-Chile seit der Spanischen Eroberung* (Stuttgart, 1929), may be compared with James, P. *Latin America* (New York, 1969), 715–17 and Sternberg, H. O'R. 'Man and Environmental change in South America', in Fittkau, E. J. *et. al.* (eds) *Biogeography and Ecology in South America*, 1 (The Hague), 418–21

54 França, A. *A marcha do café e as frentes pioneiras* (São Paulo, 1956) ; Monbeig, P. *Pionniers et planteurs de São Paulo* (Paris, 1952) ; Papy, L. 'En marge de l'empire du café: la façade atlantique de São Paulo', *Las Cahiers d'Outre-Mer*, 5 (1952), 357–98 ; James, P. 'The coffee lands of southeastern Brazil', *Geographical Review*, 22 (1932), 235–44

55 Parsons, J. J. 'Antioqueño Colonisation in Western Colombia', *Ibero-Americana*, 32 (1949)

56 Butland, G. J. 'Frontiers of settlement in South America', *Revista Geográfica Panamericana*, 65 (1966), 93–108

57 For a study putting Latin American temperate grassland frontiers into a world-wide context see Gulley, J. L. M. 'The Turnerian frontier: a study in the migration of ideas', *Tijdschrift voor Economische en Sociale Geografie*, 50 (1959), 65–71, 81–91. For the Bolton frontier thesis see: Bolton, H. E. 'The mission as a frontier institution in the Spanish American colonies', *American Historical Review*, 23 (1917), 42–61 ; Zavala, S. 'The frontiers of

Hispanic America' in Wyman, W. D. and Kroeber, C. B. (eds) *The Frontier in Perspective* (Madison, 1957), 35–58

58 Sauer, C. O. 'The road to Cíbola', *Ibero-Americana*, 3 (1932)

59 Momsen, R. P. *Routes over the Serra do Mar: the evolution of transportation in the highlands of Rio de Janeiro and São Paulo* (Rio de Janeiro, 1964); Ardissone, R. 'Influencia de las comunicaciones en la instalación humana de un sector pampeano cordobés', *Gaea*, 10 (1956), 191–36; Barba, E. M. 'El comercio de Salta a mediados del siglo pasado', *Trabajos y communicaciones* (La Plata), 7 (1958), 38–69; Bueno Ortíz, A. 'Los transportes, 1839–1964', *Boletín de la Sociedad Geográfica de Lima*, 82 (1964), 103–18; Sepúlveda, S. 'El trigo chileno en el mercado mundial: ensayo de geografía histórica', *Informaciones Geográficas*, 6 (1956), 6–133; and also 'Otro aspecto del tráfico colonial con la provincia de Cuyo', *Informaciones Geográficas*, 9 (1959), 7–21. For an example of similar developments in maritime and riverine routeways see Guzman Rivas, P. 'Geographic influences of the Galleon Trade on New Spain', *Revista Geográfica Panamericana*, 27 (1960), 5–81 and Robinson, D. J. 'Evolución en el comercio del Orinoco a mediados del siglo XIX', *Revista Geográfica Panamericana*, 72 (1970), 13–43

60 Robinson, D. J. 'Trade and trading links in western Argentina during the Viceroyalty', *Geographical Journal*, 136 (1970), 24–41; West, R. C. and Parsons, J. J. 'The Topia road: a trans-sierran trail of colonial Mexico', *Geographical Review*, 31 (1941), 406–13

61 Keller, C. 'El Norte Chico en la época de la formación de la República', *Revista Chilena de Historia y Geografía*, 123 (1954), 15–49; Rey Balmaceda, R. 'El primer cruce longitudinal de la Patagonia', *Revista Geográfica Americana*, No. 233–4 (1955), Randle, P. H. *Geografía Histórica*, 93

62 Houston, J. M. 'The foundation of colonial towns in Hispanic America', in Beckinsale, R. P. and Houston, J. M. (eds) *Urbanization and its problems* (Oxford, 1968), 352–90

63 Vila, P. 'Consideraciones sobre poblaciones errantes en el periodo colonial', *Revista de Historia* (Caracas), 12 (1966), 11–24

64 Stanislawski, D. 'Early Spanish town planning in the New World', *Geographical Review*, 37 (1947), 94–105; see also Carrera Stampa, M. 'Planos de la ciudad de México', *Boletín de la Sociedad Mexicana de Geografía y Estadística*, 67 (1949), 265–427

65 Deffontaines, P. 'The origin and growth of the Brazilian network of towns', *Geographical Review*, 28 (1938), 379–99; Azevedo, A. de 'Vilas e Cidades do Brasil colonial: ensaio de geografía

urbana retrospectiva', *Boletim,* No. 208 (1956), Facultad de Filosofia da Universidade de São Paulo

66 Azevedo, A. de (ed) *A cidade de São Paulo: estudos de geografia urbana* (Sao Paulo, 1958) 4 vols

67 Monbeig, P. 'O estudo geográfico das cidades', *Boletim Geográfico,* 7 (1943), 7–29 ; Araujo, E. G. P. de 'A cidade de Olímpia: estudo de geografia urbana', *Boletim Paulista de Geografia,* 9 (1951), 19–37 ; Conselho Nacional de Geografia, *Aspectos geográficos da Terra Bandeirante* (Rio de Janeiro, 1954) ; James, *Geographical Review,* 23, 271–98 ; Deffontaines, P. 'As feiras de burros de Sorocaba', *Geografia,* 1 (1935), 263–70 ; Medeiros, F. L. 'A feira de burros de Sorocaba', *Boletim Paulista de Geografia,* 1 (1949), 40–9 ; Carvalho, A. J. de 'São Paulo antigo (1882–1886)', *Revista do Instituto Histórico e Geográfico de São Paulo,* 41 (1942), 47–62 ; Ricci, T. R. 'Aspecto geográfico del antiguo San Miguel del Tucumán', in *Geografia Una et Varia,* Machatchek-Festschrift (Tucumán, 1951), 17–29 and his *Evolución de la ciudad de San Miguel de Tucumán* (Tucumán, 1967) ; Flores, M. 'Del molino "San Francisco" a los "rios subterraneos", *Revista Geográfica Americana,* 17 (1955), 1–14 ; Luque Colombrés, C. 'Referencias documentales sobre la topografía del asiento urbano de Córdoba durante los siglos XV y XVII', *Gaea,* 10 (1956), 173–89 ; Randle, P. H. *Algunos aspectos de la geografia urbana de Buenos Aires* (Buenos Aires, 1969)

68 Randle, P. H. *La Ciudad Pampeana: geografía histórica* (Buenos Aires, 1969) ; and 'El origen de la uniformidad de las ciudades pampeanas', *Nuestra Arquitectura* (Buenos Aires), No. 407 (1963), 28–35

69 Wilhelmy, H. *Südamerika im Spiegel seiner Städte* (Hamburg, 1952) ; compare Kubler, G. 'Cities and culture in the colonial period of Latin America', *Diogenes,* 47 (1964), 53–62

70 Wilhelmy, H. *Die La Plataländer* (Braunschweig, 1963) ; Chebataroff, J. *Tierra Uruguaya* (Montevideo, 1954) ; Vila, P., Brito Figueroa, F., Cárdenas, A. L. and Carpio R. *Geografía de Venezuela,* vol 2, *El paisaje natural y el paisaje humanizado* (Caracas, 1965) ; West, R. C. and Augelli, J. P. provide a comprehensive and well documented synthesis in *Middle America—Its Lands and Peoples* (New York, 1966) 61–106, 229–307 ; Almada, F. 'Geografía humana del Estado de Chihuahua', *Boletín de la Sociedad Mexicana de Geografía y Estadística,* 57 (1942), 227–300 ; Cáceres, L. C. *Chiapas: síntesis geográfica e histórica* (Mexico, 1946) ; Moreno Toscano, A. *Geografía económica de*

S

México, siglo XVI (Mexico, 1968) ; Hopkins, E. A., Crist. R. E. and Snow, W. P. *Paraguay, 1852 and 1968* (New York, 1968) ; Lowenthal, D. *An historical geography of the Guianas,* unpublished MA thesis (Berkeley, 1950)

71 Butland, G. J. *The Human Geography of Southern Chile* (London, 1957) ; Sandner, G. *La Costa Atlántica de Nicaragua, Costa Rica, y Panamá: su conquista y colonización desde principios de la época colonial* (San José, 1964) ; Schmieder, O. 'The historic geography of Tucumán', *University of California Publications in Geography,* 2 (1928), 359–86 ; McBryde, F. W. *Cultural and historical geography of southwest Guatemala* (Washington, 1947) ; Azevedo, A. de *O vale do Paraíba* (Rio de Janeiro, 1944) ; Andrade, E. L. de *Sertões da Noroeste, 1850–1946* (Sao Paulo, 1945) ; Rey Balmaceda, R. *Geografía histórica de la Patagonia,* unpublished Doctoral thesis Universidad de Buenos Aires (1961) ; Pederson, L. R. *The mining industry of the Norte Chico, Chile* (Evanston, 1966) ; West, R. C. *Colonial placer mining in Colombia* (Baton Rouge, 1952) and *The Pacific lowlands of Colombia* (Baton Rouge, 1957)

72 Robinson, D. J. 'Changing settlement patterns in colonial Latin America', in Ucko, P. J., Tringham, R. and Dimbleby G. W. (eds) *Man, Settlement and Urbanism* (London, 1972)

73 For the work of the Berkeley demographic historians see Chaunu, *Révue Historique,* 124, 339–68 ; an outline of sources is provided in Konetzke, 'Las fuentes para la historia demográfica de Hispano-América durante la época colonial', *Anuario de Estudios Americanos,* 5 (1948), 267–324 ; for models of investigation : Smith, C. T. 'Depopulation in the Central Andes in the 16th Century', *Current Anthropology,* 11 (1970) 453–64 ; Gerhard, P. *Mexico en 1742* (Mexico, 1962) ; Cook, S. F. 'The population of Mexico in 1793', *Human Biology,* 14 (1942), 499–515 ; Zelinsky, W. 'Historical Geography of the negro population of Latin America', *Journal of Negro History,* 34 (1949), 153–221 ; Cunill, P. 'Documento sobre los pueblos de indios del obispado de Santiago en 1795', *Informaciones Geográficas,* 5 (1955), 16–23 ; Borah, W. 'America as model: the demographic impact of European expansion upon the non-European world', *Actas y Memorias del 35 Congreso de Americanistas* (Mexico, 1962), 379–87

74 Griffin, C. C. *Los temas sociales y económicos en la epoca de la independencia* (Caracas, 1962) ; Moreno, N. B. 'La demografía argentina en 1810', *Anales de la Academia Argentina de Geografía,* 4 (1960), 74–82 ; Tablante Garrido, P. N. 'Provincia

de Apure: monografia del Gobernador General J. C. Muñoz, 1831,' *Revista Geográfica* (Mérida), 2 (1960–61), 67–139 ; Robinson, *Revista Geográfica*, 72 ; see also the several essays in Blakemore, H. and Smith, C. T. *Latin America: geographical perspectives* (London, 1971)

75 Brady, T. *The application of computers to the analysis of census data: the bishopric of Caracas, 1780–1830* (Manitoba, 1970)

76 Vila, *Geografía de Venezuela*, 2, 420–32

77 Morse, R. M. 'Latin American cities: aspects of function and structure', *Comparative Studies in Society and History*, 26 (1961), 473–93

78 Foster, G. *Culture and conquest: America's Spanish heritage* (New York, 1961) ; Service, E. R. *Spanish—Guaraní relations in early colonial Paraguay* (Michigan, 1954) and 'Indian-European relations in colonial Latin America', *American Anthropologist*, 57 (1955), 411–25

79 Friedmann, J. *Regional development policy: a case study of Venezuela* (Cambridge, Mass., 1966), 20–38, 126–32

80 Germani, G. 'Stages of modernization in Latin America', *Cultures et Développement*, 2 (1969–70), 275–313

81 Sarfatti, M. *Spanish Bureaucratic-Patrimonialism in America* (Berkeley, 1966)

82 Brito Figueroa, F. *La estructura económica de Venezuela colonial* (Caracas, 1963), and *La estructura social y demográfica de Venezuela colonial* (Caracas, 1961)

83 West, *Colonial placer mining ;* Gibson, C. *Tlaxcala in the sixteenth century* (New Haven, 1952) ; also Morrisey, R. J. 'Colonial agriculture in New Spain', *Agricultural History*, 21 (1957), 24–9

84 Chevalier, F. *La Formation des Grands Domaines au Méxique* (Paris, 1952) and 'The north Mexican hacienda: eighteenth and nineteenth centuries', in Lewis, A. R. and McGann, T. F. (eds) *The New World Looks at its history* (Austin, 1963)

85 Scobie, J. R. *Revolution on the Pampas: a social history of Argentine wheat, 1860–1910* (Austin, 1964)

86 Azevedo, A. de 'A obra de Gilberto Freyre examinada a luz da geografia', in *Gilberto Freyre: sua Ciência, sua Filosofia, sua Arte* (Rio de Janeiro, 1962), 55–63 ; Freyre, G. *Sobrados e mucambos: decadência do patriarcado rural no Brasil* (São Paulo, 1963) and *Casa-Grande e Senzala* (Rio de Janeiro, 1933)

87 Freyre, G. *Nordeste* (Rio de Janeiro, 1937)

88 Chaunu, P. and Chaunu, H. *Séville et l'Atlantique (1504–1650)* (Paris, 1955–60) 8 vols ; see also Villegas, D. C. 'History and the

social sciences in Latin America' in Diégues Júnior, M. (ed) *Social Science in Latin America* (New York, 1967), 121–37; and Zavala, S. 'Los aspectos geográficos en la colonización del Nuevo Mundo', *Revista Geográfica Panamericana,* 29 (1961), 51–137; an excellent account of port developments is found in Brand, D. D. 'The development of Pacific coast ports during the Spanish colonial period in Mexico', in *Estudios Antropológicos Publicados en Homenaje al Doctor Manuel Gamio* (Mexico, 1956), 577–91

89 Stein, S. J. 'Latin American historiography: status and research opportunities', in Wagley, C. (ed) *Social Science Research on Latin America* (New York, 1964), 113; for another vantage point see Colmenares, G. *Encomienda y población en la provincia de Pamplona, 1544–65* (Bogotá, 1969)

90 Borah, W. 'New Spain's Century of Depression', *Ibero-Americana,* 35 (1951)

91 Lynch, J. *The Second Conquest of America, 1765–1808,* being Chapter 1 of *The Spanish American Revolutions, 1808–1826* (New York, 1972)

92 Cook, S. F. 'Soil Erosion and Population in Central Mexico', *Ibero-Americana,* 34 (1949)

93 Frank, A. G. *Capitalism and Underdevelopment in Latin America* (New York, 1967)

94 Furtado, C. *Economic Development in Latin America* (Cambridge, 1970); see also Mauro, F. 'México y Brasil: dos economías coloniales comparadas', *Historia Mexicana,* 10 (1961), 570–87

95 Frank, *Capitalism,* 14–15

96 Humphreys, R. A. *Tradition and Revolt in Latin America* (London, 1969)

97 For urban-rural definitions see Robinson, *Man, Settlement and Urbanism*; see Hemmings, J. *The Conquest of the Incas* (London, 1970) for an outstanding revisit to early colonial Peru; for place name evidence see Holmer, N. M. 'Indian place names in South America and the Antilles', *Names* (New York, 8 1960) 133–49; 197–219; 9 (1961) 37–52; compare with Vivo, J. A. 'Geografía lingüística y política pre-hispánica de Chiapas y secuencia de sus pobladores', *Revista Geográfica Panamericana,* 2 (1942), 121–56; and Waibel, L. 'Place names as an aid to the reconstruction of the original vegetation of Cuba', *Geographical Review,* 33 (1948), 376–96; for colonial marketing see Lockhart, J. *Spanish Peru 1532–1560: a colonial society* (Madison, 1968); for an excellent revisionist work see Coy, P. 'A watershed in Mexican

rural history: some thoughts on the reconciliation of conflicting interpretations', *Journal of Latin American Studies*, 3 (1971), 59–57

98 Robinson, D. J. 'Cultural and historical perspective in area studies: the case of Latin America', in Johnson, J. H. and Cooke, R. U. (eds) *Trends in Geography* (London, 1969), 253–68

99 Robinson, *Man, Settlement and Urbanism*; Germani, *Cultures et Développement* 2, 275–313 ; Ribeiro, D. 'The culture-historical configurations of the American people', *Current Anthropology*, 11 (1970), 403–34

100 Ardissone, R. 'Plan para el estudio de la cromografía Argentina', *Boletín de Estudios Geográficos* (Cuyo), 8 (1960), 1–29

101 Kubler, G. *Mexican Architecture of the Sixteenth Century* (New Haven, 1948), vol 1, 68–102

102 Elliott, J. H. *The Old World and the New, 1492–1650* (Cambridge, 1970), 14–27

103 For the raw data see Cline, H. F. 'The Relaciones Geográficos of the Spanish Indies, 1577–1586', *Hispanic American Historical Review*, 44 (1964), 341–74 and for later surveys Altolaguirre, A. de *Relaciones Geográficas de la Gobernación de Venezuela, 1767–68* (Caracas, 1954) ; for a recent study utilising the source see Moreno Toscano, *Geografía Económica de México (Siglo XVI)*. For a general account see La Puente y Olea, M. de. *Los Trabajos geográficos de la Casa de Contratación* (Sevilla, 1900)

Chapter 10 Historical Geography in Africa

1 The survey was conducted by the author by means of a questionnaire sent to all departments of geography in African universities.

2 Leighly, J. (ed) *Land and Life, A Selection from the Writings of Carl Ortwin Sauer* (Berkeley and Los Angeles, 1967) 342

3 Herskovits, M. J. *The Human Factor in Changing Africa* (New York, 1967) 3

4 Murdock, G. P. *Africa. Its Peoples and Their Culture History* (New York, 1950) 7

5 For two opposite views, see, for example, Murdock, *Africa*, 68–70 and Baker, H. G. 'Comments on the thesis that there was a major centre of plant domestication near the headwaters of the river Niger', *The Journal of African History*, 3 (1962), 229–33

6 The cause-effect relationship between traditional strong centralised political systems and population density in Africa is the thesis of Robert F. Stevenson's *Population and Political Systems in Tropical Africa* (New York, 1968)

7 Dickson, K. B. 'The Middle Belt of Ghana', *Bulletin de l'IFAN,* 31 ser. B (1969), 689–716

8 Dickson, K. B. *A Historical Geography of Ghana* (Cambridge, 1969)

9 A brief review of source materials for Ghana down to 1850 will be found in Dickson, K. B. 'Source materials for the historical geography of Ghana from earliest times to AD 1850', *Bulletin of the Ghana Geographical Association,* 12 (1968), 19–31

10 Vansina, J. *Oral Tradition: A Study in Historical Methodology* (London, 1965)

Bibliography

The following list is not exhaustive. From well over one thousand items referred to in the chapters of this book, some of the important and accessible published studies have been selected.

Alexander, F. Moving Frontiers. *An American Theme and its Application to Australian History* (Melbourne, 1947)

Allen, A. C. B. 'Marginal settlement—a case study of the Channel County of southwest Queensland', *Australian Geographical Studies,* 6 (1968), 1–23

Allen, H. C. *Bush and Backwoods. A Comparison of the Frontier in Australia and the United States* (Michigan, 1959)

Almada, F. 'Geografía humana del Estado de Chihuahua', *Boletín de la Sociedad Mexicana de Geografía y Estadística,* 57 (1952), 227–300

Andrade, M. C. de *A Terra e o Homen no Nordeste* (São Paulo, 1963)

Andrews, J. 'The emergence of the wheat belt in southeastern Australia to 1930', in Andrews, J. *Frontiers and Men. A Volume in Memory of Griffith Taylor 1880–1963* (Melbourne, 1966) 5–65

Armstrong, R. W. 'Auckland by gaslight. An urban geography of 1896', *New Zealand Geographer,* 15 (1959), 173–89

Aydelotte, W. O. 'Quantification in history', *American Historical Review,* 71 (1966), 803–25

Bachmann, H. 'Zur Methodik der Auswertung der Siedlungs- und Flurkarte für die siedlungsgeschichtliche Forschung', *Zeitschrift für Agrargeschichte und Agrarsoziologie*, 8 (1960), 1–13

Baker, A. R. H. 'The field system of an East Kent parish (Deal)', *Archaeologia Cantiana*, 78 (1963), 96–117

Baker, A. R. H. 'Open fields and partible inheritance on a Kent manor', *Economic History Review*, 17 (1964–5), 1–23

Baker, A. R. H. 'Field systems in the Vale of Holmesdale', *Agricultural History Review*, 14 (1966), 1–24

Baker, A. R. H. 'A note on the retrogressive and restrospective approaches in historical geography', *Erdkunde*, 22 (1968), 243–4

Baker, A. R. H. 'Reversal of the rank-size rule: some nine-teenth-century rural settlement sizes in France', *Professional Geographer*, 21 (1969), 386–92

Baker, A. R. H. 'Today's studies of yesterday's geographies', *Geographical Magazine*, 43 (1970–71), 452–3

Baker, A. R. H., Butlin, R. A., Phillips, A. D. M. and Prince, H. C. 'The future of the past', *Area*, 4 (1969), 46–51

Baker, A. R. H., Hamshere, J. D. and Langton, J. *Geographical Interpretations of Historical Sources. Readings in Historical Geography* (Newton Abbot, 1970)

Baker, J. N. L. 'The geography of Daniel Defoe', *Scottish Geographical Magazine*, 47 (1931), 257–69

Baker, J. N. L. 'The development of historical geography in Britain during the last hundred years', *Advancement of Science*, 8 (1952), 406–12

Bate, W. 'The urban sprinkle: country towns and Australian regional history', *Australian Economic History Review*, 10 (1970), 204–17

Beaver, S. H. 'The development of the Northamptonshire iron industry, 1851–1930', in Stamp, L. D. and Wooldridge, S. W. (eds) *London Essays in Geography* (London, 1951) 33–58

Benthein, B. *Die historischen Flurformen des südwestlichen Mecklenburg* (Schwerin, 1960)

Bergman, J. F. 'The distribution of cacao cultivation in Pre-Columbian America', *Annals of the Association of American Geographers*, 59 (1969), 85–96

Berkhofer, R. F. *A Behavioural Approach to Historical Analysis* (Toronto, 1969)

Bernstein, H. 'Regionalism in the national history of Mexico', *Acta Americana,* 2 (1944), 305–14

Bird, J. 'The foundation of Australian seaport capitals', *Economic Geography,* 41 (1945), 283–99

Blakemore, H., Smith, C. T. (eds) *Latin America: Geographical Perspectives* (London, 1971)

Blainey, G. *The Rush that Never Ended. A History of Australian Mining* (Melbourne, 1963)

Blainey, G. *The Tyranny of Distance. How Distance Shaped Australia's History* (Melbourne, 1966)

Blaut, J. M. 'Space and process', *Professional Geography,* 13 no 4 (1961), 1–7

Bobek, H. 'The main stages in socio-economic evolution from a geographic point of view', in Wagner, P. L. and Mikesell, M. W. (eds) *Readings in Cultural Geography* (Chicago, 1962) 218–47

Bolton, H. E. 'The mission as a frontier institution in the Spanish American colonies', *American Historical Review,* 23 (1917), 46–61

Borba de Morais, R. 'Contribução para a historia povoamento em São Paulo até fins do século XVIII', *Geografia,* 1 (1935), 68–87

Borde, J. and Gongora, M. *Evolución de la propiedad rural en el Valle del Puangue* 2 vols (Santiago, 1956)

Born, M. 'Langstreifenfluren in Nordhessen?', *Zeitschrift f. Agrargeschichte und Agrarsoziologie,* 15 (1967), 105–33

Bowden, M. J. 'The perception of the western interior of the United States, 1800–1870: a problem in historical geosophy', *Proceedings of the Association of American Geographers,* 1 (1969), 16–21

Bowen, E. 'The Welsh colony in Patagonia 1865–1885: a study in historical geography', *Geographical Journal,* 132 (1966), 16–32

Brady, T. *The application of computers to the analysis of census data: the Bishopric of Caracas, 1780–1830* (Manitoba, 1970)

Brand, D. D. 'The development of Pacific coast ports during the Spanish colonial period in Mexico', in *Estudios*

Antropológicos Publicados en Homenaje al Doctor Manuel Gamio (Mexico, 1956), 577–91

Brandon, P. F. 'Medieval clearances in the East Sussex Weald', *Transactions of the Institute of British Geographers*, 48 (1969), 135–53

Braudel, F. *La Méditerranée et le monde méditerranéen à l'époque de Philippe II* (Paris, 2nd edn 1966)

Broek, J. O. M. *The Santa Clara Valley, California* (Utrecht, 1932)

Broens, M. 'Le peuplement germanique de la Gaule entre la Méditerranée et l'Océan', *Annales du Midi*, 63 (1956), 17–32

Brookfield, H. C. 'On the environment as perceived', *Progress in Geography*, 1 (1969), 51–80

Brown, R. H. *Mirror for Americans. Likeness of the Eastern Seaboard, 1810* (New York, 1943)

Brown, R. H. *Historical Geography of the United States* (New York, 1948)

Brunet, P. *Structure agraire et économie rurale des plateaux tertiaires entre la Seine et l'Oise* (Caen, 1960)

Brunet, R. *Les campagnes toulousaines. Etude géographique* (Toulouse, 1965)

Bull, G. B. G. 'Thomas Milne's land utilization map of the London area in 1800', *Geographical Journal*, 122 (1956), 25–30

Burghardt, A. F. 'The location of river towns in the central lowland of the United States', *Annals of the Association of American Geographers*, 49 (1959), 305–23

Burghardt, A. F. *Borderland. A Historical and Geographical Study of Burgenland, Austria* (Madison, 1962)

Burghardt, A. F. 'The origin and development of the road network of the Niagara peninsula, Ontario, 1770–1851', *Annals of the Association of American Geographers*, 59 (1969), 417–40

Butland, G. J. 'Frontiers of settlement in South America', *Revista Geográfica Panamericana*, 65 (1966), 93–108

Butzer, K. *Environment and Archaeology. An Introduction to Pleistocene Geography* (Chicago, 1964)

Buxton, G. L. *The Riverina, 1861–1894. An Australian regional study* (Melbourne, 1967)

Bylund, E. 'Theoretical considerations regarding the distribution of settlement in inner north Sweden', *Geografiske Annaler*, 42 (1960), 225–31

Bylund, E. 'Generationsvåger och bebyggelsespridning', *Ymer*, 88 (1968), 64–71

Cant, R. G. 'The agriculture frontier in miniature: a microstudy of the Canterbury Plains, 1850–1875', *New Zealand Geographer*, 24 (1968), 155–67

Cant, R. G. 'The dilemma of historical geography', in Johnston W. B. (ed) *Human Geography. Concepts and Case Studies* (Christchurch, 1969) 40–60

Caroe, L. 'A multivariate grouping scheme: association analysis of East Anglian towns', in Bowen, E. G., Carter, H. and Taylor, J. A. (eds) *Geography at Aberystwyth* (Cardiff, 1968) 253–69

Carter, F. W. 'An analysis of the medieval Serbian oecumene: a theoretical approach', *Geografiska Annaler*, 51 (1969), 39–56

Carter, H. 'The urban hierarchy and historical geography: a consideration with reference to north-west Wales', *Geographical Studies*, 3 (1956), 85–101

Carter, H. 'Urban systems and town morphology', in Bowen, E. G., Carter, H. and Taylor, J. A. (eds) *Geography at Aberystwyth* (Cardiff, 1968), 219–34

Carter, H. *The Growth of the Welsh City System. An Inaugural Lecture delivered at the University College of Wales Aberystwyth on 12 February 1969* (Cardiff, 1969)

Catchpole, A. J. W., Moodie, D. W. and Kaye, B. 'Content analysis: a method for the identification of dates of first freezing and first breaking from descriptive accounts', *Professional Geographer*, 22 no 5 (1970), 252–7

Chaunu, P. 'Une histoire hispano-américaniste pilote: en marge de l'oeuvre de l'Ecole de Berkeley', *Révue Historique*, 124 (1960), 339–68

Chevalier, F. *La formation des grandes domaines au Mexique* (Paris, 1952) Trans by E. Curtis as *Land and Society in Colonial Mexico* (Berkeley, 1963)

Chevalier, F. 'The north Mexican hacienda: eighteenth and nineteenth centuries', in A. R. Lewis and T. F. McGann (eds) *The New World Looks at its History* (Austin, 1963), 95–107

Clark, A. H. 'Field work in historical geography', *Professional Geographer,* 4 (1946), 13–23

Clark, A. H. *The Invasion of New Zealand by People, Plants and Animals. The South Island.* (New Brunswick, 1949)

Clark, A. H. 'Historical Geography' in James, P. E. and Jones, C. F. (eds) *American Geography. Inventory and Prospect* (Syracuse, 1954) 70–105

Clark, A. H. *Three Centuries and the Island. A Historical Geography of Settlement and Agriculture in Prince Edward Island, Canada* (Toronto, 1959)

Clark, A. H. 'Geographical change. A theme for economic history', *Journal of Economic History,* 20 (1960), 607–13

Clark, A. H. *Acadia. The Geography of Early Nova Scotia to 1760* (Madison, 1968)

Clark, W. A. V. 'Dunedin at the turn of the century', *New Zealand Geographer,* 18 (1962), 93–115

Claval, P. *Essai sur l'évolution de la géographie humaine* (Paris, 1964)

Cline, H. F. 'Mexican community studies', *Hispanic American Historical Review,* 32 (1952), 212–42

Clout, H. D. 'The retreat of the wasteland of the Pays de Bray', *Transactions of the Institute of British Geographers,* 47 (1969), 171–89

Cochran, T. C. 'Economic history, old and new', *American Historical Review,* 74 (1969), 1561–72

Colmenares, G. *Encomienda y población en la provincia de Pamplona (1549–1650)* (Bogotá, 1969)

Conzen, M. R. G. 'Alnwick, Northumberland. A study in town-plan analysis', *Institute of British Geographers Publications,* no 27 (1960)

Cook, S. F. 'The population of Mexico in 1793', *Human Biology,* 14 (1942), 499–515

Coy, P. 'A watershed in Mexican rural history: some thoughts on the reconciliation of conflicting interpretations', *Journal of Latin American Studies,* 3 (1971), 39–57

Cumberland, K. B. 'A century's change: natural to cultural vegetation in New Zealand', *Geographical Review,* 31 (1941), 529–54

Cumberland, K. B. 'Aotearoa Maori: New Zealand about 1780', *Geographical Review,* 39 (1949), 401–24

Cumberland, K. B. 'A land despoiled: New Zealand about 1838', *New Zealand Geographer,* 6 (1950), 13–34

Cumberland, K. B. ' "Jimmy Grants" and "Mihaneres". New Zealand about 1853', *Economic Geography,* 30 (1954), 70–89

Cumberland, K. B. 'Moas and men: New Zealand about AD 1250', *Geographical Review,* 52 (1962), 151–73

Cumberland, K. B. ' "Climatic change" or cultural interference? New Zealand in Moahunter times', in McCaskill, M. (ed) *Land and Livelihood. Geographical Essays in Honour of George Jobberns* (Christchurch, 1962) 88–142

Cumberland, K. B. and Hargreaves, R. P. 'Middle island ascendant: New Zealand in 1881', *New Zealand Geographer,* 11 (1955), 95–118

Cunill, P. 'Documento sobre los pueblos de indios del obispado de Santiago en 1795', *Informaciones Geográficas* (1955), 16–23

Daly, M. 'The development of the urban pattern of Newcastle', *Australian Economic History Review,* 10 (1970), 190–203

Darby, H. C. 'Domesday woodland in East Anglia', *Antiquity,* 8 (1934), 185–99

Darby, H. C. (ed) *An Historical Geography of England before 1800* (Cambridge, 1936)

Darby, H. C. *The Draining of the Fens* (Cambridge, 1940)

Darby, H. C. 'The movement of population to and from Cambridgeshire between 1851 and 1861', *Geographical Journal,* 101 (1943), 118–25

Darby, H. C. *The Theory and Practice of Geography. An Inaugural Lecture delivered at Liverpool on 7 February 1946* (London, 1947)

Darby, H. C. 'The regional geography of Thomas Hardy's Wessex', *Geographical Review,* 38 (1948), 426–43

Darby, H. C. 'The clearing of the English woodlands', *Geography,* 36 (1951), 71–83

Darby, H. C. 'The changing English landscape', *Geographical Journal,* 117 (1951), 377–94

Darby. H. C. *The Domesday Geography of Eastern England* (Cambridge, 1952)

Darby, H. C. 'On the relations of geography and history', *Transactions and Papers of the Institute of British Geographers*, 19 (1953), 1–11

Darby, H. C. 'Man and the landscape in England', *Journal of the Town Planning Institute*, 39 (1953), 74–80

Darby, H. C. 'Some early ideas on the agricultural regions of England', *Agricultural History Review*, 2 (1954), 30–47

Darby, H. C. 'The clearing of the woodlands in Europe', in Thomas, W. L. (ed) *Man's Role in Changing the Face of the Earth* (Chicago, 1956), 183–216

Darby, H. C. 'An Historical Geography of England: twenty years after', *Geographical Journal*, 126 (1960), 147–59

Darby, H. C. 'The problem of geographical description', *Transactions and Papers of the Institute of British Geographers*, 30 (1962), 1–14

Darby, H. C. 'Historical geography', in Finberg, H. P. R. (ed) *Approaches to History* (London, 1962), 127–56

Deffontaines, P. *Regiões e paisagens do Estado de São Paulo* (São Paulo, 1935)

Deffontaines, P. 'The origin and growth of the Brazilian network of towns', *Geographical Review*, 28 (1938), 379–99

Denecke, D. *Methodische Untersuchungen zur historisch-geographischen Wegeforschung im Baum zwischen Solling und Harz. Ein Beitrag zur Rekonstruktion der mittelalterlichen Kulturlandschaft* (Göttingen, 1969)

Denevan, W. M. 'The aboriginal cultural geography of the Llanos de Mojos of Bolivia', *Ibero-Americana*, 48 (1966)

De Planhol, X. "Les nomades, la steppe et la forêt en Anatolie', *Geographische Zeitschrift*, 53 (1965), 101–16

De Planhol, X. *Les fondements géographiques de l'histoire de l'Islam* (Paris, 1968)

De Planhol, X. 'Le déboisement de l'Iran', *Annales de Géographie*, 78 (1969), 625–35

De Planhol, X. and Lacroix, J. 'Géographie et toponymie en Lorraine', *Revue Géographique de l'Est*, 3 (1963), 9–14

Derruau, M. *La Grande Limagne auvergnate et bourbonnaise* (Clermont-Ferrand, 1949)

Desai, M. 'Some issues in economic history', *Economic History Review,* 21 (1968), 1–16

Dickinson, R. E. 'Rural settlements in the German lands', *Annals of the Association of American Geographers,* 39 (1949), 239–63

Dickson, K. B. *A Historical Geography of Ghana* (Cambridge, 1969)

Dion, R. *Le Val de Loire* (Tours, 1934)

Dion, R. *Essai sur la formation du paysage rural français* (Tours, 1934)

Dion, R. *Les frontières de la France* (Paris, 1947)

Dion, R. *Histoire de la vigne et du vin en France des origines au XIXe siècle* (Paris, 1959)

Dongus, H. 'Die Entwicklung der östlichen Poebene seit frühgeschichtlicher Zeit', *Erdkunde,* 17 (1963), 205–22

Donkin, R. A. 'The Cistercian order in medieval England: some conclusions', *Transactions and Papers of the Institute of British Geographers,* 33 (1963), 181–98

Donkin, R. A. 'Pre-Columbian field implements and their distribution in the highlands of Middle and South America', *Anthropos,* 65 (1970), 505–29

Duby, G. *L'économie rurale et la vie des campagnes dans l'Occident médiéval* (Paris, 1962)

Dunbar, G. S. *Historical Geography of the North Carolina Outer Banks* (Baton Rouge, 1955)

Edwards, C. R. 'Aboriginal watercraft on the Pacific Coast of South America', *Ibero-Americana,* 47 (1965)

Eidt, R. 'Aboriginal Chibcha settlement in Colombia', *Annals of the Association of American Geographers,* 49, (1959), 374–92

Elkins, T. H. 'An English traveller in the Stegerland', *Geographical Journal,* 122 (1956), 306–16

Emery, F. V. 'English regional studies from Aubrey to Defoe', *Geographical Journal,* 124 (1958), 315–25

Enequist, G. *Geographical Changes of Rural Settlement in Northwestern Sweden since 1523* (Uppsala, 1959)

Febvre, L. *La terre et l'évolution humaine* (Paris, 1922)

Fehn, K. *Siedlungsgeschichtliche Grundlagen der Herrschafts- und Gesellschaftsentwicklung in Mittelschwaben* (Augsburg, 1966)

Fel, A. *Les hautes terres du Massif Central. Tradition paysanne et économie agricole* (Clermont-Ferrand, 1962)

Flatrès, P. *Géographie rurale de quatre contrées celtiques. Irlande, Galles, Cornwall et Man* (Rennes, 1957)

Fliedner, D. *Die Kulturlandschaft der Hamme-Wümme-Niederung* (Göttingen, 1970)

Forrest, J. 'Population and settlement on the Otago goldfields 1861–1870', *New Zealand Geographer*, 17 (1961), 64–86

Forrest, J. 'Otago during the gold rushes', in Watters, R. F. (ed) *Land and Society in New Zealand. Essays in Historical Geography* (Wellington, 1965), 80–100

Foster, G. *Culture and conquest: America's Spanish heritage* Viking Fund Publications in Anthropology, No. 27 (Washington, 1960)

Franz, G. *Historische Kartographie Forschung und Bibliographie* (Hanover, 2nd edn, 1962)

French, R. A. 'Historical geography in the U.S.S.R.', *Soviet Geography Review and Translation*, 9 (1968) 551–61

Friis, H. R. 'The image of the American West at mid-century, 1840–1860: a product of scientific geographical exploration by the United States government', in McDermott, J. F. (ed) *The Frontier Re-examined* (Urbana, 1967), 49–63

Furtado, C. *Economic Development in Latin America* (Cambridge, 1970)

Fuson, R. H. 'The orientation of Mayan ceremonial centers', *Annals of the Association of American Geographers*, 59 (1969), 494–511

Galloway, J. H. 'The sugar industry of Pernambuco during the nineteenth century', *Annals of the Association of American Geographers*, 58 (1960), 285–303

Gerhard, P. *México en 1742* (Mexico, 1962)

Germani, G. 'Stages of modernization in Latin America', *Cultures et Développement*, 2 (1969–70), 275–313

Gilchrist, D. T. (ed) *The Growth of the Seaport Cities, 1790–1825* (Charlottesville, 1967)

Glasscock, R. E. 'The distribution of wealth in East Anglia in the early fourteenth century', *Transactions and Papers of the Institute of British Geographers*, 32 (1963), 113–23

Goehrke, C. *Die Wüstungen in der Moskauer Rus* (Wiesbaden, 1968)

Goheen, P. *Victorian Toronto, 1850–1900. Pattern and Process of Growth* (Chicago, 1970)

Göransson, S. 'Field and village on the island of Öland', *Geografiska Annaler*, 40 (1958), 101–58

Görannson, S. *Village planning patterns and territorial organization. Studies in the development of the rural landscape of eastern Sweden* (Uppsala, 1971)

Gottschalk, L. (ed) *Generalization in the Writing of History* (Chicago, 1963)

Gould, J. D. 'Hypothetical history', *Economic History Review*, 22 (1969), 195–207

Grenfell Price, A. *The Foundation and Settlement of South Australia, 1829–1845* (Adelaide, 1924)

Grenfell Price, A. *White Settlers and Native Peoples* (Melbourne, 1949)

Grenfell Price, A. *The Western Invasions of the Pacific and its Continents. A Survey of Moving Frontiers and Changing Landscapes, 1513–1958* (Melbourne, 1963)

Grenfell Price, A. 'The moving frontiers and changing landscapes of flora and fauna in Australia', in Andrews, J. (ed) *Frontiers and Men: A Volume in memory of Griffith Taylor 1880–1963* (Melbourne, 1966) 155–73

Grigg, D. B. 'Changing regional values during the Agricultural Revolution in South Lincolnshire', *Transactions and Papers of the Institute of British Geographers*, 30 (1962), 91–103

Grigg, D. *The Agricultural Revolution in South Lincolnshire* (Cambridge, 1966)

Gulley, J. L. M. 'The Turnerian frontier: a study in the migration of ideas', *Tijdschrift voor Economische en Sociale Geografie*, 50 (1959), 65–72, 81–91

Gulley, J. L. M. *The Wealden Landscape in the Early Seventeenth Century and its Antecedants* (unpublished PhD thesis, University of London, 1966)

Gulley, J. L. M. 'The retrospective approach in historical geography', *Erdkunde*, 15 (1961), 306–9

Gunder Frank, A. *Capitalism and Underdevelopment in Latin America: Historical Studies of Chile and Brazil* (New York, 1967)

T

Guzman Rivas, P. 'Geographic influences of the galleon trade on New Spain', *Revista Geográfica Panamericana*, 127 (1960), 5–81

Haarnagel, W. 'Die prähistorischen Siedungsformen im Küstengebiet der Nordsee', *Beiträge zur Genese der Siedlungs-und Agrarlandschaft in Europa* (Wiesbaden, 1968), 67–84

Hägerstrand, T. *Innovation Diffusion as a Spatial Process* (Chicago, 1967)

Hahn, H. *Die deutschen Weinbaugebiete. Ihre historisch-geographische Entwicklung und Wirtschafts und Sozialstruktur* (Bonn, 1956)

Hahn, H., Krings, W., Zorn, W. 'Historische Wirtschaftskarte der Rheinlande um 1820', *Erdkunde*, 24 (1970), 169–80

Hall, P. 'The location of the clothing trades in London, 1861–1951', *Transactions and Papers of the Institute of British Geographers*, 28 (1960), 155–78

Hall, P. *The Industries of London since 1861* (London, 1962)

Hannerberg, D. *Närkes landsbygd 1600–1820* (Göteborg, 1941)

Hannerberg, D. 'Solskifte and older methods of partitioning arable land in central Sweden during the middle ages', *Annales de l'Est*, 21 (1959), 245–59

Hannerberg, D. 'Die Parzellierung vorgeschichtlicher Kammerfluren und deren spätere Neuparzellierung durch "Bolskifte" und "Solskifte" ', *Zeitschrift für Agrargeschichte und Agrarsoziologie*, 6 (1959), 26–33

Hargreaves, R. P. 'The golden age: New Zealand about 1867', *New Zealand Geographer*, 16 (1960), 1–32

Harley, J. B. 'Population trends and agricultural developments from the Warwickshire Hundred Rolls of 1279', *Economic History Review*, 11 (1958–9), 8–18

Harris, A. *The Rural Landscape of the East Riding of Yorkshire 1700–1850* (London, 1961)

Harris, D. R. 'Plants, animals and man in the Outer Leeward Islands, West Indies—an ecological study of Antigua, Barbuda and Anguilla', *University of California Publications in Geography*, 18 (1965), 1–184

Harris, R. C. *The Seigneurial System in Early Canada. A Geographical Study* (Madison, 1966)

Harris, R. C. 'Historical geography in Canada', *Canadian Geographer*, 11 (1967), 235–250

Harris, R. C. 'Reflections on the fertility of the historical geographical mule', *University of Toronto Department of Geography Discussion Paper Series*, no 10 (1970)

Hart, J. F. 'Loss and abandonment of cleared farm land in the eastern United States', *Annals of the Association of American Geographers*, 58 (1968), 417–440

Harvey, D. W. 'Locational change in the Kentish hop industry and the analysis of land use patterns', *Transactions and Papers of the Institute of British Geographers*, 33 (1963), 123–44

Harvey, D. W. 'Models of the evolution of spatial patterns in human geography', in Chorley, R. J. and Haggett, P. (eds) *Models in Geography* (London, 1967), 549–608

Heathcote, R. L. 'Changes in pastoral land tenure and ownership', *Australian Geographical Studies*, 3 (1965), 1–16

Heathcote, R. L. *Back of Bourke. A Study of Land Appraisal and Settlement in Semi-arid Australia* (Melbourne, 1965)

Helmfrid, S. (ed) 'Morphogenesis of the agrarian landscape. Papers of the Vadstena Symposium at the XIXth International Geographical Congress', *Geografiska Annaler*, 43 (1961), 1–328

Helmfrid, S. 'The storskifte, enskifte and lagaskifte in Sweden: general features', *Geografiska Annaler*, 43 (1961), 114–29

Helmfrid, S. 'Östergötland "Västanstång". Studien über die ältere Agrarlandschaft und ihre Genese', *Geografiska Annaler*, 44 (1962), 1–277

Helmfrid, S. *Gutsbildung und Agrarlandschaft in Schweden im 16–17 Jahrhundert* (Stockholm, 1965)

Hemming, J. *The Conquest of the Incas* (London, 1970)

Henderson, H. C. K. 'Agriculture in England and Wales in 1801', *Geographical Journal*, 118 (1952), 338–45

Hewes, L. and Schmieding, A. C. 'Risk in the central Great Plains: geographical patterns of wheat failure in Nebraska, 1931–1952', *Geographical Review*, 46 (1956), 375–87

Higman, B. W. 'The regional impact of the sugar industry in New South Wales, 1870–1912', *Australian Geographical Studies*, 6 (1968), 43–58

Higounet, C. 'La méthode cartographique en histoire', *Relazioni X Congresso Internationale di Scienze Storiche*, 7 (Rome, 1955), 104–6

Higounet, C. 'Une carte agricole de l'Albigeois vers 1260', *Annales du Midi*, 65 (1958), 65–72

Hilliard, S. B. 'Pork in the ante-bellum south: the geography of self sufficiency', *Annals of the Association of American Geographers*, 59 (1969), 461–80

Hilliard, S. B. 'Hog meat and corn-pone: food habits in the ante-bellum south; *Proceedings of the American Philosophical Society*, 113 (1969), 1–13

Hopkins, E. A., Crist, R. E. and Snow, W. P. *Paraguay 1852–1968* (New York, 1968)

Hoskins, W. G. *The Making of the English Landscape* (London, 1955)

Houston, J. M. 'The foundation of colonial towns in Hispanic America', in R. P. Beckinsale and J. M. Houston (eds) *Urbanization and its Problems* (Oxford, 1968), 352–90

Hudson, J. C. 'A location theory for rural settlement', *Annals of the Association of American Geographers*, 59 (1969), 365–81

Humphreys, R. A. 'British merchants and South American Independence', *Proceedings of the British Academy*, 51 (1965), 151–74

Humphreys, R. A. *Tradition and Revolt in Latin America* (London, 1965)

Hunt, E. H. 'The new economic history: Professor Fogel's study of American railways', *History*, 53 (1968), 3–18

Jäger, H. 'Zur Geschichte der deutschen Kulturlandschaften', *Geogr. Zeitschr.*, 51 (1963), 90–143

Jäger, H. 'Wüstungsforschung und Geographie', *Geogr. Zeitschr.*, 56 (1968), 165–80

Jäger, H. 'Reduktive und progressive Methoden in der deutschen Geographie', *Erdkunde*, 22 (1965), 245–6

Jäger, H. *Historische Geographie* (Braunschweig, 1969)

Jäger, H., Krenzlin, A., Uhlig, H. (eds) *Beiträge zur Genese der Siedlungs- und Agrarlandschaft in Europa* (Wiesbaden, 1968)

Jakle, J. A. 'Salt on the Ohio Valley frontier, 1770–1820', *Annals of the Association of American Geographers,* 59 (1969), 687–709

Jakle, J. A. and Wheeler, J. O. 'The changing residential structure of the Dutch population in Kalamazoo, Michigan', *Annals of the Association of American Geographers,* 59 (1969), 441–60

James, P. E. 'Belo Horizonte and Ouro Preto: a comparative study of two Brazilian cities', *Papers of the Michigan Acad. of Sci., Arts and Letters,* 18 (1932), 239–58

James, P. E. 'The coffee lands of southeastern Brazil', *Geographical Review,* 22 (1932), 225–44

James, P. E. 'Rio de Janeiro and São Paulo', *Geographical Review,* 23 (1933), 271–98

James, P. E. 'The changing pattern of population in São Paulo State', *Geographical Review,* 28 (1938), 353–62

Jeans, D. N. 'The breakdown of Australia's first rectangular survey', *Australian Geographical Studies,* 4 (1966), 119–28

Jeans, D. N. 'Territorial divisions and the location of towns in New South Wales 1826–1842', *Australian Geographer,* 10 (1967), 243–55

Jennings, J. N. 'Man as a geological agent', *Australian Journal Science,* 28 (1965), 150–6

Jobberns, G. 'Geography and national development', *New Zealand Geographer,* 1 (1945), 6

Johnson, B. L. C. 'The charcoal iron industry in the early eighteenth century', *Geographical Journal,* 117 (1951), 167–77

Johnson, H. B. 'The location of German immigrants in the Middle West', *Annals of the Association of American Geographers,* 41 (1951), 1–41

Johnson, H. B. 'French Canada and the Ohio Country: a study in early spatial relationship', *Canadian Geographer,* 3 (1958), 1–10

Johnston, R. J. 'An outline of the development of Melbourne's street pattern', *Australian Geographer,* 10 (1968), 453–65

Johnston, W. B. 'Pioneering the bushland of lowland Taranaki: a case study', *New Zealand Geographer*, 17 (1961), 1–18

Jones, G. R. J. 'Early territorial organisation in England and Wales', *Geografiska Annaler*, 43 (1961), 174–81

Jordan, T. G. *German Seed in Texas Soil. Immigrant Farmers in Nineteenth Century Texas* (Austin, 1966)

Juillard, E. *La vie rurale dans la plaine de Basse Alsace* (Strasbourg, 1953)

Juillard, E., Meynier, A., de Planhol, X. and Sautter, G. *Structures agraires et paysages ruraux: un quart de siècle de recherches françaises* (Nancy, 1957)

Kaatz, M. R. 'The Black Swamp: a study in historical geography', *Annals of the Association of American Geographers*, 45 (1955), 1–35

Kirk, W. 'Historical geography and the concept of the behavioural environment', *Indian Geographical Journal*, Silver Jubilee Volume (1952), 152–60

Kirk, W. 'Problems of Geography', *Geography*, 48 (1963), 357–72

Kirikov, S. V. *Ptitsy i Mlekopitayushchiye v Usloviyakh Landshaftov Yuzhnoy Okonechnosti Urala* (Moscow, 1952)

Kirikov, S. V. *Promyslovyye Zhivotnyye, Prirodnaya Sreda i Chelovek* (Moscow, 1966)

Kniffen, F. B. 'The American agricultural fair: the pattern', *Annals of the Association of American Geographers*, 39 (1949), 264–82

Kniffen, F. B. 'The American agricultural fair: time and place', *Annals of the Association of American Geographers*, 41 (1951), 42–57

Kniffen, F. B. 'The American covered bridge', *Geographical Review*, 41 (1951), 114–23

Kniffen, F. B. 'Folk housing: key to diffusion', *Annals of the Association of American Geographers*, 55 (1965), 549–77

Kniffen, F. B. *Louisiana: Its Land and People* (Baton Rouge, 1968)

Kollmorgen, W. M. 'The woodsman's assaults on the domain

of the cattleman', *Annals of the Association of American Geographers,* 59 (1969), 215–39

Krause, A. *Mennonite settlement in the Paraguayan Chaco.* Univ. of Chicago, Dept. of Geography Research Paper 25 (Chicago, 1952)

Krenzlin, A. *Historische und wirtschaftliche Züge im Siedlungsformenbild des westlichen Ostdeutschland* (Frankfurt, 1955)

Kroeber, C. B. *The Growth of the Shipping Industry in the Rio de la Plata Region, 1794–1860* (Madison, 1957)

Kubler, G. A. 'Cities and culture in the colonial period in Latin America', *Diogenes,* 148 (1964), 53–62

Lambert, A. M. 'The agriculture of Oxfordshire at the end of the eighteenth century', *Agricultural History,* 29 (1955), 31–8

Lambert, J. M., Jennings, J. N., Smith, C. T., Green, C., and Hutchinson, J. N. 'The making of the Broads: a reconsideration of their origin in the light of new evidence', *Royal Geographical Society Research Series,* 3 (1960)

Langton, J. 'System theory and the study of change in human geography', *Progress in Geography,* vol 4 (1972)

Lautensach, H. 'Otto Schlüter's Bedeutung für die methodische Entwicklung der Geographie', *Petermanns Geogr. Mitt.,* 96 (1952), 219–31

Lawton, R. 'The economic geography of Craven in the early nineteenth century', *Transactions and Papers of the Institute of British Geographers,* 20 (1954), 93–111

Lawton, R. 'Population changes in England and Wales in the later nineteenth century: an analysis of trends by Registration Districts', *Transactions of the Institute of British Geographers,* 44 (1968), 55–74

Le Roy Gordon, B. 'Human geography and ecology in the Sinú country of Colombia', *Ibero-Americana,* 39 (1957)

Le Roy Ladurie, E. *Les paysans du Languedoc* (Paris, 1962)

Le Roy Ladurie, E. *Histoire du climat depuis l'an mil* (Paris, 1967)

Lewis, G. M. 'Changing emphasis in the description of the natural environment of the American Great Plains area', *Transactions and Papers of the Institute of British Geographers,* 30 (1962), 75–90

Lewis, G. M. 'Regional ideas and reality in the Cis-Rocky

Mountain West', *Transactions of the Institute of British Geographers*, 38 (1966), 135–50

Lewis, G. M. 'William Gilpin and the concept of the Great Plains region', *Annals of the Association of American Geographers*, 56 (1966), 33–51

Lewis, P. 'A numerical approach to the location of industry exemplified by the distribution of the paper-making industry in England and Wales from 1860 to 1965', *University of Hull Occasional Papers in Geography*, 13 (1969)

Lewis, R. A. and Rowland, R. H. 'Urbanization in the U.S.S.R., 1897–1966', *Annals of the Association of American Geographers*, 59 (1969), 770–96

Lindquist, S.-O. *Det förhistoriska kulturlandskapat i östra Östergötland* (Stockholm, 1968)

Linge, G. J. R. 'Manufacturing in Auckland: its origins and growth 1840–1936', *New Zealand Geographer*, 14 (1958), 47–64

Livet, R. *Habitat rural et structures agraires en Basse Provence* (Gap, 1962)

Lockhart, J. *Spanish Peru 1532–1560: a Colonial Society* (Madison, 1968)

Lowenthal, D. 'Colonial experiments in French Guiana, 1760–1800', *Hispanic American Historical Review*, 32 (1952), 22–43

McBryde, F. W. *Cultural and Historical Geography of South West Guatemala*. Smithsonian Institution, Institute of Social Anthropology, Pub No 4 (Washington, D.C., 1947)

McCaskill, M. 'Man and landscape in North Westland', in Eyre, S. R. and Jones, G. R. J. (eds) *Geography as Human Ecology* (London, 1966) 264–90

McManis, D. R. *The Initial Evaluation and Utilization of the Illinois Prairies, 1815–40* (Chicago, 1964)

McManis, D. R. *Historical Geography of the United States. A Bibliography, Excluding Alaska and Hawaii* (Ypsilanti, Michigan, 1965)

Mead, W. R. 'Pehr Kalm in the Chilterns', *Acta Geographica*, 17 (1962), 1–33

Meinig, D. W. 'A comparative historical geography of two railnets: Columbia Basin and south Australia', *Annals of the Association of American Geographers,* 52 (1962), 394–413

Meinig, D. W. *On the Margins of the Good Earth. The South Australia Wheat Frontier, 1869–1884* (Chicago, 1962)

Meinig, D. W. *The Great Columbia Plain. Historical Geography, 1805–1910* (Seattle, 1968)

Meinig, D. W. *Imperial Texas* (Austin, 1968)

Meinig, D. W. *Southwest: Three Peoples in Geographical Change* (New York, 1971)

Merrens, H. R. *Colonial North Carolina in the Eighteenth Century. A Study in Historical Geography* (Chapel Hill, 1964)

Merrens, H. R. 'Historical geography and early American history', *William and Mary Quarterly,* 3rd Ser, 22 (1965), 529–48

Meynier, A. 'La genèse du parcellaire breton', *Norois,* 13 (1966), 595–610

Mikesell, M. W. *Northern Morocco. A Cultural Geography* (Berkeley, 1961)

Mikesell, M. W. 'Geographic perspectives in anthropology', *Annals of the Association of American Geographers,* 57 (1967), 617–34

Mitchell, J. B. *Historical Geography* (London, 1954)

Mitchell, R. D. *The Upper Shenandoah Valley of Virginia During the Eighteenth Century. A Study in Historical Geography* (Madison, 1967)

Momsen, R. P. 'Routes over the Serra do Mar', *Revista Geográfica Panamericana,* 32 (1965), 5–167

Morrill, R. L. 'Migration and the spread and growth of urban settlement', *Lund Studies in Geography Series B,* 26 (1965)

Morrisey, R. J. 'Colonial agriculture in New Spain', *Agricultural History,* 31 (1957), 24–9

Morse, R. M. 'Some characteristics of Latin American urban history', *American Historical Review,* 17 (1962), 317–38

Mortimore, M. J. 'Landownership and urban growth in Bradford and its environs in the West Riding conurbation', *Transactions of the Institute of British Geographers,* 46 (1969), 105–19

Müller-Wille, W. *Eisenzeitliche Fluren in den festländischen Nordseegebieten* (Münster, 1965)

Nelson, H. J. 'Walled cities of the U.S.A.', *Annals of the Association of American Geographers*, 51 (1961), 1–22

Nelson, J. G. 'Man and landscape in the western plains of Canada', *Canadian Geographer*, 11 (1967), 251–64

Newcomb, R. M. 'Twelve working approaches to historical geography', *Yearbook of the Association of Pacific Coast Geographers*, 31 (1969), 27–50

Newcomb, R. M. 'An example of the applicability of remote sensing: historical geography', *Geoforum*, 1 (1970), 89–92

Nitz, H.-J. 'Siedlungsgeographische Beiträge zum Problem der fränkischen Staatskolonisation in süddeutschen Raum', *Zeitschr. f. Agrargesch. u. Agrarsoziol.*, 11 (1963), 34–62

Ogilvie, A. G. 'The time-element in geography', *Transactions and Papers of the Institute of British Geographers*, 18 (1952), 1–16

Olsson, G. 'Complementary models: a study of colonisation maps', *Geografiska Annaler*, 50 (1968), 115–32

Otremba, E. *Atlas d. deutschen Agrarlandschaft* (Wiesbaden, 1962)

Overbeck, H. *Kulturlandschaftsforschung und Landeskunde* (Heidelberg, 1965)

Parsons, J. J. 'Antioqueño colonization in western Colombia', *Ibero-Americana*, 32 (Berkeley, 1949; revised edition 1968)

Parsons, J. J. 'Antoquia's corridor to the sea: an historical geography of the settlement of Urabá', *Ibero-Americana*, 47 (Berkeley, 1967)

Paterson, J. H. 'The novelist and his region: Scotland through the eyes of Sir Walter Scott', *Scottish Geographical Magazine*, 81 (1965), 146–52

Pattison, W. D. *Beginnings of the American Rectangular Land Survey System, 1784–1800* (Chicago, 1957)

Peltre, J. D. 'Premiers enseignements d'une étude métrologique des terroirs lorrains', *Bulletin de l'Association de Géographes Français*, nos 352–3 (1967), 11–19

Perry, P. J. 'H. C. Darby and historical geography: a survey and review', *Geographische Zeitschrift*, 57 (1969), 161–78

Perry, P. J. 'Working class isolation and mobility in rural Dorset, 1837–1936: a study of marriage distances', *Trans-*

actions of the Institute of British Geographers, 46 (1969), 115–35

Perry, P. J. 'Marriage-distance relationships in north Otago 1875–1914', New Zealand Geographer, 25 (1969), 36–43

Perry, P. J. 'Twenty five years of New Zealand historical geography', New Zealand Geographer, 25 (1969), 93–105

Perry, T. M. Australia's First Frontier. The spread of settlement in New South Wales, 1788–1829 (Melbourne, 1963)

Perry, T. M. 'Climate and settlement in Australia 1700–1930: some theoretical considerations', in Andrews, J. (ed) Frontiers and Men: a Volume in memory of Griffith Taylor 1880–1963 (Melbourne, 1966) 138–154

Pfeifer, G. 'The basin of Puebla-Tlaxcala in Mexico', Revista Geográfica Panamericana, 64 (1966), 85–107

Pillsbury, R. 'The urban street pattern as a culture indicator. Pennsylvania, 1682–1815', Annals of the Association of American Geographers, 60 (1970), 428–46

Pitts, F. R. 'A graph-theoretical approach to historical geography', Professional Geographer, 17 no 5 (1965), 15–20

Porteous, J. D. 'The company town of Goole. An essay in urban genesis', University of Hull Occasional Papers in Geography, 12 (1969)

Pounds, N. J. G. 'North western Europe in the ninth century: its geography in the light of the polyptyques', Annals of the Association of American Geographers, 57 (1967) 439–61

Pounds, N. J. G. 'The urbanization of the classical world', Annals of the Association of American Geographers, 59 (1969), 135–57

Powell, J. M. 'The Selection Acts of Western Victoria, 1860–1880', in Steel, R. W. and Lawton, R. (eds) Liverpool Essays in Geography. A Jubilee Collection (London, 1967) 293–314

Powell, J. M. 'Victoria's woodland cover in 1869; a bureaucratic venture in cartography', New Zealand Geographer, 23 (1967), 106–16

Powell, J. M. 'Farming conditions in Victoria, 1857–1865: a prelude to selection', Australian Geographer, 10 (1968), 346–54

Powell, J. M. *The Public Lands of Australia Felix* (Melbourne, 1970)

Pownall, L. L. 'Metropolitan Auckland 1740–1945', *New Zealand Geographer*, 6 (1950), 107–24

Pred, A. *The Spatial Dynamics of U.S. Urban-Industrial Growth, 1800–1914. Interpretative and Theoretical Essays.* (Cambridge, Massachusetts, 1966)

Pred, A. 'Behaviour and location. Foundations for a geographic and dynamic location theory', *Lund Studies in Geography Series B*, 27, 28 (1967, 1968)

Prince, H. C. 'Historical geography', being Report of Section VI, *20th International Geographical Congress Proceedings* (London, 1967), 164–72

Prince, H. C. 'Relict landscapes', *Area*, no 1 (1969), 29–31

Prince, H. C. 'Progress in historical geography', in Cooke, R. U. and Johnson, J. H. (eds) *Trends in Geography. An Introductory Survey* (London, 1969), 110–22

Prince, H. C. 'Real, imagined and abstract worlds of the past'. *Progress in Geography*, 3 (1971), 1–86

Prost, G. 'Dans le Nord-Est du Brésil: les pionniers du Cariris dans la Borborema semi-aride', *Les Cahiers D'Outre Mer*, 20 (1967), 367–93; 21 (1968), 78–102

Randle, P. H., *Geografía Histórica y Planeamiento* (Buenos Aires, 1966)

Reps, J. W. *The Making of Urban America. A History of City Planning in the United States* (Princeton, 1965)

Reps, J. W. *Town Planning in Frontier America* (Princeton, 1969)

Ribeiro, D. 'The culture-historical configurations of the American people', *Current Anthropology*, 11 (1970), 403–34

Rippel, J. K. 'Eine statistische Methode zur Untersuchung von Flur- und Ortsentwicklung', *Geografiska Annaler*, 43 (1961), 252–63

Robinson, D. J. 'Changing settlement patterns in colonial Hispanic America', in P. J. Ucko, R. Tringham and G. W. Dimbleby (eds) *Man, Settlement and Urbanism* (London, 1972)

Robinson, K. W. 'Processes and patterns of urbanization in

Australia and New Zealand', *New Zealand Geographer,* 18 (1962), 32–49

Roden, D. and Baker, A. R. H. 'Field systems of the Chiltern Hills and of parts of Kent from the late thirteenth to the early seventeenth century', *Transactions of the Institute of British Geographers,* 20 (1954), 113–40

Ross, E. *Beyond the River and the Bay* (Toronto, 1970)

Rostlund, E. 'The myth of a natural prairie belt in Alabama: an interpretation of historical records', *Annals of the Association of American Geographers,* 47 (1957), 392–411

Rothstein, M. 'The cotton frontier of the antebellum south: a methodological battleground', *Agricultural History,* 44 (1970), 149–5

Rubinshteyn, N. L. *Sel'skoye Khozyaystvo Rossii vo Vtoroy Polovine XVIIIv.* (Moscow, 1957)

Sauer, C. O. 'The personality of Mexico', *Geographical Review,* 31 (1941), 353–64

Sauer, C. O. 'Foreword to historical geography', *Annals of the Association of American Geographers,* 31 (1941), 1–24

Sauer, C. O. 'Colima of New Spain in the XVI century', *Ibero-Americana,* 29 (1948)

Sauer, C. O. *The Early Spanish Main* (Berkeley, 1966)

Sauer, C. O. *Northern Mists* (Berkeley, 1968)

Saushkin, Yu. G. 'Kul'turnyy landshaft', *Voprosy Geografii,* 1 (1946), 97–106

Schlüter, O. *Die Siedlungsräume Mitteleuropas in Frühgeschichtlicher Zeit* (Remagen, 1952, 1953, 1958)

Schmieder, O. 'The Pampa—A natural or culturally induced grassland?', *Univ. of California Pub. in Geog.* 2 (1927), 255–70

Schmieder, O. 'The historic geography of Tucumán', *Univ. of California Pub. in Geog.,* 2 (1928), 359–86

Schmieder, O. 'Alteration of the Argentine Pampa in the colonial period', *Univ. of California Pub. in Geog.,* 2, 10, (1928), 303–21

Schmieder, O. 'The Brazilian culture hearth', *Univ. of California Pub. in Geog.,* 3, (1929), 159–98

Schmieder, O. *Landerkunde der Neue Welt. I. Mittel und Südamerika* (Stuttgart, 1962)

Schwarz, G. *Allgemeine Siedlungsgeographie* (3rd ed Berlin, 1966)

Sclafert, T. *Cultures en Haute-Provence: déboisement et pâturages au Moyen-Age* (Paris, 1961)

Scobie, J. R. *Revolution on the Pampas: a social history of Argentine Wheat, 1860–1910* (Austin, 1964)

Service, E. R. 'Indian-European relations in colonial Latin America', *American Anthropologist*, 57 (1955), 411–25

Sheail, J. 'Men and their money in Tudor England', *Geographical Magazine*, 42 (1970), 876–84

Sheppard, J. A. 'The pre-enclosure field and settlement patterns in an English township (Wheldrake, near York)', *Geografiska Annaler*, 48 (1966), 59–77

Shunkov, V. I. *Ocherki po Istorii Zemledeliya Sibiri (XVII vek)* (Moscow, 1956)

Simpson, L. B. 'Mexico's forgotten century', *Pacific Historical Review*, 22 (1953), 113–21

Smailes, P. J. and Molyneaux, J. K. 'The evolution of an Australian rural settlement pattern: southern New England, N.S.W.', *Transactions and Papers of the Institute of British Geographers*, 36 (1965), 31–54

Smith, C. T. 'Historical geography: current trends and prospects', in Chorley, R. J. and Haggett, P. (eds) *Frontiers in Geographical Teaching* (London, 1965) 118–43

Smith, C. T. *An Historical Geography of Europe before 1800* (London, 1967)

Smith, C. T. 'Depopulation in the Central Andes in the sixteenth century', *Current Anthropology*, 11 (1970), 453–64

Smith, C. T. Denevan, W. M. and Hamilton, P. 'Ancient ridged fields in the region of Lake Titicaca', *Geographical Journal*, 134 (1968), 353–67

Smith, D. M. 'The British hosiery industry at the middle of the nineteenth century: an historical study in economic geography', *Transactions and Papers of the Institute of British Geographers*, 32 (1963), 125–42

Smith, R. H. T. 'The development and function of transport routes in southern New South Wales 1860–1930', *Australian Geographical Studies*, 2 (1964), 47–65

Solomon, R. J. and Goodand, W. E. 'Past influences in present townscapes: some Tasmanian examples', *New Zealand Geographer*, 18 (1956), 177–84

Sporrong, U. *Kolonisation, bebyggelseutbeckling och administration* (Lund, 1971)

Stanislawski, D. 'Early Spanish town planning in the New World', *Geographical Review*, 37 (1947), 94–105

Stanislawski, D. *The Individuality of Portugal. A Study in Historical-Political Geography* (Austin, Texas, 1959)

Stanislawski, D. *Landscapes of Bacchus. The Vine in Portugal* (Austin and London, 1970)

Sternberg, H. O'R. 'Man and environmental change in South America', in *Biogeography and Ecology in South America*, E. J. Fittkau, *et al.* (ed) Vol 1, The Hague, 1968, 413–45

Sternberg, H. O'R. 'Geographic thought and development in Brazil', *The Professional Geographer*, 21 (1969), 12–17

Taylor, E. G. R. 'Leland's England' and 'Camden's England', in Darby, H. C. (ed) *An Historical Geography of England before 1800* (Cambridge, 1936), 330–53 and 354–86

Temple, E. D. 'Panorama geográfico del Perú en 1839', *Boletín de la Sociedad Geográfica de Lima*, 82 (1964), 23–52

Thomas, D. *Agriculture in Wales during the Napoleonic Wars* (Cardiff, 1963)

Thomas, D. 'Climate and cropping in the early nineteenth century in Wales', in Taylor, J. A. (ed) *Weather and Agriculture* (Oxford, 1967), 201–12

Thomas, W. L. (ed) *Man's Role in Changing the Face of the Earth* (Chicago, 1955)

Thompson, K. 'Insalubrious California: perception and reality', *Annals of the Association of American Geographers*, 59 (1969), 50–64

Thompson, K. 'Irrigation as a menace to health in California: a nineteenth century view', *Geographical Review*, 59 (1969), 195–214

Thrower, N. J. W. *Original Land Subdivision. A Comparative Study of the Form and Effect of Contrasting Cadastral Surveys* (Chicago, 1966)

Uhlig, H. 'Old hamlets with infield and outfield systems in

Western and Central Europe', *Geografiska Annaler*, 43 (1961), 285–312

Vance, J. E. 'Emerging patterns of commercial structure in American cities', *Lund Studies in Geography*, Ser B 24 (Lund, 1962)

Vance, J. E. *Geography and Urban Evolution in the San Francisco Bay Area* (Berkeley, 1964)

Vance, J. E. *The Merchant's World. The Geography of Wholesaling* (Englewood Cliffs, 1970)

Wacker, P. O. 'Early street patterns in Pennsylvania and New Jersey: a comparison', *Proceedings of the Association of American Geographers*, 3 (1970), 1–13

Wade, R. C. *The Urban Frontier* (Chicago, 1967)

Wade, R. C. and Mayer, H. M. *Growth of a Metropolis* (Chicago, 1969)

Walker, R. B. *Old New England: a history of the Northern Tablelands of New South Wales, 1818–1900* (Sydney, 1966)

Wallwork, K. L. 'The calico printing industry of Lancastria in the 1840s', *Transactions of the Institute of British Geographers*, 45 (1968), 143–56

Walsh, G. P. 'The English colony in New South Wales: AD 1803', *New Zealand Geographer*, 18 (1962), 149–69

Ward, D. 'The pre-urban cadaster and the urban pattern of Leeds', *Annals of the Association of American Geographers*, 52 (1962), 150–66

Ward, D. *Nineteenth Century Boston. A Study in the Role of Antecedent and Adjacent Conditions in the Spatial Aspects of Urban Growth* (unpublished PhD thesis, University of Wisconsin, 1963)

Ward, D. 'A comparative historical geography of streetcar suburbs in Boston, Massachusetts and Leeds, England, 1850–1920', *Annals of the Association of American Geographers*, 54 (1964), 477–89

Ward, D. 'The industrial revolution and the emergence of Boston's central business district', *Economic Geography*, 42 1966), 152–71

Ward, D. 'The emergence of central immigrant ghettoes in American cities, 1840–1920', *Annals of the Association of*

American Geographers, 58 (1968), 343–59

Ward, D. *Cities and Immigrants. A Geography of Change in Nineteenth Century America* (London, 1971)

Warkentin, J. *The Western Interior of Canada. A Record of Geographical Discovery, 1612–1971* (Toronto, 1964)

Warner, S. B. *Streetcar Suburbs. The Process of Growth in Boston, 1870–1900* (Cambridge, Massachusetts, 1962)

Warner, S. B. *The Private City. Philadelphia in Three Periods of Growth* (Philadelphia, 1968)

Watson, J. W. 'Relict geography in an urban community: Halifax, Nova Scotia', in Miller, R. and Watson, J. W. (eds) *Geographical Essays in Memory of Alan G. Ogilvie* (London, 1959), 110–43

Webb, W. P. *The Great Plains* (Boston, 1931)

West, R. C. *The Pacific Lowlands of Colombia* (Baton Rouge, 1957)

West, R. C. and Parsons, J. J. 'The Topia Road: a Trans-Sierran Trail of Colonial Mexico', *Geographical Review*, 31 (1941), 406–13

Wightman, W. R. 'The pattern of vegetation in the Vale of Pickering area c. 1300', *Transactions of the Institute of British Geographers*, 45 (1968), 125–42

Williams, M. *The Draining of the Somerset Levels* (Cambridge, 1966)

Williams, M. 'The spread of settlement in south Australia' in Gale, F. and Lawton G. H. (eds) *Settlement and Encounter. Geographical Studies Presented to Sir Grenfell Price* (Melbourne, 1969), 1–50

Williams, M. 'Places, periods and themes: a review and prospect of Australian historical geography: a review article', *Australian Geographer*, 11 (1970), 403–16

Wise, M. J. 'On the evolution of the jewellery and gun quarters in Birmingham', *Transactions and Papers of the Institute of British Geographers*, 15 (1949), 58–72

Woronoff, D. 'Vers une géographie industrielle de la France d'Ancien Régime', *Annales Economies Sociétés Civilisations*, 95 (1970), 127–30

Wrigley, E. A. *Industrial Growth and Population Change* (Cambridge, 1961)

U

Wrigley, E. A. 'A simple model of London's importance in changing English society and economy 1650–1750', *Past and Present,* 37 (1967), 44–70

Wrigley, E. A. *Population and History* (London, 1969)

Wührer, K. 'Die agrargeschichtliche Forschung in Skandinavien seit 1945', *Zeitschrift für Agrargeschichte und Agrarsoziologie,* 5 (1957), 198–220

Yates, E. M. 'History in a map', *Geographical Journal,* 126 (1960), 32–49

Zavala, S. 'The frontiers of Hispanic America', in W. D. Wyman and C. B. Kroeber (eds), *The Frontier in Perspective* (Madison, 1957)

Zelinsky, W. 'Changes in the geographic patterns of rural population in the United States, 1790–1960', *Geographical Review,* 52 (1962), 492–524

Zelinsky, W. 'Classical town names in the United States: the historical geography of an American idea', *Geographical Review,* 57 (1961), 463–95

Index

The intention of this index is to locate references in the text to people and to the main ideas common to many of their writings. No attempt has been made to index the incidental references to place-names.

Abrahamczik, W., 58
Acland, L. G. D., 157
Aerial photographs, 35, 51, 84, 177
Agrarian Landscape Research Group, 103
Aleksandrov, V. A., 126
Allen, A. C. B., 152
Ambrosiana, B., 71
Améen, L., 82
Andersson, H., 78
Andrews, J., 147, 149
Anthropology, 15, 16, 20, 43, 139, 149, 169, 181, 204; economic, 16; social, 15, 24, 25
Anuchin, V. A., 114-15
Applied geography, 114, 123
Archaeology, 15, 25, 45, 54, 60, 69, 84, 139; archaeological evidence, 37, 39, 50, 71, 121, 149, 160, 204
Ardissone, R., 177
Armstrong, R. W., 161
Arpi, G., 82
Arrhenius, O., 83
Aschmann, H., 138
Association analysis, 109
Association method, 48
Atlases, historical, 39, 56, 62, 155, 159-60: see also Maps
August, O., 56

Aydelotte, W. O., 15, 21
Azevedo, A. de, 178, 183

Bachmann, H., 48
Baker, A. R. H., 11, 12, 46, 90
Baker, J. N. L., 95
Baton Rouge group, 133
Behavioural approaches, 12, 24-8, 88, 93-4, 95, 110, 148, 165: see also Decision-making; Perception studies
Belov, M. I., 113, 127
Benthien, B., 56
Bergen Symposium (1964), 72
Bergman, J. F., 139
Berkeley 'school', 138, 139, 154, 155, 173, 174, 175, 179, 183
Berkhofer, R. F., 14, 16, 25
Bernshteyn-Kogan, S. V., 125, 126
Blalock, H. M., 22
Blaut, J. M., 24
Bloch, M., 28, 98
Biogeography, 117-19: see also Vegetation changes; Fauna, changing distribution of
Bobek, H., 53, 54
Bockh, A., 176
Borah, W., 182, 183
Borcherdt, C., 57
Born, M., 56, 70
Bowden, M. J., 12, 141

303

Bowman, R., 154
Brandon, P. F., 102
Braudel, F., 37
Brito-Figueroa, F., 182
Broadbent, S. R., 85
Broek, J. O. M., 96, 98, 142, 147
Brookfield, H. C., 93
Brown, R. H., 134, 140, 143, 161
Brunet, P., 33
Brunet, R., 33
Buchanan, K. M., 155
Burghardt, A. F., 133, 135, 136, 141
Butland, G. J., 178
Butlin, R. A., 12, 103
Butzer, K., 139
Bylund, E., 75, 87-8

Cain, N., 151
Campbell, W. J., 101
Cant, R. G., 163
Carter, F. W., 109
Carter, G., 138, 142
Carter, H., 101, 108
Chang, K. C., 25
Change through time, 15-17, 38, 63, 104, 124-5, 130-1, 152, 154, 159, 167, 190: *see also* Diachronic studies; Dynamic approaches; Geographical change; Evolutionary approaches
Changing geographies, 1, 35, 137-8, 143, 160, 184: *see also* Geographical change
Changing landscapes, 92, 93, 94, 95, 100, 102, 120-3, 127, 144, 149, 155-6: *see also* Vegetational changes
Chevalier, F., 176, 182
Chevalier, M., 32
Chorley, R. J., 27
Christaller, W., 153
Clark, A. H., 129, 133, 137, 138, 139, 141, 154, 159, 161
Claval, P., 31
Climatic change, 36, 38, 52, 58, 60, 119, 120-21, 123, 151, 164

Clout, H. D., 102
Colonisation, studies of, 34, 38-9, 40, 55, 73-5, 87-8, 117, 119, 144-8, 159, 162, 177-8: *see also* Frontier thesis; Rural settlement studies
Comparative method, 14, 16, 19, 24, 27-8, 47-8, 55, 78, 98, 102, 117, 148, 176
Computers, use of, 109, 110, 135, 166, 181
Condliffe, J. B., 157
Connectivity analysis, 109
Content analysis, 26
Conzen, M. P., 137
Cook, S. F., 183
Co-ordinates of time and place, 130-1
Cotton, C., 154
Counterfactual method, 19, 106
Cross-sections, 13, 15, 38, 46, 61, 62, 94, 96, 102, 103, 111, 123, 124, 137, 147, 160-1, 179, 184, 204: *see also* Reconstructions of past geographies; Synchronic studies
Cultural geography, 46, 102, 133, 138-9, 140, 190
Cultural landscape, 53, 58, 61, 84, 89, 114
Culture area, concept of, 193
Cumberland, K. B., 154, 155, 157, 158, 160, 164
Cunningham, J. K., 162
Curry, L., 136

Darby, H. C., 91, 94, 95, 96, 100, 103, 104, 112, 142, 174
Dating methods, 47, 78, 85, 92, 100; phosphate mapping, 83; pollen-analysis, 51, 83, 123; radio-carbon, 69, 83: *see also* Morphogenetic analysis; Typological method; Retracing, method of
Daveau, S., 32
Decision-making, 24, 26-7, 88-9, 110, 150, 153-4: *see also*

Behavioural approaches; Perception studies
Deductive method, 22, 181
Deffontaines, P., 172, 178
De Graft Johnson, J. W., 205
De La Blache, P. V., 29
De Lemps, A. H., 32
De Martonne, E., 172
De Mattos, L., 172
Denecke, D., 50
Denevan, W. M., 103, 138
De Planhol, X., 29, 32
Derruau, M., 32
Deserted settlements, 49-50, 53-4, 69-70, 72, 84
Desplanques, H., 33
De Vorsey, L., 136
Diachronic studies, 15, 16, 22: *see also* Change through time; Changing geographies; Changing landscapes; Geographical change
Dickson, K. B., 187
Diffusion, 16, 20, 22, 69, 70, 76, 101, 117, 127, 139, 162, 166, 168, 193-5
Dinsdale, E., 162
Dion, R., 22, 39-44, 98, 172
Dongus, H., 52
Donkin, R. A., 100
Dunbar, G., 133, 137
Duncan, J. S., 162
Durand, L., 142
Dynamic approaches, 38, 86, 89, 104, 120, 178: *see also* Change through time; Changing geographies; Changing landscapes; Geographical change; Diachronic studies

East, W. G., 91, 92
Ecological changes, 148-9, 177, 195
Economic geography, 30, 31, 112, 113, 114-15, 123-6
Economics, 20, 26, 146, 148, 181
Eitzen, G., 54
Elkins, T. H., 95

Emery, F. V., 95, 101
Enequist, G., 73, 75
English, P. W., 133
Ericsson, G., 82
Ethnos, 120-1, 128
Evolutionary approaches, 15, 16, 32, 38, 46, 65, 69, 70, 76-7, 88, 92, 105, 136, 148, 156, 164, 165, 171, 177-8: *see also* Change through time; Genetic approaches
Explanation, 12, 13, 21, 88, 96, 104, 105-6, 108, 133, 203

Faegri, K., 84
Fat'yanov, A. S., 118
Fauna, changing distribution of, 118-19, 127, 149, 157
Febvre, L., 36
Fehn, K., 56
Fel, A., 33
Fels, R., 52
Fenner, C., 147
Field work, 49, 69, 71, 80, 83, 118, 171, 204
Firbas, F., 51, 83
Flatrès, P., 33
Flohn, H., 52
Florin, S., 84
Folklore studies, 45, 54
Forrest, J., 161, 163
Fossier, R., 35
Frank, A. G., 183
Franklin, S. H., 162
Franz, G., 62
French, R. A., 103, 111
Freyre, G., 183
Friberg, N., 81
Friedmann, J., 181-2
Fries, M., 84
Frödin, J., 73
Frontier thesis, 98, 125-6, 148, 153, 178, 181
Fricke, W., 60
Friis, H. R., 141
Furtado, C., 183
Fuson, R. H., 139

Gaignard, R., 173
Galloway, J. H., 135
Gallusser, W. A., 56
Gedymin, A. V., 118
Genealogical methods, 48, 75
Generalisation, 14-15, 21, 22, 23, 24, 27-8, 87, 131, 132, 137, 204, 205
Genetic approaches, 46, 53, 54, 62, 76-7, 91, 92, 94, 96, 154: *see also* Evolutionary approaches
Gentilcore, L., 141
Geographical change, 13, 15, 22, 28, 104, 108, 137-8, 144, 158, 161-5: *see also* Change through time; Changing geographies; Dynamic approaches
Geographical imagination, 101
Geography behind history, 35-7, 95, 147
Geology, 146, 169; man as a geological agent, 149
Geomer, 46
George, D., 26
Germani, G., 182
Gibson, J. R., 133
Glässer, E., 52
Goehrke, C., 53
Goheen, P., 135
Göransson, S., 76-7
Grenfell Price, A., 146, 147, 148
Grey, A. H., 136
Grigg, D., 99
Grund, A., 53
Gulley, J. L. M., 96, 98
Gumilev, L. N., 120-23, 126, 127, 128
Guthrie-Smith, H., 157, 159
Guyan, W. U., 50, 61

Haarnagel, W., 52
Hafeman, D., 52
Hägerstrand, T., 22, 87
Hahn, H., 57, 58
Hall, P., 101
Hamilton, P., 103
Hamshere, J. D., 12

Hannerberg, D., 34, 69, 70, 72, 76-80, 81, 85-6, 87
Hansen, J. C., 82
Hansen, R., 80
Hard, G., 52
Hargreaves, R. P., 160, 161, 163, 164
Harris, A., 96-8, 99
Harris, R. C., 12, 129, 133, 134, 141-2
Hart, J. F., 138
Hartshorne, R., 158
Harvey, D., 12, 19, 101, 105, 136
Hastrup, F., 75, 81
Hatt, G., 69
Heathcote, R. L., 110, 144, 152, 154
Heerdegen, R. G., 162
Helmfrid, S., 63, 65, 72, 73, 76-7, 84
Hendinger, H., 58
Hepple, L. W., 12, 106
Herold, A., 56
Herskovits, M. J., 193
Herzog, F., 61
Hewes, L., 137
Higounet, C., 35
Hill, R. D., 161
Hilliard, S. B., 134
Historical demography, 37, 124: *see also* Population studies
Historical geography in Africa, 187-206; Australia, 144-54, 165-7; Austria, 45-62; Britain, 90-110, 142; Canada, 129-30, 141-2; Europe, 45-62, 127, 136, 142, 145, 173-5; France, 29-44, 98, 172-3; Germany, 45-62, 67, 72, 173; Latin America, 168-86; New Zealand, 144-5, 154-67; North America, 127, 129-43, 145, 173-5; Scandinavia, 63-89; Sweden, 34, 51, 63-89; Switzerland, 45-62; USSR, 103, 111-28
'Historical language', 27, 106
Historical scholarship, 12, 13-14, 18-19, 21, 22, 105, 132-3, 139, 183

Historic present tense, 161
History, 12, 16, 25, 27, 29, 30, 35-6, 44, 45, 93, 95, 108, 111, 112, 114, 115, 125, 130, 143, 146, 148, 169, 181, 204; art, 164; culture, 185, 195, 205; economic, 14, 16, 18, 24, 26, 45, 80, 125, 139, 147, 151, 157; local, 55, 156; regional, 55, 151-2, 156; social, 14, 18, 45, 80, 139
History behind geography, 31-5
Hjulström, F., 82
Hoskins, W. G., 123
Hough, R. F., 138
Houston, J. M., 93
Hudson, J. C., 24
Hultblad, F., 75
Huttenlocher, F., 60
Hütteroth, W. D., 54, 61
Hypothetical historical geography, 109

Innes, F., 141
Institutional policies, 59, 64, 76, 79, 87-9, 148, 150, 163
International Geographical Union (1964 meeting), 103
Isaac, E., 133, 138
Iversen, J., 84

Jäger, H., 44, 45, 51, 52, 57, 58, 61, 142
Jakle, J. A., 138
James, P. E., 173
Janin, B., 32
Janssen, W., 53
Jeansson, N. R., 84
Jobberns, G., 154, 155, 162
Johnson, H. B., 136
Johnsson, B., 85
Johnston, W. B., 161, 163
Jones, G. R. J., 100
Jordan, T. G., 133, 134
Juillard, E., 33
Jutikkala, E., 73

Kalesnik, S. V., 115-16

Katzman, M. T., 138
Käubler, R., 49
Keyser, E., 54, 55
Kharitonychev, A. T., 123
Kirikov, S. V., 114, 118-19, 127
Kirk, W., 26, 93-4, 95
Kirsten, E., 61
Kniffen, F. B., 133, 139, 140
Kochin, G., 125
Koelsch, W. A., 12
Kollmorgen, W. M., 141
Krausch, D., 51
Krausch, H., 58
Krenzlin, A., 48, 54, 55, 56
Kroeber, C. B., 173
Krüger, H., 50
Kuls, W., 56

Lamping, H., 60
Landscape histories, 60-2, 69-70, 92, 93, 94, 116, 120-1, 157, 162, 172, 177, 182: *see also* Changing landscapes
Land survey systems, 77-8, 85-6, 140, 150
Langford-Smith, T., 152
Langton, J., 12, 16, 108
Leach, E. R., 15
Lebeau, R., 32
Leister, I., 54
Lemon, J. T., 133, 134
Lerat, S., 32
Le Roy Ladurie, E., 36
Lewis, G. M., 101, 110, 141
Lewis, J. P., 24
Lewis, R. A., 138
Lewthwaite, G., 162
Lichtenberger, E., 54
Lindquist, S. O., 68-70, 72, 83, 88
Linge, G. J. R., 164
Livet, R., 33
Lombard, M., 37
London 'school', 155
Lowenthal, D., 110, 140
Lucas, C. P., 205
Lynch, J., 183

Mackinder, H., 91

Madison 'school', 133, 134, 139
Mager, F., 46, 58, 61
Maps, as means of presenting results of research, 34, 38, 49, 59, 75, 102, 117, 118, 147, 157, 159 ; as evidence, 48, 65, 69, 76, 77-8, 80, 85, 117, 118, 128, 161: *see also* Atlases, historical
Markov, K. K., 116
Marsh, G. P., 156
Marxist interpretations, 112, 113, 122, 126
May, P. R., 161
Mayer, H. M., 134
McCaskill, M., 144, 161, 162
McLintock, A. H., 159-60
McManis, D. R., 133, 143
Mead, W. R., 101, 163
Meinig, D. W., 133, 148, 149, 153, 154
Merrens, H. R., 133
Merrill, G., 141
Meteorological methods, 51, 85: *see also* Morphometric analysis
Metz, F., 60
Meyer, A. H., 133
Meynier, A., 34
Middendorf, A. F., 118
Mikesell, M., 138, 139
Millotte, J. P., 39
Mitchell, J. B., 91, 92-3, 101
Models, 11, 17, 19, 20, 22, 23, 24, 26, 27, 65, 82, 86-9, 106, 108, 127, 132, 133, 136-7, 153-4, 164, 165, 181-3, 205: *see also* Theoretical approaches
Module test, 85
Monbeig, P., 172
Morawetz, S., 58
Morphogenetic analysis, 47, 50, 75-81, 89, 101
Morphographic studies, 50: *see also* Morphological studies
Morphological studies, 139-40, 191
Morphometric analysis, 34, 72, 78-9 81, 85
Morrill, R. L., 82, 136
Mortensen, G., 46, 61

Mortensen, H., 46, 47, 49, 60, 61
Mortimore, M. J., 102
Müller-Wille, W., 47, 50, 56
Murton, B. J., 162
Myklebost, H., 82

Narrative method, 13, 14, 108, 147 ; introductory narrative, 96
Nearest neighbour analysis, 88, 109
Neef, E., 52
Nelson, H. J., 135
Nelson, J. G., 141
Newcomb, R. M., 12, 84
Niemeier, G., 83
'Noosphere', concept of, 128
Norborg, K., 82
Nordholm, G., 69
Nordstrom, O., 82
Nougier, L. R., 38
Numerical techniques, 46, 108: *see also* Quantification ; Statistical approaches

Oberbeck, G., 61
Ogilvie, A. G., 92, 100
Olsson, G., 19, 24, 87-8
Oral tradition, 204
Otremba, E., 173
Outline for an historical geography of Africa, 190-203 ; of Latin America, 184-5
Overbeck, H., 59, 60

Palaeogeography, 115, 121
Pape, H., 57
Parker, W. H., 141
Parsons, J. J., 133
Past geographies: *see* Cross-sections ; Reconstructions of past geographies
Past in the present, 91, 92, 95, 103: *see also* Relict features
Paterson, J. H., 110
Patten, J. H. C., 12
Pattison, W. D., 140
Pazhitnov, K. A., 125
Pedology, 45, 50, 51, 58, 60, 118

Peltre, J., 34
Perry, P. J., 103, 158, 166
Perry, T. M., 152
Perception studies, 26-7, 93, 95, 101, 110, 127, 140-1, 152, 154, 185-6: *see also* Behavioural approaches ; Decision-making
Pfeifer, G., 60, 62, 173
Phillips, A. D. M., 12
Philippson, A., 61
Philological methods, 43
Physical geography, 30, 49, 51-3, 112, 114-19, 120-1, 139, 146, 170
Place-names, 38, 39, 123
Pillsbury, R., 139
Pitts, F. R., 136
Pokshishevskiy, V. V., 124
Political frontiers, 32, 41
Political geography, 59-60, 162
Population studies, 81-2, 87-8, 102, 185: *see also* Historical demography
Postdiction, 106
Pounds, N. J. G., 90, 136
Powell, J. M., 152, 154
Pownall, L. L., 162, 163, 164
Pragmatic methodology, 103, 104
Pred, A., 135
Prehistoric continuity problem, 67-9, 84
Preobrazhenskiy, A. A., 86
Price, E. T., 140
Primitive (natural) landscape, 112, 175
Prince, H. C., 12, 13, 14, 22, 26, 27, 98, 101, 103, 106, 110, 142
Probabilistic explanations, 19-20, 48, 88
Prospective approach, 31
Prunty, M., 142
Psychology, 23, 93, 94: *see also* Behavioural approaches

Quantification, 17, 18-20, 21, 51, 65, 77, 80, 88, 118, 119, 127, 166, 167, 204: *see also* Statistical approaches

Randle, P., 174-5
Ranking of settlements, 109, 164
Rashin, A. G., 126
Raup, H., 142
Reconstructions of past geographies, 13, 31-2, 33, 35, 37-8, 60-2, 80, 91-2, 93-4, 102, 107, 112, 126, 149, 158, 160-1, 171, 175, 194: *see also* Cross-sections
Regional studies, 30, 31, 39, 45, 60-2, 65-6, 92, 99, 113, 131-4, 137, 138, 141, 151-2, 161, 173, 175, 179
Regressive method, 46, 53, 61
Relict features, 35, 49-50, 67, 70, 72, 78, 93, 100-101, 102, 150, 153, 177: *see also* Past in the present
Religion, 36-7, 39
Remote sensing techniques, 84
Reps, J. W., 135
Retracing method, 48
Retrogressive method, 23-4, 33, 46, 69, 72, 98, 101
Retrospective method, 23-4, 30, 33, 35, 37, 40, 46, 48, 61, 87, 96, 98, 101, 127, 152
Reusch, L., 55
Rimmer, P. J., 163, 166
Rippel, J. K., 48
Ritter, G., 59
Roberts, S. H., 147
Robinson, D. J., 103, 168
Rohmeder, W., 173, 176
Rønneseth, O., 69, 70-1
Rose, A. J., 153, 164, 166
Ross, E., 134, 141
Ross, S. H., 139
Rostlund, E., 138
Rowland, R. H., 138
Rubinshteyn, N. L., 125
Rubner, H., 51, 58
Rudberg, S., 75
Ruggles, R., 141
Rühl, A., 147
Rural settlement studies, 33, 41, 48, 52, 54, 55, 56-7, 64, 65, 67-

77, 124, 140, 163, 165: *see also* Colonisation, studies of

Sahlgren, N., 86
Samuelson, P. A., 22
Sarfatti, M., 182
Sauer, C. O., 106, 133, 138-9, 140, 143, 154, 173-4, 175-6, 177
Sauchkin, Y. G., 114, 115, 124
Scharlau, K., 70
Schlüter, O., 53, 58, 60
Schmeider, O., 173, 176
Schmieding, A. C., 137
Schöller, P., 54, 60
Schröder, K. H., 54, 57
Schutten, A., 60
Schwarz, G., 55
Scobie, J. R., 182
Semenova-Tyan-Shanskaya, A. M., 117
Semmel, A., 50
Sequent occupance, 93, 96, 127, 161-2
Shunkov, V. I., 125
Sibley, D., 24
Simoons, F., 138
Simulation procedures, 19, 86, 88-9, 106, 153
Sinskaya, Ye. N., 117, 126
Slicher van Bath, B. H., 81
Smith, C. T., 12, 103, 104-5, 142
Smith, D. M., 102
Sociology, 16, 26, 28, 181
Solomon, R. J., 152, 166
Sopher, D., 138
Sources, 18, 25, 26, 44, 46, 51, 60, 63, 64, 65, 80, 81, 82, 85, 98-9, 103, 110, 119, 144, 150-1, 158, 160, 166-7, 171, 180, 203-5
Spate, O. H. K., 153
Spatial patterns, 19, 25, 26, 92, 104, 106, 125, 149, 154, 162, 167, 206
Spelt, J., 135, 141
Spencer, J., 138
Sperling, W., 56
Sporrong, U., 70, 80, 83

Stanislawski, D., 133
Static approaches, 38, 124, 177: *see also* Cross-sections; Reconstructions of past geographies
Static-formal analysis, 46-7
Statistical approaches, 17-20, 48, 85-6, 101, 104, 105, 108-110, 131, 132, 136-7, 166: *see also* Numerical techniques; Quantification
Steensberg, A., 80
Sternberger, M., 67
Stewig, R., 55
Stochastic models, *see* Probabilistic explanations
Strumilin, S. G., 125
Sverdlov, M. B., 125
Symbolic logic, 20
Synchronic studies, 15: *see also* Cross-sections; Reconstructions of past geographies; Static approaches
System theory, 17, 22, 108

Taylor, E. G. R., 95
Taylor, G., 146
Technological change, 149, 182
Theoretical approaches, 12, 13, 21-4, 65, 75, 87-8, 101-2, 103-4, 107-8, 132, 135, 136, 153, 164-5, 166-7, 206: *see also* Models
Thomas, D., 99, 101
Thomas, W., 138
Thrower, N. J. W., 140
Tichy, F., 58, 62
Tikhomirov, M. N., 124
Tisowsky, K., 57
Topology, 20
Torbrand, D., 72
Trindell, R. J., 140
Troll, C., 58
Trusov, Yu.P., 128
Tsvetkov, M. A., 125, 126
Turner, F. J., 98, 126, 135, 148
Typological method, 47

Universities in Africa, 187-90; Australia, 146, 148; Latin

America, 169-70; New Zealand, 154-5, 161
University of Buenos Aires, 174; California (Berkeley), 138, 139; California (Los Angeles), 142; Chicago, 139; Cuyo (Mendoza), 173; John Hopkins, 142; London (University College), 174; Paris, 44; Rennes, 34; São Paulo, 172; Stockholm, 69, 83, 89; Wisconsin (Madison), 139
Unstead, J. F., 91
Urban studies, 54-5, 57, 82, 134-5, 153-4, 178-9
Urlich, D., 162

Vadstena Symposium (1960), 77
Vance, J. E., 27, 138
Vandermeer, C., 133
Vegetation change, 36, 51, 52, 58, 60, 73-5, 117-19, 125, 148-9, 157, 175-7, 194
Vertical themes, 13, 15, 61, 92, 94, 123, 152, 179
Visby Symposium (1971), 72
Viticulture, 32, 41-3, 57-8, 172
Vitov, M. V., 124
Von Thünen, J. H., 153, 163
Vorob'yeva, T. N., 123

Wacker, P. O., 133, 139
Wade, R. C., 135
Wagner, P., 138
Waibel, L., 173
Wallwork, K. L., 102

Walsh, G. P., 152
Ward, D., 23, 134
Warkentin, J., 134, 141
Warner, S. B., 135
Watson, J. W., 100, 141
Weaver, J. C., 137
Webb, W. P., 141
Weiss, R., 54
West, R. C., 133, 179, 182
Wheeler, J. O., 138
Whitney, H., 136
Whittlesey, D., 96
Wightman, W. R., 102
Wilhelmy, H., 52, 55, 173, 179
Williams, M., 99, 152
Winkelmann, R., 57
Winkler, E., 47, 61
Wirth, E., 55
Wood, J. D., 141
Wood, P. A., 102
Wooldridge, S. W., 91, 92
Wrigley, E. A., 99, 108
Würzburg Symposium (1966), 54

Yates, E. M., 100
Yatsunskiy, V., 111-14, 123, 126, 127
Yugay, R. L., 114, 126, 127, 128

Zagorovskiy, V. P., 125
Zamorano, M., 177
Zelinsky, W., 136, 138
Zhekulin, V. S., 116
Zigrai, F., 56
Zoology, 118, 119